LIBERTARIANS AND LIBERALISM

*Gerard Radnitzky reading 'Hayek on Hayek' to Olga, his poodle,
in the garden of his residence in Korlingen, Germany*

Libertarians and Liberalism

Essays in Honour of Gerard Radnitzky

Edited by
HARDY BOUILLON

Avebury

Aldershot · Brookfield USA · Hong Kong · Singapore · Sydney

© Hardy Bouillon 1996

Published by
Avebury
Ashgate Publishing Ltd
Gower House
Croft Road
Aldershot
Hants GU11 3HR
England

Ashgate Publishing Company
Old Post Road
Brookfield
Vermont 05036
USA

British Library Cataloguing in Publication Data

Libertarians and liberalism : essays in honour of Gerard
        Radnitzky. - (Avebury series in philosophy)
        1.Liberalism
        I.Bouillon, Hardy
        148

        ISBN 1 85972 460 4

Library of Congress Catalog Card Number: 96-86407

Printed in Great Britain by the Ipswich Book Company, Suffolk

Contents

Introduction 7

CHAPTER I: **Libertarians and Liberalism: of Laps, Links and Lapses**

Libertarian Perspective on Political Economy
Walter Block 16

Liberalism and Libertarians
Gerd Habermann 48

On the Law and Economics of Socialism and Desocialization
Hans-Hermann Hoppe 85

Defining Libertarian Liberty
Hardy Bouillon 95

Libertarians and the Rule of Law
Arthur Seldon 104

Value, Economic Efficiency, And Rules: Some Implicit Biases Against Individual Liberty
Louis De Alessi 112

The Böhm-Bawerkian Foundation of the Interest Theory
Hans F. Sennholz 123

CHAPTER II: **The Fatal Franchise of Freedom: of Social Choice-Democracy**

The Bitter Medicine of Freedom
Anthony de Jasay 148

Social Democracy and the Myth of Social Justice
Antony Flew 170

Nothing New Under the Sun: the Disguised Return of Totalitarianism
Roland Baader 184

Is There a Morality in Redistribution?
Angelo M. Petroni 195

Competition Among Systems – An Ordo Liberal View
Gerhard Schwarz 211

Competition Among Systems as a Defence of Liberty
Manfred E. Streit 236

CHAPTER III: **The Future of Freedom: of Facts and Fiction**

The Austrian School – Its Significance for the Transformation Process
Václav Klaus 253

Economic Dynamism: Lessons From German Experience
Herbert Giersch 260

Down with the Bishops?
Lord Harris of High Cross 274

Ideas and the Future of Liberty
Antonio Martino 288

What do Liberals Have to Say About the Future of International and Inter-ethnic Relations?
Victoria Curzon Price 298

Civilized Ants
Gordon Tullock 319

A Dog's Choice: Which Constitution Is the Best?
Detmar Doering 330

Abstracts 346

Authors 355

Introduction

The book ...

Libertarians and Liberalism is a book *by* Libertarians. It echoes 20 individual views on liberalism in the classical English (not the American) sense and its relevance for the most important aspects of our life.

There is no definite agreement on the protective measures nor on the extent of freedom. Canadian Walter Block and German Gerd Habermann make this clear right from the beginning. Block, advocating anarchism, and Habermann, pleading for minimal government, represent the two contrasting libertarian wings and put the reader into the right mood. He will find a varied spectrum of pleas for no government, minimal government, or limited government in this collection. The essays are arranged according to what might be called the three main concerns of libertarianism:

1. What is the conceptional and theoretical basis of libertarianism?
2. How is libertarianism prepared to meet the challenges of its current main opponent: mainstream democracy?
3. What are the chances for libertarian societies in the future?

These concerns are reflected by the chapter headlines.

Chapter One, *Libertarianism and liberalism: of laps, links, and lapses* mainly deals with theoretical conceptions and misconceptions among libertarianism and their opponents.

Walter Block starts the chapter by describing in clear prose the libertarian-anarchist view of the most important liberal conceptions, such as self-ownership, private property, socialism, capitalism, unions, free trade, pay equity, minimal wage, developing countries, pollution, etc. He also provides the reader with telling statistics from Canada and beyond.

Gerd Habermann, with a huge bibliography on board, distinguishes between different libertarian approaches and questions their practicability. Although estimating many merits of libertarian anarchism, he misses its contribution to activities beyond market and politics, and criticises its condemnation of the state.

After the general outline of the pros and cons of no government and of minimal government, the reader's attention is drawn to liberty's main adversary: socialism. Hans-Hermann Hoppe explains that, while eroding the sources of wealth (homesteading principle, production, and contracting) and suppressing prices and incentives, complete socialism makes us all poor. Addressing to Eastern Europe, he recommends complete privatisation to EE to make it become free and wealthy.

The success of libertarianism as a political theory relies heavily on the precision of its core conceptions, especially on a precise conception of freedom. Hardy Bouillon purges a logical defect in the definition of negative freedom. The conception of coercion used in the definition makes it circular. Separating two decision levels, inherent in free offers as well as in coercive ones, he comes up with a solution and a libertarian definition of liberty that avoids becoming discredited as self-contradicting.

Arthur Seldon addresses a liberal conception that experienced discredit in the past. He argues that democratic government discredited the rule of law during the last two centuries and shows how to recall the liberal reverence for the rule of law in Jeffersonian spirit.

Beside in the sphere of law it is in the domain of economics where libertarian conceptions are reversed and discredited by socialist thinking. Louis de Alessi reveals that mainstream economists routinely fail to separate normative from positive economics. They camouflage normative criteria that favour rules limiting individual liberty and open markets.

Hans Sennholz frees the conception of interest from its socialist condemnation as "unearned income". His historical essay stresses the importance of Eugen von Böhm-Bawerk in the Theory of Interest and draws links with current Austrian economists.

Chapter Two *The fatal franchise of freedom: of social choice-democracy* is on the tension between liberty and democracy. After the socialist collapse, at the latest, it became obvious that the intellectual debate should concentrate on mainstream democracy, its negative repercussions on liberty, and the measures to roll back the public domain.

Anthony de Jasay argues that the political decision mechanism in democracy, the "social choice rule" invites groups to decide "politically" at the expense of the rest. Freedom, unseparable from self-responsibility, is a bitter medicine, but the only one to stop the intrusion of the social into the domain of individual choice.

Democracy as it stands, is still often assumed to be just and, as if it were self-evidently, compatible with social justice. Antony Flew shows this assumption to be wrong. He attacks John Rawls for labelling social justice "just", since social justice allows unjust transfer of justly acquired property to those who were not unjustly deprived of it.

8

As Anthony de Jasay once remarked, recent literature tends to reinterpret justice as everything except what it is: justice. Such, social justice is accompanied by political justice, ecological justice and the like. Roland Baader reveals this tendency toward political totalitarianism in Germany. Case studies in the ecology movement as well as in political correctness serve as ample evidence for typical outcomes of the social choice-rule.

One reason for perverting justice as social justice goes back to the egalitarian interpretation of redistribution. Angelo Petroni, following Bertrand de Jouvenel, distinguishes two concepts of redistribution: one to provide people in need with the means of subsistence, and the other to flatten inequalities in means. He judges the first to be the only one morally compatible with a liberal order.

Egalitarianism is typical of redistributionist measures *inside* political systems, but also *among* political systems. The European Community is one of the most striking features of this tendency. Gerhard Schwarz, juxtaposing arguments for ex-ante-harmonisation in Europe with those favouring competition among systems, elaborates some of the advantages of competition, such us error limitation, deregulation and liberalisation pressure, and taking the preferences of the people seriously.

Manfred Streit steps a little bit further back in the history of European treaties. He explores the general effects of competition among systems by analysing the Rome Treaty. Referring to the modern form of Law Merchant, he demonstrates the spontaneous process of substituting formal rules of national private law for informal ones.

Chapter Three is on *The future of freedom: of facts and fiction*. It reflects on experiences, theories, and ideas, past and present, to shape the future of a liberal society. The first four essays are on the practical lessons taught by the history of policies in the respective countries of the authors as well as by the history of theories and ideas in general. The remaining three essays highlight special aspects for the future of liberty, i.e. competition, cooperation and constitution.

Czech Prime Minister Václav Klaus starts by giving credit to the "Austrian School" for proving that the communist episode was not accidental, but rather the outcome of the ideas of the main opponents to that school. He explains how restoring the "Austrian" ideas helps in the transformation process in Eastern Europe.

Moving a little bit "west", Herbert Giersch teaches us some lessons from the German experience after World War II. He recommends reliance on spontaneous growth with technological progress in a modern capitalist economy, economic dynamism for short, to achieve prosperity and growth in the future.

Shifting even further "west" and from secular observations to more ecclesiastical ones, Lord Harris of High Cross attacks the lofty and self-righteous rejection of the liberal market by leading spokesmen for the Church of England. He reminds them that liberal capitalism is the best shield against poverty, tyranny and inhumanity that imperfect man can have.

Back from the specific to the general, former Italian Foreign Minister Antonio Martino sketches the intellectual climate and its changes since the 1940s. Reflecting on the most recent experiences in his native Italy, he is optimistic on the future of liberty on a world-wide scale.

Victoria Curzon Price is concerned about the Great Society's own genius for creating wealth, since only wealthy societies can afford big government, great armies, great wars, oppressive systems and the like. In information and competition on a global scale she sees a slender hope for freedom.

Gordon Tullock observes successful cooperations of ants as the outcome of an appropriate response of their simple preference function to changes in the environment by others. He recommends man to learn his lesson from these and other highly successful social insects.

Doering searches for the best constitutional defence of property rights among different political orders. Neither anarchy, nor aristocracy, nor monarchy, nor democracy turn out to be the best safeguard, but small communities.

Starting his essay with Phaedrus' fable "Canis parturiens", Doering charmingly alludes to the affection for dogs he shares with the man to which this volume is dedicated: Gerard Radnitzky.

I will close my introduction with a short biographical sketch of his life up to now. Thus I complete my prologue on **The book**

... and the man to whom it is dedicated.

Gerard Radnitzky characterizes himself as an individualist in a collectivist age. Gerard Alfred Karl Norbert Maria Hans Radnitzky was born on 2 July 1921 in Znaim, a medieval town in Southern Moravia close to the border with Austria. In 1918 Southern Moravia had become incorporated in the first Czechoslovak Republic. Since the region had for centuries been a part of Lower Austria, its population, consisting of Lower Austrians, were German-speaking. But it had equally intimate contacts with other parts of Moravia. In Moravia Czechs and Germans had lived together in peaceful cooperation for centuries. The Jews were fully integrated, and they had been among the most loyal subjects of the Habsburg monarchy. Moravia was a typical Central European region and a culturally fertile ground.

Names that come to mind are Gregor Mendel, Sigmund Freud, Edmund Husserl, Ernst Mach, Joseph Schumpeter, and Kurt Gödel. To make their career they had to leave the province and typically gravitate to Vienna.

Radnitzky grew up in a family background that emotionally remained attached to the Austro-Hungarian Empire. The house of Habsburg had defended those regions for centuries, against the French, the Russians, and the Germans, and, as Golo Mann pointed out, the Empire was for most of the time far from an interventionist state. At the end of W.W. I the population of Southern Moravia had placed its hopes in a confederal system for "Mitteleuropa" (Central Europe – like the one that crown prince Rudolf had conceived as a pupil and disciple of Carl Menger). The newly constituted Czechoslovak Republic, in which they suddenly found themselves after Southern Moravia had been annexed in 1918 by the then emerging Prague government, which at the time had the required military power, held out the promise of a state of several nationalities after the Swiss model, but it turned out to be a nation state. In 1945 the region disappeared behind the Iron Curtain.

Nonetheless, as Radnitzky uses to point out, the Czechoslovakian Republic (CSR) offered more economic freedoms and above all more of the all-important small freedoms of everyday life than, for instance, Germany and Austria of the time did and now do. In the 30's Germany became the totalitarian Third Reich, and the Austrian Republic was plagued by a latent civil war that sometimes became manifest (in 1934 and 1937). By contrast, the CRS was open to influences from the Anglo-Saxon world. Therefore, in retrospect, Radnitzky considered it a stroke of good look to have grown up rather there than in one of the neighbouring countries. This happy coincidence – one of many in his life – laid the foundation for a lifelong admiration of the Anglo-Saxon tradition, the root of classical liberalism, which had made possible the evolution of countries that are more free, or today less unfree, than most others. Also now he sees that part of the world (in spite of the fact that these countries have also lost much of their original freedom) as a pleasing contrast to the traditionally statist and dirigist climate of countries like Germany and France, not to speak of Russia. Radnitzky's first reading language was Czech, and he was taught at home. When the family's financial position progressively declined, he attended the German school as an ordinary pupil, but for a few years continued to take exams, as an external pupil, also at the corresponding Czech school.

The "Anschluss" of Southern Moravia into Niederdonau as a part of the Third Reich in October 1938 changed everything and abolished the small freedoms of everyday life. He experienced how the interventionist state penetrates more and more spheres of life, how it becomes more and more

11

pestering, enforces participation in and conformity to the national community, the "Volksgemeinschaft" of the National-Socialist German Workers Party. It was a practical demonstration of Hayek's thesis that socialism and nationalism are the greatest scourges of our century. Radnitzky took his school leaving examination at the local "Gymnasium" in 1940 (a school where once Mendel had taught as an assistant teacher). He then began to study mathematics with a retired professor. But all this was short-lived.

Then the war set the scene for all that followed and shaped the second part of his formative years. Since he had always been fascinated by flying, he joined the Air Force, graduated from various flying schools, was briefly a flight instructor, then a combat pilot and eventually an interceptor. Again, as he points out, as a stroke of luck, on the Me 262, the jet fighter than was far superior to any aircraft of the time. He uses to summarise his life as a soldier by the confession: I was a bad soldier, but a good fighter. He considered and still considers compulsory military service as a form of modern slavery to which you are condemned without trial. Nonetheless, the experience was at least in part rewarding. In a single-seater jet fighter you could preserve some of your individuality in an otherwise meaningless grind. The excitement of a dog fight was a worthwhile experience for an adventurous youth. After all, nationality means nothing in a sporty endeavour. The war taught him about uncertainty, about the transitoriness of life, and in that way war experience laid the background for his interest in philosophy, understood as reflection on existential themes. After an assignment to the Academy of the Air Force (at the centre of the cyclone), he defected, and on 19 April 1945 landed in Sweden.

Since then he has seen himself as a "skilled" expatriate, a sort of wanderer. The largest part of his life he spent in Sweden and acquired Swedish citizenship. He still remains attached to post-war Sweden, which he remembers as an idyllic milieu with friendly and charming people, who displayed a natural honesty that he never found again in his later domiciles. The young man completely uninterested in politics could not see below the surface, did not learn about the scheming of politicians who, like Gunnar Myrdal, the maître à penser of the Swedish Social Democratic Party, in 1947 made an attempt to introduce in Sweden central planning after the Soviet model (an attempt which failed largely thanks the influence of Hayek's *The Road to Serfdom*, which had been translated into Swedish just in time before the decisive election.) After W.W. II Sweden was the richest country in Europe, and in income per capita, of the world. Hence it could live for a long time on the fat accumulated during the capitalist years. But creeping socialism then slowly undermined the economy and even began to erode the Rule of Law. This again taught him a useful lesson that Radnitzky uses to observe that he has witnessed the decline of a state more than once: first the fall of the first CSR, then the collapse of the Third Reich, and then the slow-working poison of socialism ruining Sweden (which prompted his eventual emigration). He thinks that Germany is going the way of Sweden, or, to express it more cautiously (since the future is open and uncertain), of Sweden before 1991. These experiences have made him suspicious of every tendency to corporatism and collectivism, which he now observes also in Germany.[1] With respect to his present domicile Germany, he would echo Hayek, who in 1983 wrote that to his dismay he came to recognise that liberalism in Germany is a wafer-thin layer. Fortunately, in modern times it becomes increasingly less important where you live, since you can be connected world-wide with a circle of friends, with people who share your ideals or, to put it more generally, with the friends of the free society.

When Radnitzky tried to take up academic studies in Sweden, it turned out that for a foreigner it was impossible to embark on studying engineering (aeronautical engineering had been his original plan and interest). He studied instead statistics, psychology and philosophy at Stockholm university. At the time philosophy in Sweden meant mathematical logic, formal semantics, logical empiricism. That was not much food for thought for a young man interested in existential problems, but it was a useful training. He would regard it as indispensable. His teachers were logicians and theoreticians of physics. In 1968 he published a book *Schools of Metascience* (Humanities Press and later Regnery), a critique of logical empiricism (in which he claims that its philosophy of science does not even fit physical theories) and a discussion of continental hermeneutics. Surprisingly the book became a sort of "best-seller" in Scandinavian countries. Being dissatisfied with both "schools" he became more and more a disciple of Karl Popper, of whom he also became a life-long personal friend. Although he had been converted to critical rationalism, he kept close contacts with Imre Lakatos and in particular with Paul Feyerabend, whom he always appreciated as a friend with whom you could talk about everything, about any problem (even if you never knew whether he was serious or joking). However, he is convinced that both are not a progress but rather a regress compared to Popper's theories. William Bartley, III also belonged to his inner circle of friends. He says that he misses all of these friends severely. Radnitzky's merits in the philosophy of science and the way in which he arrived at Critical Rationalism is summarized in the first *Festschrift*, edited by Gunnar Andersson.[2] The contributors to that volume are philosophers of science.[3] Significantly, the contributors to the present *Festschrift* are economists and political philosophers. This development mirrors his intellectual odyssey.

13

Rather late in life Radnitzky discovered that political philosophy and economics interested him more than other fields of knowledge. The turning point came again through a stroke of good luck. He met Hayek and had the privilege of becoming his friend. Hayek became a source of inspiration for him and a friend with whom he shared many things, from an ancestry in Southern Moravia, to the admiration for the Scottish School, the British tradition, the ideal of the free society, and, last but by no means least, the dread of the "fatal conceit". As he used to say: "The trouble is not so much what people don't know, the trouble is what people know but know wrong." The "fatal conceit", the presumptuousness of all those who claim to possess certain knowledge, is the root of constructivism, which, in politics, tends to combine with socialist elements, a combination that leads to unlimited, totalitarian democracy.

He also claims to have learned much from the publications of the Institute of Economic Affairs in London, in particular from one of its founding presidents, Arthur Seldon, whom he now also counts among his personal friends. In the last few years Radnitzky became increasingly attracted by the work of Anthony de Jasay, in particular by his lucid analysis of the dynamics of the democracy, his criticism of contractarianism in all of its forms, and of the thesis that the state or at least a legal framework is, logically and hence historically, prior to the market. Jasay's analysis of social-choice democracy shows that it relentlessly leads to government growth and to an interventionist state that invades more and more spheres of life and progressively reduces individual freedom. All this made Radnitzky move more and more toward libertarian anarchism as represented in the work of Murray Rothbard, Walter Block, H.-H. Hoppe, and others around the Ludwig von Mises Institute.

Thus, in spite of all meandering in intellectual endeavours, there is a leitmotif that runs through the history of his intellectual life, namely the love of freedom and the quest for a state – if we must have one – that leaves it to the individuals to shape their own lives and lets them take the responsibility for it. This preference, of course, runs counter to the trends in the contemporary world.

Having worked with Radnitzky for 12 years, I am fairly sure that so far as his self-understanding goes, he would epitomise his position roughly as follows: in theology, as an agnostic; in the philosophy of science, as a critical-rationalist who emphasises pervasive fallibilism, and who sees the point of intellectual effort of analysis to a large extent residing in the activity itself – always provided it is fun and seen as an unfinished agenda; in economic theory he stresses, of course, methodological individualism and the subjectivist value theory of Austrian economics; in ethics, he believes that some deontological morality (respect for property rights, for truth, etc.) is indispensable for "strict" liberalism and hence for the free society; in meta-ethics, he adheres to non-cognitivism; in political theory, he is a libertarian; with respect to world view a nostalgic and a misanthrope. Philosophy he conceives as the intellectualised art of resignation.

Charming and gentle, Gerard Radnitzky has made many friends in and outside academia over the years. The reader will find many of them in this book. The Editor wishes to express his deep gratitude to all those who have contributed to this volume dedicated to Gerard Radnitzky's 75th anniversary, as a tribute to a ceaseless champion of individual freedom.[4]

THE EDITOR

Notes

1   See, for instance, his introductory remarks in Gerard Radnitzky and Hardy Bouillon, *Ordnungstheorie und Ordnungspolitik*, Heidelberg, Springer 1991, pp. XIII-XXVI.
2   See his contribution in *Rationality in Science and Politics*, Boston Studies, Dordrecht, Reidel 1984, pp. 289–294.
3   The contributors to the second Festschrift (in German) are scientists. It was intended to mark Radnitzky's becoming a Professor Emeritus. It was edited by Hardy Bouillon and Gunnar Anderson, and entitled *Wissenschaftstheorie und Wissenschaften*, Berlin, Duncker & Humblot 1991. (This biographical sketch is in part an abridged translation of my Prologue to that volume: "Gerard Radnitzky: Kritischer Rationalist und Klassischer Liberalist", pp. 9–19.)
4   My special thanks go to Roland Baader, who had the idea of compiling these essays in honour of Gerard Radnitzky, and to Heinrich P. Delfosse and Birgit Grandjean for their careful preparation of a camera-ready printout.

Chapter I:
Libertarians and Liberalism:
of Laps, Links and Lapses

Libertarian Perspective on Political Economy

Walter Block

In this Essay I shall try to set out the basic premises of libertarianism, and to apply them to issues such as socialism, capitalism, unionism, free trade, pay equity, minimum wages, underdeveloped countries and pollution. It is important that this be done since if we are to discuss this philosophy, we do well to have a clear account of it before us. In that way, whether we accept it or not, we shall not have to fear talking at cross purposes; we will at least all be undertaking a dialogue on the same issue. Perhaps we shall only achieve informed disagreement, but this is a far better result than misunderstanding, the condition that plagues much of dialogue on economic questions.

Self Owners

The first basic premise of libertarianism is that we are all self owners. That is to say, it is improper for anyone else to invade our bodies, whether through enslavement, murder, rape, assault and battery or any other such act. An implication of this moral axiom is that it is illegitimate for anyone to initiate coercion against a person who does not first himself undertake a physically abusive act. This is the non aggression axiom, a defining characteristic of libertarianism.[1] One may defend oneself against attack, or even retaliate – libertarianism is not equated with pacifism – but one may not be the first to assault another.[2]

What are the alternatives to self ownership? One possibility is some variant of autocracy or monarchy or totalitarianism. Here, one person, or a small group of people, would possess the right to dispose of the lives of all others. But this is in stark violation of the moral requirement of generalizability or universalizability: what is so (ethically) special about this person or small group such that they deserve to rule everyone else? Since there is no such distinguishing moral characteristic in existence,[3] this scenario falls to the ground. The only other option besides self ownership is that we all own 1/n share of everyone on earth, where n equals the total population. In this vision, or rather nightmare, no one would be allowed to do as much as scratch himself, without obtaining the permission to do so from the rightful owners of his body, that is, everyone else. If 'direct democracy' were practiced under these conditions, the human race would quickly die out (relieving us of the problem of solving this dilemma) since it would be too cumbersome to get everyone else's permission to do anything. If indirect, i.e. 'representative democracy' were observed, the situation would soon deteriorate into the first, or autocratic scenatio, which we have already rejected.

Private Property

A second premise is that a person's legitimately held private property shall likewise be safe from invasion. Before going on to an extended analysis of private property rights, we do well to consider the objection that there can be no justification for them, because property itself is intrinsically an illegitimate institution. This sentiment is often buttressed by citing Prouhdon, who is widely quoted as having held that 'Property is theft.'[4] But there is something logically incongruous about this statement. 'Property is theft' is used to denigrate the legitimacy of property, but in actual point of fact the very concept of 'theft' makes no sense whatever in the absence of legitimate property. If there were no legitimately owned private property, there logically could be no such thing as theft. Consider an act which might otherwise be considered to be stealing. Without a perspective of property rights, if someone were to take an object out of the possession of another person, and place it into his own possession, we could not call this theft, and by implication label it as illegitimate. Rather, we would have to unsatisfactorily (and morally) describe it as 'transferring,' or 'conveying,' or

17

'relocating' or some such. But to do so would be to eviscerate the ordinary meaning of the word.

The sixth commandment states 'Thou shalt not steal!' This commandment makes absolutely no sense outside the assumption of private property rights.

All we mean by private property rights is that human beings can utilize physical items of the earth without necessarily committing an invasive act. If people do not have such rights, and yet insist upon acting noninvasively, we must all perish, for we cannot live without using earth, air, water, fire, and all the things we can create out of them. If we are to survive under such a flawed understanding of property, then we must all act intrusively: we must use that which according to the theory we have no right to use.

The real question, then, is not whether human beings have property rights; it is, How shall they be divided up? May they be individual, or must they be communal? These are the questions to which we now turn.

Justification

We can justify private property rights along similar lines as we used for individual self ownership of our bodies, and for rejecting communal ownership. In this case there again exist the three identical options: individual ownership of property, group ownership of everything in common, and autocratic control. Autocratic control is non universalizable, and if each of the 6 billion of us had to get the permission of the other 5,999,999,999 before anyone could begin to use the resources of the earth, we would all starve, or deteriorate into a system of autocratic rule.

Utilizing the non aggression axiom, we may say that any means of obtaining property which is strictly *voluntary* is justified.[5] For example, trade, gifts, gambling, inheritance, charity, investments, employment, borrowing, repayment of debts, etc. The point is, if A has legitimate title to property y, and trades it for B's similarly legitimately held z, then A becomes the new and proper owner of z, and likewise B of y.

And how do unowned parts of nature pass into ownership by humans? Although this answer is less fully settled than those elements of the libertarian philosophy already introduced, the answer is, through homesteading. In the words of John Locke, one mixes one's labor with the land,[6] and thereby obtains rightful title.[7]

One way to justify this procedure is again to contrast it with its alternatives. How else, then, can property pass from a state of nature into human ownership? There seem to be but three alternatives: claims, govern-

18

ment sales and communal ownership. According to the first, we can establish rightful title to land merely by claiming it. The difficulty with this is that many people may claim 'the sun, the moon and the stars,' leaving these properties in dispute. Moreover, this seems unsatisfactory to our moral sense: the claimers did nothing to earn this property; why should they be able to own it, and thus prevent others from using it? A drawback to the second is that government is only composed of flesh and blood people, none of whom can justify their claim to unowned land. What is so special about the bureaucrat that he should be entitled to possess unowned land, merely because he is a part of the government?[8] As for the third alternative, the case for it again dissolves when we realize that in practice, it would mean either that such resources could not be used (the costs of agreeing to its use, on the part of billions of people, would be catastrophic) or that they would end up, in effect, being owned by a few rulers.

Despite the foregoing, it is of the utmost importance to realize that libertarianism by no means implies a capitalist means of organization. We totally and adamantly reject the view that private property rights logically implies a capitalist mode. Instead, we assert that libertarianism is *every bit* as compatible with socialism as it is with capitalism.[9] How is this possible? Let us clarify this point with reference to the following diagram:

	Socialism	*Capitalism*
Voluntarism	Voluntary Socialism	Laissez-Faire Capitalism
Coercivism	Coercive Socialism	State Capitalism

Although most political economic theorists identify as polar opposites socialism and capitalism, and play off the one against the other, we shall completely reject this mode of analysis. For us, the relevant distinction is not between socialism and capitalism, but between voluntarism and coercivism. The major combatants on the field thus are not socialism vs. capitalism, but rather voluntary socialism, together with voluntary capitalism on the one side, arrayed against the evil forces of coercive socialism and coercive capitalism, in unholy alliance, on the other.

Before considering each of the inhabitants of the four boxes in the diagram, let us begin by describing the rows, and then the columns. We have already touched upon the distinction between voluntarism and coercivism. The former is the condition wherein the libertarian axiom of non aggression against non aggressors is respected and upheld; the latter is the situation where it is violated. It is clear, then, that a strictly voluntary system is compatible with libertarianism – indeed, the two are equated – and that coercion is the diametric opposite of libertarianism.

Socialism

Now for the columns. By socialism I understand adherence to the familiar Marxian doctrine 'From each according to his abilities, to each according to his needs,' as well as the view that all property (or at least all capital goods) shall be held in common. But the crucial question for libertarianism is whether these socialistic perspectives are put into effect on a voluntary or on a coercive basis. We are all familiar with coercive or state socialism (communism). Here, the socialistic doctrines are upheld, at least in theory,[10] but this is done on a coercive basis. Individuals have no right to opt out of the system, nor is their consent necessary in order to begin it or to justify its continued existence.

In sharp contradistinction to coercive socialism is its polar opposite, voluntary socialism. Examples include the kibbutz, the cooperative, the commune, the (voluntary) labor union, the Hutterite colony,[11] the monastery, etc. The typical nuclear family, moreover, is a (voluntary) socialist commune![12] All members of the family consume not in accordance with their ability to earn, but based on their needs. The parents may earn the entire income, but certainly do not consume it all; the (young) children earn none of it, but consume on the basis of their needs. In all these cases, voluntarism is strictly upheld. No one is dragged, kicking and screaming, into voluntary socialism, nor prevented from leaving. Nor does the voluntary commune seize the private property of those who have not joined it of their own free will. On the contrary, the property of the commune is based on the pooling of the legitimately owned resources of the individuals who compose it. In all regards, then, this form of socialism fully lives up to the requirements of voluntarism. Hence, it is entirely compatible with libertarianism.

Capitalism

By capitalism I understand that system of interaction based on trade, employment, interest rates, business firms, profits, etc. An aphorism similar in form to the socialist one considered above might be 'From each according to his abilities, to each according to his abilities.' Just as for socialism, there is a similar bifurcation in capitalism. Under the laissez-faire or voluntary variety, the businessman earns his profits only from the consensual purchases of the consumers; 'consumer sovereignty' is the catchword of the free enterprise system.[13] And whenever a trade takes place – whether one good for another (barter), or a good or service for money (sale), or money for labor services (employment) – *both* parties gain, at least in their own *ex ante* expectations, compared to the situation which obtained before the trade took place, and would have continued on in the absence of the trade. If I trade you one hour of my time for a salary of $5.00, this must mean that I value that hour as worth less to me than the $5.00, and that you value the services you expect to obtain from me more highly than that amount of money. Thus, we *both* gain in welfare from the trade.[14] The free market consists of nothing but the totality of all such voluntary trades which take place in a given area. Thus, we are in a position to claim that the market benefits all participants![15]

But not all versions of capitalism are quite so benign. The system of state capitalism (or monopoly capitalism, or economic fascism, or corporate capitalism, or, paradoxically, national socialism – Naziism) retains a thin veneer of adherence to free enterprise institutions. But this is only a mask of the underlying reality. In actual fact, the corporate interests seize, through government, that which would be unavailable to them through the market. For example, if the customers purchase a given product in sufficient quantity and at a high enough price to allow the ruling class the profit it deems adequate, well and good. Free markets may well be allowed to obtain for that one small sector. But if not, then through a series of protections, payoffs, taxes, subsidies, bail-outs, franchises, permits, licenses, quotas, bribes, exemptions, tariffs, favors, etc., the capitalist-rulers will expropriate these funds from the general public. Consider the typical business bail-out, for instance. Here, the corporation confiscates, through taxes from the citizenry, those funds which were not forthcoming to them in the form of voluntary purchases. In effect, the corporation does an end run around the consumer. It asks its agent, the government[16] to appropriate monies from all members of society, in the form of taxes, and then to turn this wealth over to the corporate interests in the form of a bailout.[17]

This distinction between laissez-faire capitalism and state monopoly capitalism (between the two boxes on the right side of the diagram) is subtle, and difficult to understand. It is even harder to perceive than that between voluntary and coercive socialism (the two boxes on the left side of the diagram.) Yet it is one of the most fundamental of all distinctions in political economy. Its importance would be hard to overestimate. So let us try once again. There is all the world of difference between defending *a system* of competition, the free marketplace, in which all businesses must sink or swim depending upon how well they satisfy consumers, and defending *particular* business enterprises (as for example, by giving them a monopoly franchise or a protective tariff). The latter, indeed, can fairly be characterized as a 'running dog' policy in behalf of capitalist interests. But not the former, the libertarian vision. If this is the running dog of anything, it is of the consumer; if it speaks in behalf of anything, it is of liberty, justice, and individual rights, not special business interest groups.

In the felicitous phrase of Robert Nozick,[18] laissez-faire permits all 'capitalist acts between consenting adults.' But for the philosophy of libertarianism, a system which allows all 'socialist acts between consenting adults' is equally legitimate. The point is, it is not the capitalism or the socialism which is important.[19] This has been, for all too long, a red-herring which has been allowed to obfuscate serious analysis. On the contrary it is the coercion or voluntarism of a system which is really at issue.

Now that we have set the stage with this introduction to libertarianism, we are ready to consider applications to several public policy issues.

Unionism

Just as for socialism and capitalism, unionism is a complex phenomenon, which admits of a voluntary and a coercive aspect. And, following the pattern introduced above, libertarianism is fully consistent with voluntary unionism, and diametrically opposed to coercive unionism. What do all varieties of unionism have in common, both the coercive and voluntary types? Unions are associations of employees, organized with the purpose of bargaining with their employer in order to increase their wages.[20]

What, then is the distinction between invasive and non invasive unions? The latter obey the libertarian axiom of non aggression against non aggressors, and the former do not. Legitimate unions, in other words, limit themselves to means of raising wages which do not violate the rights of others, while illegitimate unions do not so proscribe themselves.

Mass Walkout

This of course leads us to the $64,000 question. Which arrows in the quiver of organized labor are invasive, and which are not? We can start off with a legitimate technique: threatening, or organizing, a mass walk out, unless wage demands are met.[21] This is not an infringement of anyone's rights, since the employer, in the absence of a contract, cannot compel people to work for him at wages they deem too low. Nor is it any valid objection to this procedure that the workers are acting in concert, or in unison, or in collusion, or in 'conspiracy.' Of course they are. But if it is proper for one worker to quit his job, then all workers, together, have every right to do so, en masse. This follows directly from our defense of voluntary socialism, of which voluntary unionism is merely one facet. True, the group has no more rights than those of the individuals who make it up, but if one person has the right to quit a job, he does not lose that right merely because others choose to exercise their identical rights to quit at the same time.

There are numerous 'right wing' economists[22] who take the view that anti trust and anti combines law ought to be applied to unions.[23] Thus, even what we have been describing as voluntary unions would be for them illegitimate, because they claim that 'collusive actions' on the part of unions 'exploit' the community as a whole,'[24] in their violation of consumers' sovereignty.[25] But this only shows that there is all the world of difference between what we have been calling laissez-faire and state capitalism.

Back to work legislation

If it is proper for unions to threaten or stage a mass walkout, it is improper for governments to enact legislation forcing them back to work. Certainly, this follows from the basic libertarian premise of self ownership. In the words of Murray Rothbard:

'On October 4, 1971, President Nixon invoked the Taft-Hartley Act to obtain a court injunction forcing the suspension of a dock strike for eighty days; this was the ninth time the federal government had used the Act in a dock strike. Months earlier, the head of the New York City teachers' union went to jail for several days for defying a law prohibiting public employees from striking. It is no doubt convenient for a long suffering public to be spared the disruptions of a strike. Yet the 'solution' imposed was forced labor, pure and simple; the workers were coerced, against their will, into going back to work. There is no moral excuse, in a society claiming to be opposed to slavery and in a country which has outlawed involuntary servitude, for any legal or judicial action prohibiting strikes – or jailing union leaders who fail to comply. Slavery is all too often more convenient for the slavemasters.'[26]

Boycott

Another legitimate union activity is the boycott, whether primary or secondary. A boycott is simply the refusal of one person to deal with another.[27] All interaction in a free society (whether voluntary socialist or voluntary capitalist) must be on a mutual basis, but there is no presumption that any particular interaction must take place. I, for example, may refuse to associate with you for any reason that seems sufficient to me. Since a boycott is merely an organized refusal to deal with, and each person has a right to so act, then people may act in this way in concert. Says Rothbard in this regard:

'A boycott is an attempt to persuade other people to have nothing to do with some particular person or firm – either socially or in agreeing not to purchase the firm's product. Morally, a boycott may be used for absurd, reprehensible, laudatory or neutral goals. It may be used, for example, to attempt to persuade people not to buy non-union grapes *or* not to buy union grapes. From our point of view, the important thing about the boycott is that it is purely voluntary, an act of attempted persuasion, and therefore that it is a perfectly legal and licit instrument of action ... a boycott may well diminish a firm's customers and therefore cut into its property values; but such an act is still a perfectly legitimate exercise of free speech and property rights. Whether we wish any particular boycott well of ill depends on our moral values and on our attitudes toward the concrete goal or activity. But a boycott is legitimate *per se*. If we feel a given boycott to be morally reprehensible, then it is within the rights of those who feel this way to organize a counter boycott to persuade the consumers otherwise, or to boycott the boycotters. All this is part of the process of dissemination of information and opinion within the framework of the rights of private property.

'Furthermore, 'secondary' boycotts are also legitimate, despite their outlawry under our current labor laws. In a secondary boycott, labor unions try to persuade consumers not to buy from firms who deal with non-union (primary boycotted) firms. Again, in a free society, it should be their right to try such persuasion, just as it is the right of their opponents to counter with an opposing boycott.'[28]

Picketing

Now let us consider an illegitimate union activity. These are acts which coercive unions engage in, but which non coercive unions totally eschew. Picketing, for example, is illicit, and therefore should be outlawed, because it is equivalent to a threat or an initiation of physical force. This must be clearly demarcated from a boycott. In picketing, the object is to prevent people who would like to deal with the struck employer (suppliers, customers, competing laborers – 'scabs,' or strikebreakers) from so doing. In a boycott, in contrast, the aim is to mobilize those who already agree with the strike, to refrain from making the relevant purchases. True, one may try to convince neutral parties, but in a boycott the means of doing so are strictly limited to non invasive techniques. Once encroachments are resorted to, a boycott becomes converted into picketing.

Only Informational

There are those who characterize picketing as merely 'informational'. In order to see the utter ludicrousness of such a claim, try to imagine what our response would be were McDonald's to send its agents, hundreds of them, carrying big sticks with signs attached to them (picket signs), to surround the premises of Burger King, or Wendy's, in order to give 'information' to their customers or suppliers. In like manner, we do not allow Hertz to picket Avis, or General Motors to picket Ford. There is absolutely no doubt that such activities would be interpreted, and properly so, as an attempt to intimidate. If any of these firms wish to convey information, they have other avenues open to them: advertising, direct mail, contests, give-aways, bargains, etc. And the same applies to a union. If it wishes to communicate, it must restrict itself to these methodologies.

It is sometimes asserted that the pickets are only at a job site in order to impart the information that a strike is in progress, and it is 'conceded' that the picketers become enraged if they see anyone (customers, suppliers, strike breakers) engaging in commercial endeavors with the struck employer. The attempt, here, is to claim that picketing is merely informational, and that these 'interferences' are responsible for the violence which is endemic on a picket line. But one cannot have it both ways. Either there is only knowledge being given out, or there is not. If there is, then how do we account for the typicality with which violence arises on the picket line? Are its members just so 'sensitive?' But this is all beside the point. Even if violence was never associated with picket lines, this would only prove they were so successful in their intimidation that none was necessary. As we have seen, the libertarian non aggression axiom precludes both the actual initiation of violence as well as the threat thereof, and even picketing which is (so far) non violent is a threat to all would be crossers of the picket line.

Job Ownership

Another defense of picketing concedes that it is a violent activity, but asserts that it is not an initiation of coercion, but rather a defense of private property rights, namely the jobs of the striking coercive unionists. There is some superficial plausibility in this rejoinder. After all, libertarians are not pacifists, and certainly they defend the right of people to protect their property against theft. However, the 'scab' is not stealing the job of the striking coercive unionist. A job, by its very nature, cannot be owned by any one person. Rather, it is the embodiment of an agreement between *two* consenting parties. In the case of the strike, organized labor is unsatisfied with the offer of the employer. It is publicly renouncing this offer. It therefore cannot be said that these workers still 'have' these jobs.[29] Under laissez-faire, *all* people are allowed to compete for jobs in a free labor market. It is a vestige of the properly repudiated caste system, or guild system, to think that there are two groups of people with regard to employment at any given plant: the coercive unionists, who own the jobs, or have a right to them, and all other people, who must refrain from bidding for them.

To some extend we are fooled by the very language we use in order to describe this situation. We speak of 'my' job, or 'your' job, or 'his' job, or 'her' job; this use of the possessive pronoun seems to indicate real possession, or ownership. But this is a complete mistake We also speak of 'my' spouse, or 'my' tailor, or 'my' employee, or 'my' customer, and yet it would be nothing short of grotesque to assign ownership rights to any of these relations. All of them are based on mutuality, not ownership on the part of either person. For example, if it is 'my' spouse, and she wants to divorce me, then I would be just as warranted in picketing her home, to make sure that she did not enter into a new relationship with a replacement for me, as would be the coercive unionist in protecting 'his' job against the similar 'incursions' of the 'scab.' If it is 'my' employee, then I could forbid him to quit his job. If it is 'my' customer, I could prevent him from taking his business elsewhere, to a competitor. And if it is 'my' tailor, it would be a violation of my rights if he moved to another city, retired, or entered a new occupation.

Sweat Shops

What of the claim that without picketing, coercive unions would be rendered virtually powerless, and in the absence of strong coercive labor organizations, the working people would be forced back into the 'sweat shops.' First of all, even if this claim were true, picketing would still be unjustified, and a violation of the basic libertarian premise against the initiation of violence. Secondly, even if coercive unions were all that stood between the sweat shop and present living conditions for their members, it still does not follow that the lot of *working people* would be improved by picketing. For this activity is aimed not so much at the employer as at the cometing worker, the strike breaker. The major aim of the picket line is to prevent alternative workers from attaining access to the job site. Indeed, the very terminology employed by coercive unionists to describe him, 'scab,' is indicative of the extreme denigration in which he is held. But these people are *working people* too. Further, they are almost always poorer[30] than the striking coercive unionists. This is seen by the fact that the 'scabs' are usually more than happy to take the offer spurned by the strikers. So if there is anyone who needs to be protected from the spectre of the 'sweat shop,' it is not the coercive unionist, but the scab.

Thirdly, it is profoundly mistaken to believe that the modern level of wages depends upon coercive union activity. As any introductory economic textbook makes clear,[31] wages depend, to the contrary, on the productivity of labor. If wages are bid above productivity levels, bankruptcy and consequent unemployment will tend to result.[32] However, if wages somehow find themselves below the rate of marginal revenue productivity, other employers can earn profits from bidding these workers away from their present employers – by continually improving the job offer until wages and productivity levels come to be equated.

There is abundant evidence to support the view that coercive unionism cannot be credited with the explosion of wages and living standards. For one thing, the modern coercive labor movement has only been with us in this century, and only gained much of its power (in the U.S.) with the advent of special legislation in the 1930s, when its share of the labor force rose from 5% to 20%.[33] And yet wages, welfare and standards of living have been on this increase for hundreds of years before that. For another, the economies of countries of southeast asia such as South Korea, Taiwan, Hong Kong, Singapore, have been burgeoning in the last several decades, in the virtual absence of unionism, coercive or voluntary.[34] As well, there have been sharp wage increases in industries – within countries with a strong labor movement – which are completely unorganized. Examples include banking, computers, housecleaners.

The comparison between the U.S. and Canada is also instructive. In 1960, the (coercively) unionized sector in both countries was about 30%; by 1983, labor organizations represented fully 40% of the Canadian work force, but only some 18% in the U.S. If the union-as-the-source-of-all-prosperity hypothesis were correct, we would have noted a slippage toward sweat shop labor conditions in the U.S., and an era of extreme affluence in Canada. Needless to say, that has not at all been the case.[35]

Unequal Bargaining Power

Let us consider one last possible defence: there exists unequal 'bargaining power' between employer and employee, and that only coercive unionism can redress this imbalance. The usual reason for supposing that there is unequal bargaining power is that there are more employees than employers.[36] If so, this is hardly sufficient to establish the case. I assume that bargaining power is defined in such a way so that when there is a difference of opinion, or a dispute, the person with the greater bargaining power is more likely to attain his goal than is the person with the lesser bargaining power. But in actual point of fact, the likelihood of attaining one's goal in a bargaining situation depends almost entirely on whether the wage is above, below, or equal to equilibrium.[37] In the first case, the employer will have more 'bargaining power,' as wages will tend to fall in any case; in the second case, the employee will have more 'bargaining power,' as the market will dictate an increase in wages. One may say, if one wishes, that in the third case 'bargaining power' is equal, since wages will tend not to change. But on the basis of Ocham's Razor it would be more scientific to dispense with the concept of bargaining power entirely, and confine our purview to basic supply and demand analysis in the labor market.[38]

Labor Legislation

It follows from our analysis of coercive unionism that much or our present labor legislation is mischievous and misguided. If voluntary association and mutual consent are the only legitimate foundations of employment; if it should be strictly forbidden for one group of workers to forcibly prevent another (scabs) from competing for jobs; then it follows that government-made laws which are inconsistent with these principles are incompatible as well with the libertarian legal code. For example, there should be no laws which compel the employer to 'bargain in good faith'; with any one set of employees; he should be allowed to deal with anyone he wishes. Further, all legislation prohibiting an employer from firing striking workers, and hiring replacements on a permanent basis, should be repealed. Says Rothbard:

'It is true that the strike is a peculiar form of work stoppage. The strikers do not merely quit their jobs; they also assert that somehow, in some metaphysical sense, they still 'own' their jobs and are entitled to them, and intend to return to them when the issues are resolved. But the remedy for this self-contradictory policy, as well as for the disruptive power of labor unions, is not to pass laws outlawing strikes; the remedy is to remove the substantial body of law, federal, state, and local, that confers special governmental privileges on labor unions. All that is needed, both for libertarian principle and for a healthy economy, is to remove and abolish these special privileges.

'These privileges have been enshrined in federal law – especially in the Wagner-Taft-Hartley Act, passed originally in 1935, and the Norris-La-Guardia Act of 1931. The latter prohibits the courts from issuing injunctions in cases of imminent union violence; the former compels employers to bargain 'in good faith' with any union that wins the votes of the majority of a work unit arbitrarily defined by the federal government – and also prohibits employers from discriminating against union organizers. ... Furthermore, local and state laws often protect unions from being sued, and they place restrictions on the employers' hiring of strikebreaking labor; and police are often instructed not to interfere in use of violence against strikebreakers by union pickets. Take away these special privileges ...

'It is characteristic of our statist trend that, when general indignation against unions led to the Taft-Hartley Act of 1947, the government did not repeal any of these special privileges. Instead, it added special restrictions upon unions to limit the power which the government itself had created ... the government's seemingly contradictory policy on unions serves, first, to aggrandize the power of government over labor relations, and second, to foster a suitably integrated and Establishment-minded unionism as junior partner in government's role over the economy.'[39]

Free Trade

The moral case against trade barriers on libertarian grounds is total, complete, and straightforward. All owners of legitimately owned property have a right to trade it, on a voluntary basis, with whomever they wish. It matters not one whit that a trading partner resides in another country: human rights do not stop at national borders.

In addition to the moral argument for full free trade, there is also an economic one: trade barriers reduce economic welfare. Unfortunately, most people are not aware of the economic harm created by the policy of squelching international trade. Self-imposed banishment from the benefits of specialization and the international division of labor is a serious mistake for a large country which contains within its own borders a global scale market and many of the skills, raw materials and capital available in the entire world; for a small country this is folly indeed.[40]

Even the very term 'protectionism' is a vast misnomer. It implies that the citizens are being defended against economic exploitation somehow made even more sinister by its foreign genesis. In fact, nothing could be further from the truth.

In order to see this clearly, let us start not with a nation which refuses to trade with others, but with an individual who sets up trade barriers between himself and all other people. Such a person, of course, will have to provide for all of his needs.

He will have to grow his own food, make and mend his own clothing, build a house for himself, minister to himself when he falls ill, entertain himself, and so on. Not being able to specialise in any one thing, his productivity will not be able to attain viable levels. He will be a 'jack of all trades, master of none.'

If everyone tried the path of economic solipsism, this fertile earth, which today can support the lives of more than four billion people, might possibly be able to keep at most a few million snarling savages living on a miserable semi-starvation basis.

On a national level, one argument for protectionism is that a policy of free trade would mean the loss of jobs for Canadians. And this, it must be conceded, is true. If buyers are offered the choice between a made-in-Canada sweater for $50, and an identical one manufactured in southeast Asia for $10, there is little doubt that virtually all consumers will choose to be thrifty and save 40 of their hard-earned dollars. The inevitable result will be the loss of Canadian jobs – in sweater production.

But let us not stop here, as do the protectionists, for there are several more effects to be considered. What, pray tell, will the consumers do with the extra $40? They may spend it on other Canadian products, but if they do, some of the now unemployed sweater workers can find jobs in these other lines. They can save this money, but then the banks will be able to make loans on easier terms, thus creating additional jobs in construction, house building, and heavy industry. Alternatively, they could purchase four additional foreign sweaters (or other imports from other countries) for the same amount.

What will the foreign suppliers do with the $10 (or $50) paid to them by Canadians? One possibility is to buy Canadian products, strengthening domestic industry. They might also spend the dollars in third countries, whose nationals can turn around and purchase Canadian goods, again giving our country a boost in employment.

But what if the foreigners, perhaps determined to wreck our economy, decide instead to merely sit on their newly acquired Canadian funds? What if they merely stuff this money into their mattresses? If they were so foolish, they would only succeed in giving us their sweaters for free! By this policy, they would present us with valuable commodities, and receive in return pieces of paper their own actions render worthless. This form of financial reparation would, of course, make our sweater industry superfluous, but all Canadians saving on their clothing bills would not be able to afford additional goods – and jobs would be created in the industries catering to these new desires.

If another country can make sweaters more cheaply than we can, it makes sense to concentrate on what we do best, allow then to do the same, and then to trade – utilizing the special skills and factor endowments of each region of the globe. We're not going to be a very rich nation if we make people work at jobs others can do more cheaply.

Who Loses?

The main sufferers from a policy of free trade are not the lower paid workers with generalized training, which is as applicable to sweater production as to anything else. They will find alternative employment at comparable wages.

The real losers are the protected factory owners, and the highly paid, heavily unionized workers with a great investment in skills specific to sweater manufacture. It is only they who will suffer losses unless retrained. As a result, the unions support the manufactorers in their bid for more protection and more assistance.

Why is it, if the case for free trade makes so much sense, that we nonetheless find ourselves barricaded from affluence by high tariff walls? Although this can only be speculative, the answer seems to be in our social and economic organization. As producers, our interests are highly concentrated.[41] It is the rare person who has more than one source of employment; most investors focus on one or just a few industries. But as consumers, we typically purchase literally tens of thousands of items. Our interests, here, are staggeringly diffuse.

It is little wonder then, that when it comes to considering a tariff on shoes or tooth-brushes or paper clips or bubblegum, the producers, both owners and employees, can easily mobilize on their own behalf.

The trade 'protection' may cost the general public billions, and be worth only millions to the manufacturers. Yet because of their diffuseness as consumers and because of the fact that the tariff will cost each of us only a few pennies, Canadians have little individual incentive to organize a resistance.

The populace is so befuddled by the media blitz of the real beneficiaries of trade barriers – the protected manufactures and unionized workers – that it has come to feel, vaguely, that trade barriers are really in their own and in the public interest.

Unilateralism?

A unilateral declaration of free trade on the part of Canada is hardly at the top of the agenda of most governments. But it is of the utmost importance to examine this public policy alternative.

Consider this issue from the Canadian perspective vis-à-vis that of the U.S.

A unilateral end to all tariffs, quotas and other such interferences has at least the advantage that it could be attained without the co-operation of the inward-looking Americans. Moreover, it would undoubtedly bring great benefits to this country. (To say that it would be difficult to convince Canadians of the merits of such a move, however, would be the understatement of the century).

Under a regime of this sort, Canadian consumers would be able to avail themselves of goods at hitherto unimaginably low prices. This alone would be a magnificent spur to our standard of living, and would probably do more for the well-being of the poor than the welfare program on the books put together.

Further, this boon to consumers would likely spill over to our export sector. For the additional funds spent in the U.S. would eventually return here, in the form of domestic purchases. And this could not help but spur additional employment opportunities in Canada.

Pay Equity

Canada is in the process of promoting 'equality in employment,' as called for most notably by Judge Rosalie Abella. The main finding of the Abella Royal Commission[42] is that the female-male wage ratio of 63.9 percent is largely due to sexual discrimination on the part of the nation's employers, both public and private. Its chief recommendation is that a new affirmative action policy of 'employment equity' be implemented, which would require business and Crown corporations to change their hiring and promotion practices, until balanced job representation and equal pay have been much more nearly attained.

However, this is the wrong solution to a non-existent problem. The major finding of the Fraser Institute study is that the income gap between genders is not due to employer discrimination, but rather to differences in productivity. There is no determination that these differences are inherent, or based on genetics. Rather, one major factor is the asymmetrical effect of marriage on earnings. It raises the earnings of the husband, and reduces those of the wife. This, in turn, is because unequal child care and house management responsibilities, different psychic attachments to the labor force vs. home and hearth. The proof? Women who have never been touched by the institution of marriage, and who thus can be presumed to have productivity levels similar to those of men, do not suffer from lower incomes.

The statistics are revealing. In 1981, the female-male ratio for Canadians who have never been married was 83.1 percent. But even this is an underestimate of the true relationship, because the statistics have not been corrected for labor force experience, age, education, unionization, etc. When just one of these corrections is made, for example, and we compare female to male incomes ratios for never-marrieds with a university degree, the figure rises to 91.3 percent. (For 1971, such university educated never-married females actually earned 9.8 percent more than their equally accomplished make counterparts!)[43] In other words, when we consider only males and females who have never been touched by the productivity-differentiating institution of marriage, that is, compare men and women who are likely to have similar market productivities, we find no statistically significant differences in their earnings.[44]

Nor are these findings a statistical aberration. An intensive study of the data collected over five censuses (1941–1981) shows that the female-male ratio for the never-married has not fallen below the 80 percent level, and has not risen above 47 percent for those who have been ever-married.[45]

The recommendations of the Abella Royal Commission Report, predicated as they are on the role of employer discrimination as the cause of the income gap, will not solve the basic problem; instead, they will cause considerable mischief. For if the reason women on average are receiving only $6.50 for every $10.00 of male earnings is lower average productivity, it is easy to see the effect of legislation which requires they be paid on an 'equitable' basis: they will be priced out of the labor market, and hence become unemployed.[46]

The tragedy of the matter is that on the market, discrimination on the basis of sex, or race, is simply not viable.[47] Were equally productive male and female employees to be paid widely varying salaries, strong profit incentives would tend to wipe out the differential. Entrepreneurs would seek to hire the underpaid women and fire the overpaid men. For example, suppose you, as an employer, were faced with two job applicants, each with a productivity level of $10.00 per hour. Assume that the male had to be paid $10.00, while the woman, thanks to the magic of 'discrimination,' need only be paid $6.50. Who would you choose? Well, unless you were an extreme sexist, you would hire the woman, because you could make an additional hourly profit of $3.50 per hour from her labor. If you were an extreme sexist, and hired the man instead, you would soon enough go broke, as your competitors, with cheaper female labor, could underprice you.

Minimum Wage

Consider the plight of the low-wage worker, and the government's response, the minimum wage law. Public critisism of this initiative generally has been limited to carping that the minimum-wage level is not high enough, or rising sufficiently quickly. This is particularly unfortunate since the long-run effect of the minimum-wage laws, paradoxically, is not to raise take-home pay of workers with lesser skills, but often to make it well nigh impossible for them to find any jobs at all.

The major impetus behind this legislation is the fear that, in its absence, employers would be completely free to dictate the level of wages paid. In this view, it would be a calamity for governments to leave remuneration decisions for the lowest-paid workers to the tender mercies of the capitalist class. And enlightened opponents of minimum-wage laws do not deny that employers will try to pay as little as possible.

On the contrary, those like myself fully accept the self-serving attitude of employers. But we also accept the harsh reality that there is an inexorable tendency for wage levels to reflect the productivity of workers. Wage levels below worker productivity are pushed up, and those above are pushed down by self-serving employees.

Take, for example, a laborer who creates value of $2 per hour and who is now being paid only 25 cents per hour. This means the employer makes a pure profit of $1.75 for each hour of employee toil. This sounds bad for the worker – but it is a situation unlikely to exist in the real world, and even if it did, completely impossible to sustain.

It could not last because the $1.75 profit per hour would act like a vacuum, sucking in competing uses of such profitable labor. Every other employer would like nothing better than to woo this worker away from his present boss and seize these extraordinary profits to himself. But the new employer, of course, could entice the downtrodden worker only with a better wage.

And so, the upward march of wages toward $2 per hour would cease only when the profits to be gained by attracting such a worker begin to fall below the costs of seeking him out and employing him. Therefore, we must conclude that in the absence of government intervention, a worker worth $2 per hour will earn, at the very least, a wage not significantly below this $2 productivity level.

But what happens with the passage of a law that says that if a firm hires this worker, it must pay, say $3.40 per hour? He will be forced into a life of unemployment.

For the prospective employer, taking on this laborer would be a financial disaster: $3.40 per hour would have to be paid out, while only $2 per hour would be taken in. A firm might decide to act so unwisely in a few cases, perhaps out of charity; but if the firm persisted on a large scale, it would succeed only in driving itself toward bankruptcy.

The tragedy and the shame is that though the low-productivity worker, if given a chance of employment, usually can raise his skill levels above those rates now called for by law, with minimum wage legislation, he is effectively barred from employment in the first place. He is consigned to a life of enforced idleness, which brings in its wake many other problems: crime, alcoholism, despair, illness.

Who are these people with low economic productivity who are so mistreated by this unwise public policy? They are largely to be found among teenagers, school dropouts, native and other rural peoples, immigrants, alcoholics, the handicapped. When two or more of these categories are combined, unemployment rates rise to astounding levels.

Unemployment rates for downtrodden groups such as black, poorly educated, rural teenagers have run as high as 50%. And even these figures under-estimate the true problem, because they ignore those who have left the labor force in despair.

Nor is this country any exception to the general economic law. Minimum-wage laws in Canada have reduced employment opportunities for those at the bottom of the income scale.

Why, if the minimum-wage law is such a mistake, do Ottawa and the provinces continue this policy? The first reason is the public's fear of exploitative employers. This fear is one of the elements played on by unions.

But the key point here is that unionized labor is always in competition with non-organized and usually lower-productivity workers. Every time unions increase their wage demands, employers are to that degree more tempted to substitute nonunion labor. What better way to preclude this possibility than by lobbying for a minimum-wage law, which substantially increases the price of these alternative workers, and thus makes them uncompetitive?

Naturally, unions attach their support of such a law to their efforts 'to raise wage levels for those at the bottom of the pay scale.' But if this were really their position, they could have no objection to a minimum-wage law that applied only to unions, one that would prohibit unionists alone from early any less, say, than $30 per hour. However, no responsible union leader could accept this challenge, because he would be massive unemployment for his members and a new, less remunerative career for himself.

How can we illustrate the economic principle that high minimum wage levels lead to relatively increased unemployment rates for unskilled workers? One way is to calculate the unemployment rates of youthful Canadians as a percentage of those of the more highly productive adult employees, and compare them with the minimum wage levels in each of the provinces. (For our table, we choose workers between 20 and 24 as our control, because this is the youngest group of people subject to the 'adult' minimum wage law.)

	Unemployment rate for 20–24 year olds as % of rate for those 25 and over %	Minimum wage $
Manitoba	289	4.30
Saskatchewan	257	4.25
Ontario	251	4.00
New Brunswick	237	3.80
Nova Scotia	213	4.00
Quebec	206	4.00
Newfoundland	204	4.00
British Columbia	190	3.65
Alberta	182	3.80
Prince Edward Island	n.a.	3.75

Source: Statistics Canada, Labor Department, May 1985

The results are painfully obvious. Manitoba, with the highest minimum wage level ($4.30) has an unemployment rate for its young workers that is 1.9 times as high as that for the rest of the population. Saskatchewan, with the next greatest level ($4.25) weighs in with the second biggest relative unemployment rate for youth – 1.6 times as high as the rest of the population. And at the bottom of the pack in terms of the disenfranchisement of their young people, come British Columbia and Alberta with two of the country's lowest minimum wage levels. Here, youthful unemployment is only 90%+82%, respectively, higher than adult levels.

Third World Development

At first blush, aid to underdeveloped countries seems noble, humanitarian, and serendipitously, in our own national interests as well. After all, Canadian aid to the less fortunate nations surely must save people from starvation, encourage the development of primitive economies, increase our exports and enhence freedom by forestalling the spread of communism.

There is much evidence, however, showing aid programs to be questionable means towards these worthy ends. Further, there are indications that private trade and investment, currently shackled and hampered by tariff and import barriers in the Western industrial countries may be more efficacious than inter-governmental transfers.

Food grants are a major part of foreign aid, and Canada is the world leader here, meeting about 30% of its bilateral commitments in this form. (Canada funnels 70% of its total donations bi-laterally; 30% is given through multilateral channels such as the Organization for Economic Co-operation and Development.)

Foodstuffs are obviously basic, because the malnutrition which unfortunately prevails in many less developed countries is one of the blocks to economic betterment. But compelling humanitarian requirements in cases of actual famine aside, even this sort of aid is fraught with danger. Massive gifts can take the profit incentive out of local agriculture; with fewer farmers and less land under cultivation, this can paradoxically worsen, not improve, the long-term prospects of food production and hence safety from future starvation.

Capital grants are likewise destructive to long-term productivity. Although the ancient Egyptian pyramids were an extraordinary instance of capital accumulation, they resulted in no economic gain in the basic sense of contributing to the well-being of the great masses of people.

Even more wasteful are the modern equivalents of such monument-building made possible by foreign aid: the steel mills in Egypt, the modern chemical plants in India, the tractors given to aboriginal people who cannot operate them, the automatic assembly plants scattered widely throughout the Third World (which are the result of protective tariffs on automobile imports as well).

These are wasteful because the products fabricated in this highly techno-logical manner actually cost the underdeveloped countries more to manu-facture themselves than they could have paid by importing the finished product from more developed countries.

Many people deduce from the fact that the rich countries have much capital and the poor ones little that what is required is vast capital infusion. But this wet-sidewalks-cause-rain reasoning points to almost the exact op-posite of what is really needed. Capital, in and of itself, does not create wealth. It is rather the *result* of a process of economic development that also includes, as complementary factors, such things as the willingness to work, the skill and education of the labor force, and relatively free and private markets protected by a stable code of laws.

One indication of the importance of these other phenomena is the fact that a large proportion of the very limited capital generated in the poor countries is actually invested in the more advanced nations, where private property rights are far more secure.[48]

Then there is foreign aid in the form of technological and other educa-tion. Canada ranks third among the donor nations in this category, behind only France and New Zealand, meeting just over 15% of its bilateral com-mitments to the underdeveloped world in this form. But the difficulty is that in the absence of such facilities as fully equipped laboratories, libraries, computer centres, and without the mutual support of thousands of other similarly educated scientists and technologies, such aid cannot be efficiently utilized. And the proof can be seen in the immigration patterns of the educated classes in the Third World a 'reverse brain drain,' toward the more advanced countries.

Foreign aid of whatever variety – food, capital, technology, or outright cash grants – moreover sets up a welfare-like dependency status on the recipient country. In much the same manner as domestic welfare programs sap the economic ambition, vitality and progress of their local clients, so do programs on international levels have similar effects.

If foreign aid is unlikely to help the recipient, can it at least help the donor? Pragmatic considerations would seem to support this view. For one thing, the Canadian International Development Agency requires that about 80% of its bilateral disbursements be spent on Canadian goods and ser-vices.

But behind the bookkeeping legerdemain, this amounts only to a free gift of goods and services from Canada to other countries, with no offsetting returns. No one is foolish enough to suppose that German reparations to Israel actually benefited the economic self-interest of Germany – even though much of it took the form of exporting domestic items. Nor does the defendant in a civil case rejoice in his new-found wealth when he is forced by a court decision to compensate the plaintiff – even in the form of goods he himself produces.

Will Canadian aid to other countries at east make it more likely that they will choose the path of democracy and market institutions rather than fall into the communist and coercive collectivist ambit? Unfortunately, not only will Western foreign aid not attain this end – it is likely to undermine it, and instead to encourage coercive socialism and totalitarianism in the Third World.

First of all, Canadian aid is traditionally in the form of government-to-government grants. This strengthens the role of the public vs the private sector in the underdeveloped countries. But political freedom is a delicate and precious flower; it cannot live where the bulk of economic activity is carried on in the public sector.

Second, Canadian foreign aid has been given to countries that have made explicitly totalitarian avowals in their centralized economic plans – and our largesse has in no small degree shielded them from the repercussions of such policies and allowed them to continue unchecked down this patch. For example, we find in the five-year plan of India, a country which continues to receive strong Canadian support, the view that 'planning should take place with a view to the establishment of a socialistic pattern of society where the principal means of production are under social ownership or control.'

The Alternative

Of far greater benefit to the nations of both North and South is a policy of free trade and unregulated international flows of capital. This will greatly benefit the Canadian standard of living, as we can purchase many goods such as clothing from the less developed world for far less than it costs to make them ourselves. But of far greater importance, such policies will truly lead to Third-World economic development – and to tighter integration with our own economy.

How can we describe the leaders of a nation which loudly proclaims its interest in economic development for the poor countries of the world, and yet remains steadfast in its determination to maintain protective tariffs, quotas and other impediments to economic intercourse with the Third World? Only as hypocritical.

Pollution

Whatever its other accomplishments, the free market is commonly blamed for pollution and other environmental disasters. The critics – Greenpeace, self-styled environmentalists, the Sierra Club, 'Green' Parties around the world – all hold the laissez-faire capitalist system responsible for acid rain, unclean air, and other such problems.

A superficial response would be that there is pollution behind the Iron Curtain as well, and much of the mischievous interference with nature in the west is caused directly by government operations, such as utilities.

A more basic answer, however, is that Yes, capitalism is indeed responsible for pollution, but the fault lies with the coercive elements of the system, not with the voluntary, or libertarian aspects.

In the 1830s and 1840s there were a spate of law suits in the U.S. and Great Britain which are very pertinent to our modern experience. Typically, a woman would go to court, under the common law provision of nuisance, and complain that a factory, in belching forth smoke, was dirtying the laundry she had hung out to dry. Or a farmer would object to a railroad car passing by with sparks flying, which would burn his hay stacks.[49] The plaintiff, in other words, alleged that his private property rights were being violated, and appealed to the judiciary for an injunction to stop the affront.

The courts, in a long series of decisions which established the precedents which rule us even now, admitted that private property rights were indeed being violated by the defendants. However, they commonly held that there was something even more important than private property rights, namely, 'the public good.' And what did the 'public good' consist of, you may ask? It consisted of encouraging manufacturing! With this doctrine in mind, the case of the plaintiff was summarily dismissed, and the manufacturer was given carte blanche to use the atmosphere as he saw fit.

There are several points which must be made with regard to this sorry tale. First of all, it should be clear that this was an instance of the workings of coercive capitalism, not the free market. In the latter, but not the former, the rights of the individual and his property are sacrosanct; they are not rendered inoperable by philosophically meaningless concepts such as the 'public good,' or the 'common good.'[50] Secondly, it is clear that the concept of private property rights, although much reviled by self-styled defenders of the environment, is the key to its protection. What we have here is a dramatic instance of the 'tragedy of the commons.' When people are allowed full title to property, they treat it as if they own it; that is, they tend to protect it. But when property rights are unprotected, and others may violate them with impunity, they do so, and spoilation of the environment is the result. Thirdly, with this series of judicial decisions, even a public spirited manufacturer would be forced into engaging in pollution. For if he alone invested in expensive smoke prevention devices, while his competitors invaded the property of their neighbors with dust particles, they would be able to undersell him, and eventually drive him from business. As a result, the entire economy was encouraged to engage in pollution intensive technologies. That is, had the judges found for the plaintiffs in these cases, the economy would have invested more in methods which had less pollution as a by product. More research and development funds would have gone into the creation of better smoke prevention devices. Legal institutions which would have diminished the negative effects of environmental despoliation – such as restrictive covenants – might have sprung up and/or been strengthened. The sort of manufactoring process which had smoke particles as an almost inevitable result would have been forced to locate further away from population centres. In short, the environmental crisis could have been vastly reduced, or eliminated entirely, had the precepts of free enterprise been incorporated into our legal findings. That they were not is due to elements of coercive capitalism, not to the market system.

Notes

1   Other perspectives, to be sure, would agree with the non aggression axiom. Even public opinion is overwhelmingly in support of such a view. The distinctiveness of libertarianism is not that it, too, upholds the axiom, but that it makes it a basic premise of it entire system, and rigorously adheres to it. See in this regard Murray N. Rothbard, *The Ethics of Liberty*, N.J. Atlantic Highlands, 1982.

2   Libertarianism is a political philosophy, not a philosophy of life. It asks one single solitary question – under which conditions is the use of physical force justified? – and gives one single solitary answer – only when a prior use of physical force was engaged in.

3   Being a member of the Aryan race, or having red hair, or being able to run a mile in less than four minutes, are certainly characteristics which distinguish those to whom they apply from most other people, but they are not morally relevant, and thus cannot be used to justify rule of one over another.

4   Joseph Proudhon, *What is property?*, Trans, B. Tucker, New York, Humboldt, 1890.

5   For a full explication of this, see Robert Nozick's adumbration of legitimate process, in his *Anarchy, State and Utopia*, New York, Basic Books, 1983.

6   See John Locke, *An Essay concerning the True Original Extent and End of Civil Government*, in E. Barker, ed., *Social Contract*, New York, Oxford University Press, 1948, pp. 17–18.

7   Homestanding theory has been subjected to a thorough going critique by Robert Nozick, op.cit. For a defense against this attack, see Jeffrey Paul, ed., *On Reading Nozick*, New York, Rowan and Littlefield, 1983.

8   There are those who will claim that the government represents us all, especially the democratic variety. For a critique of this view, see Lysander Spooner, *No Treason*, Larkspur, Colorado, (1870) 1966.

9   Those theologians who are looking for a 'third way' which is confined neither to socialism nor to capitalism could do worse than consider libertarianism.

10 The egalitarian code is far from achieved in places like Cuba, the Soviet Union, the People's Republic of China, Eastern Europe, the Marxist dictatorships in Africa, etc.

11 See Walter Block, 'The Hutterites,' *Grainews*.

12 At least with regard to the adult members, who, in any case, are the only people to whom the concept 'voluntary act' could apply fully.

13 The market is set up so as to satisfy the consumer. But sometimes (ofttimes) the consumer demands products that are (properly) considered immoral. Examples such as pornography, prostitution, certain 'recreational' drugs come to mind. But it would be improper to blame the free enterprise system for this occurrence. Presumably, a voluntarily socialist system could produce these goods and services, were its members interested in them. The libertarian view on this phenomenon is thus *not* that the market (or economic freedom) always precludes the production of items of questionable morality (See the Morality of the Market: Religious and Economic Perspectives, Walter Block, Geoffrey Brennan and Kenneth Elzinga, eds., Vancouver, The Fraser Institute, 1985, especially chapter VI), but only that since the production of these items does not necessarily involve the initiation of violence, it should not be made a jailable offence.

14 True, I may have been in a bad state beforehand. This is indicated, perhaps, by the fact that my position is improved through employment at $5 per hour. But this is not (necessarily) the fault of my new employer! Assume that it is not. Assume, that is, that my unfortunate pre-employment conditions was due to some other source. Then it is clear that my employer is my benefactor, even if my position with him is a very humble one.

15 Consider a possible objection. When Henry Ford began mass pro-

ducing the 'horseless carriage,' he undoubtedly benefited millions of people. For the first time in the history of the world, this item became more than a plaything for the rich: the middle class, and then even the poor, were able to own automobiles. But what about the capitalists and workers in the horse and buggy industry: the horsebreakers and trainers, the carriage, bridle and buggy whip manufacturers, the skilled artisans who created saddles, etc. Weren't they hurt by the free market? The answer is 'no.' The market consists *solely* of the voluntary trades which actually take place. After the advent of Ford, virtually no one was willing to engage in any sorts of trades for the particular skills of the members of the horse and buggy industry. By definition, they were no longer part of the market (although, to be sure, before the automobile they were an integral part of the market.) After the introduction of the car, these people had a choice: to remain outside the market, and not benefit from it, or to orient themselves to the market, and begin supplying things that the consumers now wanted to purchase. The market thus benefits all participants, but not everyone necessarily always chooses to be a part of the market.

16 See Walter Williams, *The State Against Blacks*, New York, Mc Graw-Hill, 1982.

17 When this occurs in the third world, it is particularly vicious. There are numerous cases on record where the indigenous people were relative happy in their pre-(coercive) capitalist tribal life, and/or at least unwilling to work for a multinational enterprise for money wages. Whereupon the local government, at the behest of the MNE, began taxing the natives, and forced them to pay in the form of money, not goods – which was only available 'courtesy' of the (coercive) capitalist. In this way the MNE could in effect enslave (force unwilling persons to become employees) the natives. See Parker T. Moon, *Imperialism and World Politics*, New York: Diamond, 1927.
But these are *coercive* MNEs. If our analysis is to be coherent and rational, they must be sharply distinguished from voluntary multinational corporations, which can only benefit all those with whom they come in contact, since by stipulation they are part of the mutually beneficial free enterprise system. See in this regard Peter Bauer, *Equality, the Third World, and Economic Delusion*, Cambridge: Harvard University Press, 1981; and Michael Novak, *Will It Liberate? Questions about Liberation Theology*, New York, Paulist Press, 1986.

18 Robert Nozick, *Anarchy, State and Utopia*, New York, Basic Books, 1983.

19 It is ofttimes claimed that cooperation takes place under socialism, and

competition under capitalism. Limiting our vision, now, to only the voluntary versions of both these systems, we can see that there is a grain of truth in this assertion. That is, *explicit* cooperation takes place only in voluntary socialism, not voluntary capitalism. But *implicit* coopertaion takes place in the latter system. For example, in the market, if everyone wanted to be a carpenter, and no one a plumber, the wages of the former would fall calamitously, and those for the latter would rise sharply. This would induce at least some people to give up a life of carpentering, and embrace one of plumbing. If the allocation between these two callings still did not match the relative desires of consumers for their services, there would yet remain a wage gap, ever inducing further changes. It takes no great insight to see that the market system is really enticing people into *cooperating* with each other in this regard. As Adam Smith said, each person is only attempting to further his own private interest. But in so doing, he is led, *as if by an invisible hand*, to benefit the public, which was no part of his intention. Theologians see the hand of God in every part of our existence, even in the most unlikely of places: in a sunset, in music, in mathematics, in a baby's smile. Why is it that there is very little appreciation that the free market, too, is part of God's plan, and that the invisible hand indentified by Adam Smith is part of it. (For further elucidation and elaboration of this point, see Walter Block, *The U.S. Bishops and Their Critics*, Vancouver, The Fraser Institute, 1985.)

20 Since money wages are funds which the employees take home, and working conditions embody funds which are spent, at least in part, in behalf of the employees while on the job, there are really two desiderata here. One, the total of money wages and working conditions, and two, the allocation between them. As I have elsewhere analyzed the latter issue (*The U.S. Bishops and Their Critics*, po. cit., pp. 30–32), I shall assume the problem away for present purposes, and hence concentrate only on total wages in the present context.

21 I assume that there is no valid employment contract in effect at this time which prohibits such an act.

22 As opposed, of course, to libertarian oriented economists.

23 In contrast, libertarians take the view that anti trust and anti combines legislation ought not be applied to anyone, neither unions nor business firms. See below.

24 W. H. Hutt, *The Strike Treat System: The Economic Consequences of Collective Bargaining*, New Rochelle, N.Y., Arlington House, 1973, p. 3. Also see Emerson P. Schmidt, *Union Power and the Public Interest*, Los Angeles, Nash, 1973; Henry C. Simons, *Economic Policy for a Free Society*, Chicago, University of Chicago Press, 1948.

In sharp distinction, for a libertarian analysis which *defends* the right of organized labor to threaten or to quit in unison, see Sylvester Petro, *The Labor Policy of the Free Society*, New York, Ronald Press, 1957; Morgan Reynolds, *Power and Privilege: Labor Unions in America*, New York, Universe, 1984.

25 For a critique of Hutt, see Murray N. Rothbard, *Man, Economy and State*, Los Angeles, Nash, 1970, pp. 561–566.

26 See Murray N. Rothbard, *For New Liberty*, New York, Collier, 1978, pp. 83–84.

27 A 'hot edict,' whereby a union declares the handling of certain products to be prohibited by members of organized labor, is a special case of the boycott. Provided that there is no contract in force which is incompatible with such a declaration, it, too, is entirely compatible with the libertarian legal code.

28 Murray N. Rothbard, *The Ethics of Liberty*, Atlantic Highlands, N.Y. Humanities Press, 1983, p. 131.

29 I assume that there is no longer a valid employment contract in force between the employer and employees. If there is, then the workers do indeed 'own' these jobs, but only because of the contract, not because of any superior status they may claim as members of the union caste.

30 The Canadian and U.S. bishops are on record as supporting the 'preferential option for the poor.' Yet, inconsistently, they support coercive unionism as against the 'scabs,' who are their major victims. As I stated in another context, 'It is no exaggeration to consider the scab as the economic equivalent of the leper. And we all know the treatment with regard to lepers urged upon us by ecclesiastical and biblical authorities.' See Walter Block, *The U.S. Bishops and Their Critics: An Economic and Ethical Perspective*, Vancouver, the Fraser Institute, 1986, p. 22; see also Walter Block, *On Economics and the Canadian Bishops*, Vancouver, the Fraser Institute, 1983.

31 Even those written by authors who are far from sympathetic to the free enterprise system. See for examples Paul Samuelson, *Economics*, New York, McGraw-Hill, 8th edition, 1970, chapter 29.

32 This was the fate of West Virginia, which fell victim to the activities of John L. Lewis, and organized labor in the coal fields.

33 See *For a New Liberty*, op. cit., p. 84.

34 See Michael Novak, *Will it Liberate? Questions about Liberation Theology*, New York, Paulist Press, 1987.

35 This data is taken from Herbert G. Grubel and Josef Bonnici, *Why is Canada's Unemployment Rate So High?*, Vancouver, the Fraser Institute, 1986, pp. 40–43. As well as the differing unionization rates, the

two countries also experienced widely divergent unemployment insurance policies. In 1970, the U.S. and Canada both spent about 0.9% of their G.N.P. on unemployment insurance benefits; by 1983, the U.S. had maintained its previous level of 0.9%, but Canada's had risen to 3.4%, an increase of 277%! (pp. 44–47). These two events had a profound effect upon the unemployment rates of the two North American neighbors. Traditionally, U.S. and Canadian unemployment rates have moved together within a narrow range. In 1963 for example, they were both slightly less than 6%. But as the disparate unionization and unemployment policies began to take effect, the Canadian rate began to exceed that for the U.S. In the early 1980s a gap of some 4% opened up (p. 2).

36   Other reasons are that employers are typically more wealthy than employees, and that it is easier for the former to replace the latter than the inverse.

37   See W. H. Hutt, *The Strike-Threat-system: The Economic Consequences of Collective Bargaining*, New Rochelle, N.Y.: Arlington House, 1973, ch. 5.

38   There are more customers than merchants (and more whites than blacks, more right handed persons than southpaws, more brunettes than blondes). Does this mean that the latter have more 'bargaining power' than the former whenever the two embroiled in competition, or in a dispute over the terms of trade? Not a bit of it. Customers have more 'bargaining power' than merchants when prices are presently above equilibrium, that is, when goods are in surplus, because prices tend to be fall in such cases. Likewise, merchants have more 'bargaining power' than customers when prices are below equilibrium, i.e., when there is a shortage of the good in question, because prices tend to rise in such cases.

39   See Murray N. Rothbard, *For a New Liberty*, op. cit., pp. 84–85: (This statement follows his ringing defense of employee rights to collude, and to engage in quits en masse – see endnote 25 above).

40   The best defense of free trade as a means toward human prosperity is still probably Adam Smith, *An Inquiry into the Nature and Causes of the Wealth of Nations*, New York, Penguin, 1974 (1776); for an eloquent modern statement, see Milton Friedman, Capitalism and Freedom, Chicago, University of Chicago Press, 1962, ch. 3.

41   See *ibid*.

42   Walter Block and Michael Walker, *Focus: On Employment Equity*, Vancouver, The Fraser Institute, 1985, is a response to *Equality in Employment*, the Royal Commission report released in 1984.

43 Ibid., p. 54.

44 Research indicates that out of fear that these changes will threaten their marriage or social relationships, females refuse promotions, salary raises, and job relocations which could enhence their careers. As well, the early childhood socialization of girls, not boys, is to be less competitive, and to defer in matters of business to the opposite sex. It is little question but that these different socialization patterns are capable of influencing choices that affect incomes. See *Discrimination, Affirmative Action, and Equal Opportunity*, Walter Block and Michael Walker, eds., Vancouver: the Fraser Institute, 1982, p. 245.

45 *On Employment Equity*, op. cit., p. 43

46 See the section, below, on the minimum wage law.

47 See ibid.

48 See Michael Novak, *Will it Liberate?: Questions about Liberation Theology*, New York, Paulist Press, 1985; Peter T.Bauer, *Equality, the Third World, and Economic Delusion*, Cambridge, Harvard University Press, 1981.

49 See Morton J. Horwitz, *The Transformation of American Law: 1780–1860*, Cambridge, Harvard University Press, 1977.

50 There is no such thing as the 'public good' or the 'common good,' or the best interests of 'society.' There are only individuals on this planet. Such a doctrine is not equivalent to 'atomism,' because these individuals can voluntarily interact with one another through groups, clubs, churches, and other mediating institutions. For further reading on the philosophy of methodological individualism, see Ludwig von Mises, *Human Action*, Chicago, Regnery, 1963, pp. 44–46.

Liberalism and Libertarians

Gerd Habermann

> Know all men by these presents, that I, Henry David Thoreau, do not wish to be regarded as a member of any incorporated society which I have not joined.
>
> (Thoreau)

America remains – despite the Prussian-type welfare bureaucracy that has spread since the New Deal[1] – the land with the strongest traditions of freedom. Debates still are conducted in this great country on freedom and government as well as on democracy and constitutionality with a fundamental intensity only rarely to be found in statist, bureaucratic Europe, where, if such debates at all occur, then only in reaction to the American discussion. Debates in the Old World, particularly in Germany, all too often pall and turn into learned philological exchanges or, owing to their technicized-specialized jargon, are comprehensible only to the initiated. The last time debates like those in America took place in Europe was in the shadow cast by the totalitarian dictatorships of Hitler and Stalin. It was during this period that Ludwig von Mises wrote his "Nationalökonomie" (1940), Friedrich August von Hayek in London his "Weg zur Knechtschaft" (1944), Wilhelm Röpke in Geneva his "Civitas Humana" (1944), and Bertrand de Jouvenel, while in Swiss exile, his "Über die Staatsgewalt" (1945). It is no coincidence that Ludwig von Mises and Friedrich August von Hayek enjoyed more recognition and popularity in America than in their own native countries, as seen in the taking up and elaboration of typically neo-liberal discussion topics (see in particular Viktor Vanberg, cf. 1994).

The radical-individualist traditions of America are practically unknown in Europe. No German translations exist of the works of Lysander Spooner, for example, or of Benjamin R. Tucker, Albert Jay Nock, and David Friedman. In historical studies of anarchism, these thinkers are mentioned only in passing. At best, the master of modern American "anarchist capitalism," Murray Rothbard, who died in 1995 (cf. Rockwell, 1995), caused something of a stir in the Old World owing to the voluminous extent and especially the rhetorical vehemence of his publications. Yet not a single book of Rothbard's has been translated into German.

Modern American individualist anarchism reached its apogee in Rothbard.[2] This paper is primarily a critique focusing on Rothbard and his followers, but also includes a descriptive survey of the positions of Rothbard's school and its natural-law criticism of the state. This is unavoidable in view of the extent to which Rothbard's thinking is unknown, or even regarded as outlandish, in Germany.

I. Concepts

It is well known that in America the word "liberalism" has lost its European connotation (see von Hayek, 1971, p. 492f.). The word was misappropriated there for social democratic, statist objectives. What Europeans regard as "liberal" is regarded as "conservative" by Americans. The coining of the word "libertarian," or "libertarianism," was an attempt to restore the European meaning of "liberal." The term "libertarianism" comprehends all liberal schools of thought, ranging from Adam Smith's "moderate" liberalism (cf. David Friedman, 1989, p. 245), Wilhelm von Humboldt's or Herbert Spencer's conceptions of the minimal state, proponents of an ultra-minimal state like Robert Nozick or Arthur Seldon, to the American school of individualist anarchism. Recently, the expression "libertarian" has come to find limited application to a certain direction within liberalism (or, depending on the way in which liberalism is understood, "outside" liberalism) – namely specifically to that sphere of ideas represented by the names of Murray Rothbard, David Friedman, and, in recent years, more and more to Hans-Hermann Hoppe (a German academic in the USA). In this group, not the classic-liberal but individualist-anarchist tradition is being carried on, which has the goal of a stateless society in which any coercion exercised by persons over other persons is seen as basically "illegitimate" with the exception of self-defense (here this school differs from, among others, the strict pacifism of the anarcho-communist Tolstoi). These thinkers are committed to elimination of the state as a coercive organization, no matter what form it may have, with the goal of replacing it by free contractual relationships on the basis of private property, competition, and markets (this ideal is elaborated with varying degrees of precision and consistency). Regarded from this point of view, evolutionist-oriented classic liberals like Friedrich August von Hayek and particularly the German

"Ordo Liberals" are "statists" since they remain committed to the role of the state in maintaining order, and some even see competition as a sort of governmental function. The point has been reached where anarcho-capitalists make a sport of finding social-democratic inconsistencies in the writings of such classic liberal thinkers as, for example, Friedrich August von Hayek (cf. Hoppe, 1994, de Jasay, 1995b).[3] German representatives who more or less follow this school of thought include, for example, the theoretician Gerard Radnitzky (cf. 1995a-d), the publicists Detmar Doering (cf. 1995a, for example), or Stefan Blankertz (cf. 1980, 1988, 1995).

II. The Place of Radical "Libertarians" in Intellectual History[4]

In intellectual history, the "libertarian" school is part of the tradition of "individualist anarchism," which as a radical-liberal fringe movement achieved prominence in the last two centuries. In Germany, individualist anarchism found a philosophical spokesman in a bizarre egomaniac, the leftist Hegelian Max Stirner (1845: "Der Einzige und sein Eigentum"), who for a brief time was highly regarded (about Stirner, see particularly Gide/Rist, 1923, pp. 673–676). At a time when the radical-liberal French publicist Frédéric Bastiat was still declaring that "All justified interests are harmonious," Stirner said rather bluntly that "All interests are justified … to the extent that they have power." And: "It is right for the tiger to attack me, but it is also right for me to strike the tiger down." Or: "Whoever has the power, is right; if you lack one, you lack the other." His slogan is characteristic: "I exalt nothing more highly than myself." For Stirner, all collective entities (state, society, and so on) and ossified abstractions of principles, rights, duties, the "sacredness of private property," are idées fixes that have the sole purpose of shackling the self-justified egotism of the individual. Stirner calls for the war of all against all: "Seize the opportunity to take what you need." Stirner was indeed "unique" in Europe in forwarding his variety of exaggerated individualism. His name appears again and again in libertarian-anarchist literature.[5]

Much more attention, typically enough, was given by Europeans to the collectivist anarchism, which is close to anarcho-communism; the movement's most important representatives were Michael Bakunin, Peter Kropotkin, and Sergei Netschajev. Collectivist anarchism shared with liberalism a preference for basic liberty, contractual principle, and faith in the spontaneous emergence of order, and the collectivist anarchists also vehemently criticized the state for moral and economic reasons. Like individualist anarchists, collective anarchists sought total elimination of the state;

they differed from individualist anarchists in wanting to replace the state not by free markets and private property, but by voluntary communes and cooperatives – that is, by a kind of decentralized and collective economy based on shared property. The collective anarchists aimed to reestablish every area of society on the basis of "voluntary associations." In forwarding this anarchist goal, they had some influence on Marxism and Leninism (see Gide/Rist, 1923, pp. 701–714). The great political demands of collective anarchism contrast sharply with its rudimentary economic foundation. Moreover, collective anarchism is subject to contradiction in its aim of realizing a realm of fraternal freedom and cooperative self-organization by means of revolutionary terrorism and violence. (The most recent attempt to do this just came to an end.)

One movement of thought, in its methods a pacifist and individualist form of anarchism, has failed to attract much notice either in Germany or in the rest of Europe. This movement, despite its occasional use of an extremely aggressive language, relies on passive resistance and the power of persuasion. In the 19th century and at the opening of this century, its impressive representatives included the above-mentioned Lysander Spooner (1992, on Spooner, see Doering, 1994) as well as Benjamin R. Tucker (cf. Brooks, 1994, and Eltzbacher, 1987). These thinkers wanted a social order free of government and based on private property, a market economy in which even the privatization of currency – anyone may open a bank – was one of its more moderate measures. Worthy of mention is also the Belgian-born French thinker Gustave Molinari ([1849], 1977), who drew up a scenario for a privately organized "security industry" and hoped that this scheme would lead to lasting and effective maintenance of peace. After elimination of the state, citizens could use private services in its stead, proposed Molinari. He disputed this point, among others, with the radical liberal Frédéric Bastiat.

Pacifist anarchism also included some "moderate" members who wished to retain the state as a voluntary institution: the astute Briton Auberon Herbert (1838–1906), for example, proposed that the state be financed by voluntary contributions (see Herbert, 1978). Some pacifist anarchists also thought that state services should be provided only to those who had entered into contracts individually with public agencies supplying the services and had paid for them directly. Even the sometimes far-from-moderate Thomas Jefferson proposed financing of national defense by lottery (cf. Blankertz, 1988, p. 122).

Contemporary libertarian anarchism, as forwarded by Rothbard, David Friedman, and others, is characterized by its bolstering of traditional individualist-anarchist positions with a modern economic foundation; this form of anarchism generalizes traditional individualist-anarchist principles in assigning them to the state and political agencies. For this reason, the movement prefers to call itself anarchist capitalism or "100–percent capitalism" (Hans-Hermann Hoppe).[6]

III. Premises

What are the premises of anarchist capitalism? Most, but not all, of its followers support individual liberty based on natural law. They absolutize John Locke's principle that everyone's "natural" right to life, freedom, and property is, as reason shows, logically necessary and eternally valid. A person has absolute rights to his body (the precept of universal "self-ownership"). He also has the absolute right to claim as his property the material resources that he produces or transforms. Finally, he has the absolute right to transfer ownership of his property to another person in order to receive an adequate recompense for his labor. By this, he acquires the dignity of an absolute sovereignty which can be limited only to the extent that he himself consents to it and does no harm to his neighbor ("harm principle"): not the "state," but the individual, is and remains sovereign, who does not transfer this sovereignty to governments or other collective organizations by any kind of mysterious "social contract." The "law of equal freedom" is incontestable. Society, traditionally held together by political coercion, is to be bound only by free contract. A further important premise: nobody has a right to use coercion against anyone else, means of force are out of the question, non-domination and non-aggression are the rule. The individual has merely the right to arm himself for self-defense. To sum up in the words of this movement's leading figure, Murray Rothbard: "The libertarian creed can now be summed up as (1) the absolute right of every man to the ownership of his own body; (2) the equally absolute right to own and therefore to control the material resources he has found and transformed; and (3) therefore the absolute right to exchange or give away the ownership to such titles to whoever is willing to exchange or receive them. As we have seen, each of these steps involves property rights, but even if we call step (1) "personal" rights, we shall see that problems about 'personal liberty' inextricably involve the rights of material property or free exchange. Or, briefly, the rights of personal liberty and 'freedom of enterprise' almost invariably intertwine and cannot really be separated" (*Rothbard*, 1994, S. 68/69).

While John Locke (and in this tradition Ludwig von Mises and Friedrich August von Hayek) thought individual freedom should be guaranteed by governmental (or, by analogy, pre-governmental) obligatory rules ("Freedom under the law"), the radical libertarians saw law itself as the greatest threat to freedom. The state did not make personal freedom possible, but is its greatest opponent, even the most liberal of states. This radical natural-law foundation supports the school's arguments against utilitarian positions: absolute freedom of the individual – to be granted immediately and without restriction – is the ultimate criterion, not vague quantities like efficiency, the cost-benefit ratio, amount of transaction costs, or even criteria of evolutionary efficiency, such as self-assertion and growth of a group in a competitive situation (cf. Rothbard, 1994, p. 16, pp. 26–27). Evolutionism, in Hayek's sense, is dismissed as "consequentialism" (cf. Radnitzky, 1995d, Hoppe, 1994). This, because Hayek, for the most part, defends liberty not for its own sake but because of its benevolent "consequences" (supply of goods, growth, self-assertion of the group, and so on). By adopting this point of view, anarchist capitalism seeks to ward off the "historical" argument and the political temptation of a reformist "gradualism." It refuses to enter into any compromises under any conditions, and this is the main reason for its charisma. Rothbard makes no bones about calling himself an "abolitionist"; he calls for the immediate elimination of "state slavery."

IV. Links with "Classic Liberalism"

For the "classic liberal," the state is a necessary evil to assert "equal liberty" for all its citizens, particularly the protection and freedom of its weaker members in a world of universal competition. The state, according to liberals, must provide guarantees against the enduring temptation of individuals and particularly of well-organized groups to assert their interests by violence, fraud, or blackmail. Never would a liberal regard the state (or "society") as an end-in-itself in the manner of the Hegelian collectivist school. No genuine liberal has ever take part in the swindle involving "collective concepts" ("holism"). He is protected from doing so, particularly if he has background in economics, to the extent that he subscribes to "methodological individualism" or "nominalism" – which, after all, is nothing other than scientific methodology applied to the social realm. He will, therefore, support even Max Stirner's radical criticism of metaphysical personifications of concepts like state, society, monarchy, church, and so on. Every liberal would doubtlessly regard the economic efficiency of the state much as does Albert Jay Nock ([1935], 1992, p. 83): "State power has an unbroken record of inability, to do anything efficiently, economically, disinterestedly or honestly, yet when the slightest dissatisfaction arises over any exercises of social power, the aid of the agent least qualified to give aid is immediately called for".

Liberals and anarchists question state monopolies and regulations, no matter of which kind. Liberals are also always critical of the number of compulsorily financed public goods and wish to keep that number as low as possible. Compulsory public education, especially in a governmentally organized educational system, is for every genuinely "strict liberal" (de Jasay) as much as a problem as it is for the anarcho-capitalists who conjure up appealing visions of private educational pluralism (cf. Blankertz / Goodman, 1980, Blankertz, 1989, Rothbard, 1994, Richman, 1994). In principle, liberals have as little difficulty accepting privatization of social insurance as does Auberon Herbert, even if they unlike the anarcho-capitalists, wish to retain an unavoidable, compulsorily financed, public system of social benefits as a "last anchor" while keeping benefits at an unattractive level and providing for examinations of need – note that they "wish," not "have to"; examples include von Humboldt, ([1792], 1962) or Herbert Spencer (1892, 1950), who, like Rothbard, in this respect have full confidence in private initiative. The privatization and deregulation of public infrastructure-monopolies is also no problem in principle provided that no technical problems obstruct it. In case of doubt, the liberal, along with Milton Friedman, prefers a private monopoly (with the state as counterweight) to a public monopoly. If need be, a liberal would even consider privatization of the local road system.[7] Other monopolies or privileges as well also are under continual pressure to justify themselves (patent rights, customs duties, and so on). In so far as a liberal is true to his principles, he will call for the decriminalization of all delicts that harm no one but the wrongdoer ("Vices are not crimes": Lysander Spooner on, for example, use of drugs). The liberal favors, as did Adam Smith (1978, pp. 587–600), voluntarily recruited, professional armed forces, which in fact are relied upon today by classic-liberal states like England and the USA in times of peace. The liberal would object to compulsory military service in any event, and would tolerate it at best as a temporary necessary evil. It is likewise clear that a liberal would support the reduction of the powers of a state through internal decentralization, preferring in place of a "big nation state" a federation of small states with an efficient system of local competition. Wilhelm Röpke (1966, p. 338), for example, suggested using the word "decentrism" instead of liberalism. Not only Spooner, Tucker, and Rothbard (1990),[8] but also Friedrich August von Hayek (1977) have proposed plans for privatizations of currencies. The liberal would also see difficulties in negative taxation, like that of Milton Friedman's or of Joachim Mitschke's (meaning a governmentally guaranteed minimum income without any examination of need), because of its compulsory redistribution and blatant violation of the principle of subsidiarity.

Natural-law arguments have also had an important role in liberalism – from the Stoics on (cf. Hasbach, 1891). However, some liberals would find a fundamental contradiction (for example, through conflicting interpretations of natural law) in the elimination of legally prescribed monogamy or the demand for unrestricted abortion rights. Rothbard (1994, p. 107f.) speaks of an unwanted pregnancy as a "parasite" to be destroyed because it obstructs self-determination. In any case, a clear dividing line exists between liberals and anarcho-capitalists in the question of comprehensive assertion of a "universal King's peace" and "equal liberties" by coercive measures of government as well as in the securing of collective self-assertion by state authority in a world of competing peoples. In any case, debating is intense on the question of whether markets are capable by themselves of bringing forth warrantable forms of regulating use of force, indeed, whether markets are at all capable of being the only frame of reference used to decide the question. Incidentally, this does not mean that private firms could not have a greater part in enforcing law and order – in fact, some already do.[9]

V. Government as a Band of Gangsters

The use of physical means of coercion against other people is, according to leading libertarian thinkers, legitimate only in defense against encroachments on property rights (including rights over one's own body). Such defense can take the form of taking the law into one's own hands for self-help (hence the emphatic support, which Europeans find so odd, of gun rights by many theorists[10]) or of resorting to private contracts with commercial security services. From the libertarian point of view, involuntary and governmental monopoly of means of physical coercion is fundamentally illegitimate. It is precisely here that the dividing line is drawn between liberalism and anarchism: for the classic liberals, the state (or other governing body) is "legitimate," because the state, by regulating use of means of physical coercion makes it possible for its citizens to live in peace and liberty. The anarcho-capitalists, on the other hand, regard the state per se as an illegitimate restriction of liberty. As Rothbard says: "Liberty is not the daughter but the mother of order" (1993, p. 880). To a liberal, this is putting the cart before the horse (de Jasay, 1994, who, however, tends to follow Rothbard in his arguments; also see Walter Lippmann's polemic against a misinterpreted laissez-faire philosophy, 1945, pp. 249–258). For the liberal, it is not so important whether the peace is kept by a professional government apparatus or by some non-governmental association (like Swiss militia democracy).

The anarchist view of the state leads to a complete "transvaluation of values": government is seen as an organization that monopolizes crime for its own purposes. Government has, so to speak, a monopoly on illegitimate use of physical force. It is an organization that serves the interests of only the few in power while engaging in robbery and plundering (taxes), murder (police and military), servitude (liability for military service), or kidnaping (compulsory education). Government is illegitimate even when it merely protects the property and freedom of citizens. As Benjamin R. Tucker once wrote: "How is it possible to reconcile the principle of equal liberty for all with the fact that the fruits of my labor are confiscated to pay for a protection which I neither asked for nor want?" (cited in: Eltzbacher, 1987, p. 172). The French anarchist Pierre Proudhon characterized government in unrivaled language.[11] American individualist anarchists of this century, however, hardly lag behind Proudhon, as shown, for example, by Albert Jay Nock (cited in: Rothbard, 1994, p. 51): "the State claims and exercises the monopoly of crime. ... It forbids private murder, but itself organizes murder on a colossal scale. It punishes private theft, but itself lays unscrupulous hands on anything it wants, whether the property of citizen or of alien."

Or let us quote the master himself, Rothbard: "But if we look at the state naked, as it were, we see that it is universally allowed, and even encouraged, to commit all the acts which even nonlibertarians concede are reprehensible crimes. The State habitually commits mass murder, which it calls 'war', or sometimes 'suppression of subversion'; the State engages in enslavement into its military forces, which it calls 'conscription'; and it lives and has its being in the practice of forcible theft, which it calls 'taxation'. The libertarian insists that whether or not such practices are supported by the majority of the population is not germane to their nature: that, regardless of popular sanction, war is Mass Murder, Conscription is Slavery, and Taxation is Robbery. The libertarian, in short, is almost completely the child in the fable, pointing out insistently that the emperor has no clothes."

Even Leonard Liggio, otherwise more often moderate than not, wrote (cited in: Blankertz, 1995, p. 176): "Laws are not based on consensus. If there were a consensus, then laws would not be necessary. Laws represent civil war." Spooner speaks flatly of the state as a "band of robbers and murderers." Hans-Hermann Hoppe (1987, p. 86) regards public law not as law in the true sense of the word but in some areas as institutionalized aggression against property claims of private persons. "Taxation" is said to be in the same legal category as "robbery"; statutory duties or obligations involuntarily entered into for social or defense aims amount to "slavery for a set time"; and socio-political measures have their twin in the "forced appropriation of property titles and redistribution or resale of unrightfully gained property," amounting, in short, to "theft and handling of stolen goods" (Hoppe, 1987, p. 87).

VI. Delegitimizing Democracy

Since the state, for anarcho-capitalists, is per se an illegitimate organization of criminals, it does not make much difference how its political will is formed, which is in any case illegitimate: the compulsory character of governmental measures cannot be neutralized no matter by what form of state, whether monarchy, oligarchy, or democracy. "The voice of the majority saves bloodshed, but it is subject to the arbitrariness of forceful means just as much as is the rule of an unqualified despot backed by the mightiest army" (Tucker, cited in: Eltzbacher, 1987, p. 172). The difference from totalitarian regimes is just a matter of degree. It is always a case of taking a step on the "Road to Serfdom." What is the qualitative distinction between the coercive measures of a sole monarch or of a Stalinist dictatorship and the coercive measures mandated by a tiny minority of a parliament or by referendum, when in extreme cases 50.01 percent may vote Yes and 49.99 percent vote No? This is the reason for Auberon Herbert's aversion toward collective decisions.[12] For this reason, according to Spooner (1992, p. 81/82), a constitution cannot be binding for anybody who does not agree to it freely and in writing: "The constitution not only binds nobody now, but it never did bind anybody. It never bound anybody, because it was never agreed to by any body in such a manner as to make it, on general principles of law and reason, binding upon him ... The constitution was not only never signet by anybody, but it was never delivered by anybody to anybody, or to anybody's agent or attorney. It can be therefore be of no more validity as a contract, than can any other instrument, that was never signet or delivered".

Democracy is a particularly aggressive means for reducing liberties. Hoppe (1987, p. 154) speaks of democracy as "an administrative measure carried out with strategic considerations in mind to supplement the revenue of the corporation state from forced appropriations." The form of control may have changed, but democracy is also control; and encroachments on existing property rights, even if backed by a majority vote, amount to aggression. He calls democracy "the most important administrative innovation for broadening public authority" (1987, p. 25). Even hereditary monarchy, which he sees as "private owned government," has shown more reserve in plundering its subjects.[13]

Consequently, for these thinkers there can be no "legitimate" rule unless it is based on freely given agreement and is fully revocable. They dismiss as naive the contractual design of political theory and – recently – the public choice school, although they also share many critical approaches with public choice theorists, as in characterizing politicians as egotistical income maximizers. Anarcho-capitalists regard the principal defect of every democracy – coercion of a minority by a majority – as beyond remedy. According to Anthony de Jasay, who calls himself "strictly liberal" although the forms of his argumentation clearly put him in the individualist anarchist camp, democracy, mainly as a consequence of equal voting rights, ends in destruction of the free-market economy and ultimately sinks into "battletank socialism" (cf. Weede, 1990, p. 139).[14]

How is it possible in view of the above considerations for the masses, apparently voluntarily, to regard democracy as "legitimate"? This poses no special difficulty to anarcho-capitalist theorists, who claim that intellectuals serving state purposes spread misleading myths to legitimize the interests of those in power as well as to defend their own sinecures (cf. Rothbard, 1994, pp. 54–69, and Hoppe, 1995a). Anarcho-capitalists regard as legitimate only those conditions of power that are in agreement with "objective" anarchist conceptions of legitimacy. An empirical theory of legitimacy, like Weber's theory of legitimacy types, is regarded as irrelevant in determining "true," or ethically compelling, legitimacy.[15] This is a form of argumentation that provides a justification for the use of force to "liberate" persons having "false awareness" just as this occurred in the second phase of the French Revolution. Yet anarcho-capitalists, unlike the anarcho-communists, remain true to their principles in renouncing the use of force to assert their conception of legitimacy. They rely on peaceful means of persuasion and the "power of ideas." However, in this connection "elections" are not an appropriate instrument because of the illegitimacy of power exercised by majorities. According to anarchists, the struggle to broaden suffrage, for example by giving women the right to vote, was not worth fighting. Yet it must be noted that in the meantime a libertarian party has come into existence, and there have been libertarian presidential candidates (cf. D. Friedman, 1989, pp. 226–229): this, strictly speaking, is an inconsistency.

VII. A Society without Government and Majority Rule[16]

"In trying freedom, in abolishing the state, we have nothing to lose and everything to gain." (Rothbard, 1994, p. 237)

The ideal, then, is elimination of state and democracy. However, as emphasized above, not by means of violence, because this would not be in agreement with central libertarian principles. What is relied upon here, rather, is use of "evolutionary," intellectual means of persuasion and the slow replacement of the politically ordered segments of society by markets. As Hoppe (1995b, p. 67) wrote: "If – and only if – this recognition of states (governments) as fundamentally evil and wasteful returns and prevails in public opinion will the power of the central state crumble devolve onto smaller and smaller territorials, and ultimately whither away and make room for a system of ordered and self-reinforcing private property anarchy as required by ethics and economics".

According to anarcho-communists, national states will split up into autonomous communes and cooperatives and enter into non-federative agreements with another, while according to individualist anarchists private firms, for example arbitration commissions, security services, or privately operated prisons, could settle disputes and, if need be, take measures to apprehend and arrest violators. A "Murderer's Incorporated," so to speak, could compete with and replace public agencies. The service of providing security would no longer be a public service, but would be offered by private firms in free competition. One would then, for example, have the choice between a firm willing to carry out death penalties and another firm that contents itself with financial penalties or arrests. Even the standards of protection for the client would be subject to competitive market conditions. The awarding of contracts on the basis of residential districts determined by geography or other priorities could take place in such a manner that individuals who are highly interested in the protection of their property could take the initiative; their neighbors could participate, if they wished. Probably unavoidable bandwagonners would profit from increased security at neighboring premises, but they would not enjoy any real security guarantee. For the client, however, the cost-benefit ratio of the security measures would change only marginally so that the awarding of contracts to private security firms could remain feasible.

The "citizen," if it is at all possible to speak of one under such circumstances, would conclude a sort of legal protection agreement with a private court, and possibly also decide to engage the services of a commercial arbitration only when needed for specific cases, thus securing for himself the most favorable conditions.

Let us, along with Rothbard, imagine the following scene in a de-politicized market economy: a citizen is robbed. He asks his private court to take action, which could apprehend the "thief" and decide on his guilt. If the thief recognizes this decision, two options result: if the thief is provided with legal protection by the same court as the citizen's, or decides to employ the same court, then the thief must recognize the decision of his court, which is also the citizen's. If, however, the thief decides to employ a different private court, then this other court will reach its own decision. If this court also finds the thief guilty, then judgment will be final. If the thief's court finds him innocent, then recourse would be made to a court of appeal. In this case, both courts would agree to apply to a third instance, and both courts would recognize the decision of this third instance. If the thief decided to evade justice, then both the court and the citizen could commission a detective to find the thief and, if necessary, to detain him in a privately operated detention facility or prison. In addition, a "bounty" could be offered for his capture.

The private court's own interest in its good reputation will make it less susceptible to corruption. If suspicion arose, then this court would no longer survive in a competitive market because it would lose the confidence of its clients – not less so than any other firm would if its reputation were damaged.

And Foreign Policy?

In a world governed by anarchist ideals, there would be no more national states, only competing private firms with clients and markets surrounded by no borders whatever. One would then be rid of the vexing problems of "reason of state" (cf. Meinecke, 1957) and of foreign policy. The problem of "dual national standards" would be ended (Is the state allowed to do what is forbidden to the private individual?). Only private law would exist – and violations of private law. No monopoly government could force its citizens, as "slaves", to war against citizens of other nations. Admittedly, it is conceivable that an individual could commission a private security agency to commit a violent act against another individual, but such conflicts would automatically contain themselves. At first, it would be difficult to find any private armies or security firms who would be willing to use violence against an innocent third party or against the third party's own security firm. The result here would be at most a locally restricted conflict, with damage to the reputation of the firm commissioned to engage in a violent act resulting in the ultimate bankruptcy of the firm after loss of its clients.

The transitional phase may be difficult, when, perhaps, ungoverned regions may have formed while monopoly governments still in existence would continue to pose a threat at borders. Yet even in this case interested parties could join forces to hire the necessary protective troops (mercenary firms) for their defense. David Friedman (1989, p. 173), however, says it would be justified in extreme cases to introduce universal conscription: temporary slavery would be better than lasting slavery under a victorious foreign country.

Even if "civil wars" of private security firms would break out, according to Stefan Blankertz (1995, p. 185) they would be less harmful than civil wars fought under conditions of national statehood. He justifies this assumption by pointing out the low losses of private militia in Lebanon as compared to losses of the governmentally financed armies in the former Yugoslavia. The private militia recruit mostly volunteers and have no funding from tax revenues. That minimizes their range of options.

"Strong" and "quiet" states, according to the writer (1995, p. 185) are not at peace, but merely show that one party to the civil war emerged victorious. In other words: strong and expansive countries, including democratic ones, carry out continual, if latent, civil war against its population. If the population fails to recognize this, then this is due to the fact that the anti-capitalist mentality continually attempts to portray peaceful markets as places of battle and warring states as strongholds of peace.

VIII. Historical Confirmation

Is the anarchist ideal of a state-free society an utopian illusion? Murray Rothbard says it is not: a goal is utopian to the extent that it contradicts human nature and physical laws. Thus, the communist goal could not be attained not only because it failed to take into account human nature and social rules but also because it ignored the uniqueness and individuality of human beings and of their interests and also, lacking a realistic economic base, ruined its own industry. In implementing anarchist ideals, however, it is crucial to persuade a sufficient number of people to support the anarchist program; and this, it is claimed, would lead to the withering away of the state. The libertarian ideal does not deny human diversity; on the contrary, libertarians wish full expression of human diversity in a world of total freedom (Rothbard, 1994, p. 303).

Libertarians make use of examples from both the past and the present in order to show that their ideals can be realized in the future and are already even beginning to be realized in the present. They call attention to the time before nation states were established: no government monopolies existed in the world of the Celt, Teuton, or Icelandic peoples. The legal system developed through free courts that often competed with another. The Common Law, for example, was the result of "private" empirical legal production, not of any central legislation like that on the continent (cf. especially Benson, 1990). A collectivist anarchist, Kropotkin (1975), called attention in a splendid book to the many existing forms of autonomous organization of state-free societies, particularly in the Middle Ages. The ancient Greek city-state, the Polis, was "state-free" as well. England, classic country of freedom and capitalism, is also the country in which it took a very long time for a bureaucratic-monopolist coercive system, patterned after Continental models already in existence, to establish itself. Even today, the concept of "state" or administrative law in the Continental-European sense is officially unknown. The state in England is neither a legal entity nor does it have any real public authority. It has neither a uniform civil servant class nor a uniform national territory. Only the "Crown," not the state, can be sued. A fictitious vassalage and "parliamentary rights" takes the place of citizenship (see Brunner, 1965, pp. 154–155). The historic background of this special development: because it is an island, England was able to preserve the mediaeval foundation that military states on the Continent had to give up.

Fritz Kern, whom the libertarians (and von Hayek) like to quote, writes in a paper of fundamental importance that in the Middle Ages "law," not the "state" or the "people," was sovereign. Taxation took place only on a voluntary basis. A permanent tax was considered confiscation of assets (Kern, 1965, p. 73).

For libertarians, an impressive example for autonomous organization to ensure protection of freedom and property is the Wild West, as accordingly described by Terry Anderson and P. J. Hill (1989). Notwithstanding popular Wild West mythology, there was no more violence in the West than in areas under government administration. Anderson and Hill write: "The West during this time often is perceived as a place of great chaos, with little respect for property or life. Our research indicates that this was not the case; property rights were protected and civil order prevailed. Private agencies provided the necessary basis for an orderly society in which property was protected and conflicts were resolved. These agencies often did not qualify as governments because they did not have a legal monopoly on 'keeping order'. They soon discovered that 'warfare' was a costly way of resolving disputes and lower cost methods of settlement (arbitration, courts, etc.) resulted. In summary ... a characterization of the American West as chaotic would appear to be incorrect" (Anderson/Hill, 1989, p. 9; cf. also Benson, 1990, pp. 312–321).

The practices of social boycotting, ostracism, social disapprobation, and, in extreme cases, outlawing in that pre-governmental period curbed crime.

Today, the many forms of private arbitration and private police show that anarchist ideals can be realized, if only partly, in a nationally governed society. Particularly Bruce Benson (1990, pp. 173–268; cf. also Doering 1995b) points this out. It can be seen in every sphere of activity that free trade, because it is in its own interest, spontaneously develops its own "private" forms of universally oriented law and arbitration. Commercial law originally developed without government influence and gave rise to a social order that up to the present day still finds its raison d'être in the interests of those who share in it. Freely agreed forms of private arbitration are more efficient than any government monopoly court with its lengthy trials and inefficient procedures. For libertarians, commercial law before it came partly under government control is the ideal law-system.

IX. Critique[17]

Every liberal sympathizes with the ideal of freedom from government control, of living free of any form of coercion. However, a liberal should remain a "critical" rationalist obligated to employ scientific methods and accountable for his premises and logical argumentation, empiric evidence, and practical consequences of implementing his ideals.

On the Premises

First of all, what is the situation regarding the purportedly "objective" (that is, derived from "human nature") premise of "equal liberty" as "natural law"?[18] The view that natural-law postulates are formed thanks to scholarly discernment or ethically "universal" principles of human behavior is simply erroneous.[19] It is possible to posit "rights" as norms – as an ideal "ought," just as liberals have and the public choice school has in its contract theory (yet libertarians often criticize the public choice school). This amounts, however, to a departure from the realm of facts for the realm of subjective fancies. This has little to do with "science" or any scientifically grounded system of ethics. Science cannot tell an individual what ideals he should live by, whether, for example, accumulation of goods or maximizing of liberties or even life itself is of any "objective" positive value. Indian ascetics or Christian penitents, as is well known, have their doubts about this position. An advocate of the "Austrian" (subjectivist, that is) national economy shouldn't find any grounds to dispute this. It is obviously circular reasoning to claim that every "reasoning" person would see that is only logical to promote unrestricted self-ownership and that, for this reason, use of force is illegitimate. There are more than enough "unreasoning" groups that pay little attention to such arguments and in the name of ideals contrary to natural law (or varying interpretations of natural law, cf. Max Weber, 1964, pp. 634–643) even glorify the use of force – for example, in the name of "holy war" or "social justice" or national glory. Conquerors, colonizers, political demagogues, religious fanatics again and again have showed that they value not logically sound, ethically "objective" conduct, but rely on the pleasurable thrill of appropriating the goods of others or exploiting their bodies in the absence of any contractual agreement whatsoever, without any adequate recompense – they may also rely on murder, even if this takes place "in the name of God," as it did during the Crusades. One need only glance at the history of imperialism: war functioned, and still functions, more like the prima than the ultima ratio (cf. Schumpeter, 1953, Durant, 1969, pp. 90–97). It shouldn't detract from the value of a purely normative principle to admit that it is inherently subjective. Max Weber, himself an adherent of strict neutrality in science and the separation of "is" and "ought," nevertheless enthusiastically forwarded his own liberal and democratic ideals. The claim that an individualist natural law, as interpreted in Western countries, is universally applicable is simple presumption. Confucianism, for example, has nothing in common with this type of natural law (cf. Kühnhardt, 1987), and yet the Chinese civilization is one of the most successful in human history. The skeptical von Hayek, however, would call this kind of thinking "social constructivism." He proceeds from the assumption that all relevant facts can be known to an individual and that it should be possible for the individual to derive from the knowledge thus gained a definitively "right" and eternally valid social order (cf. Zeitler, 1995, p. 253).

Anarcho-capitalist theory suffers from the one-sided fiction of basically peaceful market participants mainly interested in maximizing profits and friendly exchange of goods. It closes its eyes to the role of force as used by collective organizations for purportedly "legitimate" aggressive force applied both internally and externally, as often occurs before states begin to expand; it also ignores the diversity of human motives. Such a rigorous and logically consistent view of an assumed ethical-objective natural law actually is recognized only by a very small minority of the libertarians themselves – and even they are at odds about it.

Furthermore, who is the "individual" posited by this theory? The "methodological individualism" of social scientists is one instrument of interpretation, the normative exaggeration of maximization of individual liberties, regarded as an end in itself and apart from any social or traditional context, is another. Even Edmund Burke ([1792], 1967) disagreed with the fiction of the "individual" of the French Revolution. Most anarcho-capitalists are rightly criticized for regarding human beings as isolated, as atoms or islands, in ignorance of their most basic social bonds. Charles Rist once commented on this: "It is as little possible to imagine the individual outside of his society as it is to imagine a fish out of water. Without water, the fish will, it is true, remain a fish, but in any case a dead fish" (Gide/Rist, 1923, p. 689). This is a matter of that type of "false" individualism that von Hayek (e.g. 1976, pp. 9–48) was right to criticize so sharply. According to this theory, society is built together like a wall of bricks. But the theory takes little notice of the cement of traditional rules and traditional sentiments of belonging that has a very strong imprint on society. The ideal society should be like Stirner's "association of egotists." Every newborn human being, in entering society, merely comes to participate in an association that had already long been in existence and which will survive him. As de Jouvenel once noted in opposition to this point of view (1963, p. 302): "How blind the individual must be and how impudent not to realize that he depends on what others have put together and not to recognize how miserable he would be in every respect if he did not have a share in this capital and the organization, how little this organization depends on his small contribution and how much he depends on it." It may well be that the extensive significance of social community, group rivalries, and traditional heritage, apart from the factors of market and state, is not completely overlooked. Nevertheless, it is not given consideration commensurate with its importance. The same subject comes up for discussion with insistent monotony: the individual and his property. Discussion is limited to economic questions.

Idealization of the Age Before the State

What about the personal sovereignty of the individual before emergence of states? Haven't the sort of practical anarchies favored by the anarcho-capitalists already been in existence? In any case, before the rise of national government there was no comprehensive "monopoly on legitimate use of force" enjoyed by any political professional elite. Historical sociology and comparative historical research, however, show that in every social community a mechanism of coercion existed to keep the peace, a system of rules that, if need be, can be asserted by use of force against criminals. Nowhere is there mention of "equal liberty" in the age before emergence of states. Regulated use of force within one's own group gives way to more or less regulated warfare against foreign groups. Max Weber (1964, p. 660) wrote: "The use of force by a community is something that appears to be intrinsically and absolutely elemental; from the level of domestic arrangements to the level of political parties, every community has availed itself of means of physical force, whenever it had to or could, to protect the interests of its members. An outcome of social development is the monopolization of legitimate force by political subdivisions." According to the libertarian analysis, the origin of the state is be found in the use of force or plunder against foreign groups. German sociologist Franz Oppenheimer[20] is often quoted in support of this view. But this phenomenon – recourse to violent means or theft – can likewise be found in pre-governmental political bands. Moreover, this is also what gave rise to property. Ludwig von Mises (1981, p. 17) writes: "All property has its origin in occupation and force ... All law is founded on real force, and all property was originally appropriated or stolen." Von Mises rightly points out that this leaves much unsaid on the present necessity, suitability, or moral justification of property and state.

Before the state regulated the use of force, at least internally, and began offering social and legal protection, fighting raged between and within political groups ranging from the household, clan, race, Polis, city, confederation to feudal or patrimonial monarchy. It is false to characterize conditions before the emergence of states as "anarchic" in the sense of "free from tyranny" or free from illegitimate coercion: use of force, for example by the household patriarch, was extensive. It included, as Max Weber wrote in his economic history (1958, p. 58), the absolute, life-long, and hereditary despotism of the pater familias. The head of the household was a despot who had total control over wife, children, slaves ("instrumentum vocale"), cattle, work tools, and the familia pecuniaque of Roman law. His "dominion" was absolute. The rights of the master of the house, subject only to certain ritual restrictions, extended so far as to include the right to kill and sell his wife or even to sell or to hire out his children. The household patriarch, whether under Babylonian, Roman, or Germanic law, could adopt children to add to his own whenever he wanted to. A woman was by definition a slave or a concubine, children slaves.

Before modern states emerged, the use of physical force against criminals was cruel and extensive.[21] The clan elevated revenge to the level of sacred duty, of a cult. The aim was to exact fitting revenge, to destroy the opponent. When criminals were caught in the act of committing crimes, they were killed regardless of the seriousness of the crime. Feuds were essentially organized revenge in the form of vendettas; later, they were replaced by a system of fines, but the choice of action against the insolvent debtor was free. The extreme case was "outlawry," an excessive reaction of society as a whole against a violation of law: the disrupter of social order was killed without any opportunity given for repentance, like a predatory animal. A price could be put on his head, and he was given no burial and was left to be devoured by predatory animals. All his legal ties were severed: his wife became a widow, his children orphans; he lost all title to his property; he was denied any human fellowship. Nobody could protect him without risking accusations of complicity. Public executions spared no measures of cruelty, ranging from stoning to running the gauntlet or forcing the condemned to build their own gallows or pyre. Who would prefer such conditions to those in a publicly controlled legal system?

Moreover, the Middle Ages, which anarchists often idealize, was a time of constant feuding. Even commerce used means of force, often amounting to piracy. In ancient Greece, wars were fought constantly among the Poleis. War and military achievements were downright glorified (cf. Burckhardt, 1940, pp. 139–147). Feuds in the Middle Ages were not considered illegitimate but a normal means to settle conflicts at a time of extremely decentralized use of force.

A particularly serious flaw in anarcho-capitalist argumentation is the failure to see that it has always been in the interest of the commercial middle class, the merchants and cities, to have church and state control feuding and maintain the peace by the church and state. 500 years ago, in the Germany of Emperor Maximilian, a lasting "proscription of feuds" ("ewiger Landfrieden") was welcomed in particular by commercial interests (cf. Becker, 1995).[22]

To regard conditions in the Middle Ages as ordered by an anarchic private law, as for example Benson or de Jasay do, means assuming a distinction between private and public that did not exist at that time.[23] Public law had not yet achieved independence with respect to the political power of household heads, local leaders, confederations, and other groups. No difference could be found between the public and private realms. There still were no institutionalized political forces capable of carrying out measures of coercion. But this is the only difference existing between that time and the present. Commercial law was, and remains, at least partly, a law that merchants themselves create – but it has always been supplemented by a penal code that employs means of physical coercion or the martial "law" at work in conflicts between clans, races, nations, or cities. Commercial interests depend on political protection, aside from those cases where they themselves have the capacity, like the Hanseatic League, to use political means of coercion.

Anarchy in the sense of a social order not based on any coercion, hierarchies, and legal inequalities has never existed. The functions performed by law and justice today to uphold social morals and customs were once performed by social morals, conventions, and traditions themselves (cf. Jellinek, 1966, pp. 221–228).

It is striking that the natural-law dogmatism of libertarians ignores everything except for the individual and humanity. Humanity, however, happens to be split up in competing peoples, ethnic entities, religious groups, and other units. And these have always showed willingness to use force of arms as a means to assert their interests if this seemed profitable to them, even going so far as to secure trade monopolies, as in mercantile republics. One need only study, among others, Carthaginian, Venetian, or English history. From the day of birth, every "individual" already is tied into the specific affiliations that make up his identity. This is a fact that the social constructivism of this school fails to take into consideration.

And the Anarchy of the Future?

If the monopolist use of legitimate force by the state could be eliminated in accordance with the libertarian ideal, then governmental force could be shifted to private firms (security agencies, for example). Armed with physical means of coercion, these agencies, as experience shows, might attempt to establish monopoly positions and force the paying of rents, thus turning business clients into "private subjects." Such organizations would legitimize their existence not by performing services on a voluntary basis but through compulsory measures of protection. The history of disintegrating empires and states shows this clearly. A sort of re-feudalizing of society would set in, with the difference that the former feuding lords would be transformed into the heads of corporations. The existing international dimensions of the Mafia give an idea of what it would be like. The rare, large-scale wars fought between competing national entities would be replaced by many one-to-one conflicts between competing firms. Perhaps the result of this unpeaceful competition would be the emergence of large private enterprises with regional monopolies. What difference would there be between these entities and national states? And what would actually be gained by this form of "anarchy"? It is only wishful thinking without basis in practical experience to speculate like David Friedman (1989, p. 116) that "wars are very expensive and Tannahelp and Dawn Defense (two private firms, GH) are both profit-making corporations, more interested in saving money than face". Friedman, however, also admits (1989, p. 147) that private firms could possibly turn into conventional governments ("rules"); he conceded that private corporations could assume the role of conventional governments ("rules") and that anarchist institutions could not guarantee that this would not happen.

Reprivatization, during which competition would allocate the use of force (occupational franchises for every member of this branch), will be of great significance for the functioning of market economy and for the currently excessive division of labor and "just-in-time" production. This can be better appreciated after reading Max Weber's (1968) observations on the prerequisites of "modern capitalism." These prerequisites included, according to Weber, a "rational state" with a monopoly on use of force and a reliable formalist law. Those active in a market economy have always been important supporters of a "general proscription of feuding" ("ewiger Landfrieden").

Ethnic groups and peoples fighting among another for power, prestige, influence, and economic opportunities, which regard themselves as "united" because of parentage or a shared history and feel entitled to use legitimate use of force against competing groups, are either never mentioned in the social models forwarded by libertarians or dismissed as annoying, but temporary, disturbances. Only markets and "the state" exist. Occasionally, in a metaphysical manner, the state is personified as an evil demon. "Foreign policy" is officially eliminated, since there are no more states and thus no nations, either (on the current "disposition" of states and nations, read Fukuyama 1992 and Lukacz, 1996). This is a blatant manifestation of constructivist thought. If the military arm of the state were abolished, then existing ethnic communities could hire private firms to wage their wars (as, in fact, they already have done many times). Commercial enterprises would doubtlessly make the fighting of war more efficient. Even Adam Smith supported professional armies. But the problem of rival peoples and their conflicts would not be solved (not to mention the problem of privately owned weapons of mass destruction, which anarchist literature fails to take into sufficient consideration).

Further Points

Ultimately, what is really more important – the absolute freedom of the individual or, under the right conditions, the keeping of social order with the resulting peaceful maximization of the well-being of the individuals who depend on this order? Should the question really be: Fiat libertas et pereat mundus? Even a writer like David Friedman has his doubts about this. Furthermore: is not democracy, with its rule by majority, a useful invention to settle conflicts of opinion without bloodshed as well as to help to solve the problems of succession that led monarchies to fight such devastating wars so often? As long as democracy is constitutionally restricted, it ideally supplements the market. If, like de Jasay or Rothbard, it is claimed that democracy cannot be held in check by constitutional restrictions or is itself illegitimate, thus dismissing democracy entirely, most of us would not accept the social ideals of these thinkers because of the predictable consequences of their realization.[25] Nevertheless, compared to the claim that constitutional control of democracy is utopian, the anarchist program for elimination of state and democracy is certainly much more utopian.

Digression: Ludwig von Mises on State, Anarchism, and Democracy

The libertarians, principally Rothbard, often refer to Ludwig von Mises. There is a Ludwig von Mises Institute at Auburn University in Alabama that keeps up anarcho-capitalist traditions. Indeed, Rohbard's monumental opus "Man, Economy, and the State" (1993) appears to be a continuation of Ludwig von Mises's "Human Action" (1966, see also Rothbard, 1988). Ludwig von Mises actually opposed anarchism and firmly defended the necessity of state and democracy (see Mises, 1927, pp. 32–39).[26] Von Mises argued that the observance of social morals and customs was in the interest of all because all are interested in strengthening social cooperation; however, there are persons who lack the insight or requisite will to obey customs and traditions of their own accord. Coercive measures and use of force against forces hostile to a society, however, would make it impossible for its members to live with another harmoniously and government and its organs would still be required to enforce the laws. Liberalism, writes von Mises, is not anarchism; they share no common ground. Von Mises is convinced that without use of force the existence of society would be endangered and that laws which need to be followed must be backed up by means of force. Liberals give the state the role of protecting property, freedom, and peace. This state must be organized in such a way that its progress could continue calmly and peacefully, unimpeded by civil war, revolution, or coups. Von Mises goes on to argue that a lasting economic upswing is not possible if the making of transactions, which require stability and order, were repeatedly impeded by internal unrest. It would take only a few days for political conditions like, for example, those in England during the War of the Roses to inflict terrible distress on the England of our day. As for democracy, von Mises says that is a constitutional form that reconciles government with the wishes of the governed without this leading to violent struggle. Elections and parliamentarism ensure that changes of government proceed smoothly without use of force or bloodshed. It may not be below one's dignity to be ruled at all by others. There may be people, who claim, that this was his view in the Twenties. But even in his later writings, no indication exists that von Mises, regardless of his scathing and sometimes sarcastic criticism of the state, ever changed his basic opinion (cf. Mises, 1983).

X. Anarchist capitalism and the Communitarian Ideal

The harshest critics of the abstractions of anarcho-capitalist theory are members of a new and rather heterogeneous American school of thought: the so-called communitarians.[27] Although some of its members are not averse to social democratic welfare traditions – even the most appealing among them, such as Michael Walzer and Amitai Etzioni – in essence they advocate ideas that have always been part of the liberal tradition. This tradition has always had theoreticians who not only designed models to promote liberties and free exchange but also gave thought to how social and historical facts could form a framework or infrastructure for the preservation of freedom. This is in the tradition of the school of "critical rationalists," which includes as members in the 18th century particularly Adam Ferguson and Edmund Burke, in the 19th century Benjamin Constant, Lord Acton, or Alexis de Tocqueville, in the 20th century Bertrand de Jouvenel, Wilhelm Röpke, and especially Friedrich August von Hayek (see von Hayek 1971, pp. 65–88, 1981, pp. 76–79 and 189–199).

Michael Walzer criticizes, very much as these authors do,[28] the fiction of an autonomous individual who creates his individuality ex nihilo so to speak, who is grounded in his own private will and who, being free of all social bonds (although his identity was formed by those bonds), recognizes no community values, no permanent relationships, no collective morals, customs, or traditions. Walzer speaks polemically of the "mythical figures" of this theory, "without eyes, without teeth, without taste, without anything ..." Everything that the individual does not freely choose and agree to is regarded as an arbitrary, oppressive burden. Individuals have no original attachment to society, are literally free and independent, themselves the only ones to create and shape their own lives without criteria, unaided by collective norms and standards. Just as de Jouvenel would, Walzer asks how it is possible for a group to exist whose members are strangers to another when obviously every member of this group has parents at birth and these parents in turn have friends, relatives, neighbors, colleagues, fellow church members and fellow citizens – links and bonds that, when examined, reveal themselves to be relations that are not freely chosen, but passed on and

71

inherited (Honneth, 1990, p. 162). Certainly, we live today, as another communitarian writes, in a pluralist or individualist "mosaic culture," but the mosaic has to be held together by cement of some kind or else it will fall apart (Etzioni, 1995, p. 20). Although some writers are close to social democracy in their thinking, the state is never glorified but keenly criticized as a destroyer of free social bonds and as a juggernaut of centralization (weakening of federalism and self-government). Etzioni and other writers firmly support a revaluation of self-responsibility and the responsibility of free communities – all those pluralist forms standing between the individual and the state. Smaller, decentralized units that can govern themselves much as the ancient Polis governed itself are the ideal (an ideal that shares common ground with Hans-Hermann Hoppe's positions). For all communitarians, the "market" cannot be alone responsible for the forming of relationships in view of primary existential associations ranging from the family, club, and school to the nation. Even if in large national political entities the glue holding society together is highly diluted, nonetheless it exists, as is shown by the free and uncoerced feeling of citizens of that they "belong." The recent process of German reunification is a highly instructive example of this. Public organizations rely on this primary feeling of fellowship (often exploiting it in the name of fictive and coercive ideals of solidarity).

We are unable to find in communitarianism – at least grosso modo and with regard to its principal advocates – a movement that truly opposes classic liberalism; rather, it is its complement. However, there does exist a polemic front concerning individualist anarchism. It may be possible to disqualify this school by labeling it "romantic" (just as von Hayeks views themselves once were called). But this sort of romanticism can also be the basis of social cohesion. On the other hand, the anarchist ideal of the lonely gunfighter "going it alone" also has romantic appeal.

A Concluding Appreciation

The type of anarchist capitalism discussed here is a generalization of the free market model and economic motivation, which have given all liberals such an extraordinary abundance of ideas. Anarchist capitalism compels examination of everything not rooted in the market or in individualism – whether the state, the nation, or the family household. There have never been severer critics of the state than those of this school – this is in itself is a useful lesson for Continental Europeans and particularly for Germans. Thinking of this kind that is consistent with natural law provides impressive protection against the suggestive power and lure of the state. Liberals will also subscribe to the natural-law argument (of their type) for its own sake. Indeed, anarcho-capitalist criticism of the welfare state and public economy is of inestimable value. Of course, anarchist capitalism fails to find application in areas of society where market forces are not at work – beyond or before the market and state. It gives little attention to such problems. Its theory hinders appreciation of the value of communities founded on real fellowship and of their claims in a world in which groups compete with another. Anarchist capitalism also succumbs to overexaggeration of economic incentives. Tending to indulge in a certain demonization of the collective concept of the "state," anarchist capitalism sometimes falls prey to the same evil that it otherwise so vehemently criticizes: the personification of concepts. Every liberal will gain much from an intensive study of this current of thought, but its limits should be equally clear to him, limits also known by all forms of constructivism.

Notes

1 Cf. Felix Somary (1994, p. 278): "Fighting about social policy took place everywhere in this huge realm, and it amused me to rediscover all the German social measures that had already been in existence for fifty years under such high-sounding names as New Deal."

2 "His work constitutes perhaps the most powerful and sophisticated case for individualistic anarchism in this century, if not in the entire history of this particular social philosophy." (Barry, 1986, p. 173). Cf. also the quoted rhapsodic volume of commemorative articles of Rothbard's "followers" (Rockwell, 1995).

3 In an aggressive paper, Hoppe gives what amounts to a devastating critique of Hayek's social philosophy: "Hayek's view regarding the role of market and state cannot be systematically distinguished from that of a modern social democrat" (p. 127). Hoppe's review deserves its own critical response. In particular, von Hayek's evolutionist approach is misunderstood. Cf. on criticism of Hayek also Rothbard, 1995, pp. 40–42, 370–379. Anthony de Jasay clearly points out the dificulties of setting an exact limit to "legitimate" redistribution if it is admitted, as it is by most liberals, that the state is responsible for securing at least subsistence level support ("public assistance" or the like). And, of course, redistribution already takes place whenever the state finances itself by taxation. For genuine anarchists, the elimination of the state is only the logical consequence of their postulate of the absolute freedom of the individual.

4   General surveys of the intellectual history of anarchism are made by, among others, Cantzen (1987), Eltzbacher (1987), Göhler / Klein (1991), Lösche (1977, 1991), Stowasser (1995), Woodcock (1962), von Zencker (1985). In these surveys, individualist anarchism is mentioned only in passing. Particulars on the tradition of American anarchism: Brooks (1994), Martin (1970), Barry (1986, pp. 161–191). A systematic introduction to individualist anarchism is given by Bergland (1990). On the thought of the Rothbard school see in particular Rockwell (1990). I thank Detmar Doering for his generous bibliographical assistance.

5   Cf. for example Brooks (1994). It is said that it would be too great an honor for this tedious pedant of the German idealist school to classify him as a "predecessor" of that incomparably more fertile source of ideas, Friedrich Nietzsche.

6   In particular, Rothbard and his circle rely on the work of the "Austrian School," whose members include Menger, Böhm-Bawerk, Mises, von Hayek (cf. Taylor, 1988; on controversies within this school, cf. in particular Selgin, 1990).

7   Cf. Rothbard (1994, pp. 201–214). The unavoidable counterargument of high transaction costs (for private roads within local communities) does not dismay Libertarians; absolute freedom always has priority.

8   Rothbard vehemently supports a gold standard on a private basis. He rejects, along with Hans-Hermann Hoppe, von Hayek's privatization model.

9   Cf. Benson (1990, pp. 179–268), and Habermann (1994). In German administrative law, for example, the figure of the "commissioned entrepreneur" ("beliehener Unternehmer") has long been known and is also widely seen in action, ranging from inspectors of the Technical Control Association (roughly equivalent to the American Underwriters' Laboratories) to captains on board of their ships (cf. Achterberg, 1986, pp. 388–389; Wolff / Bachof, 1976, pp. 452–457).

10   Cf. Bergland (1990, pp. 82–83): "Americans have the right to decide how best to protect themselves, their families, and their property. Millions of Americans have guns in their homes and sleep more comfortably because of it. Studies show that where gun ownership has been made illegal, more residential burglaries are committed. No one has anything to fear from the person who keeps a gun in his or her home for protection, except burglars." Cf. also Halbrook, in: Rockwell (1990, pp. 153–157).

11   "Whoever is governed is, in every action, every transaction, every movement, noted, registered, counted, appraised, stamped, measured,

classified, estimated, taxed, assessed, authorized, endorsed, warned, hindered, improved, set right, and corrected. Under the pretext of the public good or general welfare, he is plundered, harrassed, imprisoned, exploited, monopolized, licensed, impoverished, mystified, or robbed; if he offers the slightest resistance, then even in beginning action he is oppressed, punished, vituperated, annoyed, hounded, scolded, beaten to death, disarmed, muzzled, jailed, shot, torn apart, sentenced, condemned, deported, sacrificed, sold, and betrayed; and, to make sure that the list is complete, he is also duped, fooled, insulted, disdained, and disgraced. Such is government, such is its justice and morality." (Quoted in: Gide / Rist, 1924, p. 681).

12 Against a Mr. Hobson: "Does he satisfy us that three men may rightly do whatever they please with the minds, bodies, and property of two men?" and so forth (Herbert, 1978, p. 239).

13 Hoppe believes that hereditary monarchy ("privately owned government") ensures protection of property and freedom better than modern mass democracy, since the holder of monarchic power had a natural interest in the long-term use of his private resource, namely the state, while democratic politicians give priority to immediate expenditure during their terms of office. Cf. Hoppe (1996); for a critique of Hoppe, see Habermann (1996).

14 That he actually regards himself as a "strict liberal" is shown by his book: "Liberalismus, neu gefasst" (de Jasay, 1995a) or his 1991 paper. In the meantime, the logic of his arguments has drifted toward a state-free society, meaning anarchy; cf. recent de Jasay (1995c).

15 Cf. Max Weber, "Wirtschaft und Gesellschaft" (1964, pp. 22–24, 157–160). Whether in past or present times, most of humanity have not subscribed to the anarchist conception of legitimacy; they have no difficulty accepting the binding force of acts of state or of majority decisions. They are willing to subordinate themselves not only for reasons of coercion, calculation, interest, fear, or force of habit, but also because they regard the given social and political order as "having model character" – a tragic error, according to anarchists.

16 The final goal of a society free of state, an anarchic global economy, has been described by, among others, David Friedman (1989, pp. 109–164: "Anarchy is not chaos") or by Rothbard (1994, pp. 215–241, pp. 263–294). In the following discussion, talks with my colleague Erwin Siweris have been greatly helpful.

17 The intellectual debate with the anarchist capitalists is conducted mainly in America, particularly by members of the public choice school (cf. Buchanan, 1984) and the communitarians (see below). Cf.

also Gray (1994) and de Jasays's response (1994), Zeitler (1995, pp. 238–268) and Barry (1986, pp. 161–191); cf. also earlier writings focusing on leftist anarchism, including Gide / Rist (1924), Mosca (1950), Jellinek (1966), Herzog (1971) in addition Zippelius (1988). A review of Rothbard's criticism of von Hayek was given by Heuß and Mestmäcker in "Ordo-Jahrbuch" (32, 1981, pp. 103–107, pp. 109–115). Boger's criticism (1990) was reserved.

18 An obvious objection is that the expression natural law is misleading: nature does not grant any rights. The many who have suffered untimely deaths as the result of violence, illness, or disaster, indeed, all of human and natural history, constitute dramatic proof of the ethical indifference of "nature." Nature paid court to Jenghiz Khan and nailed Christ to the cross. Attention is drawn to the age-old "theodicy" discussion ranging from the Upanishads to the book of Job (cf. Durant, 1969, pp. 46–56; Max Weber, 1964, pp. 405–411).

19 Reference is made in general to the discussion on freedom of value judgment in the social sciences, both the earlier one between Max Weber and the Schmoller school and more recent debates, like that between Hans Albert and Jürgen Habermas.

20 In particular, his book on the "state" ([1927], 1990) with its lengthy, moralizing section on the origin of the state and a brief but bloated part that describes a future "free citizenship" (without "political means" but with a civil service). A somewhat more adequate analysis of the establishment of states is given by Max Weber (1964, pp. 660–664: "Entwicklungsstadien politischer Vergesellschaftung"). Anarchism lacks the distinction between a modern state with its professional administrative personnel and a "political assocation" without such professionalization. As a result, he draws the erroneous conclusion that "anarchy" or a private legal system existed before the state. Cf. on the origin of states also Will Durant (1969, pp. 75–89, and 1981, pp. 36–42).

21 Cf. surveys in legal histories, for example, by Heinrich Mitteis (1966) or Hermann Conrad (1962). We rely greatly here on Mitteis's survey.

22 In this context, it is worthwhile to quote Max Weber again: " ... By these means, the political community monopolized the legitimate use of force for their coercive apparatus, transforming it gradually into an institution providing legal protection. In doing so, it received powerful and crucial support from all those groups that had direct or indirect economic interests in the expansion of the market community as well as in religious powers ... From the economic point of view ... those interested in peace are primarily those with market interests, particu-

larly the bourgeoisie of the cities, then all those with interests in tolls exacted for passage along rivers, roads, and under bridges as well as in the taxable capacity of tenants and subjects. Even before political authority imposed restrictions on feuding to serve its power interests, in the Middle Ages steadily growing groups of those interested in developing a money economy along with the church limited feuding and sought to establish temporary, periodic, or lasting alliances to end feuding. Moreover, as the expanding market increasingly ... undermined monopolist groups economically so that their members themselves became interested in the market, the market deprived them of the base of that community of interests on which they had developed a legitimate claim to use of force. Parallel to the spreading of peace and expanding of the market, therefore, first of all the monopolization of legitimate use of force was continued by the political association as perfected within the framework of the modern conception of state as the authoritative source of any legitimacy of physical force and second of all simultaneously within the framework of the rationalization of rules for use of force in the concept of a legitimate legal order." (1964, p. 663)

23 In German historical studies, a detailed discussion has been held on this question and on the nature of the "state in the Middle Ages." Cf. Kämpf (1964), Brunner (1965).

24 In the author's view, this is the weakest area of anarchist social theory. Cf. the discussion among Tullock, Bernholz, and Walter Block, in: Radnitzky (1992, pp. 301–428).

25 The Italian political scientist Gaetano Mosca (1950, pp. 243–244) described these consequences impressively: "Assuming ... that neither nations nor governments exist any longer, and the army, the bureaucracy, the courts, and particularly the police and prisons also vanished, then ... there would still be weapons as well as enterprising and determined persons who would use them to subjugate others. As a result, small social groups would form rapidly, and a majority of workers would be exploited and protected by a minority of armed persons. The armed would live from the labor of the unarmed. This would amount to a return to a simple, primitive social order in which every armed group would have absolute power over a small parcel of land and over those cultivating it as long as the group managed to keep its power. We have called this type "feudal." In brief, exactly the same thing would occur that occurred in Europe when Charlemagne's empire broke up and its fragments were absorbed into the system of the Roman empire, when the Mogul empire of India collapsed, and that

occurs in every civilized society that falls apart for internal or external reasons. The bold and the strong, who have nothing to lose, would doubtlessly exploit such a radical change, which could only end by enhancing the role of force and personal courage. The overwhelming majority of peaceful individuals would suffer, perhaps 90 percent of all people, who would reject this "rule of the sword," preferring instead a little peace and security in which to enjoy at least some of the fruits of their labor ... De Gourmont writes on this: "If there are no laws, the superiority of superior individuals would be the only law, and nobody could dispute their just despotism. This despotism is necessary in order to muzzle the fools; for a man without intellect bites." (It is not relevant that Mosca criticizes anarchist communists here.)

26 Although Hoppe differs from von Mises in this crucial point, he wrote a rather persuasive introduction to an unchanged new edition (1993) of the book by von Mises on liberalism that is quoted here.

References

Achterberg, Norbert (1986), *Allgemeines Verwaltungsrecht*, 2nd ed., C. F. Müller, Heidelberg.

Anderson, Terry und Hill, P. J. (1979), 'An American Experiment in Anarcho-Kapitalism: The Not so Wild Wild-West', in: *Journal of Libertarian Studies*, 3, pp. 27ff.

Baader, Roland (ed.) (1995 a), *Die Enkel des Perikles. Liberale Positionen zu Sozialstaat und Gesellschaft*, Resch, Munich.

Baader, Roland (ed.) (1995 b), *Wider die Wohlfahrtsdiktatur. Zehn liberale Stimmen*, Resch, Munich.

Barry, Norman (1986), *On Classical Liberalism and Libertarianism*, Mac Millan-Press, London.

Becker, Hans-Jürgen (1995), 'Das Gewaltmonopol des Staates und die Sicherheit des Bürgers', *Neue Juristische Wochenschrift*, 32, pp. 2077ff.

Beierwaltes, Andreas (1995), 'Das Ende des Liberalismus?' in: Supplement of the journal *'Das Parlament'* 43.

Benson, Bruce L. (1990), *The Enterprise of Law, Justice without the State*, Pacific Research Institute for Public Policy, San Francisco.

Bergland, David (1990), *Libertarianism in one Lesson*, 5th ed., Orpheus Publications, Costa Mesa.

Blankertz, Stefan und Goodman, Paul (1980), *Staatlichkeitswahn*, Büchse der Pandora Verlags GmbH, Wetzlar.

Blankertz, Stefan (1988), *Politik der neuen Toleranz, Plädoyer für einen radikalen Liberalismus*, Büchse der Pandora Verlags GmbH, Wetzlar.

Blankertz, Stefan (1989), *Legitimität und Praxis*, Büchse der Pandora Verlags GmbH, Wetzlar.

Blankertz, Stefan (1995), 'Eingreifen statt übergreifen. Über die Privatisierbarkeit der Polizei', in: Doering/Fliszar, pp. 176ff.

Block, Walter (1991), *Defending the Undefendable*, Fox and Wilkes, San Francisco.

Block, Walter (1995), 'Freiheit und Umwelt: Wege und Irrwege in der Umweltpolitik', in: Baader (1995 b), pp. 171ff.

Boger, Horst Wolfgang (1990), 'Anarchismus und radikaler Liberalismus', in: *Jahrbuch zur Liberalismusforschung*, 1990, pp. 47ff.

Brooks, Frank H. (ed.) (1994), *The Individualist Anarchists*, New Brunswick, Transaction Publishers, New Jersey.

Brunner, Otto (1965), *Land und Herrschaft*, 5th ed., Rudolf M. Rohrer, Vienna.

Buchanan, James M. (1984), *Die Grenzen der Freiheit*, J. C. B. Mohr (Paul Siebeck), Tübingen.

Burke, Edmund (1967), *Betrachtungen über die Französische Revolution*, Suhrkamp, Frankfurt/M.

Cantzen, Rolf (1987), *Weniger Staat – mehr Gesellschaft*, Fischer Taschenbuch, Frankfurt/M.

Conrad, Hermann (1962), *Deutsche Rechtsgeschichte*, vol. 1, C. F. Müller, Karlsruhe.

Constant, Benjamin (1948), *Über die Gewalt*, Reclam, Stuttgart.

Doering, Detmar (1994), 'Lysander Spooner und die Freiheit ohne Staat', in: *liberal* (German journal), 37, pp. 74ff.

Doering, Detmar (1995 a), 'Nicht vertrauenswürdig: der Staat als Garant der Freiheit', in: Baader (1995 a), pp. 107ff.

Doering, Detmar (1995 b), 'Recht durch Markt', in: Doering/Fliszar (1995), pp. 165ff.

Doering, Detmar and Fliszar, Fritz (eds.) (1995), *Freiheit: die unbequeme Idee*, Deutsche Verlagsanstalt, Stuttgart.

Durant, Will (1981), *Kulturgeschichte der Menschheit*, vol. 1, *Der alte Orient und Indien*, Ullstein, Frankfurt/M., Berlin, Vienna.

Durant, Will und Ariel (1969), *Die Lehren der Geschichte*, Francke-Verlag, Bern and Munich.

Eltzbacher, Paul (1987), *Der Anarchismus*, Libertad-Verlag, Berlin.

Etzioni, Amitai (1994), *Jenseits des Egoismusprinzips*, Schaeffer Poeschel, Stuttgart.

Etzioni, Amitai (1995), *Die Entdeckung des Gemeinwesens*, Schaeffer Poeschel, Stuttgart.

Frei, Christoph und Nef, Robert (eds.) (1994), Peter Lang, *Contending with Hayek*, Bern.

Friedman, David (1989) *The Machinery of Freedom*, 2nd ed., Open Court Publishing Company, La Salles, Illinois.

Fukuyama, Francis (1992), *Das Ende der Geschichte*, Kindler, Munich.

Fukuyama, Francis (1995), *Konfuzius und Marktwirtschaft*, Kindler, Munich.

Gide, Charles and Rist, Charles (1923), *Geschichte der volkswirtschaftlichen Lehrmeinungen*, 3rd ed., Gustav Fischer, Jena.

Göhler, Gerhard and Klein, Ansgar (1991), 'Politische Theorien des 19. Jahrhunderts, Der Anarchismus', in: Hans Joachim Lieber (ed.), *Politische Theorien von der Antike bis zur Gegenwart*, Bundeszentrale für politische Bildung, Bonn, pp. 577ff.

Gray, John (1994), 'Hayeks Spontaneus Order and the Post-Communist Societies in Transition', in: Frei/Nef (eds.), pp. 29ff.

Habermann, Gerd (1994), 'Privatisierung – hoheitliche Prinzipien kein Tabu!', in: *Schlanker Staat, schlanke Kommunen, schlanke Unternehmen, 3. Privatisierungstagung der Arbeitsgemeinschaft zur Förderung der Partnerschaft in der Wirtschaft*, 1994, pp. 148ff.

Habermann, Gerd (1996), 'Commentary on Hoppe', in: Gerard Radnitzky (ed.), *Values and the Social Order*, vol. 3, Aldershot, forthcoming.

Halbrook, Stephan P. (1990), 'Afraid to Trust the People With Arms', in: Rockwell (1990), pp. 153ff., Auburn, Alabama.

Hasbach, Wilhelm (1891), 'Die allgemeinen philosophischen Grundlagen der von F. Quesnay und Adam Smith begründeten Politischen Ökonomie', in: Gustav Schmoller (ed.), *Staats- und Sozialwissenschaftliche Forschungen*, vol. 10.

Hayek, Friedrich August von (1944), *Der Weg zur Knechtschaft*, Erlenbach, Zürich (reprint, Olzog Munich 1994).

Hayek, Friedrich August von (1971), *Die Verfassung der Freiheit*, J. C. B. Mohr (Paul Siebeck), Tübingen.

Hayek, Friedrich August von (1976), 'Wahrer und falscher Individualismus', in: *Individualismus und wirtschaftliche Ordnung*, Wolfgang Neugebauer, Salzburg, pp. 9ff.

Hayek, Friedrich August von (1977), *Entnationalisierung des Geldes*, J. C. B. Mohr (Paul Siebeck), Tübingen.

Hayek, Friedrich August von (1979), *Liberalismus*, J. C. B. Mohr (Paul Siebeck), Tübingen.

Hayek, Friedrich August von (1981), *Recht, Gesetzgebung und Freiheit*, 3 vls., Verlag moderne industrie, Landsberg am Lech.

Herbert, Auberon (1978), *The Right and Wrong of Compulsion by the State*, Liberty Fund, Indianapolis.

Herzog, Roman (1971), *Allgemeine Staatslehre*, Athenäum, Frankfurt/M.

Heuss, Ernst (1981), 'Wie man Sozialwissenschaften nicht betreiben soll', in: *Ordo, Jahrbuch für die Ordnung von Wirtschaft und Gesellschaft*, vol. 32, Stuttgart, New York, pp. 109ff.

Honneth, Axel (ed.) (1993), *Kommunitarismus*, Campus, Frankfurt/M.

Hoppe, Hans-Hermann (1987), *Eigentum, Anarchie und Staat*, Westdeutscher Verlag, Opladen.

Hoppe, Hans-Hermann (1994), 'F. A. Hayek on Government and Social Evolution: a critique', in: Frei/Nef, pp. 127ff.

Hoppe, Hans-Hermann (1995 a), 'Ein Liberalismus von unerhörter Radikalität', *Neue Zürcher Zeitung*, January, 14, 1995.

Hoppe, Hans-Hermann (1995 b), *Natural Elites, Intellectuals and the State*, Broschüre, Mises-Institute, Auburn, Alabama.

Hoppe, Hans-Hermann (1995 c), 'The Western State as a Paradigm: Lerning from history', *Lecture on the Conference of the Mont Pélérine-Society in Capetown*, Southafrica.

Hoppe, Hans-Hermann (1996), 'The Political Economy of Monarchy and Democracy and the Idea of Natural Order', in: Gerard Radnitzky (ed.), *Values and the Social Order*, vol. 3, Aldershot, forthcoming.

Humboldt, Wilhelm von (1962), *Versuch, die Grenzen der Wirksamkeit des Staates zu bestimmen*, Verlag Freies Geistesleben, Darmstadt.

Jasay, Anthony de (1991), 'Zur Möglichkeit begrenzter Staatsgewalt', in: Radnitzky/Bouillon, pp. 77ff.

Jasay, Anthony de (1991), *Choice, Consent, Contract: a Restatement of Liberalism*, Institute of Economic Affairs, London; German: (1995 a), *Liberalismus neu gefaßt*, Ullstein Propyläen, Berlin and Frankfurt/M.

Jasay, Anthony de (1994), 'The Cart before the Horse', in: Frei/Nef (eds.), pp. 49ff.

Jasay, Anthony de (1995 b), 'Freiheit und Umverteilung', in: Baader (1995 b), pp. 19ff.

Jasay, Anthony de (1995 c), 'Conventions: Some Thoughts on the Economics of Ordered Anarchy', *Lectiones Jenenses, Vortragsreihe des Max-Planck-Instituts zur Erforschung von Wirtschaftssystemen*, No. 3, Jena.

Jellinek, Georg (1966), *Allgemeine Staatslehre*, 3rd ed., Max von der Gehlen, Bad Homburg v.d.H., Berlin, Zürich.

Jouvenel, Bertrand de (1945), *Über die Staatsgewalt* (German transl., Rombach, Freiburg 1972).

Jouvenel, Bertrand de (1963), *Über Souveränität*, Luchterhand, Neuwied.

Kämpf, Hellmut (ed.) (1964), *Herrschaft und Staat im Mittelalter*, Wissenschaftliche Buchgesellschaft, Darmstadt.

Kern, Fritz (1965), *Recht und Verfassung im Mittelalter*, Wissenschaftliche Buchgesellschaft, Darmstadt.

Kropotkin, Peter (1920), *Gegenseitige Hilfe in der Tier- und Menschenwelt*, Thomas, Leipzig.

Kühnhardt, Ludger (1987), *Die Universalität der Menschenrechte*, Bundeszentrale für Politische Bildung, Bonn.

Lippman, Walter (1945), *Die Gesellschaft freier Menschen*, A. Francke, Bern.

Lösche, Peter (1977), *Anarchismus*, Wissenschaftliche Buchgesllschaft, Darmstadt.

Lösche, Peter (1991), 'Artikel Anarchismus', in: Dieter Nohlen (ed.), *Wörterbuch Staat und Politik*, Bundeszentrale für politische Bildung, Bonn, pp. 7ff.

Lukacs, John (1996), *Die Geschichte geht weiter*, Heyne, Munich.

Martin, James J. (1970), *Men against the State*, Ralph Myles, Colorado Springs.

Meinecke, Friedrich (1963), *Die Idee der Staatsraison*, 3rd ed., R. Oldenbourg, Munich.

Mestmäcker, Ernst Joachim (1981), 'Vom Bürgerkrieg als Utopie', in: *Ordo, Jahrbuch für die Ordnung von Wirtschaft und Gesellschaft, vol. 32, Stuttgart, New York, pp. 103ff.*

Mises, Ludwig von (1927), *Liberalismus*, Gustav Fischer, Jena.

Mises, Ludwig von (1966), *Human Action*, 3rd ed., Fox and Wilkes, San Francisco.

Mises, Ludwig von (1981), *Die Gemeinwirtschaft*, Untersuchungen über den Sozialismus, 2nd ed., Philosophia Verlag, Munich.

Mises, Ludwig von (1983), *Vom Wert der besseren Ideen*, 6 Vorlesungen über Wirtschaft und Politik, Poller-Verlag, Stuttgart.

Mitteis, Heinrich (1966), *Deutsche Rechtsgeschichte*, 10th ed., C. H. Beck'sche Verlagsbuchhandlung, Munich and Berlin.

Molinari, Gustave de (1977), *The Production of Security* (brochure), The Center for Libertarian-Studies, New York.

Mosca, Gaetano (1950), *Die herrschende Klasse, Grundlagen der Politischen Wissenschaft*, Leo Lehnen-Verlag, Munich.

Nock, Albert Jay (1992), *Our Enemy the State*, 4th ed., Fox and Wilkes, San Francisco.

Oppenheimer, Franz (1990), *Der Staat*, Libertad-Verlag, Berlin.

Radnitzky, Gerard and Bouillon, Hardy (eds.) (1991), *Ordnungstheorie und Ordnungspolitik*, Springer, Berlin, Heidelberg, New York, Tokio.

Radnitzky, Gerard (1991), 'Marktwirtschaft: frei oder sozial?', in: Radnitzky/Bouillon, pp. 44ff.

Radnitzky, Gerard (ed.) (1992), *Universal Economics*, Icus, New York.

Radnitzky, Gerard (1995 a), 'Die demokratische Wohlfahrtsdiktatur', in: Baader, pp. 187ff.

Radnitzky, Gerard (1995 b), 'Freiheit und Wohlfahrtsdemokratie, Information und Mobilität können die Umverteilungsdemokratie zähmen', in: Baader (ed.), pp. 87ff.

Radnitzky, Gerard (1995 c), 'On the Passage to a Less unfree Society', in: Radnitzky/Bouillon, *Values and the Social Order*, Aldershot, Avebury, vol. 1, pp. 135ff.

Radnitzky, Gerard (1995 d), 'The 'Churning Society' and its perversities', *Journal of Social and Evolutionary systems*, 18 (4), 1995.

Reese-Schäfer, Walter (1994), *Was ist Kommunitarismus?*, Campus, Frankfurt/M., New York.

Richman, Sheldon (1994), *Separating School and State*, The Future of Freedom Foundation, Fairfax, Virginia.

Rockwell, Llewellyn H. (1990) (ed.), *The Economics of Liberty*, Mises-Institute, Auburn, Alabama.

Rockwell, Llewellyn H. (1995) (ed.), *Murray N. Rothbard, In Memoriam*, Mises-Institute, Auburn, Alabama.

Röpke, Wilhelm (1944), *Civitas Humana*, Erlenbach, Zürich, 4th ed., Paul Haupt, Bern 1979.

Röpke, Wilhelm (1966), *Jenseits von Angebot und Nachfrage*, 4th ed., Eugen Rentsch, Erlenbach, Zürich and Stuttgart.

Rothbard, Murray N. (1988), *Ludwig von Mises: Scholar, Creator, Hero*, Mises-Institute, Auburn, Alabama.

Rothbard, Murray N. (1990), *What has Government done to our Money?*, Mises-Institute, Auburn, Alabama.

Rothbard, Murray N. (1991), *Freedom, Inequality, Primitivism and the Division of Labor*, Mises-Institute, Auburn, Alabama.

Rothbard, Murray N. (1993), *Man, Economy and State*, Mises-Institute, Auburn, Alabama.

Rothbard, Murray N. (1994), *For a New Liberty, the Libertarian Manifesto*, 3th ed., Fox and Wilkes, San Francisco.

Rothbard, Murray N. (1995), *Making Economic Sense*, Mises-Institute, Auburn, Alabama.

Schumpeter, Josef A. (1953), 'Zur Soziologie der Imperialismen', in: *Aufsätze zur Soziologie*, J. C. B. Mohr (Paul Siebeck), Tübingen, pp. 72ff.

Schwarz, Gerhard (1995 a), 'Marktwirtschaft ohne Wenn und Aber', in: Doering/Fliszar (1995), pp. 117ff.

Schwarz, Gerhard (1995 b), 'Die Schalmeienklänge des Kommunitarismus', *Neue Zürcher Zeitung*, April, 15/16 1995.

Seldon, Arthur (1994), *The State is Rolling Back*, Economic and Literary Books, London.

Selgin, George A. (1990), *Praxeology and Understanding, An Analysis of*

the *Controversy in Austrian Economics*, Mises-Institute, Auburn, Alabama.

Sennholz, Hans F. (1995), 'Freiheit und Gleichheit: Über den Abbau von
Armut und Ungleichheit' in: Baader (1995), pp. 121ff.

Smith, Adam (1978), *Der Wohlstand der Nationen*, Deutscher Taschen-
buch-Verlag, Munich.

Spencer, Herbert (1978), *Principles of Ethics*, 2 vls., Liberty Fund, Indianapolis.

Spencer, Herbert (1950), *The Man versus the State*, The Beacon Press, Boston

Spooner, Lysander (1992), *The Lysander Spooner Reader*, Fox and Wilkes,
San Francisco.

Stowasser, Horst (1995), *Freiheit pur. Die Idee der Anarchie, Geschichte
und Zukunft*, Eichborn, Frankfurt/M.

Taylor, Thomas C. (1988), *An Introduction to Austrian Economics*, Mises-
Institute, Auburn, Alabama.

Vanberg, Viktor (1994), *Wettbewerb in Markt und Politik – Anregungen
für die Verfassung Europas*, Comdok, St. Augustin.

Weber, Max (1958), *Wirtschaftsgeschichte*, Duncker and Humbloth, Berlin.

Weber, Max (1964), *Wirtschaft und Gesellschaft*, Kiepenheuer and Witsch,
Cologne and Berlin.

Weede, Erich (1990), *Wirtschaft, Staat und Gesellschaft*, J. C. B. Mohr (Paul
Siebeck), Tübingen.

Winterberger, Andreas K. (1995), 'Freiheit und Politik: Von der liberalen
Demokratiekritik zur liberalen Verfassungsreform' in: Baader (1995),
pp. 191ff.

Wolff, Hans J. und Bachof, Otto (1976), *Verwaltungsrecht*, vol. 2, 4th ed.,
C. H. Beck'sche Verlagsbuchhandlung, Munich.

Woodcock, George (1962), *Anarchism*, World Publication Company, Cle-
veland, Ohio.

Zeitler, Christoph (1995), *Spontane Ordnung, Freiheit und Recht*, Peter
Lang, Frankfurt/M.

Zenker, E. V. (1984), *Der Anarchismus*, Rixdorfer Verlagsanstalt, Berlin.

Zippelius, Reinhold (1988), *Allgemeine Staatslehre*, 10th ed., C. H.
Beck'sche Verlagsbuchhandlung, Munich.

On the Law and Economics of Socialism and Desocialization

Hans-Hermann Hoppe

I.

Wealth can be brought into existence or increased in three and only three ways: by perceiving certain nature-given things as scarce and actively bringing them into one's possession before anyone else has seen and done so (homesteading); by producing goods with the help of one's labor and such previously appropriated resources; or by acquiring a good through voluntary, contractual transfer from a previous appropriator or producer. Acts of original appropriation turn something which no one had previously perceived as scarce into an income-providing asset; acts of production are by their very nature aimed at the transformation of a less valuable asset into a more valuable one; and every contractual exchange concerns the exchange and redirection of specific assets from the hands of those who value their possession less to those who value them more.

From this it follows that socialism can only lead to impoverishment:[1]

(1) Under socialism, ownership of productive assets is assigned to a collective of individuals regardless of each member's prior actions or inactions in relation to the owned assets. In effect, then, socialist ownership favors the non-homesteader, the non-producer, and the non-contractor and disadvantages homesteaders, producers, and contractors. Accordingly, there will be less original appropriation of natural resources whose scarcity is realized, there will be less production of new and less upkeep of old factors of production, and there will be less contracting. All of these activities involve costs. Under a regime of collective ownership the cost of performing them is raised, and that of not performing them is lowered.

(2) Since means of production cannot be sold under socialism, no market prices for factors of production exist. Without such prices, cost-accounting is impossible. Inputs cannot be compared with outputs; and it is impossible to decide if their usage for a given purpose has been worthwhile or has led

to a squandering of scarce resources in the pursuit of projects with relatively little or no importance for consumers. By not being permitted to take any offers from private individuals who might see an alternative way of using a given means of production, the socialist caretaker of capital goods simply does not know what his foregone opportunities are. Hence, permanent misallocations of production factors must ensue.

(3) Even *given* some initial allocation, since input factors and the output produced are owned collectively, every single producer's incentive to increase the quantity and/or quality of his individual output is systematically diminished; and likewise, his incentive to use input factors so as to avoid their over – or underutilization is reduced. Instead, with gains and losses in the socialist firm's capital and sales account socialized instead of attributed to specific, individual producers, everyone's inclination toward laziness and negligence is systematically encouraged. Hence, an inferior quality and/or quantity of goods will be produced and permanent capital consumption will ensue.

(4) Under a regime of private property, the person who owns a resource can determine independently of others what to do with it. If he wants to increase his wealth and/or rise in social status, he can only do so by better serving the most urgent wants of voluntary consumers through the use he makes of his property. With collectively owned factors of production, collective decision making mechanisms are required. Every decision as to what, how and for whom to produce, how much to pay or charge, and who to promote or demote, is a political affair. Any disagreement must be settled by superimposing one person's will on another's view, and invariably creates winners and losers. Hence, if one wants to climb the ladder under socialism, one must resort to one's political talents. It is not the ability to initiate, to work, and to respond to the needs of consumers that assures success. Rather, it is by means of persuasion, demagoguery, and intrigue, through promises, bribes, and threats that one rises to the top. Needless to say, this politicalization of society, implied in any system of collective ownership, contributes even more to impoverishment.[2]

II.

The manifest bankruptcy of socialism all across Eastern Europe since the late 1980's, after some 70 – and in most cases only 40 – years of 'social experimentation' provides the sad illustration of the validity of economic theory. What does the theory that long ago predicted this result as inevitable[3] imply now regarding how Eastern Europe can rise most quickly from the ruins left by socialism? Since the ultimate cause of her economic misery is the collective ownership of factors of production, the solution and key to a prosperous future is privatization. Yet how should socialized property be privatized?[4]

An elementary yet fundamental moral observation must precede the answer to this question. Since socialism cannot arise without the expropriation of assets originally 'created' and owned by individual homesteaders, producers, and/or contractors, all socialist property, ill-begotten from the very start, should be forfeited. No government, even if freely elected, can be considered the owner of any socialist property. For a criminal's heir, even if himself innocent, does not become the legitimate owner of illegitimately acquired assets. Because of his personal innocence he remains exempt from prosecution; but all of his 'inherited' gains must immediately revert to the original victims, and their repossession of socialist property must take place without their being required to pay anything. In fact, to charge a victimized population a price for the reacquisition of what was originally its own would itself be a crime and once and forever take away any innocence that a government previously might have had.

More specifically, all original property titles should be recognized immediately, regardless of who presently owns them. Insofar as the claims of original private owners or their heirs clash with those of the current assets' users, the former should override the latter. Only if a current user can prove that an original owner-heir's claim is illegitimate – that the title to the property in question had been acquired initially by coercive or fraudulent means – should a user's claim prevail and should he be recognized as owner.[5]

Regarding socialist property that is not reclaimed in this way, syndicalist ideas should be implemented. Assets should become owned immediately by those who use them – the farmland by the farmers, the factories by the workers, the streets by the street workers or the residents, the schools by the teachers, the bureaus by the bureaucrats, and so on.[6] To break up the mostly over-sized socialist production conglomerates, the syndicalist principle should be applied to those production units in which a given individual's work is actually performed, i.e., to individual office buildings, schools, streets or blocks of streets, factories and farms. Unlike syndicalism, yet of the utmost importance, the property shares thus acquired should be freely tradeable and a stock market established, so as to allow a separation of the functions of owner-capitalists and non-owning employees, and the smooth and continuous transfer of assets from less into more value-productive hands.[7]

Two problems are connected with this privatization strategy. First, what is to be done in the case of newly erected structures – which according to the proposed scheme would be owned by their current productive users – built on land that is to revert to a different original owner? While it may appear straightforward enough to award each current producer with an equal property share, how many shares should go to the land owner? Structures and land cannot be physically separated. In terms of economic theory, they are absolutely specific complementary production factors whose relative contribution to their joint value product cannot be disentangled. In these cases there is no alternative but to bargain.[8] Yet this – contrary to the first impression that it might lead to permanent, unresolvable conflict – should hardly cause many headaches. For invariably there are only two parties and strictly limited resources involved in any such dispute. Moreover, to find a quick, mutually agreeable compromise is in both parties' interest, and if either party possesses a weaker bargaining position it is clearly the landowner (because he cannot sell the land without the structure owners' consent while they could dismantle the structure without needing the landowner's permission).

Secondly, the syndicalist privatization strategy implies that producers in capital intensive industries would have a relative advantage as compared to those in labor intensive industries. For the value of the property shares received by the former would exceed the wealth awarded to the latter, and this unequal distribution of wealth would require justification, or so it seems. In fact, such justification is readily available. Contrary to widespread 'liberal' beliefs, there is nothing ethically wrong with inequality.[9] Indeed, the problem of privatizing formerly socialized property is almost perfectly analogous to that of establishing private property in a 'state of nature', i.e., when resources previously had been unowned. In this situation, according to the central Lockean idea of natural rights which coincides with most people's natural sense of justice, private property is established through acts of homesteading: by mixing one's labor with nature-given resources before anyone else has done so;[10] and insofar as any differences between the quality of nature-given resources exist, as is surely the case, the outcome generated by the homesteading ethic is inequality rather than equality.[11] The syndicalist privatization approach is merely the application of this homesteading principle to slightly changed circumstances. The socialized factors of production are already homesteaded by particular individuals. Only their property right regarding particular production factors has so far been ignored, and all that would occur under the proposed scheme is that this unjustifiable situation would finally be rectified. If such rectification results in inequalities, this is no more unfair than the inequalities that would emerge under a regime of original, unadulterated homesteading.[12]

Moreover, our syndicalist proposal is economically more efficient than the only conceivable privatization alternative in line with the basic requirement of justice (that the government does not legitimately own the socialized economy and hence its selling or auctioning it off should be out of the question). According to the latter alternative, the entire population would receive equal shares in all of the country's assets not reclaimed by an original, expropriated owner. Aside from the questionable moral quality of this policy,[13] it would be extremely inefficient. For one thing, in order for such country-wide distributed shares to become tradeable property titles, they must specify to which particular resource they refer. Hence, to implement this proposal, first a complete inventory of all of the country's assets would be required, or at least an inventory of all its distinctively separable production units. Secondly, even if such an inventory were finally assembled, the owners would consist by and large of individuals who knew next to nothing about the assets they owned. In contrast, under the non-egalitarian syndicalist privatization scheme no inventory is necessary. Furthermore, initial ownership comes to rest exclusively with individuals who, because of their productive involvement with the assets owned by them, are by and large best informed to make a first realistic appraisal of such assets.

In conjunction with the privatization of all assets according to the principles outlined, the government should adopt a private property constitution and declare it the immutable basic law for the entire country. This constitution should be extremely brief and lay down the following principles in terms as unambiguous as possible: Every person, apart from being the sole owner of his physical body, has the right to employ his private property in any way he sees fit so long as in so doing he does not uninvitedly change the physical integrity of another person's body or property. All interpersonal exchanges and all exchanges of property titles between private owners are to be voluntary (contractual). These rights of a person are absolute. Any person's infringement on them is subject to lawful prosecution by the victim of this infringement or his agent, and is actionable in accordance with the principles of the proportionality of punishment and of strict liability.[14]

As implied by this constitution, then, all existing wage and price controls, all property regulations and licensing requirements, and all import and export restrictions should be immediately abolished and complete freedom of contract, occupation, trade and migration introduced. Subsequently, the government, now property-less, should declare its own continued existence unconstitutional – insofar as it would have to rest on non-contractual property acquisitions, that is, taxation – and abdicate.[15]

III.

The result of this complete abolition of socialism and the establishment of a pure private property society – an anarchy of private property owners, regulated exclusively by private property law – would be the quickest economic recovery of Eastern Europe. From the outset the population would, by and large, be made amazingly rich. For while the economies of Eastern Europe are in shambles, the countries are not destroyed. High real estate values exist, and in spite of all the capital consumption of the past there are still massive amounts of capital goods in existence. With no government sector left and the entire national wealth in private hands, the people of Eastern Europe could soon become objects of envy among their West European counterparts.

Moreover, releasing factors of production from political control and handing them over to private individuals who are allowed to use them as they see fit provided only that they do not physically damage the resources owned by others, provides the ultimate stimulus for future production. With an unrestricted market for capital goods, rational cost-accounting is made possible. With profits as well as losses individualized, and reflected in an owner's capital- and sales-account, every single producer's incentive to increase the quantity and/or quality of his output and to avoid any over – or underutilization of his capital is maximized. In particular, the constitutional provision that only the physical integrity of property (not property values) be protected guarantees that every owner will undertake the greatest value-productive efforts – efforts to promote favorable changes in property values and to prevent and counter any unfavorable ones (as might result from another person's actions regarding his property).

Specifically, the abolishment of all price controls would almost instantaneously eliminate all present shortages; and output would immediately begin to increase, quantitatively as well as qualitatively. Temporarily, unemployment would drastically increase. Yet with flexible wage rates, without collective bargaining, and without unemployment subsidies it would quickly disappear. Initially, average wage rates would remain substantially below Western rates. But this, too, would soon begin to change. Lured by comparatively low wages, by the fact that East Europeans will expectedly show a great need for cashing in (liquidating) their newly acquired capital assets so as to finance their current consumption, and above all by the fact that East Europe would be a no-tax, free-trade haven, large numbers of investors and huge amounts of capital would begin to flow in immediately.

The production of security – of police protection and of a judicial system – which is usually assumed to lie outside the province of free markets and be the proper function of government, would most likely be taken over by major Western insurance companies.[16] Providing insurance for personal property, police-action – the prevention and detection of crime as well as the exaction of compensation – is in fact part of this industry's 'natural' business (if it were not for governments preventing insurers from doing so and arrogating this task to itself, with all the usual and familiar inefficiencies resulting from such a monopolization). Likewise, being already in the business of arbitrating conflicts between claimants of competing insurers, they would naturally assume the function of a judicial system.

Yet more important than the entrance of big business, such as insurance companies into the field of security production, would be the influx of large numbers of small entrepreneurs, in particular from Western Europe. Facing not only a heavy load of taxation in the welfare states of Western Europe, but being stifled there by countless regulations (licensing requirements, labor protection laws, mandated working and shop-opening hours), an unregulated private property economy in Eastern Europe would be an almost irresistible attraction. The large-scale import of entrepreneurial talent and capital would soon begin to raise real wage rates, stimulate internal savings, and lead to a rapidly accelerating process of capital accumulation. Rather than people leaving the East, migration would quickly take place in the opposite direction, with increasing numbers of West Europeans abandoning welfare socialism for the unlimited opportunities offered in the East. Finally, faced with increasing losses of productive individuals, which would put even more pressure on their welfare budgets, the power elites of Western Europe would be forced to begin desocializing Western Europe as well.

Notes

1   See also H. H. Hoppe, *A Theory of Socialism and Capitalism Economics, Politics and Ethics* (Boston: Kluwer Academic Publishers, 1989).

2   Contrary to widespread beliefs the lack of democracy has essentially nothing to do with socialism's inefficiency. It is not the selection principle for politicians that constitutes the problem. It is politics and political decision-making as such. Instead of each producer deciding independently what to do with particular resources, as under a regime of private property and contractualism, with socialized factors of production each decision requires a collective's permission. It is irrelevant to the producer how those giving permission are chosen. What matters to him is that permission must be sought at all. As long as this is the

case, the incentive for producers to produce is reduced and impoverishment will continue. Private property is as incompatible with democracy, then, as with any other form of political rule. Rather, with the institution of private property an 'anarchy of production' is established, in which no one rules anybody, and all producers' relations are voluntary, and thus mutually beneficial.

3   L. v. Mises, *Die Gemeinwirtschaft: Untersuchungen ueber den Sozialismus* (Jena: Gustav Fischer, 1922). The first English translation appeared in 1936 under the title *Socialism: An Economic and Sociological Analysis*. The latest edition is from 1981 (Indianapolis: Liberty Fund). See also idem, *Human Action. A Treatise on Economics* (Chicago: Henry Regnery, 1966), chs. XXV, XXVI, where Mises provides a definitive answer to critics of his earlier work (such as O. Lange and H. D. Dickinson).

4   While a vast body of literature dealing with the socialization of private property exists, little has been written on how to de-socialize. Most likely, one would suspect, because of explicit or implicit socialist predilections popular among Western intellectuals, which preclude any treatment of this problem as simply irrelevant. For why should anyone ever want to go back from an allegedly 'higher stage of social evolution', i.e., socialism, to a lower one, i.e., capitalism? But even within the Mises-School at best only implicit advice on this most pressing problem presently confronting the people of Eastern Europe can be found. For one of the few exceptions see M. N. Rothbard, "How To Desocialize?" and "A Radical Prescription for the Socialist Bloc" in: L. Rockwell, ed., *The Economics of Liberty* (Auburn, Al.: Auburn University, Ludwig von Mises Institute, 1990).

5   In those cases in which current users actually bought expropriated assets from the government, they should seek compensation from those responsible for this sale, and the government officials accountable for it should be compelled to repay the purchase price.

6   On the economics and ethics of privatization see M. N. Rothbard, *For A New Liberty;* for the privatization of streets in particular W. Block, "Free Market Transportation: Denationalizing the Roads", *Journal of Libertarian Studies*, 1979; idem, "Public Goods and Externalities: The Case of Roads", *Journal of Libertarian Studies*, 1983.

7   For an economic analysis of syndicalism see L. v. Mises, *Socialism*, ch. 16.4.

8   On the economic theory of bargaining see L. v. Mises, *Human Action*, pp. 338–39; M. N. Rothbard, *Man, Economy and State*, pp. 308–12.

9   See M. N. Rothbard, *Egalitarianism As A Revolt Against Nature and*

other Essays, (Washington D.C.: Libertarian Review Press, 1974); also: R. Nozick, *Anarchy, State and Utopia* (New York: Basic Books, 1974), ch. 8; H. Schoeck, *Der Neid. Eine Theorie der Gesellschaft* (Munich, 1966); idem, Das Recht auf Ungleichheit (Munich, 1979); E. v. Kuehnelt-Leddhin, *Freiheit oder Gleichheit* (Salzburg, 1953).

10 See J. Locke, *Two Treatises of Government*, P. Laslett, ed (Cambridge: Cambridge University Press, 1960), pp. 305–307.

11 For an attempt to justify an 'egalitarian' homesteading ethic see H. Steiner, "The Natural Right to the Means of Production", *Philosophical Quarterly*, 27 (1977); for a refutation of this theory as inconsistent see J. Paul, "Historical Entitlement and the Right to Natural Resources", in: W. Block / L. H.Rockwell, eds., *Man, Economy and Liberty. Essays in Honor of Murray N. Rothbard* (Auburn, Al.: Ludwig von Mises Institute, 1988); F. D. Miller, "The Natural Right to Private Property", in: T. R. Machan, ed., *The Libertarian Reader* (Totowa: Rowman & Littlefield, 1982).

12 For the most consistent and complete Lockean property rights theory see M. N. Rothbard, *The Ethics of Liberty*; idem, "Law, Property Rights, and Air Pollution", *Cato Journal*, Vol. 2/1 (Spring 1982); for a theoretical justification of the homesteading principle in particular, as the indisputable, axiomatic foundation of ethics: H. H. Hoppe, *Eigentum, Anarchie und Staat*, ch. 4; idem, A Theory of Socialism and Capitalism, chs. 2, 7; idem, "From the Economics of Laissez Faire to the Ethics of Libertarianism", in: W. Block / L. H. Rockwell, eds., *Man, Economy and Liberty*; idem, "The Justice of Economic Efficiency", *Austrian Economics Newsletter*, Vol. 9/2 (Winter 1988).

13 How can one justify that ownership of productive assets should be assigned without considering a given individual's actions or inactions in relation to the owned asset? More specifically, how can it be justified, for instance, that someone who has contributed literally nothing to the existence or maintenance of a particular asset – and who might not even know that any such asset exists – should own it in the same way as someone else who actively, objectifiably contributed to its existence or maintenance?

14 On the proportionality principle of punishment see M. N. Rothbard, *The Ethics of Liberty*, ch. 13; H. H. Hoppe, *Eigentum, Anarchie und Staat*, pp. 106–28; on the principle of strict liability also: R. A. Epstein, "A Theory of Strict Liability," *Journal of Legal Studies*, 2 (January 1973); also idem, *Medical Malpractice: The Case for Contract* (Burlingame, Ca.: Center for Libertarian Studies, Occasional Paper Series No. 9, 1979); J. J.Thomson, *Rights, Restitution, and Risk* (Cambridge:

Harvard University Press, 1986), esp. chs. 12 (Remarks on Causation and Liability), and 13 (Liability and Individualized Evidence).

15   On the ethics and economics of state-less societies see M. N. Rothbard, "Society Without a State", in: J. Pennock / J. Chapman, eds., *Anarchism (Nomos XIX)* (New York: New York University Press, 1978); B. Benson, *The Enterprise of Law. Justice Without the State* (San Francisco: Pacific Institute, 1991).

16   On the economics of competitive, private security production see G. d. Molinari, *The Production of Security* (New York: Center for Libertarian Studies, Occassional Paper Series No. 2, 1977); M. N. Rothbard, *Power and Market*, ch. 1; idem, *For A New Liberty*, ch. 12; M.& L. Tannehill, The Market For Liberty (New York: Laissez Faire Books, 1984); W. Wooldridge, *Uncle Sam the Monopoly Man* (New Rochelle: Arlington House, 1970); B. Leoni, *Freedom and the Law* (Princeton: Van Nostrand, 1972); H. H. Hoppe, "Fallacies of the Public Goods Theory and the Production of Security", *Journal of Libertarian Studies*, Vol. IX/1, 1989; B. Benson, *The Enterprise of Law.*

Defining Libertarian Liberty

Hardy Bouillon

Classical liberals distinguished negative freedom and positive freedom from the beginning. We find the negative concept of liberty already in a terse remark by Thomas Hobbes. "A free man is he that ... is not hindered to do what he hath the will to do."[1] Antony Flew has commented on this: "It is a pity that he apparently failed to notice both that, always supposing that people would in fact intervene to constrain or coerce someone, then that person must remain in that particular respect unfree; and that this is the case regardless of whether or not "he hath the will to do" whatever it may be."[2]

Flew brings to our attention that Hobbes's definition is obviously too narrow for it excludes two kinds of situations which surely go for coercion. The first one is a situation in which a person is not actually hindered but would be coerced if he acted in a particular way, and the second one is a situation in which a person is hindered (actually or potentially) to do what he has not the will to do but could do if he had the will to do it. In other words, Hobbes definition is not convincing. Hence, it does not meet the clever remark by Bruno Leoni on the definition of freedom.

"Everybody can define what he thinks freedom to be, but as soon as he wants us to accept his formulation as our own, he has to produce some truly convincing argument."[3]

Nowadays, most thinkers, liberal and others, share the conviction that individual liberty presupposes the absence of coercion. They also consent that unintentional restraint or intervention does not count as coercion. "Coercion implies the deliberate interference of other human beings within the area in which I could otherwise act. ... This is what the classical English political philosophers meant when they used this word."[4] However clarifying this is, Berlin's explication is incomplete.[5] It does not say what is meant by deliberate interference or by coercion. As Hayek noticed, it is the concept of coercion on which thinkers most widely differ.[6]

Friedrich A. Hayek, in his *Constitution of Liberty* (1960), undertakes an exploration of what is meant by coercion, acknowledging that a clear concept of liberty presupposes a clear concept of coercion. "Our definition of liberty depends upon the meaning of the concept of coercion, and it will not be precise until we have similarly defined that term." (Hayek 1960, p. 20) Furthermore, Hayek pointed out that freedom "refers solely to a relation of men to other men, and the only infringement on it is coercion by men. This means, in particular, that the range of physical possibilities from which a person can choose at a given moment has no direct relevance to freedom. The rock climber on a difficult pitch who sees only one way out to save his life is unquestionably free, though we would hardly say he has any choice." (p. 12)

Apparently, Hayek was very much aware of the distinction between freedom and power. Nonetheless, he himself confused freedom and power on several occasions, obviously mislead by a residue of consequentialist ethics. He wrote, "So long as the services of a particular person are not crucial to my existence or the preservation of what I most value, the conditions he exacts for rendering these services cannot properly be called "coercion". A monopolist could exercise true coercion, however, if he were, say, the owner of a spring in an oasis. Let us say that other persons settled there on the assumption that water would always be available at a reasonable price and then found, perhaps because a second spring dried up, that they had no choice but to do whatever the owner of the spring demanded of them if they were to survive: here would be a clear case of coercion." (p. 136) And Hayek goes on, "So long as the services of a particular person are not crucial to my existence or the preservation of what I most value, the conditions he exacts for rendering these services cannot properly be called "coercion." (p. 136)

What is "crucial to my existence or the preservation of what I value most"? What is an "unreasonable price"? Hayek gives no answer. Murray Rothbard rightly remarked that Hayek failed attempting "to distinguish, merely quantitatively, between "mild" and "more severe" forms of coercion."[7] A monopolist has the right under freedom to refuse any exchange he likes to refuse, however disastrous the consequences may be.[8] Mitigating the consequences of those who suffer under the economic power of others is honourable. Doing it by confusing the terms is intellectually inappropriate.

Even more entangling than Hayek's confusion of freedom with power is his definition of coercion. "By 'coercion' we mean such control of the environment or circumstances of a person by an other that, in order to avoid greater evil, he is forced to act not according to a coherent plan of his own but to serve the ends of an other." (Hayek, 1960, pp. 20f.) This definition creates confusions in at least two respects.

1. Hayek's definition neglects cases in which coercion that makes a person serving an other person's ends goes along with the coherent plan of that person. An old movie, starring Henry Fonda as lieutenant and John Wayne as recruit, illustrates such cases in which men are coerced – but coherently with their own plan. The troop reaches an old abandoned fortress. Some soldiers find a left cask filled with whiskey. Asked what to do, the lieutenant gives order to annihilate the whiskey. It goes without saying that the soldiers were happy to follow that order. It also goes without saying that the soldiers had clear order to do so and, hence, were coerced to annihilate the whiskey.

2. It is unclear which part of the environment and of the circumstances has to be changed by another in order to produce possible coercion. Hayek is more precise on this elsewhere. "Freedom thus presupposes that the individual has some assured private sphere, that there is some set of circumstances in his environment with which others cannot interfere." (p. 13)

However, to Hayek, not only that strictly private sphere should be protected from coercion, "reasonable expectations" should be protected too. "In determining where the boundaries of the protected sphere ought to be drawn, the important question is whether the actions of other people that we wish to see prevented would actually interfere with the reasonable expectations of the protected person." (p. 145)

But which expectations are reasonable in Hayek's view? He gives two examples. "The enforcement of religious conformity, for instance, was a legitimate object of government when people believed in the collective responsibility of the community toward some deity and it was thought that the sins of any member would be visited upon all." (p. 145) Moreover, Hayek follows Bertrand Russell's opinion on the treatment of homosexuality. Russell wrote: "If it were still believed, as it once was, that the toleration of such behaviour would expose the community to the fate of Sodom and Gomorrah, the community would have every right to interfere." Hayek adds: "But where such factual beliefs do not prevail, private practice among adults, however abhorrent it may be to the majority, is not a proper subject for coercive action for a state whose object is to minimise coercion." (p. 451, note 18)

Hayek seems to ignore or neglect that the private sphere of one person easily can collide with the protected sphere of an other. He does not provide an analytic criterion of reasonable expectations. Hence the protected sphere becomes arbitrary. Religious freedom and homosexuality do not limit the private sphere of possible and legitimate actions of others, though it might infringe with others "protected sphere", if these fear religious freedom or homosexuality to influence their interests in a negative way.[9] A related and no less fatal consequence is that the protected spheres of all individuals cannot be upheld in a non-contradictory way, since in a world of different minds the protected sphere of one necessarily overlaps with the protected spheres of others.

Thus, Hayek conception of the private sphere is self-contradictory and, hence, unacceptable.[10] To avoid such contradictions, we should recapitulate what we had before we were mislead by Hayek. We said that liberals of all kinds consent that freedom is the absence of coercion in a person's private sphere. Before we go on, let us reflect on what we necessarily assume when we talk of coercion and of a private sphere. Let us start with two very plain remarks.

1. If coercion takes place then it cannot but interfere in the sphere of possible actions of another person.

2. If a person acts then he cannot but consume goods. Whether these goods are objects, living beings, or even the person's body does not matter.

However, with respect to the relation between men and goods, we usually tell private from non-private goods, namely goods from which others are excluded and goods open to joined consumption. Though we could think of a world without non-private goods, we cannot imagine a world without private goods. Our conceptions and our use of speech presuppose at least some goods, e.g. human beings, to be private. Otherwise it would not make sense to say, for instance: "I am playing piano." If I would not own my body exclusively, I would give a false statement, for it was not me, but me and others who played piano. Despite from that, goods enable us do things we could not do if they were absent. If Andrew hinders Bruce to use a good, then Bruce lacks an advantage he otherwise had. This is so no matter whether the good is private or non-private.

However, we distinguish these two possible cases for good reasons. Recall the case of Diogenes. Alexander approached him while he lay in the sun. Being asked what Alexander could do for him, he answered: "Step out of the sun." Alexander hindered him from using a non-private good (sun). Though cases like these can be unpleasant, we do not say that they can constitute coercion. Otherwise we constantly could claim that others coerce us as soon as they make or want to make use of any non-private good. Vice versa, they could claim the same when we opt to use that very non-private good. Hence, mutual exclusive claims of coercion were not only possible. They were both valid. Thus, we had no analytic criterion to decide on the superiority of these claims.

If, in turn, the good was private, then mutual exclusive claims of that kind could not be equally valid. Private goods have an analytic criterion by which the superiority of mutual exclusive claims can be decided, i.e. exclusion. Private goods are exclusive by definition.[11] Of private goods we can say that they are owned by one person exclusively. Though it seems redundant to note, we should state for the sake of clarity that we assume that the use of *own* private goods cannot constitute coercion. Otherwise the word "coercion" in a similar way would become useless. All could claim that others coerce them when these use their own goods, and vice versa. For instance, I could claim Steve to coerce me to walk when he prefers to ride his car alone. He could claim, in turn, that I would coerce him to buy expensive gas, for I use my power exclusively to walk rather than to push his car.

Thus, we may conclude that the term "coercion" presupposes not only the assumption of private goods. It also presupposes that someone is in certain way obstructed by another or by others to use one or more of *his* private goods. Of course, saying that "someone is obstructed by another or by others in a certain way" needs some specification.

It goes without saying that an obstruction constitutes coercion only, if it is done intentionally, and if it sufficiently causes the objection. Saying so, in turn presupposes some other assumptions.

1. It presupposes that man can act. Otherwise we would not talk of coercion and connotate this word with moral assumption, e.g. that coercion is morally bad.

2. It also presupposes that the "coercer" as well as the "coercee" can act. If an act, though intended to be coercion, forces an other person to react like a physical object, then we do not talk of coercion at all. To keep the definition "freedom is the absence of coercion" free from self-contradictions, we have to conclude the following: Coercion is possible only if it is an intentional act that sufficiently causes an interference in another person's private sphere. Of course, from what we said the private sphere of a person is nothing else than the sum of all possible ways of consuming the goods owned by that person. Otherwise the private sphere of Andrew could overlap with the private sphere of Bruce. This possibility is excluded by the definition of a private good (good used by one person exclusively).

As we said in the beginning, freedom is the absence of coercion. Taking into consideration the above made explications, we can specify that definition as follows: *Freedom is the absence of an intentional interference in the private sphere of another person, sufficient to produce the intended effect.* Though this definition is much clearer than that of Hayek, it is certainly not the final word on that subject. With the help of that very definition we cannot distinguish between interventions in a private sphere to which the owner of that sphere agrees and those to which he does not. It goes without saying that only the latter can entail coercion whereas the former cannot.

Suppose, a husband asks his wife to take away his cookies for he feels too weak to resist the smell. Doing so, the wife interferes in her husband's private sphere (for the cookies are his). Her action is sufficient to cause what she intended. However, we would not call her action coercion, simply because the husband wanted her to do what she did. The same holds for Odysseus sailing through the Sirens.[12] To eliminate these cases, we have to specify the definition of freedom a little bit more.

If freedom is the absence of an intentional interference in the private sphere of another person, sufficient to produce the intended effect, then why not simply add: *to which that person does not freely agree?* The reason for this is quite obvious. The italicised supplement introduces the definiendum (free, freedom, freely and the like) into the definiens and, hence, makes the definition worthless. The hitherto developed definition needs another supplement which avoids this disastrous consequence.

The crucial task is to express the same without smuggling in the definiendum into the definiens. How can this be achieved? How can the useless phrase "to which that person does not freely agree" be substituted by a fruitful one? Certainly, it would be of no help to use instead the formula, "which means no costs to that person", because a person might freely agree to that an other person interferes into his private sphere and creates costs, e.g., a husband agrees to be deprived of his cookies. Hence, what we are looking for is a criterion that distinguishes two types of costs of intervention in private spheres by others; one that involves coercion and one that does not.

In search for that criterion one ought to notice a very simple fact, i.e., that the perception of a new information creates a new decision. As soon as we perceive a new information we cannot but decide whether or not to change our plans because of the new data. This happens every day hundreds of times. These situations constitute what we might call "either-or-choices". Of course, these "either-or-choices" of our daily life are often routinized. Nonetheless, they call for decisions caused by new information. For instance, when we start to cross a street and perceive an approaching car, then we have to decide either to pursue the existing plan or to change it. When we read a sales offer, then we cannot but decide either to react to it or to stay to the status. When we on our way to our home, cross the market and being asked by the merchant to buy either apples, oranges, or bananas, then again we cannot other than decide whether to stay to our original plan or to change it, i.e., to "react" to that offer. Of course, this decision, we will make, will be somehow influenced by the offer itself, e.g. by the price and quality of the fruits. Nonetheless, the decision either to react to the offer or not is *not* to be confused with the choice between apples, oranges, or bananas. It was even there if there was no choice between apples, oranges, and bananas, for instance, if the merchant spoke to us in a foreign language or too faint to be clearly understood. If it was the case that the merchant conveyed no choice between apples, oranges, or bananas, then we still had to decide whether we deviated from our original plan (i.e., react to the foreign speaking merchant) or stayed to our original intention (i.e., going home unflustered). The first decision precedes the second analytically, although it might coincide with it chronologically.

To distinguish these two types of decision a terminological distinction is useful. It is also useful to start with the description of the second decision of the example mentioned above. The second decision (choice between three different fruits) is characterised by the fact that it constitutes a decision among different objects. I propose to call that second decision an *object-decision*. The number of objects does not influence the character of an object-decision. With respect to the fact that the content (objects) does not matter in this case, and in order to distinguish the two types of decisions clearly, I propose to call the first decision *meta-decision*. The first decision (meta-decision) is a decision between staying to the original plan or deviating from it, hence an "either-or-choice". Having these two, and only these two, alternatives is a constitutional character of a meta-decision. The decision is necessarily no other then a decision between "either" "or", independent of the content of the plan to which one either stays or from which one deviates.

However, what is the distinction between object-decision and meta-decision good for, beside from the fact that it might serve as an analytical insight of decision-processes? The decision helps us out of our circular definition. To use that help, let us look, firstly, at a typical case of coercion and, secondly, at that very case transformed into a typical case of free choice.

(A) Suppose, you liked to keep your money and your life. Suppose also, an armed robber asked for your "Money or your life!". That would be a clear case of what we use to call coercion.

(B) Suppose now, that, ceteris paribus, the same person would be unarmed and obviously unable to threat or extort you in any possible way, and suppose, that very person would kindly ask you to give him either your money or your life. Then we would not say that he coerces you. We would classify his saying as a case in which he offers you a free choice. (Although it does not matter analytically, we also would classify his saying as silly.)

Now, let us separate the meta-decison from the object-decision. With regard to the object-decision, the two cases (A and B) do not differ. In both cases you have the choice either to give your money or your life. Hence, in both cases the costs of your object-decision will be the same.

With respect to the possible meta-decisions, we notice a difference. The costs of a positive meta-decision (i.e., to consider the offer of the person), however huge, are the same in both cases. Nonetheless, the costs of a negative meta-decision (i.e., to ignore the offer of the person) differ decisively. In the first case you have to expect additional costs by the person (e.g., being shot or hurt). In the second case you do *not* have to expect such costs. Hence, under the above mentioned preconditions the difference between a case of coercion and a case of free choice is in the artificial costs[13] which are to be expected in case of a negative meta-decision.

We now have found a *differentia specifica* that moves our provisional definition out of the vicious circle. Freedom, we defined provisionally, is the absence of an intentional interference in the private sphere of another person, sufficient to produce the intended effect. To abridge this definition, I propose to speak of "artificial interference" instead of "intentional interference, sufficient to produce the intended effect". Hence, the short version of our previous provisional definition would be: Freedom is the absence of artificial interference in the private sphere of another person.

Considering our final reflections on non-circular definitions and the two levels of decision we can resume: *Freedom is the absence of artificial interference in the private sphere of another that would mean artificial costs to him if he opted for a negative meta-decision.*

Notes

1   Thomas Hobbes, *Leviathan*, 1651, II (xxi).
2   Antony Flew, *Equality in Liberty and Justice*, London: Routledge 1989, p. 5.
3   Bruno Leoni, *Freedom and the Law*, expanded 3. edition, reprinted by Liberty Fund, Indianapolis 1991, p. 4.
4   Isaah Berlin, *Two Concepts of Liberty* (1958), cited after *Liberty*, ed. by David Miller, Oxford: OUP 1991, p. 35.
5   Berlin later said what he had meant. Unfortunately he introduced more vagueness by saying that freedom is "absence of obstacles to possible choices and activities" put by "alterable human practices." (See Isaah Berlin, *Four Essays on Liberty*, Oxford: OUP 1969, pp. xxxixf.) This comes close to confusing "freedom" with "opportunity". On this see William A. Parent, "Some recent work on the concept of liberty", in: *American Philosophical Quarterly*, July 1974, pp. 149–153

and Murray Rothbard, *The Ethics of Liberty*, Atlantic Highlands, N.J.: Humanities Press 1982, pp. 216ff.

6   See Friedrich A. Hayek, *The Constitution of Liberty*, Chicago 1960, p. 19.

7   Murray Rothbard, *The Ethics of Liberty*, loc. cit., p. 223.

8   I abstain from intruding into this argument any deeper. For further criticism see Ronald Hamowys book review of *The Constitution of Liberty* in: *New Individualist Review*, 1961, 1,1, p. 28ff. and William Meckling, Michael Jensen, "Human rights and the meaning of freedom", unpublished manuscript 1985, S. 19, and David Miller, "Introduction" in the anthology *Liberty*, loc. cit., p. 15: "Finally, Hayek appears to put the cat among the pigeons when he concedes that in certain circumstances economic power might be used in a coercive manner. Once the possibility has been conceded, why restrict the circumstances as narrowly as Hayek does, confining them to extreme cases where an individual enjoys a monopoly of a vital resource? Why not admit that the distribution of resources is always going to be relevant to the distribution of negative liberty in a society?"

9   Obviously, you cannot have both. Forbidding homosexuality or religious freedom means interfering with other's privacy. It reduces the possible and legitimate actions of others. Vice versa, respecting their privacy leaves the domain of interests of those who have reasonable expectations – whatever these may be – of the "right" behaviour unprotected.

10   For an extended version of my critique see my *Freiheit, Liberalismus und Wohlfahrtsstaat*, Baden-Baden: Nomos 1996, chapter two.

11   See Anthony de Jasay, *Choice, Contract, Consent: A Restatement of Liberalism*, London: Institute of Economic Affairs 1991, p. 75.) "... collective ownership defeats the very purpose of property, which is to vest individuals the sovereignty over employment of scarce resources. Sovereignty over certain types of decisions may be delegated revocably, or transferred for good, but it cannot be shared ..."

12   As we know from Homer, Odysseus asked his men to tie him at the mast of his ship. With their help he was able to listen to the seductive singing of the Sirens without becoming a victim of their tempting melodies. Of course, although his men hindered him to move, they did not coerce him, because he agreed to what they did.

13   It goes without saying that these costs must be intended and sufficiently caused by that person in question. Therefore, I call them artificial costs, for short.

Libertarians and the Rule of Law

Arthur Seldon

1. A Philosopher's Stimulus to Adventurous Thinking

In my relatively recent acquaintance with Gerard Radnitzky he has emerged as the scholarly entrepreneur of European and American studies in the obstacles to the development of the free society. His seminars and publications have assembled many of the most original and fearless thinkers in the natural and 'social' sciences, the renowned and the unknown, for uninhibited refinement of their contributions to the understanding of human and humane society.

As an economist untutored in the refinements of philosophy, and with knowledge of German largely confined to the undergraduate requirements of a subsidiary first degree subject, I could not easily follow all his recent writings. But the English rendering of his train of thought revealed his instinctive understanding of the refinements of classical liberal economic thinking. The exposition in his writings and the discussions with the scholars he assembled have encouraged me to pursue venturesome thoughts on the failure of the democratic political process to liberate the economic potential of Western society to benefit the people by the accelerating social progress and technological advances of the 20th century.

A new approach to the role of politics in economic life will have to be forged in the 21st century. In these reflections I attribute to Radnitzky only stimulus, not necessarily endorsement.

2. The Diminishing Respect for the Rule of Law

An unquestioned principle of the free society is the liberal reverence for the rule of law. The reverence has been weakened in recent decades. The culprit is over-government.

The essential recept was formulated by Thomas Jefferson: if a citizen found the law objectionable or unacceptable his remedy was to change it by discussion and persuasion rather than to defy or break it by unlawful conduct.

The precept once seemed unquestionable. No liberal would accept that even objectionable laws should be broken. He would see resulting disorder, the weakening of justice, perhaps anarchy, the end of civilised society.

Western liberal society rests on economic systems that are supposed to be buttressed by government to make spontaneuos voluntary contracts enforceable at law. Yet the law is increasingly defied by otherwise law-abiding citizens. In principle their general instinct is to respect the law as a fundamental element of their conduct in a liberal democratic society. In everyday practice they reject Thomas Jefferson in their domestic and working lives.

And they reject this principle of Jeffersonian political philosophy on a large and accelerating scale. The law is broken not only by small bands of habitual law-breakers who are discovered and punished by the law to general public acclaim. The main offenders are the large numbers of generally law-abiding citizens themselves who otherwise live blameless lives and would be shocked to be told they were guilty of undermining the conduct of democratic government and civilised society.

Yet the citizen law-breakers no longer see law-breaking as destroying civilised society. They speak openly among themselves of their experiences in being quoted lower charges for work paid by unrecorded cash, in claiming expenditures on partly or largely private purposes as expenses necessarily incurred in earning incomes, in working for payment despite registering as 'unemployed' in order to qualify for national insurance unemployment compensation, and most lately in exchanging goods or services in virtually barter arrangements between firms or individuals that are in effect substitutes for buying and selling at market prices yielding taxable incomes.

There is no reverence but unconscious implicit contempt for the rule of law in such transactions. The participants would be dismayed to think of themselves as law-breakers. Yet the conscious or unconscious evasion of taxes is spreading far enough for a Swiss scholar studying comparative national economies to speak clinically and objectively of the 'parallel' (legal and illegal) economies as *both* contributing to national production and raising living standards.

3. The Moral Dilemma

Spontaneous exchange between individuals or firms adds to production whether it is conducted with observance or in defiance of the rule of law. It increases the sum total of the flow of goods and services available for immediate or delayed consumption, for investment to improve the human or technical means of production, for voluntary charity to the poorer members of family or neighbours, for building schools, hospitals, sports facilities, churches, even for the minimum of government that may be desirable or indispensable. The increased flow of goods and services can reduce avoidable inequalities in incomes by creating opportunities for the culturally weak to add to their earnings even though they lack the family, occupational or political conections widely used by the generality. And it can ease the sense of injustice among the 'under-privileged' – a term, though much abused in sociology, that can graphically express the disabilites of the millions in welfare states who lack the cultural ability to argue a case with middling or minor officials in claiming entitlements in schooling, medical care, housing, pensions or other 'social benefits'.

Ironically the economic underground has become, or by *force majeure* has been made, a vehicle of compassion and social justice. The dilemma is that breaking the rule of law has made possible some rectification of the inequities of the welfare state and other government fabrications. And repressing 'unrecorded' transactions by severe penalties would thus exacerbate the inequities.

The wartime French underground was a rebellion against legalised tyranny. The peacetime world-wide underground market is a rebellion against the clumsy legal ravages of the over-inflated state by enabling its victims to escape. But for liberals it creates a moral dilemma. The expansion and enforcement of the rule of law by over-government has created avoidable inequities. And its strict enforcement would intensify them.

4. The Genesis and the Remedy

The roots of the dilemma are clear. And the remedy follows from the identification of the roots.

As long as government confined itself to the supply of goods and services that could not be generated by private agreements in the open market, the writ of government – the rule of law – was accepted and respected. Since government has demonstrated in the past century its failure to withdraw to its indispensable minimum territory as changing technology, rising incomes, and advancing aspirations since the 1880s made it superfluous, public respect for it has evaporated.

The attempt by government to enforce its oppressive laws when the citizens can easily escape from them is futile, wasteful, undignified and dangerous for democracy. The failing respect for the sanctity of the law is typified by the attitude to the payment of taxes. The attempt by government to distinguish between permissible and impermissible rejection of taxes is necessary but itself undermines the efforts of government to collect what it regards as essential revenues. The cititzen is taught to distinguish between tax 'avoidance' and tax 'evasion'. But to the individual the effect is the same: both increase the amount of income left for the citizen to use as he or she thinks best, not as government directs. Both appear as restrictions on the freedom of the individual.

Moreover, the skills developed to reduce taxes by lawful 'avoidance' tend to teach further skills to reduce taxes by unlawful 'evasion'. Taxes are reduced lawfully by turning from work that yields income taxed at higher rates to work that yields income taxed at lower rates. The emphasis is no longer exclusively on work that earns the highest incomes as the measure of its value to other citizens and society.

But if efforts to minimise taxes are approved by government and its laws, the 'official' approval is easily transferred by the citizen to other methods of minimising taxes. The effort turns from seeking work that attracts the lowest rates of taxes to work that carries the process to its logical conclusion in attracting no taxation. And the easiest method is to attract the least attention. In the mind of the taxpayer who resents taxes *per se* legal tax rejection merges imperceptibly into illegal tax rejection. The distinction between acceptable 'avoidance' and unacceptable 'evasion' changes from a difference of principle to a difference of degree.

Nor does the process subject the citizen to the risk of certain attention and detection, with fines or other penalties, if many other citizens accept the transition from avoidance to evasion as increasingly common and therefore in a moral sense permissible by general practice.

This is the condition to which over-government has reduced the distinction between the legal and the illegal, the moral and the immoral. It is the cause of the failing rule of law created by a political process that induces government to pass too many laws which cannot be enforced. Changing conditions of supply and demand enable them to be escaped by individuals in the sucessful search in free markets for higher living standards for families and their private voluntary co-operative and charitable causes which once flourished before they were suppressed.

But there is no escape for politicians and government from the political, economic and moral dilemmas they have created for themselves except by reducing the number and extent of the laws they have myopically enacted. They will have to learn that it is futile to pass laws that are easy to escape. And escapes will become even more common if taxation is raised further to finance services that the people learn are obtainable at lower costs and with better quality in the market. Government will have to yield to the market.

5. The Blockage in the Political Process

'The rule of law' has become a ritualised political incantation. 'Democracy' is propounded as an unquestioned political ideal – by politicians. The good word 'public' has been debased into a cynical question-begging misdescription for the power-seeking by individuals who would fail in the competitive test of the market-place.

For many decades government of all parties in Britain and elsewhere in Europe spoke of 'public' services in education, health services, insurance against sickness and unemployment, transport and fuel and local government activities that *ignored* 'public' preferences, sensitivities, aspirations. The 'new' British New Labour Party promises 'public' control and 'public' accountability – the new language of socialism – in the railway system that is now being belatedly desocialised after years of decreasing efficiency. Political profligacy is camouflaged by the government extravagance that is misdescribed by the title 'public sector borrowing requirement' (PSBR) which is not a 'requirement' but a conscious decisions by Ministers to spend more than they dared to raise in taxes. The 'national insurance fund' has been a post-war fraud to avoid the political unpopularity of raising taxes by pursuading millions of employees and employers to pay 'contributions' into a non-existent 'fund' that paid them out as 'insurance benefits' almost as soon as they were received.

I have little doubt that these political misdemeanours, which politicians would denounce if they were practiced by 'commercial' sellers and buyers in the market-place, are the everyday tools of the 'democratic' process in other countries in Europe, America and every other continent.

Yet there is a blockage in the political system that perhaps unconsciously connives at concealment of the fundamental flaw.

The political parties engage in apparently unrestrained criticism of one another but not of the political system that enables them all to achieve the elected power to mislead the people. Governments and legislatures of 'the Right' have recently be elected after long periods of office by governments of 'the left' in Canada, the U.S.A., Australia and Spain. There may be more such political reversals or 'revolutions' in the near future.

Yet the political fiction remains that it is to government that the people must look for the solutions to its problems. Even the new non-socialist Congress in the U.S.A. promises that the 'right' politicians will find the solutions in government. Few politicians teach that the market is the supreme mechanism that cures the limitations and imperfections, the failures and excesses, of over-government.

The market is the physician that cures itself. Its power of recuperation is the essence of its mechanism. Much though it may try to suppress change in order to favour their supporters who have an interest in resisting progress, government cannot endlessly suppress the changes in supply and demand that derive from the irrepressible activity of the human brain. In time the market rids itself of monopoly, restrictive practices, inequality, fraud, and its other frailties by its inborn power of economic recovery. Even the so-called public goods and the activities with supposed severe 'externalities' that were once thought to be the essentials of government are being increasingly supplied in the market.

It often takes time. The monopoly of the railways lasted almost a century before it was broken by the internal combustion engine. But it was democratic politics that added decades to its life before government could no longer hide from its long-suffering public the potential benefits from road and air travel.

The stubborn long life of 'public' services and political power is the result of the absence of the advocacy of economic libertarianism – the view that government could do less good by patching up its past mistakes than it could by liberating economic life from its propensity to socialise, control and regulate. It is the only political creed to teach that the acknowledged but temporary defects of the market are to be preferred to the certain and long-lived defects of over-government.

The last epoch of libertarian thinking was the emergence of the classical liberal school of the late 18th and early 19th century that won recognition and support, notably from some far-sighted politicians, for its demolition of the case for government control of economic life *per se*. Its large blatant target was the centuries of medieval mercantilism. The present-day but no less blatant target is the century of socialism.

The failure of the liberal intelligentsia of our times has been that it finds fault with government but recommends different powers for government. It may urge less government, but mostly it is different government – which means different powers for the same politicians.

But government rarely learns promptly from its mistakes. Much legislation by democratic legislatures is too late to correct its own legislation, much of which have inflicted grievous suffering on the people. But politicians do not apologise or ask forgiveness for their blunders. They are essentially professionals who must believe in the ultimate ability of their profession to find the solutions. Few other professions claim infallibility: the political profession is the universal claimant of infallibility.

The exceptions are rare: isolated individual Labour politicians in New Zealand; Vaclav Klaus in Europe. But which big-government politician, in all parties, has confessed abject, costly, long-lasting failure? Where is the statesman or stateswoman who prolonged the welfare state beyond its plausible excuses but who has at long last taken the veil and retired from 'public' life with a promise never to return?

6. A New Laissez-faire

There is no body of scholarship that teaches the acceptance of market imperfections, even abuses, as the temporary lesser evil than long-lasting political solutions introduced by short-lived government that leave the consequences of their blunders *apres la deluge*. The requirement is for a school that teaches the essentials of liberation – not least from over-government.

It is not sufficient to regret the breakdown of the rule of law. The task for philosophers and economists has become to explain it more fundamentally. The rule of law, the extent to which it is respected and observed, is not solely the creation of the representative government produced by the democratic political process. It is also the product of the market. The interplay of supply and demand does not emerge wholly within the limitations set by the political law. The natural urge of supply to discover demand and of demand to generate supply are deep-lying human instincts. They obey the intensely personal urge to express natural or acquired faculties to produce goods or services or to satisfy subjective preferences or the very desire to reject the preferences of the mass.

The 'natural' instinctive market does not operate solely within the political law as it happens to have emerged at a given time or place. The instinctive market that satisfies natural human preference could in time spread to generate increasing fundamental deep-rooted opinion and a philosophy that requires government to reform the laws that inhibit suppliers from meeting growing demands, or to pass new laws that facilitate new sources of supply.

Even if the required law is passed or the obstructive law is reformed, it is not itself likely to create the flexible conditions in which supply can be varied to satisfy the myriad demands. Government is too clumsy an instrument to enable the 'legalised' supplies to satisfy the 'legalised' demands. If the industrial revolution of the 18–19th centuries in the West had to wait for government to 'authorise' craftsmen in primitive workshops to invent the simple machinery that accelerated spinning and weaving and created the new textile industries it would have delayed the improvements in clothing and living standards for half a century.

The market could enable natural supply to meet natural demand and negotiate deals or bargains to satisfy both parties as much as technical conditions make possible. It would have to advance faster than the political process to enable individual differences in supply to meet individual differences in demand and so maximise the advancement of the human condition.

The rule of law is essential for civilised human cooperation. It has been weakened by the over-ambitions of the political process taught by socialist thinkers. It now requires a new era of less government that is enforceable because it is confined to the very small part of life where it is indispensable. And it requires the liberal dream to become libertarian.

Value, Economic Efficiency, And Rules: Some Implicit Biases Against Individual Liberty

Louis De Alessi[1]

1. Introduction

The failure to separate normative from positive economics continues to bedevil economists, leading to analyses and policy recommendations that are value-loaded and biased against individual liberty and open markets. Menger (1883) and J. N. Keynes (1890) were among the first modern writers to stress that normative economics deals with what ought to be, and thus is embedded in moral and ethical values, while positive economics deals with what is, and thus – at least in principle – is value-free. Friedman (1953) emphasized this distinction in his famous essay on methodology, and since then generations of economists have paid lip service to it. In practice, however, even highly theoretical explorations of alternative institutional arrangements typically rely – often implicitly – on social welfare functions that tilt the results in favor of government intervention to reduce individual liberty by limiting private property rights and open market processes.

Economic theory provides a powerful set of tools for examining the evolution and economic consequences of alternative institutional and contractual arrangements, including the informal rules that arise from a society's customs and ethical values. Economic theory even allows economists to explain why and how certain norms of moral behavior arise, evolve, and interact with a society's institutions (Benson, 1995). The conclusion that one institution is superior to another, however, rests on value judgments concerning the information to be taken into account (Hayek, 1945, 1988) and the benchmark to be used in comparing alternative distributions of welfare. Economics does not provide objective criteria for determining which rules and ethical values are preferable.

Welfare economists seeking a base for policy recommendations proposed Pareto criteria as a benchmark: a rule change is an improvement if it makes someone better off without making someone else worse off. Although the choice of Pareto criteria entails a value judgment, it is one that – some argue – is relatively weak.[2] More damaging is the recognition that, in the absence of unanimity, any non-trivial change in a rule that makes some people better off typically makes other people worse off, raising the twin problems of knowledge and interpersonal utility comparisons that make Pareto criteria inapplicable. Skirting some of these issues, Kaldor (1938) and Hicks (1939) argued that a change is an improvement if the gainers can fully compensate the losers – whether or not the compensation is paid. Kaldor and Hicks seemed satisfied, even if the uncompensated losers would not be. Scitovsky (1941), however, exposed a logical flaw in the argument: if the compensation is not paid, then the losers in principle can compensate the gainers to return to the initial situation, in which case the original change is not an improvement. In a futile subterfuge to resolve the impasse, many economists simply use a social welfare function that they judge suitable.

A social welfare function defines a set of ethical norms, and individuals who share these norms may find the analysis and recommendations based on it compelling. Other individuals may justifiably reject both the analysis and the recommendations. Unfortunately, the nature of the social welfare function used often is not made clear or, even worse, is masked by misleading assumptions and supposedly objective criteria of economic efficiency.

The failure to distinguish between normative and positive economics is abetted by the nature of theory. Economic theory, like any scientific theory, abstracts from the infinite details of reality to focus on a few relationships relevant to the field of inquiry. Pure theory deals with the behavior of idealized variables under highly stylized circumstances, where the distinction between the axioms (initial hypotheses) of the theory and the conditions ("if ... then ...") that describe the relevant state of the world is crucial but rarely understood or made clear. Not surprisingly, the solutions found under various idealized sets of conditions offer tempting standards of efficiency.[3] The choice of any such standard of efficiency as a benchmark for comparing alternative rules, however, is not value-free – like any other choice, it entails a value judgment. Implicitly, the perception of the world, including the ethical norms, adopted by the analyst and embedded in the benchmark is substituted for the perceptions and values of the individuals affected by the rule. The resulting analyses and policy recommendations ignore individuals' knowledge and values; accordingly, they favor the use of third parties to impose rules and limit individual choices.

The present paper examines the flaws and biases inherent in analyses purporting to show that, on economic grounds, one rule or institution is superior to another. Topics include the value judgments that are implicit in criteria of efficiency, the use of (antecedent) conditions that are empirically false, the perception that values can be measured objectively by outside observers, the failure to specify rules of correspondence for key theoretical terms, and the focus on equilibrium conditions rather than on the process of adjustment and discovery.

2. Comparative Institutions

Individuals compete for resources in a world of scarcity. Accordingly, the fundamental economic problem within any society is to adopt a set of institutions that provide the rules to control competition.[4] These institutions establish the system of property rights, which are the rights of individuals to the use, income, and transfer of resources. These property rights bound the choices that are permissible and determine how the consequences – the benefits and the harms – of a decision are allocated between the decision maker(s) and other individuals. In a world of private property rights and zero transaction costs, for example, individuals bear the full economic consequences of their decisions: there are no external effects.

Alternative systems of property rights provide individuals with different constraints, that is, with different structures of costs and rewards. Because changes in constraints affect choices systematically and predictably, economics can be used to analyze the nature and consequences of alternative institutional and contractual arrangements. The comparison of these alternatives, however, raises a number of difficulties.

2.1. Economic Efficiency

Economists deal frequently and casually with the concept of efficiency. From the perspective of positive economics, efficiency can be defined as the equilibrium solution to an optimization problem given a specific set of constraints (De Alessi, 1983). A position away from an equilibrium is inefficient in the sense that it is not stable; the system predictably will shift away from it and toward the equilibrium. For example, a change in the rule of product liability yields a movement toward a new equilibrium that, given the new set of constraints, is more efficient than the old one. On positive grounds, both the old equilibrium under the old rule and the new equilibrium under the new rule are efficient: economic theory does not provide a value-free basis for finding one equilibrium more efficient than the other.

The more common definition of efficiency, however, is value-loaded. Perhaps without fully realizing the normative implications involved, economists typically take the equilibrium solution associated with the purely competitive model in a world of private property rights and zero transaction costs as the benchmark of economic efficiency. On this approach, the ideal equilibrium solution – by definition – must lie on the appropriate envelope (boundary); for example, an efficient output must lie on the production possibility surface. Alternative rules then are more or less efficient depending upon how closely they approximate this ideal.

This approach is flawed.[5] First, consider the claim that a rule is inefficient if it yields an interior solution. As Stigler (1976) noted, *all* equilibrium solutions must lie on the envelope. An interior solution can arise, and appear to be inefficient, only if the analyst chooses (makes the value judgment) to disregard one or more of the relevant variables. For example, an output combination will lie inside the production possibility surface only if the analyst chooses not to measure some outputs.

Second, consider the claim that a rule is more efficient than another, and therefore preferable on economic grounds, if it yields a solution that lies closer to the envelope. This assertion, even if the rule yields more of every measured output, rests on the conditions that all relevant (to whom?) outputs have been measured and that possible changes in the distribution of income do not matter. For example, suppose that the increase in measured outputs occurs at the expense of other sources of utility (e.g., leisure, liberty) that the analyst chooses not to measure. Then the seemingly more efficient solution could be further away from the full envelope and less desirable on its own terms of reference. Or suppose that some individuals are less productive than others, so that shifting resources from the former to the latter increases measured output. If the transfer is involuntary and the losers are not fully compensated (as they see it), they are worse off. Finally, choosing one point closer to the envelope implies foregoing other points – with different combinations of outputs and different distributions of income – that are at least as close to the envelope.

Ranking alternatives using a concept of efficiency that ignores these considerations must rest on some notion of social welfare distinct from the welfare of the individual members of that society. The conclusion that a rule is preferable if it is closer to the ideal masks the value judgment that the distribution of income does not matter. Although it may not matter to the analyst, it surely matters to the gainers and losers from a proposed change in the rules.

Actual market solutions in a world of limited private property rights and positive transaction costs always appear to be inefficient relative to some ideal. The result is a bias toward government action to impose rules that, supposedly, move the system toward the ideal. As the application of economics to the analysis of public choices has shown, generations of economists have provided the rhetoric used by rent-seekers in both the private and the public sectors to coopt government regulation and redistribute income to themselves.[6]

2.2. False Antecedent Conditions and Missing Rules of Correspondence

Neoclassical economics, which provides the purely competitive model used as a benchmark of efficiency, contains three kinds of theoretical statements that analysts often – and, as shown below, inappropriately – lump together under the general rubric of assumptions (Nagel, 1963).[7] One type of theoretical statement consists of the axioms or initial hypotheses of the theory. These axioms describe the nature and relationship of the variables within the scope of inquiry of the discipline. Because the axioms abstract from reality, their validity generally can be determined only by testing their implications. If the theory works – if it is not falsified by the evidence – then the axioms are accepted provisionally.

Another type of theoretical statement consists of the implications. Implications take the form of universal conditional statements ("if ... then ..."), and here the term "assumptions" refers to the antecedent conditions. These conditions describe the state of the world in which the theory is applicable; for example, they identify the system of property rights that governs relationships (e.g., common ownership with open access). Because different antecedent conditions yield different solutions, the validity of the antecedent conditions must be determined empirically *before* the implications of the theory can be tested. If the antecedent conditions do not describe the existing state of the world, then the resulting implications and equilibrium solutions are not applicable to that world.

The third kind of statement concerns theoretical terms. These are terms that, by definition, have no empirical counterparts: they describe either the limits of processes that are theoretically endless (e.g., elasticity at a point) or entities whose existence is postulated by some other theory. In order for the theory to yield testable implications, those theoretical terms that appear in lower-level hypotheses must be related to observable events by appropriate rules of correspondence.

Unfortunately, many economists do not seem to realize that the theoretical statements labeled as "assumptions" may differ and require different kind of treatment. For example, the validity of the assumption (axiom) that individuals maximize their own utility is determined by testing some of the resulting implications. In contrast, the validity of the assumption (anteced-ent condition) that the price of some commodity has increased or that all individuals have identical preferences must be established empirically be-fore the implications can be tested. Similarly, remaining theoretical con-cepts, such as "a purely competitive market," must be related to appropri-ate observations before the theory can be tested.[8]

Failure to draw these distinctions results in analyses that are inapplicable to the real world and biased toward government intervention. For example, neoclassical economic theory contains the statement that transaction (in-cluding information) costs are zero. In the real world, transaction costs typically are positive and increase at the margin, giving rise to a wide range of contractual arrangements designed to reduce their impact. Resale price maintenance, termination at will, long-term exclusive dealings, and other seemingly unfair contracts can allow more aggressive competition by re-ducing transaction costs. Compared to the ideal benchmark, however, these contracts appear to be anti-competitive and continue to be proscribed by an array of antitrust and other government-imposed regulations.

2.3. Subjective versus Objective Values

To compare rules, an analyst must measure their economic consequences. Although the use of market prices for this purpose suggests that the appro-priate values are measured objectively, this is not the case. There is merely the pretense of knowledge (Hayek, 1988).

2.3.1. Values ultimately are subjective

To the individual making a choice, the value of an option is the value of the desirable attributes less the value of the undesirable attributes of that op-tion; the cost of an option is the value of the next best alternative foregone (Alchian, 1968). Because both value and cost depend upon the anticipations and the range of alternatives considered by the individual making the choice, they are purely private (Buchanan, 1969). Thus, value is subjective.

An analyst cannot know the circumstances of time and place that guide the choices of individuals. Not only is much information subjective, but some (tacit) simply cannot be communicated to others. Moreover, relevant information is lost in any aggregation process.

2.3.2. Prices measure value at the margin

Prices help reduce scarcity in private property systems by facilitating spe-cialization and exchange. Prices transmit information cheaply and quickly while simultaneously providing individual consumers and producers who have specific, often tacit, knowledge of their own circumstances with the incentive to respond. Prices guide the allocation of resources to their highest-valued uses, as judged by consumers, because they reveal values at the margin: the price that a resource can command in each alternative use reflects the value that the resource can yield in that use. Because the private owners of (bundles of rights to the use of) resources bear the value-consequences of their choices, they have incentive to allocate resources where their prices are highest: resources flow where they are most productive. Thus, in the absence of side conditions, equilibrium prices measure value at the margin. Precisely because prices are designed (whether spontaneously or intentionally) to perform this function, they are less useful for other purposes, including the measurement of total values.

In particular, market prices do not reveal the value that an individual – whether a consumer or an owner/manager of resources – attaches to the inframarginal units. As a result, the market price of a commodity times the quantity purchased by an individual underestimates the total value of the commodity to that individual by an amount equal to the gain from trade (consumer's surplus). If the potential gains from trade on the next best opportunity foregone are ignored, costs are underestimated as well.

2.3.3. An exchange typically involves characteristics other than price

Nonprice characteristics affect the divergence between subjective values and market prices. First, most trades include side conditions that give rise to compensating differentials. The buyer acquires a bundle of rights to the use of some resources – the bundle of rights may vary from one transaction to another – and pays a compensation that may include a bundle of other rights as well as money. For example, an employee might agree to invest in firm-specific human capital and job-related tools while the employer might agree to provide more job security and the use of a company car. Changes in circumstances can yield systematic changes in the bundles of rights exchanged. For example, individuals will attach more side conditions to an exchange if nominal prices fluctuate widely than if they are stable.

Second, choices are determined by the structure of full prices, which include all pecuniary and non-pecuniary sources of utility perceived by the choosers. For example, two grocery stores may offer the same goods at the same nominal prices. The full prices of the goods, however, will differ among consumers depending on how far they live from each store, the lengths of the queues, and so on.

If a change in a rule affects the composition and full prices of the bundles of rights being exchanged, comparisons that ignore these differences disregard relevant information.[9]

2.3.4. *The comparison of aggregates ignores distributional issues*

Economists frequently conclude that a policy is preferable if it yields a larger aggregate consumers' surplus. Setting aside the problem of measuring individuals' subjective values and other econometric difficulties, using aggregate consumers' surplus to rank alternatives implies the strong value judgment that the distribution of the gains is irrelevant. The political process suggests that such a value judgment has support largely (only?) within the community of analysts, who find it convenient.

The implicit assumptions that a third party observer can measure values objectively and that the distribution of gains and losses does not matter allow analysts to ignore the individual. This approach clearly loads the dice toward intervention by government employees – implicitly assumed to be wholly dedicated to the view of the public interest chosen by the analyst – to regulate the behavior of individual economic agents.

2.4. Relevance of the Process for Adjusting to Change

Analysts typically compare alternative rules on the basis of the static equilibrium conditions expected to exist. At best, these conditions reveal only part of the story.

Individuals live in a world of limited private property rights, positive information and transaction costs, and continuous change brought about by the vagaries of nature, new knowledge, population dynamics, and other events. When circumstances change, the economic system gravitates toward a new equilibrium. Before that equilibrium is reached, however, new unanticipated changes yield a movement toward a new solution. Because equilibrium solutions, whether static or dynamic, based on a given set of initial conditions are seldom attained, the process for coping with unanticipated changes becomes critical.

In a private property system, individuals have incentive to respond accurately and quickly to the opportunities for gain created by changes in circumstances. Moreover, they have incentive to discover new and more productive ways to use resources by introducing new commodities, new production techniques, and new organizational forms. Focusing on equilibrium conditions at the expense of the process for adjusting to changed circumstances ignores the responsiveness to change provided by individual producers and consumers in open markets and biases the comparison of institutions in favor of centralist solutions.

3. Conclusions

Hayek (1948, 1988) emphasized that the specific circumstances of time and place relevant to the choices of individuals simply cannot be known to a central bureau. Even if they were known, why would government bureaucrats have the incentive to behave according to the dictates of some ideal model? Who would choose the benchmark – and how?

The failure to appreciate these observations keeps resurfacing under different guises. It is reflected in the belief that economic efficiency can be defined to provide an objective benchmark for comparing alternative institutions, disregarding the value judgments involved and the unavailability of relevant (individual) information; that an outside observer can measure values objectively; that the conditions relevant to an application of the theory can simply be assumed to be true; and that only equilibrium conditions matter, disregarding the process for adjusting to change and discovering new and more productive ways to use resources by introducing new commodities, new production techniques, and new organizational forms. These and related beliefs provide the basis for identifying a whole range of alleged "market failures" and justifying pervasive government involvement in open markets, an involvement coopted by rent-seeking individuals within the private and public sectors to advance their own welfare and impose their values on others.[10] As private property rights and individual liberties are eroded, economies grow more slowly and eventually may fail (De Alessi, 1995a).

Economics can indicate some of the consequences associated with alternative institutional and contractual arrangements. It does not provide a benchmark for deciding which rule is superior (preferable). That choice – like any other choice – requires a value judgment as well as knowledge of individual circumstances that simply is not available to a third party.

Notes

1   This paper is a shorter version of De Alessi (1995c); it benefitted from comments by Donald J. Boudreaux, Michael L. De Alessi, Raymond P. H. Fishe, William F. Shughart II, and Walter E. Williams.

2   Pareto criteria embody some strong value judgments (De Alessi, 1992,

pp. 336–8). For example, the welfare of individuals outside the set being analyzed does not matter.

3   Demsetz (1969) decries this nirvana approach, which he finds prone to three logical fallacies: the grass is always greener, the free lunch, and the people could be different.

4   A society's constitution establishes the property rights determining the range of formal and informal contracts that individuals may form voluntarily. Whether the constitution is achieved spontaneously or not, typically it evolves through various levels of collective decisions.

5   De Alessi (1992) offers a more detailed analysis of the bias in efficiency comparisons.

6   Regulation by utility-maximizing government employees does not yield an improvement even by the standards of efficiency used to justify the intervention (De Alessi, 1995b).

7   De Alessi (1987) reviews the methodological issues at stake.

8   Rules of correspondence cannot be avoided by as-if-statements (Nagel, 1963).

9   In addition to the issue of subjective values, measuring an individual's gain from trade raises a host of econometric problems that usually are side-stepped by adopting false antecedent conditions. For example, the analyst may assume that the demand curve is linear, that the marginal utility of the commodity is independent of the quantity of other goods consumed by the individual, and that the marginal utility of income is constant.

10 For example, Yandle (1995) provides detailed documentation of the growth in regulatory takings of private property under various environmental laws.

References

Alchian, Armen A. (1968), "Cost," *International Encyclopedia of the Social Sciences*, Vol. 3, pp. 404–15. Reprinted in Alchian, Armen A., *Economic Forces at Work*, Liberty Press, Indianapolis, 1977, pp. 301–23.

Benson, Bruce (1995), "Institutions and the Spontaneous Evolution of Morality," Paper presented at the Twentieth International Conference on the Unity of the Sciences, Seoul, Korea, August 21–27, 1995.

Buchanan, James M. (1969), *Cost and Choice*, Markham, Chicago.

De Alessi, Louis (1983), "Property Rights, Transaction Costs, and X-Efficiency: An Essay in Economic Theory," *American Economic Review*, Vol. 73, pp. 64–81.

–, (1987), "Nature and Methodological Foundations of Some Recent Extensions of Economic Theory," in Radnitzky, Gerard and Bernholz, Peter (eds.), *Economic Imperialism: The Economic Method Applied Outside the Field of Economics*, Paragon House Publishers, New York, pp. 51–76.

–, (1992), "Efficiency Criteria for Optimal Laws: Objective Standards or Value Judgments?" *Constitutional Political Economy*, 3, pp. 321–42.

–, (1995a), "Institutions, Competition, and Individual Welfare," in Karlson, Niels (ed.), *Can the Present Problems of Mature Welfare States Such as Sweden Be Solved?* City University Press, Stockholm, Sweden, pp. 76–87.

–, (1995b), "The Public Choice Model of Antitrust Enforcement," in McChesney, Fred S. and Shughart, William F. II (eds.), *The Causes and Consequences of Antitrust: A Public Choice Approach*, University of Chicago Press, Chicago, pp. 189–200.

–, (1995c), "Value, Efficiency, and Rules: The Limits of Economics," Paper presented at the Twentieth International Conference on the Unity of the Sciences, Seoul, Korea, August 21–27, 1995.

Demsetz, Harold (1969), "Information and Efficiency: Another Viewpoint," *Journal of Law & Economics*, Vol. 12, pp. 1–23.

Friedman, Milton (1953), "The Methodology of Positive Economics," in Friedman, Milton (ed.), *Essays in Positive Economics*, University of Chicago Press, Chicago, pp. 3–43.

Hayek, Friedrich A. (1945), "The Use of Knowledge in Society," *American Economic Review*, Vol. 35, pp. 519–30.

–, (1988), *The Fatal Conceit*, University of Chicago Press, Chicago.

Hicks, John R. (1939), "The Foundations of Welfare Economics," *Economic Journal*, Vol. 49, pp. 696–712.

Kaldor, Nicholas (1939), "Welfare Propositions of Economics and Interpersonal Comparisons of Utility," *Economic Journal*, Vol. 49, pp. 549–52.

Keynes, John N. (1890), *The Scope and Method of Political Economy*, Reprints of Economic Classics, Kelley & Millman, New York, 1955.

Menger, Carl (1883), *Investigations into the Methods of the Social Sciences with Special Reference to Economics*, New York University Press, New York, 1985.

Nagel, Ernest (1963), "Assumption in Economic Theory," *American Economic Review*, Proceedings, Vol. 53, pp. 211–19.

Scitovsky, Tibor (1941), "A Note on Welfare Propositions in Economics," *Review of Economic Studies*, Vol. 9, pp. 77–88.

Stigler, George J. (1976), "The Xistence of X-Efficiency," *American Economic Review*, Vol. 69, pp. 213–16.

Yandle, Bruce (ed.) (1995), *Land Rights: The 1990s' Property Rights Rebellion*, Rowman & Littlefield Publishers, Lanham, Maryland.

The Böhm-Bawerkian Foundation of the Interest Theory

Hans F. Sennholz

It is difficult to imagine a more important task for economists than to explain the principles and complexities of income. Although socialism has fallen into disfavor and the socialist condemnation of interest income is in disrepute, the receipt of "unearned income" continues to offend many observers. They deplore the visible disparity between the amount of interest paid to wealthy capitalists and the meager wages paid to workers. They lament the fact that the owners of capital enjoy an unending stream of surplus income without personal toil or merit while the poor workingman ekes out a meager existence by dint of heavy labor and great sacrifice. Such descriptions invariably raise the questions of why interest income should not be extirpated and whether human welfare is not better promoted by an expropriation of all unearned income. They also may help to explain the burdensome taxation of interest income in nearly all industrial countries. U.S. tax laws even make a clear distinction between "earned" income, that is, labor income, and "unearned" income, which denotes all others. "Unearned" income is "unfair" income which is taxed repeatedly by all levels of government.

At the time when **Eugen von Böhm-Bawerk** published his pioneering *History and Critique of Interest Theories* (1884) many European scholars were explaining the interest phenomenon in terms of an "exploitation theory." The German "socialists of the chair" were echoing the writings of Proudhon, Rodbertus, and Marx. Regarding labor as the sole source of value, they looked upon interest as "an appropriation of a large portion of the product of labor" by employers and capitalists. In the English-speaking world, John Stuart Mill led the way with an eclectic explanation, a combination of an "abstinence theory" "la Nassau Senior and an "exploitation theory" that built on the Ricardian principle that labor is the chief source of all value.[1] A few other economists, following in the footsteps of John Baptiste Say, were expounding variations of a "productivity theory."

123

Today, more than a century later, the economics profession continues to be divided on the question of interest. The number of explanations is as numerous and varied today as it was during the Böhm-Bawerk era. Some theories present interest as a natural and necessary form of income; others view it as a surplus increment that springs from bargaining power and economic struggles between the market participants. Some can be classified as Keynesian Monetary Theory or derivations thereof, others as variations of the Cambridge Surplus Theory, a Schumpeterian Disequilibrium Theory, the Marginal or Neoclassical Theory, or the Austrian Time Preference Theory.

The Monetary Theory of Interest is a consistent component of John Maynard Keynes' "monetary theory of production" as he presented it in his *General Theory of Employment, Interest and Money.* (1936) In his earlier writings, in *Tract on Monetary Reform* (1923) and his *Treatise on Money*[2] (1930) he had held to the quantity theory of money and the productivity theory of interest which he had inherited from his teachers at Cambridge. In his *General Theory* he abandoned the concept of "natural interest rate" and instead presented the concept of "average" or "durable" level of interest. The most important factor in his structure is the policy of the monetary authority shaping the "common opinion" on the future of the interest rate.

The Cambridge Surplus Theory has occupied an important place in many macro-economic textbooks since the 1950s and 60s. Its spokesmen, most of whom are ardent supporters of the Keynesian system, summarily reject all neoclassical explanations. Until her passing in 1983, Joan Violet Robinson led this theoretical movement of which Piero Sraffa, Nicholas Kaldor, and Richard Kahn are eminent representatives. Pronouncing judgment on all versions of the abstinence and productivity doctrines, Robinson developed her surplus theory on the Keynesian foundation. She made investment an independent variable which passively determines total savings through the operation of the multiplier. Consequently, the rate of interest cannot be a remuneration for someone's sacrifice or productivity. This is especially true during the times of depression when thrift, which is a private virtue, becomes a public vice.[3]

The Schumpeterian Disequilibrium Theory is one of several explanations by Joseph A. Schumpeter, the Austrian enfant terrible. He admired Leon Walras as the greatest economist of all time, sounded like Böhm-Bawerk when he defined interest as "a premium on present over future means of payment," and echoed Proudhon, Rodbertus, and Marx when he called interest "a social permit" for acquiring commodities and services "without having previously contributed other commodities and services to the social stream." Having affirmed his allegiance to the exploitation theory, he then presented his Disequilibrium Theory which makes capitalist innovation "the pillar of interest." The profit which an innovation yields to a successful entrepreneur is the typical reason for his willingness to pay interest. In the short run, the actual rate of interest is merely a disequilibrium phenomenon; in the long run, the rate will be zero.[4]

The Neoclassical Theory stands on certain foundations laid by W. S. Jevons, C. Menger, L. Walras, J. B. Clark, and F. H. Knight, but is presented by many diverse, even contradictory, voices. Some see marginal productivity as an essential feature of neoclassical theory, others regard the aggregation of capital as essential. Neoclassical income theories seek to explain the levels of payment to the various factors of production – land, labor, and capital – by their marginal productivities, land yielding rent, labor earning wages, and capital reaping interest and profit. Marginal productivity determines factor rewards.

John Bates Clark engaged Böhm-Bawerk in a lengthy debate on capital and interest theories. His *The Philosophy of Wealth* (1886) and his *The Theory of Wages, Interest and Profits* (1899) made him one of the first American economists to earn an international reputation. He treated all economic resources that both directly and indirectly enter into the production of consumers goods as **capital** and viewed interest as the marginal productivity of capital. He even implied that factor payments ought to be according to their marginal productivity and that they tend to be like this in the real world of competitive enterprise. Some twenty years later Frank H. Knight in *Risk, Uncertainty and Profit* arrived at similar conclusions.[5]

The "neoclassical synthesis," a term coined by Paul Samuelson, seeks to use whatever is valuable in both the older versions and those in modern garb.[6] In particular it seeks to make proper use of monetary and fiscal policy and thus add Keynesian insight to classical truth. However, many theorists summarily reject this "neoclassical synthesis" for being fundamentally flawed failing to explain the inability of markets to clear during the 1960s and 70s and of prices and wages to adjust.[7] High rates of inflation persisted together with high rates of unemployment.

The Austrian Time Preference Theory is probably the least known and understood of all Austrian explanations. While other basic theorems have been absorbed into micro-economic thought, in particular, the methodological individualism, the importance of marginal changes, the effects of opportunity costs, the profound role played by time in all economic processes continues to be ignored by the profession. Yet some economists call themselves "Austrians" because they rest their explanations on Böhm-Bawerkian theories. Two distinct versions of "Austrian economics" are clearly discernible: **the subjectivist Mengerian School** and the **Neo-Austrian School.** The former enjoyed its greatest acceptance and acclaim during the 1920s and early 30s. It disappeared from view during the late 1930s and 40s with its flush of enthusiasm for the Keynesian Revolution. It was not until the 1940s and 50s that the School again emerged under the banner of Ludwig von Mises and Friedrich von Hayek. Since then it has grown continually and now is prospering with its representatives holding forth in various centers of learning.

During the 1970s and 80s the Austrian label began to assume a rather different connotation in many circles. The Keynesian concept of the production function had fallen into disrepute because it ignored the time structure of the production process. This obvious shortcoming led a growing number of economists to rediscover Böhm-Bawerk's capital theory and build a **Neo-Austrian School** upon his theoretical foundation. This new school soon split into three separate groups each using different elements of the Böhm-Bawerkian structure. The most numerous and vocal group is led by J. R. Hicks[8] who emphasizes Böhm's vertical time structure of the production process. Another group led by G. Tintners[9] and C. C. von Weizsäcker[10] builds upon Böhm's time preference and period of production. A third group around Professors P. Bernholz[11] and M. Faber[12] uses Böhm's concepts of superiority of roundabout methods and time preference to demonstrate the source of interest.

The Neo-Austrians reject the general subjective tradition begun by Carl Menger and continued by many illustrious Austrians. They barely acknowledge the Mengerian School which, to them, is a relic of the distant past. In their literature one searches in vain for any reference to the seminal writings of Ludwig von Mises, Murray N. Rothbard, and Israel Kirzner. F. A. Hayek's **The Pure Theory of Capital** may rate only a cursory mention.

An analysis of the interest theories of the Neo-Austrian School exceeds the scope of this study. It would require lengthy epistemological and theoretical discourse to do justice to this branch of Austrian economics. And even if such a task were undertaken, it is doubtful that both schools, the subjectivist Austrian and the Neo-Austrian, would find a common ground from which both could proceed.

In this short overview I must limit myself to the traditional school of subjectivism and return to the Böhm-Bawerkian foundation upon which these Austrians rest their deliberations. Although it is rather presumptuous to summarize the rich Böhm-Bawerkian thought in a short essay, we cannot avoid a discussion of the very foundation of modern micro-economic theory of capital and interest. Böhm himself built on the cornerstone laid by Carl Menger in his *Principles of Economics*, but carried his analysis to new heights. In the fields of capital and interest Böhm was a pioneer who did more to stimulate scholarly interest than did any other writer.

This essay cannot possibly touch on all the intricacies of the Böhm-Bawerkian structure nor can it embark upon a critical review of all the theoretical edifices and superstructures that have been added to it during the last century. Such a task would require a thorough investigation similar to Böhm-Bawerk's *History and Critique of Interest Theories*, to which he gave three of his most productive years as a young professor at the University of Innsbruck. This short essay merely sets out to sketch the field of inquiry, indicate the milestones set by a few eminent scholars, and outline the task ahead. As was the case a century ago, the phenomenon of interest income continues to be enmeshed in much controversy, which makes it one of the most open and demanding subjects of economic inquiry.

The Theoretical Problem of Interest

What is the theoretical problem of interest? On the first page of his **magnum opus** Böhm-Bawerk seeks to answer this question: "Whoever is the owner of a capital sum is ordinarily able to derive from it a permanent net income which goes under the scientific name of interest in the broad sense of the word." To explain this net income Böhm-Bawerk wrote *Kapital und Kapitalzins* which has become a classic although it is also the object of much criticism. It reads like an attorney's brief, responding conscientiously and meticulously to every criticism. His responses added much material which in time was to enlarge two slim volumes to three massive tomes.

In the first volume, *History and Critique of Interest Theories* (1884) Böhm outlines his theory by refuting and disposing of competing explanations. He seeks to prove that the rate of interest **cannot** be determined by considerations of marginal utility, but rather is circumscribed by contemplation of time preference. And he demonstrates brilliantly that the existence of interest income is not due to exploitation. As long as production is not instantaneous, but is roundabout taking time, the present value of the workers' output is necessarily less than its value at the time of completion. Böhm-Bawerk was probably the first theoretical economist to analyze critically the writings of Marx. Although it drew numerous responses by socialistic writers, his critique remained the only significant response until Mises took up the issue during the 1920s.

Böhm expounded his own theory in the *Positive Theory* which builds on the fundamental principle that present goods generally have a greater subjective value than future goods. And since the subjective value determines objective exchange value, present goods generally have greater exchange value and higher prices than future goods. This result is the first of three causes which, although they "differ markedly," exert their influence in the same direction.

The **first** principal cause for a value difference is the "difference between the relation of supply to demand as it exists at one point in time and that relation as it exists at another point in time (1889/1959, 265, 266). The beginner in every calling, especially the budding artist or Austrian instructor who is barely "breaking even," gladly consents to accept an educational loan now and promises to pay a larger sum in the future. The same is true of the person who in the present has a good income but expects to have a lower income in the future, such as in retirement, and who thus will attach a slightly higher value to present goods. The **second** cause for the value difference is the fact that "we systematically undervalue our future wants and also the means which serve to satisfy them." (268) We do this for reasons of our ignorance about the future, of lack of will power, and our consideration of the uncertainty of life. The **third** cause, finally, is the general rule that "present goods are for technological reasons preferable means to the satisfaction of wants and for that reason they are a warranty of higher marginal utility than are future goods." (273) The productive superiority of present goods produces a surplus not only in products but also in value. As a cause of surplus value entirely independent of the two other causes, the "technical" superiority emerges because present goods facilitate roundabout production that is more productive and also more remunerative than direct production.

By elevating the technological superiority of more time-consuming roundabout methods of production to an equal position in interest causation, he resuscitated various parts of the productivity theories of John Baptiste Say, Wilhelm Roscher, Lord Lauderdale, Thomas Malthus, and Henry Carey, and gave life to numerous versions of a modern productivity theory. But he also drew severe criticism by a number of writers against whom he defended his thesis meticulously and conscientiously.[13] In reaction he even elevated it to the "most important of several cooperating reasons leading to higher valuation of present goods over future goods and thus to the emergence of interest." (1912/1959, 150) But later he seems to be on the defensive when he assures his opponents that the third reason is not the only reason but merely one of three independent reasons.

The theoretical foundations so brilliantly laid by Böhm-Bawerk served other scholars as launching bases upon which they could build their own theories. Thus Fetter developed a pure time-preference theory (1902/1904). Irving Fisher (1907, 1930) forged Böhm's analysis into a theory of interest of his own. Wicksell (1893, 1901) was to turn Böhm's thesis into a theory of marginal productivity of production. Schumpeter was to present a disequilibrium theory (1939), Hicks was to seek to salvage Böhm's view of production (1965), and Faber (1973) and Weizsäcker (1971) labored to give Böhm's theory a modern, "more exact" mathematical formulation.

Several Branches of the Böhm-Bawerkian Structure

Böhm-Bawerk wrote the first edition of **Kapital and Interest** in great haste and thereafter never found the time and peace of mind to rethink his grandiose structure; yet he was much occupied in paying absorptive attention to all the criticism that was hurled at his theory. The great interest in Böhm-Bawerk's theory and the various attempts to reformulate his ideas today, a century later, prove the vitality of his thought.[14]

It was **Frank A. Fetter** who elaborated and perfected Böhm's time-preference theory during the first decade of this century. He applauded Böhm for stating the nature of the problem of interest while faulting him for failing to formulate a consistent and satisfactory theory of interest. The conception of the interest problem is one aspect of exchange value, but is only *preliminary* to the formulation of an interest theory, not as the theory itself.

Fetter took issue with all productivity explanations of interest. They demonstrate correctly that capital goods are productive in physical terms, but the problem of interest is to explain why the present value of these goods is so low that it always generates a surplus return in the future. Surely, long roundabout processes of production are physically highly productive, but why are they not always preferred to less productive, immediately fruitful processes? According to Fetter, Böhm-Bawerk failed to answer this question. In defense of his "third cause," Böhm leaped repeatedly from the concept of increased physical productivity of roundabout processes to value productivity and then back to physical productivity. In other words, he failed to separate the unquestioned increase in physical productivity from an increase in value productivity, locking him into a vicious cycle. For instance, at a market rate of 20%, a capital of 10 units is capitalized at 50; if the interest rate falls to 2%, it is worth 500. This calculation already involves the rate of interest which is to be explained. Technical productiveness does not explain it.

Fetter made his positive case for the interest phenomenon in all his early writings. In his *Economic Principles* he announced that "time is a factor in practically all economic choice and in practically all valuation. Indeed, time-value and time-preference have aspects that transcend economics; they are universal phenomena of life and conduct." (1915, p. 246) And what determines the rate of preference? It depends on individual valuation as to thrift, industry, prudence, and other personal factors. Individual time-preference is visible in the use of economic goods and services, in their care and repairs. And as economics frequently touches on the borders of ethics, personal conduct in the realm of moral values has a large place in the comparison between present and future enjoyments. Time-value is involved in prodigality as in many forms of vice. Thus the drinker exchanges his hopes for a brighter future for the exhilaration of the binge. Such indulgence is a loan from the future at usurious cost. "If no one ever paid more than a moderate premium for the gratification of his present whims and impulses, most hospitals, drugstores, and medical colleges would close, and half, if not all, the prisons would be empty." (1915, p. 255)[15]

Such startling observations which are "radical" on several counts reflect his time-preference theory. Fetter purged all features of capital productivity from his theory and thereby developed a pure time-preference theory. And he did not hesitate to apply his knowledge to fields of individual psyche and endeavor other than economic. He was considered "politically incorrect" when he wrote these passages in 1914 and surely would be perceived that way today.

Another contemporary of Böhm-Bawerk, the Swedish economist **Johann Gustaf Knut Wicksell**, too, was politically incorrect throughout most of his life. He was an eclectic par excellence who managed better than any other writer to fuse the elements of other writers and present them in a clear and integrated form. He adopted the marginal utility theory of Jevons, Menger and Marshall, added Böhm-Bawerk's theories of capital and interest, and cast them in a Walrasian general equilibrium framework. He thus became one of the founders of the marginal productivity theory of distribution.

In his *Value, Capital and Rent* (1893/1954) Wicksell built his theory on Böhm-Bawerk's "average period of production", which enables capital to introduce longer production processes and consequently the adoption of more roundabout methods of production. The greater the amount of capital, the longer the average period of production that can be applied, the greater will be the output of finished goods. Wicksell did not apply the principle of marginal productivity directly to capital and capital goods but rather to given quantities of the two original factors of production, to "saved-up labor" and "saved-up land" employed in production. These are rewarded according to their marginal productivities and are employed in the proportions determined by the equilibrium condition of a given rate of interest. In short, the relative scarcity of saved-up original factors ultimately determines the rate of interest as a reward for the delay.

Although later writers were to laud Wicksell for having espoused the time-preference theory, it seems proper to group him with the "productivity theorists." He defined capital as "produced means of production" and interest as an "organic growth out of capital, a certain percentage of capital. An increase in the efficiency of the original factors of production – man and nature – is "a necessary condition of interest; it is the source from which it flows (just as the fruitfulness of the earth is the source of rent and the productivity of labour the source of wages) (1901/1934, 150).[16] And later Wicksell sums it up in an eclectic nutshell: "Capital is saved-up labor and saved-up land. Interest is the difference between the marginal productivity of saved-up labor and land and of current labour and land" (1901/1934, p. 154).

The thesis of marginal utility is Wicksell's guiding principle of income distribution. If "marginalism" is the core of neoclassicism, Wicksell is an exemplary neoclassicist. He did not receive much recognition during his own lifetime, remaining relatively unknown in the English-speaking world until the 1930s when J. M. Keynes caused his monetary works to be translated into English. *His Interest and Prices, A Study in the Causes Regulating the Value of Money* (1898/1936) and especially his Lectures on Political Economy (1906/1935) influenced and fortified Keynes in his analyses in both his **Treatise on Money** and his **General Employment, Interest and Money.** Wicksell's stature in the world of economics has grown dramatically since then.

The economist regarded during his lifetime as the greatest economist America has ever produced was **Irving Fisher.** He attacked the problems of factor incomes in a more abstract, mathematical, and ethically neutral manner than Clark and Böhm-Bawerk. His writings were intended to participate in the heated debate in Europe and North America about the sources and the social rationale of interest and other returns to private property. In particular, he meant to lend support to the Austrian scholars who were answering the Marxian challenge to the legitimacy of property income.

Fisher is credited with having "perfected the timepreference theory". In his *The Nature of Capital and Income* (1906) Fisher stated with admirable clarity the idea that the value of capital goods is the discounted value of their income, the element of time making the great difference. The interest rate, which to Fisher was the main problem of economic theory, depends on the "time preference" of individuals for present over future goods. Fisher called it "impatience." Yet Fisher is not content with just one explanation. He defines the rate of interest in two distinctly different ways: "as the price of capital in terms of income" and also as a "premium concept" (1906, pp. 194, 195).

In both his treatises on interest, in **The Rate of Interest** (1907) and his **Theory of Interest** (1930), which was meant to be a revision of the earlier volume, Fisher dealt with Böhm's doctrines in considerable detail. He painstakingly refuted Böhm's theory of the technical superiority of present goods as the source of interest. It is the undervaluation of the future, due to psychological conditioning, Fisher contended, which produces the advantage of present over future goods. He summarized his own theory in purely psychological terms: "It is clear that the rate of interest is dependent upon very unstable influences many of which have their own origin deep down in the social fabric and involve considerations not strictly economic. Any causes tending to affect intelligence, foresight, self-control, habits, the longevity of man, family affection, and fashion will have their influence upon the rate of interest" (1906, p. 505).

These statements contain three different interest theories that may not be complementary. Fisher's substitution of "impatience" for time preference introduces a psychological explanation which places interest in the nebulous world of human understanding, calling for psychoanalysis, psychotherapy, and investigations into the psychosomatic and psychosocial behavior of the individual. Such an explanation is unlikely to fortify our understanding of the interest phenomenon. The definition of interest as a price of capital leads him straight back into a productivity explanation which makes interest the specific income derived from utilization of capital goods. The "premium concept" finally returns him to the Böhm-Bawerkian foundation of time preference. Fisher described himself as an advocate of "impatience" as the final explanation of interest.[17]

The economist who, a generation later, was to shun such excursions into psychology, physiology, sociology, and even ethics, and instead elevate the perception of time to a category of life was **Ludwig von Mises**.[18] He rejected the world of static general equilibrium of the Jevons and Walras branches of marginal utility theory for a step-by-step process analysis. He ignored the neoclassical mutual determination of mathematical functions in favor of a causal explanation from individual utilities and actions to price. In his *Theory of Money and Credit* (1912) he integrated money into microtheory, showing how the marginal utility of money affects other goods and determines money prices. He rejected all neutral-money concepts such as Fisher's "equation of exchange" and dismissed the idea of stabilizing "the price level." Mises developed his famous theory of the business cycle on the foundation of Böhm-Bawerk's theory of capital and Wicksell's distinction between natural and market rates of interest. And in order to defend economic theory against the rising tide of logical positivism, he elaborated "praxeology," the methodology that discovers economic principles by logical deduction from self-evident axioms (Mises, 1933, 1949, 1957).

Mises lauded Irving Fisher and Frank Fetter for having "perfected the time-preference theory" (1949/1966, p. 489) and then, instead of taking issue with Fisher's psychology and

productivity theories, took his great mentor, Böhm-Bawerk, to task for having committed the original errors.

"It is important to realize," Mises wrote, "that the period of production as well as the duration of the serviceableness are categories of human action and not concepts constructed by philosophers, economists and historians as mental tools for their interpretation of events. . . . It is necessary to stress this point because Böhm-Bawerk, to whom economics owes the discovery of the role played by the period of production, failed to comprehend the difference" (1949/1966, p. 480). All human action is subject to the categorical element of time and time preference which, without any exception, is operative in every instance of action. Yet, time preference is not specifically human, Mises explained in a footnote. "It is an inherent feature of the behavior of all living beings. The distinction of man consists in the very fact that with him time preference is not inexorable and the lengthening of the period of provision not merely instinctive as with certain animals that store food, but the result of a process of valuation (Mises, 1949/1966, p. 488).

Mises differed from his famous mentor on the role of capital productivity. Böhm allowed capital productivity considerations to enter his theory. In his *Positive Theory* (1889) and its enlarged third edition (1909 and 1912) Böhm proclaimed an indubitable independence of the higher productivity of longer methods of production – his third cause – from any other causes. To Mises, this was an unfortunate relapse into a subtle version of the productivity theory which Böhm had so brilliantly refuted in his *History and Critique of Interest Theories*. He denied that capital productivity plays any role at all in the source of interest. The productivity of the factors of production determines the prices that are paid for them; interest is the increment of value that arises when the factors ripen into present goods of a higher value, flowing into the hands of the owners of the factors of production (1949/1966, p. 525). Moreover, Böhm looked back, reflecting on the role played by the "average period of production" in the source of interest. To Mises, this was an empty concept. Capital goods are valued for their usefulness for the production of future goods and the satisfaction of future wants. To Böhm-Bawerk, capital was an aggregate of the produced means of production. In the Menger tradition Mises rejected this notion of capital as an aggregate of physical things. To him, capital was inextricably linked with capitalism and the market economy. It was the sum of the money equivalent of all business assets used in entrepreneurial decision making, that is, an accounting concept based on market prices. To Mises, profit and loss were the motive power of decision making and interest a basic category inherent in every human action.

The most eminent of Mises' students, a man who was to become a central figure in 20th century economic debate, a Nobel laureate, and a seminal writer in the philosophy of science, political and social philosophy, epistemology, and psychology, as well as economics, was **Friedrich von Hayek.** His achievements in these fields are widely acknowledged. His books have been translated into major languages of the world; some have become classics of the literature of liberty. In the footsteps of Adam Smith, who admired the "invisible hand" in man's division of labor, and of Carl Menger, who defined economics as "the unintended consequences of human action," Hayek marvelled at the "spontaneous order."[19] Economic institutions are the results of human action but not of human design. The use of money is an example of Hayek's spontaneous order; it has neither inventor nor designer who intended to develop the use of money. Market economies are manifestations of this spontaneous order which is always complex and intricate and in need of continuous coordination. For Hayek, economic life was a continuous coordination problem.

Hayek's theories of capital and money led him to censure and confront Keynes' theories and policies. While Keynes sought to confine the term "interest" to the rate at which money can be borrowed, that is, the actual market rate that enters into the calculations of entrepreneurs, Hayek preferred to adhere to the "real" or "commodity rates" of interest which are the object of investigation in traditional economic theory. And while Keynes regarded the rate of interest as being solely dependent on the quantity of money in circulation and on the people's desire for cash holdings, Hayek reiterated his confidence in the well-known principle that changes in the quantity of money and the demand for money (commonly known as the velocity of circulation) do deflect the rate from its real rate (Hayek, 1941, pp. 356, 359).

Hayek's contribution to the capital theory is viewed by some observers as his most significant achievement. It provided the basis and stimulus for many other discussions of the capital theory. In his *Prices and Production* (1935) he analyzed the changes in the intertemporal pattern of the capital structure. In *The Pure Theory of Capital* (1941) Hayek examined point by point the coordination process of economic activities over time (Cf. also Hayek, 1935/1967). Joining the controversy about productivity or time preference as the ultimate source of interest he visibly leaned toward the productivity side while steering a middle course. "Of the two branches of the BöhmBawerkian school," Hayek observed, "that which stressed the productivity element almost to the exclusion of time preference, the branch whose chief representative is K. Wicksell, was essentially right, as against the branch represented by Professors F. A. Fetter and I. Fisher, who stressed time preference as the exclusive factor and an at least equally important factor respectively" (Hayek, 1941, p. 420). Wicksell neglected the time preference element while Fisher gave the psychical factor "more than its due share." Having cast his vote for the Wicksellian school Hayek cites the most widely held view of Marshall's tale of the two blades of the scissors which made it "impossible to say which has the greater and which the lesser influence. (p. 420)

Through his writings and teaching, Hayek has exerted a powerful influence on the intellectual debate in economics and political science. As the first Austrian economist to appear in the English-speaking world, he became a vocal spokesman of Austrian thought, participating in the economic debates that raged throughout the Great Depression. Unfortunately, most economists readily accepted Keynes' simple message that aggregate consumption is a function of national income and that governments must adopt spending programs aimed at maintaining a high level of national income. They rejected the alien thought coming from Austria, especially Hayek's theories of capital, interest, and money.

Murray N. Rothbard never had any doubts about the sole importance of the time element. His blades were always perfectly sharp, cutting through all ambiguity and obscurity. They cut deep in his brilliant refutation of the dominant economic fallacies espoused by prominent economists such as Marshall, Fisher, Keynes, and Galbraith. Rothbard constructed an integrated and coherent body of economic knowledge shunning unnecessary and superfluous deductions. In his *Man, Economy, and State* (1962) he constructed a grand edifice on the foundation laid by his illustrious teacher, Ludwig von Mises. He concentrated on the economic ingredients of the Mises praxeology, filled in the interspaces, and explained many of its implications. The treatise meant to "add a few bricks" to the noble Mises structure, lending support to its pure timepreference theory by carefully explaining how individual time preference schedules determine the market rate of interest and how they decide the individual and aggregate proportions between consumption and savings.

Rothbard offered new insights with his observation that the interest rate must be uniform not only for each good but also for every stage of production, and that it is equal to the rate of price spread in the various stages. He made it clear that the loan market, although conspicuous, is not the only time market, but that the purchase of producers' goods and services of any kind is much more important. The time market permeates the entire production structure. Rothbard took issue especially with the notion of the permanence of capital which led J. B. Clark and Frank H. Knight to deny the very influence of time in production. In the modern, complex world, they believed, production is continuous and timeless, which denies time preference any influence on the rate of interest. If the capital structure is really permanent and there is no problem of replacing and maintaining productive capital, it is easy to conclude, as many economists have done, that the only important element that manages to maintain economic production is consumers' spending and that consumption expenditures alone are sufficient to maintain the capital structure. Rothbard responded by demonstrating that, in reality, there is no relationship between prosperity and consumer spending. The driving force for business prosperity is the rate of interest return to the capitalist. It induces him to save and invest present goods in facilities of production (1962, p. 344).

Rothbard was at his best when he exploded the dominant neoclassical doctrine that the interest rate is codetermined by time preference (which affects the supply of individual savings) and by the marginal productivity of investment (which affects the demand for funds by businessmen), which in turn is determined by the investment returns. To Rothbard, this was an unfortunate relapse into just another version of the productivity theory. Economic productivity in reality has no basic relation to the rate of return on business investments. The return depends entirely on the price spreads between the stages, which in turn depend on the time-preference schedules of all the individuals. In sum, the rates of business return are, in fact, the rate of interest, which is determined by time preference (1962, pp. 363, 364). On this point Rothbard also takes Keynes to task for his preoccupation with the relatively unimportant problems of the loan market and for confusing the rate of interest with the "marginal efficiency of capital."

Another eminent Mises student, a seminal writer in Austrian theory and Nobel laureate candidate, is **Israel Kirzner.** He refuses to view the role of capital theory as a mere adjunct to the theory of interest. We need a complete theory of capital in order to explain inputs and outputs, goods prices and interest rates. We should know how we arrived at the present state of affairs. More important, we need a theory of capital that explains the multiperiod plans continually being made and remade on the basis of a given stock and distribution of capital goods. The Clark-Knight approach to capital theory, which denies any role to time or "waiting" in production, holding that the stock of capital is permanent, does not fill this need. Kirzner rejects it together with the Dorfman "bathtub theorem" which leads to similar conclusions. Kirzner lauds Böhm-Bawerk for refusing to recognize waiting as an independent factor of production with its own marginal productivity and earning its own return. Viewing the process of production *prospectively*, we do ignore "waiting" altogether as an input and cost factor but are mindful of time preference as to the present value of future goods. The time lag that matters always is prospective, ex ante. It gives rise to the interest phenomenon in intertemporal exchanges that are guided by the time preferences of the exchanging individuals (Kirzner, 1966, pp. 73–102).

Most neoclassical economists have eliminated the entrepreneur from their deliberations and models of the competitive market order. Kirzner has returned him to the center of economic inquiry. His numerous writings explain artfully and rationally the important role played by the entrepreneur in adjusting and readjusting the structure of production through speculation and arbitrage. What distinguishes Kirzner from all other Austrian defenders of entrepreneurship is his courage to enter upon the most difficult and yet most important of all social issues: the moral justification of entrepreneurial profits and their rightful place in everyone's moral philosophy.

In his *Discovery, Capitalism and Distribution* (1989) Kirzner courageously joins several neoclassical economists who tried to defend capital income and thereby fortify the private property order. Yet he differs from all others by refraining from moral judgments and instead explains the ethical features of the competitive order. While J. B. Clark rested his precept of justice on capital productivity, F. A. Knight on uncertainty, F. B. Hawley on risk, and J. A. Schumpeter on creative destruction, Kirzner points at the process of discovery and "finding" as the ethical justification, which merely reflects the widely-held perception of justice within everyone's moral philosophy. He calls it the "ethics of finders-keepers."

An act of discovery, according to Kirzner, is an act of creation *ex nihilo* (1989, p. 47). The entrepreneur may have produced nothing, but he may have discovered an opportunity of maladjustment, a price differential that permits him to reap a profit. The finders-keepers rule "provides a direct defense of legitimacy of entrepreneurial profit" (1989, p. 124). A commodity speculator may earn a fortune in a few minutes of buying and selling, discovering price discrepancies between the cash and futures prices of live chickens and iced broilers. He is entitled to keep the gains according to the finders-keepers ethics. But is it a rationale for the justice of incomes other than pure entrepreneurial profit? Is it a rational ground also for originary interest which by far exceeds the magnitude of pure profit in any economy?

Millions of capitalists are reaping billions of dollars of interest without any individual effort of discovery and deliberate acts of creation *ex nihilo*.

What is the ethical justification of their income? To search for an answer to this question, this writer is tempted to return to those explanations that would elevate "future-orientation" and "thrift" to an ethical justification. He would advance the "ethics of futurity" to justify the interest phenomenon. Just like Kirzner, who is careful not to surrender his *Wertfreiheit* in hinting at the ethics of finders-keepers, this writer would base the "ethics of futurity" on value neutrality. Mises taught us that the interest phenomenon is a category of human action devoid of all ethical implications. An economist surely could offer advice on all matters of futurity without approving or disapproving a person's aspirations. He may warn against "wrong policies" without impugning the motives. Yet it is unlikely that he will be able to prevent his fellows from forming ethical judgments on the basis of their understanding of economic phenomena, and that he himself will be able to resist ethical judgments.

In questions of income, ethical conflicts are permeating society today just as they did a century ago. Many mainstream economists, just like the "socialists of the chair" during the age of Böhm-Bawerk, are questioning the morality of interest income. Guided by fallacious income theories and notions of economic inequality, that is, the ethical or aesthetic judgment that the present degree of income inequality is distinctly evil, they favor drastic progression of income taxation. They form judgments of value and advocate public policy harmful to intertemporal exchanges while paying lip service to the importance of value neutrality in scholarly pursuits. Austrian economists try to avoid making value judgments when they speak or write as economists. But they constitute the only school of thought that provides a logical foundation for a system of ethics favoring individual freedom and the private property order. Searching for the inexorable principles of human action, they point out that man acts purposefully, engaging in production and exchanges in which both parties expect to benefit. Intertemporal exchanges aim to benefit both the lender and the borrower. But this mutual gain and no one's demonstrated loss does not entitle Austrian economists to endorse a value system unless they themselves become ethicists affirming time-preference as a category of life and human life as an ultimate ethical value.

The economic writing of the four central figures of the Austrian School since World War II, Mises, Hayek, Rothbard, and Kirzner are impeccably value free. Nevertheless, all four made occasional value judgments in favor of individual freedom, competitive markets, and classical liberalism. Rothbard even ventured beyond economics to establish an "objective ethics" with individual liberty as the paramount value; Kirzner, the only living member of this group, intimated the finders-keepers ethics. He is working tirelessly to safeguard the Austrian tradition, add his insight to the body of Austrian thought, and counsel a growing number of young scholars such as Gerald O'Driscoll, Mario Rizzo, Laurence White, Don Lavoie, Roger Garrison, Peter J. Boettke, and several younger men and women. George G. Reisman, the youngest of Professor Mises' graduate students, is about to release his *magnum opus, Capitalism: A Treatise on Economics*,[21] which is a comprehensive and substantially original work in textbook format. The book is designed to become an effective alternative to Samuelson's *Economics* and all its clones that have contributed so much to the disparagement of the market order and the condemnation of interest income.

Synopsis

Böhm-Bawerk's magnum opus, *Kapital und Kapitalzins*, is an important milestone in the development of economic theory. It ushered in the Austrian School and helped it gain the ascendancy over classical economic theory. Elaborating on Menger's seminal contribution, it presented an intertemporal theory of value and distribution in which time plays a crucial role. This theory together with its famous application to the doctrines of Marx not only influenced the subsequent development of economic thought but also made Austrian economics the main critic and adversary of socialism.

The impact of Böhm-Bawerk's analyses was immense. Frank A. Fetter (1904, 1915) developed Böhm's theory of intertemporal valuation into a theory of interest which is based entirely on the notion of time preference. Irving Fisher (1907, 1930) transformed it into a property of utility functions, Knut Wicksell (1893, 1911) turned it into a marginal productivity theory of the rate of interest. Since then numerus attempts have been made to reformulate Böhm-Bawerk's theory in such a way that it would suit many purposes. During the 1970s when Keynesian doctrines were falling into disrepute, several writers, especially in the German-speaking world, sought to present it in a modern framework, emphasizing its static nature. The NeoAustrians John R. Hicks (1965, 1973), Gerhard Tintner (1970), Peter Bernholz (1971), and Walter Faber (1981) reject the general subjective tradition of Austrian thought which is alive in the writings of the Austrians in the English-speaking world. The works of Ludwig von Mises (1933/ 1981, 1949, 1957), Friedrich A. von Hayek (1935/1967, 1939, 1941), Murray N. Rothbard (1962, 1973, 1990), and Israel Kirzner (1966, 1979, 1989, 1995) build on the tradition begun by Carl Menger and Eugen von Böhm-Bawerk.

In question of income, the differences of theory are as great today as they were a century ago. And as before, the Austrian body of thought not only provides a logical foundation for a consistent explanation of interest income but also offers the rationale for a system of ethics that sustains the private property order against its numerous critics.

Notes

1   Ricardo, David, *The Principles of Political Economy and Taxation* (London: J. M. Dent & Sons, 1817/1937), p. 18. Ricardo did not invent the theory; it can be traced as far back as Thomas Aquinas. Ricardo clung to it throughout his life although he himself offered an important modification that seems to contradict it. In the chapter "On Value" of the Principles he writes "The value of a commodity ... depends on the relative quantity of labour which is necessary for its production." Further on he cites an exception: The value principle is "considerably modified by the employment of machinery and other fixed and durable capital." (Ricardo, 1937)

2   *The Treatise of Money* is an ambitious two-volume work which was designed to earn him an academic reputation that would match the public reputation he already had received from his earlier publications. Cf. Klein, L. *The Keynesian Revolution* (New York: Macmillan, 1947.)

3   Joan Robinson selflessly and entirely supported Keynes and placed herself in his shadow. Her Essays in the *Theory of Employment* (1937) and her Introduction to the *Theory of Employment* (1937 b) were written to clarify and popularize Keynes's *General Theory*. Cf. Pasinetti, L. L., *Structural Changes and Economic Growth* (Cambridge: Cambridge University Press, 1981).

4   Schumpeter's theory of zero-rate interest in long-run equilibrium and his message on our march into socialism which would extirpate interest income appear to be homologous and complementary.

5   During the 1930s Knight wrote a number of articles against the time preference theories and the Böhm-Bawerkian theory of capital. He denied the existence of any "primary" factors of production which contain no capital. Cf., *Capital, Time and the Interest Rate* (1934) and The *Quantity of Capital and the Rate of Interest* (1936). For an Austrian assessment of the Knight theory of the permanence of capital, see Kirzner 1966, 55–72.

6   Samuelson, P. 1948/1955. *Economics*, 3rd ed. (New York: McGraw-Hill).

7   Lucas, R., 1980. "Methods and Problems of Business Cycle Theories" in *Journal of Money, Credit and Banking*, November, 696–715.

8   Hicks, J. R. 1965, *Capital and Growth*, Oxford: Clarendon Press; *Capital and Time: A Neo-Austrian Theory*, Clarendon Press, 1973; "The Austrian Theory of Capital and its Rebirth in Modern Economics" in *Carl Menger and the Austrian School of Economics*, ed. by J. R. Hicks and W. Weber, Oxford: Clarendon Press, 1973, pp. 190–206.

9   Tintner, G. "Lineare Methoden der Nationalökonomie und die Produktionsperiode von Böhm-Bawerk" in *Zeitschrift für Nationalökonomie* 30, 1970, pp. 1–5.

10 Weizsäcker, C. C. von "Die zeitliche Struktur des Produktionsprozesses und das Problem der Einkommensverteilung zwischen Kapital und Arbeit," *Weltwirtschaftliches Archiv* 106, 1971, pp. 1–33.

11 Bernholz, P. "Superiority of Roundabout Processes and Positive Rate of Interest," *Kyklos* 24, 1971, pp. 687–721. Bernholz faults Böhm-Bawerk's analysis for not being convincing "because of crudeness and inadequacies of the methods applied." He criticizes Böhm's followers for introducing time as a factor of production, "thus hindering an integration of the capital theory proposed with the traditional theory of production." (p. 687) In his framework of a two-period model Bernholz seeks to demonstrate that, under certain conditions, the greater productivity of roundabout production processes always yields a positive interest rate. His models also show "that population growth favours the existence of a positive interest rate because it tends to impede or remove capital saturation." (p. 720) *Grundlagen der Politischen Okonomie*, Vol. 1, Tübingen: J. C. Mohr, 1972; P. Bernholz and M. Faber, "Interest Rate, Growth Rate, Roundaboutness and Impatience" in *University Basel, Discussion Paper No. 2*, December 1975.

12 Faber, M., "Die "österreichische Zinstheorie und das Neumann-Modell" in *Discussion Paper No. 10*, Department of Economics, University of Berlin, 1973. For a critique of Faber's Austrian Theory cf. Gerhard O. Orosel, "Faber's Modern Austrian Capital Theory: A Critical Survey" in *Zeitschrift für Nationalökonomie*, Vol. 41, 1981, pp. 141–155. And for Faber's reply cf. Ibid., pp. 157–176.

13 Böhm-Bawerk's most important critics who invited his assiduous rejoinders were one of Germany's most famous statisticians, L. von Bortkieroicz, and America's first mathematical economist, Irving Fisher. Cf. 1912/59, 150–193.

14 Böhm-Bawerk was in great demand as a civil servant. He served as secretary of the Austrian treasury in three different administrations as vice-president of a commission conducting hearings on a return to the

gold standard, and as chief justice of an administrative court of appeals. Cf. *Gesammelte Schriften*, 1924. ed. F. X. Weisz (Vienna: Hölder-Pickler-Tempsky).

15   Fetter's limited influence on modern economic thought must be ascribed to his withdrawal from value and distribution theory during the last three decades of his life and his preoccupation with the alleged evils of monopolistic practices.

16   Looking upon interest as flowing from "an increase in the efficiency of the original factors of production – man and nature," it is not surprising that Wicksell favored democratic socialism. In his belief, the coming of great inequities of income and wealth created severe social problems. He argued for nationalization of industry but held that farming and genuinely competitive enterprises be left in private hands. He pleaded for social programs such as social security and basic health care. His pleas were heard and acted upon in Sweden which after fifty years of Social Democratic rule is reflecting the Wicksellian vision.

17   Fisher like Wicksell was a congenital reformer, an inveterate crusader. Always aggressive and persistent, many of his contemporaries discounted his scientific work and regarded him as a "crank." Science and reform often interfused in his work. His mission was always to reform and save the world from impending disaster. His theory made him persistently optimistic about the economy and stock prices, even after the 1929 crash. It is significant that he failed to understand the economic changes of the 1920s and 30s and, therefore, lost his family wealth. As a pauper during the last fifteen years of his life and depending on Yale University charity to buy his home and save him from eviction, his explanations rightly deserve to be open to question. Cf. I. N. Fisher, 1956. *My Father Irving Fisher*. New York: Comet Press.

18   Ludwig von Mises was one of the great scholars of the 20th century and certainly its greatest economist. He taught and touched nearly all eminent economists who call themselves Austrian and through them reached an ever widening circle of young scholars who proudly acknowledge to be Austrian. There would be no vibrant Austrian school today if Mises had not stood upright when he was alone, pointing the way for generations to come. Cf. Rothbard, M. N. 1973. *The Essential von Mises*. Washington, D.C.: Ludwig von Mises Institute; Moss, L. (ed.) 1976. *The Economics of Ludwig von Mises: Toward a Critical Reappraisal*. Kansas City: Shead & Ward; Andrews, J. K. (ed.) 1981. *Homage to Mises: The First Hundred Years*. Hillsdale, Mich.: Hillsdale College Press. Kirzner, I. 1982. *Method, Process and Austrian Economics: Essays in Honor of Ludwig von Mises*. Lexington, Mass.: Lexington Books.

19   Hayek's view of economic phenomenon as "spontaneous" order seems to contradict the Mises proposition that human action is always "purposeful." If we define "spontaneous" as acting by impulse, natural feeling, temperament, or disposition, and "purposeful" as characterized by defined purpose and full of meaning, not merely instinctive but the result of valuation, both propositions run counter to each other. This writer readily identifies with the Misesian view. He must part company with Hayek on language as a spontaneous creation or money as a spontaneous medium of exchange. Surely, both man's language and monetary institutions were not invented or designed by genius creators but are the outcome of purposeful colloquial communication throughout the millennia.

20   Throughout his professional life Rothbard was a colorful scholar passionately committed to the cause of individual freedom, to Austrian economics, and the market order. He was a powerful mentor of the new libertarianism in the U.S., a popular writer who inspired millions with his vision of liberty and a vibrant scholar who made original contributions to economics, history, political science, law, ethics, and epistemology. His message was always too provocative and persuasive to be ignored.

21   Reisman questions the "discount approach" to interest income and instead credits the "demand and supply" constellations of consumers' goods and factors of production for the emergence of discounts. "The discount approach is, in fact, a denial of the law of supply and demand! I say this, because it seeks to exempt the formation of prices of factors of production from the operation of that law. In its eyes, only the prices of consumers' goods are determined by supply and demand; the prices of the factors of production are held to be determined directly by the application of a discount of the prices of consumers' goods. The truth is that the prices of factors of production are determined by supply and demand no less than the prices of consumers' goods and that the rate of discount (viz., profit) then emerges as the result of the differences between the demand / supply situation in the market for products and the demand / supply situation in the market for factors of production" (Reisman, 1996, p. 806). This writer wonders why there should be such persistent differences between the various demand / supply situations.

References

Andrews, J. K. (ed.) 1981. *Homage to Mises: The First Hundred Years.* Hillsdale, MI: Hillsdale College Press.

Bernholz, P. 1972. *Grundlagen der Politischen Okonomie*, Vol. I. Tübingen: J. C. Mohr.

Bernholz, P. and Faber, M. 1975. "Interest Rate, Growth Rate, Roundaboutness and Impatience" in *University Basel, Discussion Paper No. 2.*

Boettke, P. J. and Rizzo, M. J. 1995. *Advances in Austrian Economics.* Greenwood, CT: JAI Press, Inc.

Böhm-Bawerk, E. von. 1884/1959. *History and Critique.* Spring Mills, PA: Libertarian Press.

Böhm-Bawerk. E. von. 1889/1959. *Positive Theory.* Spring Mills, PA: Libertarian Press.

Böhm-Bawerk, E. von. 1912/1959. *Further Essays on Capital and Interest.* Spring Mills, PA: Libertarian Press.

Clark, J.B. 1886. *The Philosophy of Wealth.* Boston: Gin & Co.

Clark, J. B. 1899. *The Distribution of Wealth: A Theory of Wages, Interest and Profit.* New York: The Macmillan Co.

Dolan, E. G. (ed.) 1976. *The Foundations of Modern Austrian Economics.* Kansas City: Sheed & Ward.

Faber, M. 1973. "Die "Österreichische Zinstheorie und das NeumannModell" in *Discussion Paper No. 10.* Department of Economics, University of Berlin.

Fetter, F. 1902/1977. "'The Roundabout Process' in the Interest Theory," *Quarterly Journal of Economics.* Reprinted in *Capital, Interest, and Rent.*

Fetter, F. 1904/1977. "The Relations Between Rent and Interest," in *Papers and Proceedings of the Sixteenth Annual Convention.* American Economic Association. Reprinted in *Capital, Interest, and Rent.*

Fetter, F. 1904. *Principles of Economics.* New York: The Century Co.

Fetter, F. 1914/1977. "Interest Theories, Old and New" in *American Economic Review.* Reprinted in *Capital, Interest, and Rent.*

Fetter, F. 1915. *Economic Principles.* New York: The Century Co.

Fetter, F. 1927/1977. "Interest Theory and Price Movements," in *American Economic Review.* Reprinted in *Capital, Interest, and Rent.*

Fetter, F. 1977. *Capital, Interest, and Rent: Essays in the Theory of Distribution.* Edited by M. N. Rothbard. Kansas City: Shead Andrews and McMeel.

Fisher, I. 1906. *The Nature of Capital and Income.* New York: The Macmillan Co.

Fisher, I. 1907. *The Rate of Interest.* New York: Macmillan.

Fisher, I. 1930. *The Theory of Interest.* New York: Macmillan

Garrison, R. W. 1978. "Austrian Macroeconomics: A Diagramatical Exposition" in *New Directions of Austrian Economics.* Edited by L.M. Spadaro. Kansas City: Sheed, Andrews & McMeel.

Garrison, R. W. 1979. "In Defense of the Misesian Theory of Interest," *Journal of Libertarian Studies* 3, No. 2. (Summer, 1979), 141–149.

Garrison, R. W. 1982. "Austrian Economics as the Middle Ground: Comment on Loasby" in *Method, Process and Austrian Economics: Essays in Honor of Ludwig von Mises.* Edited by I.M. Kirzner. Lexington, MA: Lexington Books.

Gray, J. 1984. *Hayek on Liberty.* Oxford: Basil Blackwell.

Hayek, F. A. 1935/1967. *Prices and Production,* 2nd ed. London: Routledge and Kegan Paul.

Hayek, F. A. 1939. *Profits, Interest and Investment.* London: Routledge and Kegan Paul.

Hayek, F. A. 1941. *The Pure Theory of Capital.* London: Macmillan and Co.

Hayek, F. A. 1946. "The Methodology of Capital" in *Readings in the Theory of Income Distribution.* Edited by W. Fellner and B. F. Haley. Philadelphia: Blakiston.

Hayek, F. A. 1952. *The Counter-Revolution of Science: Studies on the Abuse of Reason.* Glencoe, IL: Free Press.

Hayek, F. A. 1972. *A Tiger by the Tail.* Edited by S. Shenoy, London: Institute for Economic Affairs.

Herbener, J. M. 1993. *The Meaning of Ludwig von Mises.* Norwell, MA: Kluwer Academic Publishers.

Hicks, J. R. 1965. *Capital and Growth.* Oxford: Clarendon Press.

Hicks, J. R. 1973. *Capital and Time: A Neo-Austrian Theory.* Oxford: Clarendon Press.

Hicks, J. R. 1973. "The Austrian Theory of Capital and its Rebirth in Modern Economics" in *Carl Menger and the Austrian School of Economics,* edited by J. R. Hicks and W. Weber. Oxford: Clarendon Press.

Hutchison, T. W. 1981. *The Politics and Philosophy of Economics: Marxians, Keynesians, and Austrians.* New York: New York University Press.

Kauder, E. 1965. *A History of Marginal Utility Theory.* Princeton, NJ: Princeton University Press.

Keynes, J.M. 1930/1971. *A Treatise of Money* in *The Collected Writings of John Maynard Keynes,* Vols. V and VI. London: Macmillan.

Keynes, J.M. 1936/1971. *The General Theory of Employment, Interest, and Money* in *The Collected Writings of John Maynard Keynes.* London: Macmillan.

Kirzner, I. M. 1966. *An Essay on Capital.* New York: A. M. Kelley.

Kirzner, I. M. 1979. *Perception, Opportunity, and Profit.* Chicago: The University of Chicago Press.

Kirzner, I. M. 1982.(ed.) *Method, Process, and Austrian Economics: Essays in Honor of Ludwig von Mises.* Lexington, MA: Lexington Books.

Kirzner, I. M. 1989. *Discovery, Capitalism and Distributive Justice.* Oxford: Basil Blackwell.

Kirzner, I. M. 1995. "Philosophical and Ethical Implications of Austrian Economics," in *The Foundations of Modern Austrian Economics.* Edited by E.G. Dolan. Kansas City: Sheed & Ward, Inc.

Kirzner, I. M. 1976. "Ludwig von Mises and the Theory of Capital and Interest '" in *The Economics of Ludwig von Mises.* Edited by L. S. Moss. Kansas City: Sheed & Ward.

Knight, F. H. 1921. *Risk, Uncertainty, and Profit.* Boston: Houghton Mifflin.

Knight. F. H. 1935. *The Ethics of Competition, and Other Essays.* London: Allen & Unwin.

Lutz, F. H. 1968. *The Theory of Interest.* Chicago: Aldine Pub.

Machlup, F. 1976. "Hayek's Contribution to Economics" in *Essays on Hayek.* Edited by F. Machlup. Hillsdale, MI: Hillsdale College Press.

Mill, J.S. 1848/1878. *Principles of Political Economy.* 8th ed. London: Longmans, Green, Reader, and Dyer.

Mises, L. von. 1933/1981. *Epistemological Problems of Economics.* New York: New York University Press.

Mises, L. von. 1949. *Human Action.* New Haven: Yale University Press.

Mises, L. von. 1957/1985. *Theory and History: An Interpretation of Social and Economic Evolution.* 2nd ed. Auburn, AL: Ludwig von Mises Institute.

Moss, L. (ed.) 1976. *The Economics of Ludwig von Mises: Toward a Critical Reappraisal.* Kansas City: Sheed & Ward.

O'Driscoll, G. P. 1977. *Economics as a Coordination Problem: The Contributions of Friedrich A. Hayek.* Kansas City: Shead Andrews and McMeel.

O'Driscoll, G. P. and Rizzo, M. J. 1985. *The Economics of Time and Ignorance.* Oxford: Basil Blackwell.

Orosel, G. O. 1981. "Faber's Modern Austrian Capital Theory: A Critical Survey" in *Zeitschrift für Nationalökonomie*, Vol. 41.

Pasinetti, L. L. 1974. *Growth and Income Distribution: Essays in Economic Theory.* Cambridge: Cambridge University Press.

Reisman, G. G. 1996. *Capitalism: A Treatise on Economics.* Ottawa, IL: Jameson Books.

Rizzo, M. ed. 1979. *Time, Uncertainty, and Disequilibrium.* Lexington, MA: Lexington Books, D.C. Heath & Co.

Robinson, J.V. 1937. *Essays in the Theory of Employment.* London: Macmillan.

Robinson, J.V. 1937 (b). *Introduction to the Theory of Employment.* London: Macmillan.

Robinson, J. V. 1956. *The Accumulation of Capital.* London: Macmillan.

Rothbard, M. N. 1962. *Man, Economy and State.* Princeton, NJ: D. Van Nostrand.

Rothbard, M. N. 1973. *The Essential von Mises.* Washington, D. C.: Ludwig von Mises Institute.

Rothbard, M. N. 1990. "Time Preference" in *Capital Theory.* Edited by John Eatwell, Murray Milgate, and Peter Newman. New York: W. W. Norton & Co.

Samuelson, P. A. 1978. "The canonical classical model of political economy" in *Journal of Economic Literature,* 16(4).

Schumpeter, J. A. 1939. *Business Cycles.* New York:McGraw-Hill Book Co.

Schumpeter, J. A. 1954. *History of Economic Analysis.* New York: Oxford University Press.

Sraffa, P. 1960. *Production of Commodities by Means of Commodities: Prelude to a Critique of Economic Theory.* Cambridge: Cambridge University Press.

Stigler, G. 1941. *Production and Distribution Theories: The Formative Period.* New York: The Macmillan Co.

Tintner, G. 1970. "Lineare Methoden der Nationalökonomie und die Produktionsperiode von Böhm-Bawerk" in *Zeitschrift für Nationalökonomie* 30.

Weizsäcker, C. C. von. 1971. "Die zeitliche Struktur des Produktionsprozesses und das Problem der Einkommensverteilung zwischen Kapital und Arbeit," in *Weltwirtschaftliches Archiv* 106.

White, L. H. 1977/1984. *The Methodology of the Austrian School Economists.* Auburn, AL: The Ludwig von Mises Institute.

Wicksell, K. 1893/1934. *Value, Capital and Rent.* London: Allen & Unwin.

Wicksell, K. 1901/1934. *Lectures on Political Economy,* Vol.I. Edited by Lionel Robbins. London: George Routledge and Sons.

Wicksell, K. 1911/1958. "Böhm-Bawerk's theory of interest" in *Selected Papers on Economic Theory,* edited by E. Lindahl. Cambridge, MA: Harvard University Press.

Chapter II:
The Fatal Franchise of Freedom: of Social Choice-Democracy

The Bitter Medicine of Freedom[*]

Anthony de Jasay

From the romantic age of political philosophy, many stirring images have come down to us. Some depict a people wrenching its freedom from the clutches of oppressors, native or foreign. Others show the lone individual fighting for his spiritual autonomy and material independence against totalitarian encroachment. Whatever the truth of these images in the past, their relevance for the present is fading. The issue of freedom in our civilization is changing its character. It is not so much despots, dictators or totalitarian creeds that menace it. In essence, we do.

It is far from evident that democratic control of government is usually conducive to the preservation of liberal practices and values, let alone to their enhancement. Anti-liberal ideologies gain and retain credence in as much as they suit our inclinations, legitimize our interests and warrant our policies. We love the rhetoric of freedom-talk and indulge in it beyond the call of sobriety and good taste, but it is open to serious doubt that we actually like the substantive content of freedom. On the whole we do not act as if we did. I shall presently be arguing that it is an austere substance, not unlike bitter medicine that we do not naturally relish – though it can become an acquired taste for the exceptional individual – but take only when the need presses. My object is to show that contrary to the sweetness-and-light views of freedom, it is this more austere view that best explains why we keep praising it while in our politics we are busily engaged in shrinking its domain.

Taking Freedom Easy and In Vain

Countless notions of greater or lesser woolliness attach to freedom, and a full review of its alternative definitions would be tedious. The very limited sample I choose to look at, however, seems to me representative of the main live political currents of the age. The context of each is non-Robinsonian, in that it deals with a person's freedom as constituted by the options and constraints of his social life. The subject, in other words, is not the individual facing his Creator, nor the solitary player in the game against Nature, but the person acting with or against other persons. The freedom in question is a property of one's conduct in relation to the conduct of others, rather than an affirmation of free will, 'inner' freedom or some other proposition about the causation of human actions or the state of men's minds.

The rudiments of the liberal definition identify a free person as one who faces no man-made obstacles to choosing according to his preferences, provided only that his doing so does not cause a tort to another person. This idea of freedom takes preference and choice conceptually for granted, does not worry about how preference can be recognized unless it is revealed by choice, nor does it seek to make statements about the nature of the self. It is practical political freedom. This, however, means something far more general than conventional 'political liberty,' i.e. the freedom of each to affect collective decisions to some albeit minimal extent through a regulated political process, and normally understood to consist of the freedoms of speech, assembly, press and election. Instead, it is political in the broader sense that it results from the political process, depending as it does on collectively imposed institutional restrictions of greater or lesser stringency on the opportunity set open to choice. As Frank Knight put it, it is coercion and not freedom that needs defining (Knight, 1943, p. 75).

By extention of his view, the corollary of freedom is said to be the reduction of coercion 'as much as is possible' (Hayek, 1960, p. 11, 21); in the same vein, it is independence from the 'arbitrary will' of another (p. 11). Giving the matter an ethical dimension, freedom is represented as a state of affairs that permits one to choose any feasible option provided that his doing so does not harm another person.[1] Loosely related to the principles of *noncoercion, independence* and *no-harm*, is the Kantian principle of 'equal liberty.' It appears to refer to a state of affairs where one person's options are not subjected to a man-made restriction to which those of any other person are not also subjected. This formulation, however, is incomplete. Needless to say, neither Kant nor those, notably Herbert Spencer, who followed him in employing this form of words, mean that the 'extent' or 'quantity' of freedom in a state of affairs was irrelevant and only its 'distribution' needed to be of a certain kind – i.e. 'equal.' If such a distribution were the sole criterion, it would not matter how much or how little there was to be had, as long as everybody had as much or as little as everybody else. That freedom demanded to be both 'maximized' and 'distributed equally,' was made explicit by Rawls in his adaption of Kant's principle.[2]

In these versions, freedom appears as a unitary concept. It may or may not be capable of variation by degrees. Hayek suggests more than once that it is indivisible; it is either present or absent; we either have it or we do not; we either choose freely or we are coerced. The 'size' of the feasible, uncoerced opportunity set does not affect the issue, nor does coercion vary in extent or intensity (Hayek, 1960, p. 13).

Liberals of the orthodox tradition, for whom it is a property of the relation between individual preference and choice – a relation devoid of obstacles erected by politics except where such obstacles serve to shelter the freedom of others – do not as a rule recognize a plurality of freedoms. The plural usage, on the other hand, is fairly typical of heterodox, 'redistributor' liberals who deal in numerous freedoms to accede to desirable states or activities, designated as 'positive,' as well as in 'freedom from' hunger, want, insecurity and other undesirable conditions. Dewey's freedom as 'power to do' also belongs to this category, where diverse 'freedoms' represent power to do diverse things. It is not hard to appreciate that these heterodox freedom concepts are in essence rhetorical proxies standing for diverse goods, some tangible and others intangible, that are perfectly recognizable under their everyday names and need not be described indirectly in the guise of 'freedoms.' Freedom from hunger is an oblique statement about food being a good, and about a condition in which one is not deprived of it; it can be turned into a general norm under which none must be deprived of it. Similarly, freedom of worship conveys, positively, that it is good for each to be able to profess his own faith, and normatively that none must be deprived of access to this good. Employing freedom-speak in discussing various goods can at best underline the importance we attach to them; at worst, it confuses issues of autonomy and coercion with issues of wealth and welfare. The term freedom in the classical sense seeks to express – whether successfully or not – the unhindered transformation of preference into action, the ability of each to do as he sees fit. 'Freedom to' and 'freedom from,' on the other hand, seem to refer to the extent to which options to act are available to satisfy individual or even 'social' preferences.

In a spectacular logical leap which speaks well of his insight if not of his talents of lucid explanation, Marx 'unmasks' the liberal foundation of freedom: 'The practical application of the right of man to freedom is the right of man to private property (Marx, 1843, p. 229).

Antagonistic to liberal inspiration, he turns to wholly different categories to construct a concept of freedom. The Marxist concept has nothing – or nothing explicit – to do with the passage, unobstructed or not, from individual preference to chosen action, a passage of which private property is the privileged vehicle. The corollary of Marxist freedom is not the absence of coercion of the individual by his fellow men through the political authority, but escape from the realm of material necessity, from the tyranny of things.[3] Its subject is not the individual, but mankind.[4] Self-realization – 'rehumanization' – of the latter from the 'reified' social relations of 'commodity production' *is* the state of freedom.

To the extent that this thickly metaphoric language is intelligible, it seems to mean that humanity is free when, no longer subjected to the unconscious and impersonal force of things, which is Marx's code name for the automatism of a market economy, it collectively masters its own fate by deliberate, rational planning. The passage from the realm of necessity to that of freedom is both the cause of, and is caused by, the passage from the realm of scarcity to that of plenty.

Vacuity and Moral Truism

One common feature shines luminously through these various concepts, definitions and normative principles of freedom. Each as it stands is a moral truism, impossible to dispute or reject because each is defined, if at all, in terms of indisputable superiority. Each, moreover, is defined in terms of conditions whose fulfillment cannot be empirically ascertained – when is coercion at its 'possible minimum'? – when is man not subject to the 'tyranny of things'? The proposition that a state of affairs is free is rendered 'irrefutable,' 'unfalsifiable.' Each, finally, expresses a condition which, if it prevails, one can enjoy without incurring any costs in exchange. Consequently, the question of trade-offs does not arise and it would be lunatic to say, with regard to any one of the rival concepts, that on balance one would rather not have it. Renunciation of freedom, so defined, would not bring any compensating benefit either to the self or to others, nor reduce any attendant sacrifice or disadvantage. Unlike values we buy by giving up some comparable value, it is always better to get and keep such freedom than to give it up.

No great analytical effort is needed to see that freedom concepts have this apple-pie-and-motherhood feature when they are vacuous, their stated conditions being impossible either to violate or to fulfill. They make no identifiable demand on anyone and lack any content one could disagree with. That coercion should be reduced 'as much as possible' is, *pace* Hayek, a vacuous precept unless integrated into a stringent and clear doctrine of 'necessary coercion.'[5] Only then would the precept get any definite meaning, for only then would it be referring to some recognizable standard or measure of how far it is 'possible' to reduce coercion, and only then could it identify the actual level of coercion as higher than necessary. Otherwise, any level could be as compatible with freedom as any other, and the most shamelessly instrusive dictators of this world would all be recognized as libertarians doing the best they could to avoid unnecessary coercion.

Immunity from the 'arbitrary will' of another is similarly empty, for the will of another is judged arbitrary or not, according to the reasons the judge imputes to it. If another's decision rests on identifiable reasons, it may be unwelcome to me because it restricts my ability to act as I would, but I can only have a good claim to immunity from it in the name of my freedom if I have a valid argument to rule out those reasons. Bad reasons leave the decision unjustified, and absence of reasons makes it arbitrary – surely a relatively rare case. Manifestly, however, the crux of the problem is that the claim to immunity from the will of another stands or falls with somebody's judgment of the reasons for the latter; and lest his judgment itself be arbitrary, it must be guided by an independent system of laws, customs, moral principles and whatever else goes into the determination of a person's liberties in his dealings with others. Immunity from the 'arbitrary' will of another seems to mean no more than that one's liberties must be respected; its use to define freedom is simply a recourse to a tautologous identity between it and the non-violation of liberties – whatever they are – whereas a meaningful definition should be capable to serve as a determinant, or more loosely as an argument about what those liberties ought to be. However, the rule that in a state of freedom nobody should be subject to the arbitrary will of another, does not commit anybody to anything beyond respecting well-defined rules of tort. It may in fact be that the immunity concept of freedom and the normative rule it provides is even more trivial than that, for it could be held that in these matters liberties are well-defined only if they are codified, and the rule then boils down to the banality that in a state of freedom nobody should break the law.

The harm principle turns out, on inspection, to lack specific content for much the same reason as the immunity principle. Under it, the political authority in a state of freedom does not prevent – or 'artificially' raise the cost of – acts that are harmless to others; it does not allow anyone to interfere with the harmless acts of others; and prevents and sanctions harmful acts. However, there is no very evident binary division of acts into a harmful and a harmless class.[6] Some of our acts may possibly be beneficial or at worse indifferent to everybody else, though it would no doubt be hard to make sure that this was the case. As regards these acts, there is a clear enough reason why we should be left free to commit them. But this does not take liberty very far. For there is a vast number of other acts that are harmful to somebody to some degree, having as they do some unwelcome effect on somebody's interests, ranging in a continuous spectrum from the merely annoying to the gravely prejudicial.

This must be so far a variety of reasons, the simplest one being that in any realm of scarcity – scarce goods, crowded *Lebensraum*, limited markets, competitive examinations, rival careers, exclusive friendship, possessive love – one person's chosen course of action preempts and prejudges the choices of others, sometimes helpfully but mostly adversely. The place and the prize one gets is not available to runners-up, no matter how badly they want or 'need' it. Where does 'harm' to them begin? Common sense tells us that, depending on circumstances, there are acts you must be free to engage in even though they harm my interests, hurt my feelings or expose me to risk. How to tell these acts from those which are to be prevented? Define them, and you have defined the rights that may be *exercised* – 'positive' freedom – and must not be *violated* – 'negative' freedom – the two kinds appearing as two perspectives of one and the same system of 'rights.' The harm principle is vacuous prior to a system of liberties and rights, while posterior to it all it does say is that the holders of liberties and rights are not to be deprived of them either by the state or by anybody else. Concisely, the harm principle affirms no more than that liberties are liberties and rights are rights.

The Kantian equal liberty, whether or not equipped with a maximizing clause, is baffling in its lack of guidance about what exactly is, or ought to be made, equal – and subject to equality, maximal. It appears, at first blush, to have to do with the distribution among individuals of something finite, quantifiable and variable, analogous to a stretch devoid of obstacles, a level surface, a private space, a protected sphere. If this were a possible interpretation and freedom were a quantifiable dimension – or dimensions – of states of affairs, it would make perfect sense to say that one person disposed of more of it than another – a test of equality – or could have more if another had less – a test that problems of distribution are technically soluble – and that if there were more of it altogether, at least some – and subject to solving problems of distribution, all – could have more, which may also mean that by giving some more of it, it can be maximized – a test that maximization is a practical objective. The difficulty is that the analogy between unobstructed length, surface or space, and freedom, is just that, an analogy and no more. There seems to be no apparent way in which freedom could be quantified. I suggest that two persons are 'equally free' has the same cognitive status as that they are 'equally happy' or 'equally handsome'; these are statements of somebody's judgment from the evidence, but the same evidence could have induced somebody else to pass a different judgment and it is impossible conclusively to settle, from the evidence alone, which of two contradictory judgments is more nearly right. There is no agreed arbitrator, nor is a last-resort test built into the practice of these sujective comparisons for settling contrary judgments and perceptions. On the view that interpersonal comparisons of such states of mind conditions as utility, happiness or satisfaction are a category-mistake to begin with, and that the freedom of one person, being as it is bound up with subjective perceptions, is similarly incomparable to the freedom of another, the whole practice of seeking their levels or the extent of differences between them may be logically suspect anyway. In its normative version, 'equal freedom' is no more stringent than Dworkin's 'equal concern and respect,' the central plank in his democratic ethics, rightly dismissed by Raz with the deadpan finding that it 'seems to mean that everyone has a right to concern and respect' (Raz, 1986, p. 220). Like 'equal respect,' the norm of 'equal freedom' is unexceptionable, due in no small measure to its non-committal vagueness: practically *any* feasible state of affairs can be claimed, without fear of rebuttal, to be satisfying such norms.[7]

If it is reasonable to read the Marxist concept of freedom as emancipation from the regime of 'reified relations' and mastery over one's material destiny, and then to translate this into less exalted English as the abolition of commodity and labor markets, the concept is extravagant but not vacuous. 'Abolition of the market' and 'resource allocation by the political authority' have sufficiently precise factual content that can be empirically recognized as being or not being the case. Unlike 'arbitrary will,' 'minimum necessary coercion' or 'equal liberty,' they are ascertainable features of given social state of affairs: they either obtain or they do not. A Ministry of Planning and Rationing cannot very well be 'deconstructed' and shown to be 'really' a market in thin disguise. Where Marxist freedom nevertheless convicts itself of vacuousness and moral truism is in tirelessly transforming and qualifying descriptive statements, till they cease to describe anything that is ascertainable. 'Servitude' is not to the conditions of the market, but to its 'blind caprice,' its 'irrationality'; absence of central resource allocation is a 'chaotic, self-destructive' system; 'the product is master of the producer'; 'man, too, may be commodity' and as such becomes 'a plaything of chance' (Engels, 1891, p. 680–1). Production under socialist planning is not in obedience to the instructions of the political authority – a testable statement – but 'according to need' – an irrefutable vacuity. Any situation, whatever its characteristic empirical data, can be qualified as harmonious or a tooth-and-claw jungle war; any resource allocation can safely be called socially optimal or condemned as 'bureaucratic,' hence failing to produce 'according to needs.' There is the compulsion to agree to the moral truism that rational, conscious social deliberation is more conducive to the freedom of mankind than irrational, unconscious thrashing about in the dark; but as we can never tell which is which, the agreement is easy; freedom's name is taken in vain and does not commit anyone to anything.

The Freedom That Hurts

The rough underside of freedom is responsibility for oneself. The fewer the institutional obstacles an individual faces in choosing acts to fit his preferences, the more his life is what he makes it, and the less excuse he has for what he has made of it. The looser the man-made constraints upon him, the less he can count on others being constrained to spare his interests and help him in need. The corollary of an individual's discretion to contribute to or coldly ignore the purposes of the community is that he has no good claims upon it to advance his purposes. It may be that immunity from the 'arbitrary will' of others is coextensive with freedom, but so is dependence on one's own talents, efforts and luck. As Toynbee put it, the 'road from slavery to freedom is also the road from security to insecurity of maintenance.'

The agreeable corollary of my right is the duty of others to respect it; less agreeably, *their* right entails *my* duty. Freedom, if it has ascertainable content, turns out to have attendant costs, and, if freedom has degrees, the greater it is, probably the higher is its opportunity cost. Trade-offs between freedom and other goods are manifest facts of social life, though it may be embarrassing to admit to our better selves how often we take advantage of them. By no means is it evident that men want all the freedom that tyrannical or 'bureaucratic' political systems deny them.

The less nebulous and the more matter-of-fact is the content of freedom, the more obtrusive become its costs. Nowhere is this so clear as in the matter of the most contested safeguard of freely chosen individual action, that is private property. Freedom of contract, privacy and private property rights are mutually entailed. Complete respect for either member of the triad would exclude taxation. Even when it has no deliberate redistributive function, taxation simultaneously violates privacy, property rights and the freedom of contract as the taxpayer loses the faculty to dipose of part of his resources by voluntary contract, and must permit the political authority to dispose of it by command. A reconciliation between the freedom of contract – and by implication, private property and taxation – is offered by social contract theory, whose assumptions lead to taxation, as well as political obedience in general, being recognized as if it were voluntarily undertaken.

There is a tendency, cutting across the political spectrum from left to right, to see private property as divisible into several distinct and independent rights (Alchian and Demsetz 1973, p. 18). While this position is certainly tenable, its consequence is to encourage the view that restrictions on transfers of ownership, rent, dividend and price controls, the regulation of corporate control etc., are consistent with the integrity of private property. If the latter is to be regarded as a 'bundle' consisting of a number of separable rights, any one of these measures leaves all other rights within the bundle inviolate; yet any one of them is a violation of the freedom of contract. No ambiguity about their mutual entailment arises when property is conceived as an integral, indivisible right.

Adherence to any maximizing principle of freedom[8] *prima facie* implies non-violation of the freedom of contract, for it would be extravagant to maintain that its restriction, whatever its purportedly beneficial effects on, say, efficiency or income distribution, somehow leaves intact, let alone contributes to maximize, freedom in general. Moreover, if freedom is really about the unobstructed faculty of every sane adult person to be the judge of his own interest, acting as he sees fit and 'doing what he desires' (Mill, 1848, ch. 5), freedom of contract must be its irreducible hard core. To argue in the same breath for maximized (and 'equal') freedom in general and restricted freedom of contract, seems to me to presuppose that we judge *unilateral* and potentially 'Pareto-inferior' acts not requiring the consent of a contracting party by a liberal standard, bilateral and presumably 'Pareto-superior' ones, depending on willing reciprocity of two or more parties, by a more severe one. Yet this is surely applying the standards the wrong way round. If a double standard were admissible, and necessary to sort out actions that *should* from those that should *not* be interfered with, the easier one should be applied to contracts since, unlike unilateral acts, they have passed a prior test of mutual consent by the parties most directly concerned. The chosen action of one person that is not contingent on the agreed cooperation of another and may leave the latter worse off, can hardly have a better claim to the social *laissez passer* of freedom from legalized obstruction, than the proposed action that must, for its realization, first obtain the agreement and fit in with the matching proposed action of a potential contracting party.

Insistence on freedom of contract and on its corollaries, property and privacy, is a hard position that attracts only a minority constituency of doctrinaires on the one hand, old-fogey-nostalgics of a better past that never really was, on the other. Such a constituency is naturally suspect. Its stand offends the moral reflexes of a broad public; for it is yet another moral truism that fair prices, fair rents, fair wages and conditions of employment, fair trade, fair competition are incontrovertibly better and worthier of approval than prices, rents, wages, etc. that have merely been agreed in a bargain without being necessarily fair. Anyone who contests this may be putting an ulterior motive above justice, and the onus of proving the contrary is on him.

A somewhat more clever argument that does not directly beg the question of fairness holds that even if a bargain between willing parties at some point on their contract curve is 'in itself' better than failing to agree and staying off the curve, some points are nevertheless better than others for one party, worse for the other. In two-person or two-group face-to-face dealings, the actual point they agree on is partly a matter of their relative bargaining power, which must in turn depend on the distribution or wealth, will, skill and so forth. Untrammelled freedom of contract subject only to no force and fraud thus gives 'a moral blessing to the inequalities of wealth,'[9] and, for that matter, of abilities and other advantages. Commitment to is a commitment *both* to a maximizing principle of freedom and to non-interference with a given distribution of natural and acquired assets.

An attempt to escape from this commitment, with which many feel ill at ease and vulnerable, is to promote the idea that there could be an initial distribution of advantages that would act as a 'level playing field.' Once this special distribution is achieved – by redistribution of acquired and transferable assets, such as wealth, and by compensatory measures of 'positive discrimination' in education to offset natural and non-transferable advantages, such as talent and intelligence – freedom of contract becomes not only compatible with justice but is the very means to it. It produces 'pure procedural justice,' in the same way as a game played by the rules on a level playing field by definition produces a just result. This particular distribution-cum-compensatory-discrimination amounts to a state of equal opportunity for all. Under equality and opportunity, freedom of contract gives rise to outcomes that need not be overridden in the interest of justice. Equality of opportunity, freedom of contract and just outcomes, constitute a triadic relation such that any two entail the third. In terms of causation, the first two jointly constitute the procedure whose outcome is distributive justice.

This attempt at squaring freedom with justice must clear two hurdles, the first substantive, the second analytical. The substantive hurdle concerns the practical possibility of levelling the playing-field, instead of perversely making it more uneven in the attempt. I do not intend to dicuss this problem (except to note that it is a genuine one), and could not resolve it if I did. The second hurdle consists in the argument for procedural justice proving to depend on self-contradictory reasoning. A distribution of resources and advantages is both an end-state, and a starting position leading to a new distribution. The object of a particular initial distribution D, offering equal opportunities, is to have the freedom of contract to produce just outcomes. However, whatever outcome D' it did produce will differ from the initial equal-opportunity distribution D; some people will have gotten ahead of the position – in terms of wealth, skills, reputation, place in the social network – assigned to them in the equal-opportunity distribution, others will have lagged behind it. (Countless handicap races have been run on the world's race courses but despite the best efforts of expert handicappers, there is to my knowledge no record of a single race ever producing a dead heat of *all* the runners). We need not decide whether this is an empirical law or a logical necessity. Such will be the just outcome of the first round; however, this just end-state represents a new distribution D' of assets and advantages that, unlike the initial D, no longer offers equal opportunities for the second round. Equality of opportunity must be restored by redistribution, positive discrimination and so forth. The just end-state D' generated by equal opportunities and freedom of contract in the first round offers the participants unequal opportunities for the second round, and must be overridden to secure the justice of the end-state to be generated in it, and so on to the third and all subsequent rounds to the end of time.

The contradiction in the reasoning of many liberals who want to embrace a plurality of values, seek the reconciliation of freedom and justice, and find in equality of opportunity combined with freedom of contract the joint necessary and sufficient conditions of a procedural type of social justice, resides in this: 1) a particular end-state distribution D, and only D, is consistent with equality of opportunity, 2) equality of opportunity combined with freedom of contract engenders non-D, and only non-D, 3) D is not compatible with procedural distributive justice, 4) therefore equality of opportunity, freedom of contract and procedural distributive justice are not mutually compatible.

The reader will remark that if equality of opportunity is not itself a final value, but has only instrumental value in bringing about a certain valuable end-state, yet that kind of end-state must continually be overridden because it is inconsistent with the maintenance of equality of opportunity, the instrumental value of the latter is fleeting and self-destructive. If it is to be commended, it must be on its own merits as a final value, and not for its instrumental capacity to bring about procedural justice in distribution. If no equivalent procedure suggests itself, the attempt at procedural distributive justice must be considered a failure, the justice or otherwise of a distribution must be ascertained in some other manner, such as by listening to the moral consensus of public opinion, and the just distribution either given up as too costly and awkward to achieve, or enforced by direct measures that *ipso facto* violate the freedom of contract and the corollary rights of property and privacy.

Twist it as we may, the dilemma will not go away. The hard sort of freedom that is more than moral truism and noncommittal, costless piety, forbids the exercise of social choice over questions of 'who gets what.' Yet that is the crucial domain over which voters, groups, classes and their coalitions generally aspire, and often succeed, to turn the power of the political authority to their advantage. More freedom is less scope for collective choice and vice versa; there is trade-off which democratic society has used these past hundred years or so to whittle down freedom sometimes overtly, sometimes surreptitiously and the most often fairly unconsciously. The process of whittling down has been promoted and justified by a more plausible and seductive ideology than anything classical liberals could muster.

No Hard Choices

The ideology of the expanding domain of social choice used to have, and probably has not lost, the ambition of showing how this is compatible with the avoidance of hard choices, notably the preservation of freedom. Two key theses serve as its twin pillars.

The first, put briefly, concerns the reliance on reason. It seems to affirm that, whether embodied in the knowledge of a technocratic elite or in the consensual wisdom born of democratic debate, reason is the only guide we should follow, and, in a more exacting and activist version, we should never fail to follow. Reason is in most circumstances able to detect faults in the functioning of economic and social arrangements, and can prescribe the likely remedy. This thesis is common to doctrines as disparate as Benthamite utilitarianism, Saint Simonian, Marxist or just *ad hoc* socialism, Fabian compromise, 'constructivist' system-building and Popperite trial-and-error social engineering. They are consequentialist doctrines, willing the means if they will the end: they fear no taboos and stop at no barriers of a non-reasoned and metaphysical nature.

All hold, albeit implicitly, that government whose vocation it is to elicit and execute social choices, is a uniquely potent tool which it is wasteful and inefficient not to employ to capacity for bringing about feasible improvements. Government, and it alone, can correct the deformities of markets. It can deal with unwanted externalities and regulate the conduct of private enterprise when the divergence of private and social costs and returns misguides it by false signals. Forgoing society's political power to improve results in these respects, and indeed in any others, is irrational and obscurantist.

Without actually being a series of truism, the easy plausibility of this thesis makes it near-invincible in public debate. Counter-arguments, if directed against 'excessive interference' and 'bureaucratic busybodyness,' are irrefutable but ineffective, since meliorist measures dictated by reason are never meant to be excessive or bureaucratic. A general plea to leave well alone is, to all intents and purposes, a defeatist or uncaring stance against trying to do better. Each policy, each measure is defended piecemeal by reason, on its separate merits. The perhaps unintended sum of winning piecemeal arguments for doing this and that, is a win for government intervention as a general practice. The twin of the thesis about reason is about justice. The former aims at allocative efficiency, the latter at the right distribution of the product. The dual structure of the domain of social choice suggested by this division of aims, implies that logically and temporally production comes first, distribution follows second. Things are produced, as Mill believed, according to 'the laws of economics,' and once they are there, become available for distribution according to some other law or precept. Such has been the position of Christian Socialists since high medieval times, and such is that of redistributor liberals from Mill and T.H. Green to Rawls. Distributions caused by the hazard of heredity, heritage and history may be freely altered, subject only to limits set by expediency, by social choice which is sovereign over the matter. They ought to be altered, to conform to some moral standard, because they are morally arbitrary.

The charge of moral arbitrariness, if it is upheld, means no more than it says, namely that rewards are not, or not wholly, determined by the moral features of a social state of affairs: the morally arbitrary distribution fails to fulfill the positive prediction that people's incomes, etc. depend on their deserts, as well as the normative postulate that they ought to depend on them. However, a cognitive diagnosis of arbitrariness might be applied to a distribution not only from the moral, but also from the economic, legal, social or historical points of view. A morally arbitrary distribution fails to conform to a moral theory; arbitrariness, however, may also obtain with respect to economic, legal or historical theories of distribution as well. If the actual distribution is partly determined by genetic endowments and their development, character, education, wealth and chance, which seems to me a sensible hypothesis, it has, from the point of view of any theory which does not properly account for these factors, an ineradicable property of uncaused randomness, or to use the value-loaded synonym, 'arbitrariness.' Thus, we can say that, in terms of the marginal productivity theory of factor rewards, the distribution of factor incomes in the Soviet Union is arbitrary. That, however, does not in itself condemn it. Arbitrariness is an obstacle to explaining or predicting, and it is also the absence of reasons for upholding or commending a particular distribution, but it is not a reason for changing it (Atiyah, 1979, p. 337). Some further, positive argument is needed to make the case that an arbitrary distribution ought to be purged of its random features and transformed into one that fully obeys some ordering principle drawn from a moral (or some other) theory.

It would be too easy if the ideology which, for its completeness, needed a theory of distributive justice, could validate the latter by the mere claim, however well founded, that the actual distribution was arbitrary. The theory needs the support of axioms that must be independend, difficult to reject and adequate. However, what axioms will bear the weight of a theory that must justify the subjection of who-gets-what questions to the political authority? Neither moral desert[10] nor the various versions of egalitarianism are difficult enough to reject.

Moral desert lacks independence, in that what is judged as morally deserved, obviously depends on an (at least implicit) moral theory guiding such judgments. Only prior agreement on such a theory, and notably on its implications for distributive justice, can secure agreed judgments of moral desert. They are indeterminate without the support of the theory, hence cannot serve as its antecedents.

Unlike moral desert, egalitarianism is at least not circular, and can be, though it rarely is, non-vacuous, i.e. its necessary conditions can be so defined that whether they are fulfilled or not becomes an empirical question. However, little else is left to be said for it. As an instrumental value, it used to be bolstered by consequentialist arguments, e.g. maximization of utility from a given total income, better satisfaction of 'real needs' or reduced pain of envy, that no longer enjoy much intellectual credit. As an ultimate, non-instrumental value that need not be argued for, it retains the emotional appeal it always had and probably always will have; paradoxically, however, the clearer it becomes that the appeal is essentially emotional, the more its effect fades.

On the whole, like certain seductive mining prospects that have been sadly spoiled by the drilling of core samples, distributive justice loses some of its glitter in analysis. 'A distribution ought to be just' is a plausible requirement. 'A just distribution ought to correspond to moral deserts,' or 'a just distribution ought to be equal' are a good deal easier to contradict. Moreover, attempts to put such norms into practice have not helped either, ranging as they did from the disappointing when they were ineffective, to the disastrous when they were effective. Sir Stafford Cripps, Olaf Palme and Willy Brandt have done much to make redistributive compromises unappealing. Pol Pot and Nicolae Ceauscescu have done as much for the uncompromising variety.

A more ingenious strategy proceeds by revising the order of the arguments. The usual sequence is to propose that, 1) the existing distribution is arbitrary, 2) only non-arbitrary distributions can be just, 3) a just distribution conforms to an appropriate ordering principle, 4) social choice legitimately mandates the government to realize this conformity. Instead of this roundabout route to the sovereignty of social choice over distribution, it is more efficient directly to propose that the assets, endowments and other advantages that make the existing distribution what it is, are not rightfully owned by the persons to whom they are in various ways attached, but are the property of their community,[11] and it is up to the community to decide the disposal of the fruits of its property. Genetic qualities, wealth, acquired knowledge and organization all belong to society as a whole and are *eo ipso* subject to social choice, without any need for a legitimation drawn from controversial requirements of justice, and a debatable mandate for actually imposing them.

Distributions 'chosen by society' may or may not be just. They are *ipso facto* just only in case the moral axioms that are used to define the justice or otherwise of a distribution, are taken to be the same as those that help, by fixing the choice rule, to identify an alternative as the 'socially chosen' one. This means, broadly speaking, that if in a given politial society the 'chosen' alternative is some resultant of the wishes of its members, if every member's wish 'counts for one and no more than, one,' and the majority wish prevails, then the 'just' distribution is identified by the same rule in the same way. 'Just' then means 'chosen by society,' found to be such by a democratic process of search and consultation, or, more loosely, conforming to the moral consensus. It is just that a person should be allowed to keep what he has, and only if, more people than not think that he should. This is perhaps a brutal and unsympathetic statement of what the sovereignty of social choice implies, but it is by no means a caricature of it.

The real difference between the two ideological strategies for extending the domain of social choice consists in this: if assets, in the broad sense which includes wealth, skill and character, belong to individuals in a 'capitalist free-for-all,' there is a *prima facie* implication that it is their right to dispose of the resulting income, both 'earned' and the 'unearned.' Society, however, speaking by the medium of the 'social choice rule' might declare such an income distribution unjust, refuse to countenance it and proceed to its redistribution. In doing so, it would contradict itself, for it could not in the same breath both respect and violate a given set of property rights with the attendant freedom of contract. Its solution, adopted, as Hayek called them in the *Road to Serfdom*, by 'socialists of all parties' except the genuine ones, is to chop up property rights into a variety of separate rights, recognize and attach some to certain classes of asset or asset-holder, and detach others, depending on the origin, type or size of the asset or advantage in question, finally declaring its unshaken respect for the resulting mishmash. Ownership of property and the right to use, sell, bequeath, rent or consume it thus become disjointed, fitting together as *ad hoc* 'social choices' decree. In conjunction with this solution, society or its government can affirm allegiance to any innocuous notion of freedom, and for good measure even give it 'lexicographic priority,' that requires the non-violation of rights in general without committing itself to specific and potentially inconvenient rights, and to the freedom of contract in particular.

Genuine socialists, probably no longer a very numerous or happy class, face no such contradiction between private rights and the ambition for social choice to override them, and need not have recourse to the ambiguities of redistributor liberals. With property vested in society, it is 'social choice' that by rights distributes incomes, positions and ranks in the first place; it does not need to redistribute what it has distributed, hence it does not come into conflict with any right it may have recognized to begin with; the problem of the freedom of contract does not even arise.

One way or the other, as long as freedom is allowed to be 'soft,' nebulous, innocuous, costless, and as long as the claim that it is being respected and its conditions are fulfilled, remains 'unfalsifiable' because the conditions are vacuous and commit to little, there are no hard choices. Allocative efficiency and social justice can be pursued in conjunction with the 'greatest possible' and most 'equal' freedom. We can have it all. By contrast, the painful trade-offs imposed by laying down 'hard,' specific, falsifiable conditions of freedom can be made to stand out clearly. Privacy, private property and freedom of contract strike at the heart of 'social choice,' removing as they do from its domain many of the most valuable opportunities any decisive subset of society would use for imposing on the superset the choices and solutions it prefers, considers right or just, or expects to profit from.

Non-violation of privacy, private property and freedom of contract involves massive self-denial. It demands a large measure of renunciation of the use of political processes for advancing certain interests in conflict with others. Instead of getting their way, majorities may have to bargain and buy it by contractual means. It also involves negation of plausible and well-developed ideologies that would justify the use of political power to promote one's selfish or unselfish ends in the name of allocative efficiency or social justice.[12] Small wonder, then, that these principles of freedom are systematically violated or talked out of existence. The contrary would be surprising in a civilization with a good deal of political sophistication, skills of adversarial argument and no inconvenient taboos; a civilization like our own.

Undeserved Luck

The problem is not how to explain why enlightened men do not noticeably like the more-than-rhetorical freedom that imposes upon them self-denial, renunciation, responsibility and duty. It is to account for the far stranger fact that, perhaps for the first time in a hundred-odd years, this freedom most of us do not really like is nevertheless holding its own. It seems actually to have gained in some important countries of the political West, and has ceased to retreat in most others. From an abysmal starting level, it is clearly in the ascendant in the societies of the political 'East,' that had set out really to build socialism and have found that they have inadvertently joined the Third World in the process. Why should the relentless expansion of the domain of collective choice, which has all the logic of political power behind it, now be checked and reversed in so many different places?

Each of these societies has its particular case history; each is no doubt rich in particular lessons. This is not the occasion to survey their more bizarre episodes and their high and low moments. As always, however, each case history has much in common with every other. The chief common feature, to my mind, is that the cumulative imposition by 'social choice' of reasoned solutions to an infinity of problems in production and distribution, efficiency and justice, has gradually built up perverse effects, whose total weight finally sufficed to convert the afflicted society to the bitter medicine of freedom.

It is important to admit and indeed to underline that the attempted solutions were reasoned. The caprice of the tyrant played little part in modern attempts at social problem-solving. In each instance, some sort of rational case could be constructed for them. Nothing is easier than to state with hindsight that the case for solution A was 'obviously' false and owed its adoption to the stupidity or wickedness of politicians. Nothing is more dangerous than to follow up this train of thought with the all too frequent suggestion that because A was so obviously wrong, B ought to have been chosen. This is the sort of argument that would always justify one more try[13] And would give rise to an endless chain of measures, instead of the decisive abandonment of tinkering. Often we reason as if alternative measures and policies came with labels describing the likely effects of each, and perhaps also the 'objective' probability that a particular effect will manifest itself. If this were so, the social choice of policies would be a choice between sets of specified consequences, or their probability distributions. Better policies would therefore on the whole tend to be chosen in preference to worse ones. Logically the power of the political authority to put chosen policies into practice would be beneficial at least in the long run, over large numbers of measures; collective choice equipped with such coercive power would have a good chance of yielding better results than the sum of individual choices that has lacked such power; and the enlargement of the collective domain at the expense of 'hard' freedom would augment the scope for better results. Power, chance and scope would jointly work for progress, and speed us towards the meliorist ideal.

In reality, the labels the policies carry specify only the narrow band of their effects that have reasonably good visibility. Only hindsight shows that there always is, in addition, a broader and fuzzier band of consequences whose *ex ante* predictability must have been very low, very conjectural or simply non-existent. Whether this is so because our knowledge about these matters is inadequate though capable of improvement, or because they are inherently unknowable, is perhaps immaterial at any period in time for the consequentialist evaluation of a policy. There may, in addition, be effects that are reasonably predictable but so slow to mature that they get heavily discounted at the inception of a measure – discounting, of course, is a legitimate and indeed a mandatory operation in the rational calculus – and only begin seriously to hurt when the measure that has caused them it as good as forgotten together with the men who had chosen it.

I propose to call unwelcome consequences 'perverse' in a broad sense, not only when they are direct opposite of the main aim of a policy (e.g., a redistributive measure intended to decrease inequality which in fact increases it; a policy of import substitution which makes exports shrink more than imports; government sponsorship of research that actually retards technological progress, and so forth) but also when, acting over a more diffuse area, indirectly or in unexpected directions, they impose costs and reduce benefits so as to leave society worse off than if a given policy had not been adopted. I am aware that condemning a measure on this ground may be question-begging for two reasons. First, the imputation to it of particular unwelcome effects may be too conjectural when the supposed causation is indirect. It may be that lavish spending on arms over the last decade has for roundabout reasons weakned the war making ability and fighting prowess of both the great powers, but how can the diagnosis of cause and effect be made conclusive? Second, a judgment that society is on balance worse off when certain things, say inflation or child delinquency, have gone wrong but others, say care for the old or water pollution, have gone right, is forever fated to depend on how homogenous weights are to be assigned to heterogenous variables; give greater weight to the ones which have gone right, and you find society better off.

Nevertheless there are well within our memory unmitigated disasters, utter failures and glaring disproportions between outlay and return, where a distinct policy is so clearly the prime suspect in producing perverse effects that it is bad faith or intellectual preciosity to argue the incompleteness of the proof. The collectivization of land and the attendant pursuit of 'economies of scale' in agricultural and, for that matter, in manufacturing too, is now almost unanimously recognized as an act of self-mutilation that has done irreparable damage to the Soviet Union. Strengthening the powers, disciplinary cohesion and legal immunities of trade unions, and taking them into the corporatist conspiracy of the Macmillan, Wilson and Heath years is now, albeit less unanimously, seen as a major cause of the 'English disease.' The policy of forcibly diverting investment from the rest of Italy to its Mezzogiorno has not only cost the country dear in direct and indirect ways – that transferring benefits from one part of society to another is not costless is after all quite consistent with the fond supposition that the exercise nevertheless has a 'positive sum' – but may not even have been of real net benefit to the Mezzogiorno.

There are less localized examples of once respected policies that are now highly suspect of perverse effects. Progressive taxation is one: even its natural advocates have learnt to say that it must not be 'too' progressive. Free, universal, nonselective formal education, no 'streaming,' no elitism, diplomas for all, open access for all to universities crowned by the principle of one man-one Ph.D., is another. We are discovering that it hinders the education of those who could profit from it and wastes the time of the rest, breeds student unrest and disappointment, and buys these personal and social blessing at a near-crippling cost to the community's finances. Public policies of welfare and public guarantees (including compulsory insurance) against risks and wants of various kinds in both 'mixed' and avowedly 'socialist' economies, are coming to be suspected of generating unwelcome behavioral changes: sluggishness to respond to incentives and opportunities, poor resistance to adverse conditions, a weakening of the 'work ethic,' free riding, irresponsibility for oneself and one's offspring, a falling personal propensity to save, overconsumption and waste of freely provided public goods; these costs, and the long-run damage they do to society's capacity to function, and to the character and virtue of its members, are beginning to weigh heavily against the putative gain in welfare and social justice of which they are dimly perceived to be a by-product.

Not that disillusion, suspicion and an 'agonizing reappraisal' of their costs and benefits is actually leading to the wholesale rolling back of these policies. But their easy expansion has by and large been checked, and in some areas collective choice seams to be restraining itself to give way to the operation of 'hard,' non-vacuous freedom principles. Its remaining champions, by way of last-ditch defense, design fall-back positions holding out the same old promise that we can, after all, have it both ways. Though they have mostly given up talk about the Yugoslav Road, the third Way, Indicative Planning and Social Justice In a Free Society, and though such magic passwords to coercion as 'prisoners' dilemma,' 'externality' and 'community preference ordering' may with luck soon go the way of 'the diminishing marginal utility of money' and 'pump-priming for full employment,' the intellectual advocacy of using the power of collective decisions to make a better world will never cease. There are still so many good ideas left! Assuredly, we have not heard the last of the prize inanity, market socialism.

When and where societies, and the decision-making coalitions of interests within them, renounce to use their force for allocating resources and rewards, and take the bitter medicine of freedom instead, they do so because their meliorist solutions that would violate freedom, are proving too costly in perverse effects. Contrast this with the diametrically opposite position of actually liking freedom, even if it proved costly in material sacrifice. As Roepke (1959, p. 232) has movingly put it: 'I would stay for a free economic order even if it implied material sacrifice and if socialism gave the certain prospect of material increase. It is our undeserved luck that the exact opposite is true.'

It is undeserved luck indeed. Where would we be now if socialism were affordable and whittling freedom down were not as expensive as we are finding it to be?

Notes

*   From Roger Mitchener (ed.), *The Balance of Freedom*, 1995, St. Paul, Paragon House.

1   Cf. the 1791 *Declaration of the Rights of Man*; also Mill 1848, ch. 2.

2   'The most extensive basic liberty compatible with a similar liberty for others,' Rawls, 1972, 60. Liberty, then, is to be increased as long as its further increase does not require some to have less of it than others; equality of freedom is a constraint on its maximization. This is implicit in the formula but is not spelt out by Rawls.

3   Marx, 1844, 1975, *passim.*

4   More precisely, the species, the *Gattungswesen.*

5   Whether there is any satisfactory doctrine of necessary coercion is a vast open question, which I have tried to address at length elsewhere. Hayek, at all events, has not provided one; the coercion he considers justified because necessary to raise the means for providing useful public goods and services, including a social 'safety net,' is completely open-ended. It excludes as unnecessary the coercion involved in raising the means for useless public goods and services, or those that, though usefull, could better be provided by private enterprise. This leaves a quasi-infinity of occasions for necessary coercion, or at least for coercion that can never be proven unnecessary by the loose Hayek criteria.

6   Cf., however, the approach adopted by Feinberg, 1984.

7   One of Rawl's two versions of equal liberty, that consisting of an integrated, coherent 'system ... definig rights and duties' (*op. cit.*, 202) seems to me clearly open to this charge. In the other version, the system is said to consist of a number of distinct 'basic liberties' (*op. cit.*, 302) of 'equal citizenship.' They are the conventional political freedoms ensuring democratic representation and equality before the law, and they are not vacuous. They seem to me, however, too confined in their effects and therefore inadequate to pass for a 'principle of liberty.' For one, they offer too few safeguards to minorities against the will of the majority. For another, they provide no defense of property, nor of privacy. Such 'basic liberties' leave the respective domains of individual and collective choice wholly indeterminate.

8   ' ... an equal right to the most extensive total system of equal basic liberties'; Rawls, *op. cit.*, 302.

9   For a different argument on moral arbitrariness: Nozick, 1974, 213–26.

10   There can, in any case, be no differential moral desert if all differential performance is due to some differential advantage (talent, education,

character etc.), and all such advantages are themselves underserved. Cf. Sandels, 1982, 88. Moral desert then collapses into equality, and becomes redundant.

11 G.A. Cohen in Paul, Miller, Paul and Ahrens, 1986.

12 Since 'talk is cheap' and language will adapt to anything, one can override principles of freedom to advance one's interest in the name of freedom. When in 1776, in one of the failed attempts of the century to make French society more efficient and mobile, Turgot tried to put through a program of fairly extensive deregulation, the 'duly constituted' corporations defended and saved regulation as a system of 'real freedom,' necessary for public good.

13 In a large flock of geese, the most precious ones started to languish and die one by one. The wise rabbi was asked to find a remedy. As each of his suggestions was put into practice, more geese died. When the wretched gooseherd finally reported the demise of his last bird, the rabbi, much annoyed exclaimed: 'What a shame, I had so many good ideas left!'

References

A. Alchian and H. Demsetz, 'The Property Rights Paradigm,' *Journal of Economic History*, 1973, Vol. 33.

P.S. Atiyah, *The Rise and Fall of the Freedom of Contract*, 1979.

F. Engels, 'The Origin of the Family, Private Property and the State,' 1891, in Marx and Engels, *Selected Writings*, 1968.

J. Feinberg, *Harm to Others*, 1984.

F.A. Hayek, *The Constitution of Liberty*, 1960.

F.H. Knight, 'The Meaning of Freedom,' in C.H. Perry, ed. *The Philosophy of American Democracy*, 1943.

K. Marx, 'The Jewish Question,' 1843, Economic and Philosophical Manuscripts, 1844, in *Early Writings*, 1975.

J.S. Mill, *Principles of Political Economy*, 1848.

R. Nozick, *Anarchy, State, Utopia*, 1974.

E.F. Paul, F.D. Miller, Jr., J. Paul and J. Ahrens, eds., *Marxism and Liberalism*, 1986.

J. Rawls, *A Theory of Justice*, 1972.

J. Raz, *The Morality of Freedom*, 1986.

W. Roepke, 'The Economic Necessity of Freedom,' *Modern Age*, 1959, reprinted with a foreword by E.J. Feulner, Jr., The Heritage Foundation, 1988.

M.J. Sandels, *Liberalism and The Limits of Justice*, 1982.

Social Democracy and the Myth of Social Justice

Antony Flew

Hayek published two books in 1976: A Second Edition of *The Road to Serfdom*; and *The Mirage of Social Justice*, Volume II of his trilogy *Law, Legislation and Liberty*. In his new Preface to the former he recognized the emergence of a second sense of the word 'socialism':

At the time I wrote[1] socialism meant unambiguously the nationalisation of the means of production and the central economic planning which this made possible and necessary. In this sense Sweden, for instance, is today very much less socialistically organized than Great Britain or Austria, though Sweden is commonly regarded as much more socialistic.[2] This is due to the fact that socialism has come to mean chiefly the extensive re-distribution of incomes through taxation and the institutions of the welfare state. In the latter the effects I discuss in this book are brought about more slowly, indirectly and imperfectly.[3]

In 1976 the replacement of the first sense by the second was, even in the Western democracies, by no means complete. For whereas the German Social Democratic Party – which had been the original, model Marxist party – had at its 1959 Bad Godesberg Conference categorically and completely rejected socialism as nationalization, in its conference in the same year the British Labour Party rejected its Leader Hugh Gaitskell's appeal to abandon the aim – stated on every party membership card – of achieving "the public ownership of all the means of production, distribution and exchange."[4] It was only after it had suffered defeat in four successive General Elections, and after the collapse of the USSR and its empire, that its present Leader persuaded that party to adopt a quite different statement of its aims. It is significant that, partly by way of preparation for the production of this statement, the party established an 'independent Commission on Social Justice'; while the key concept in the eventual statement, which is vague and verbose in comparison with its terse and incisive predecessor, is again social justice.

1. Is 'social' justice a kind of justice?

None of this could have reasonably been foreseen in 1976. So we should surely not be surprised to find Hayek explaining, in his Preface to The Mirage of Social Justice, how he came to conclude "that the Emperor had no clothes on, that is, that the term 'social justice' was entirely empty and meaningless", and "that the people who habitually employ the phrase simply do not know themselves what they mean by it and just use it as an assertion that a claim is justified without giving a reason for it" (Hayek, 1976, p. xi).

Certainly, as Hayek proceeded so painstakingly to show, this cant expression is usually employed quite thoughtlessly. Few if any of those who habitually employ it have even attempted to produce a systematic and consistent rationale for its application. But this is still not sufficient to show that it is "entirely empty and meaningless". For there is in fact sufficient regularity in the actual usage of the expression 'social justice' to provide it with a meaning, albeit a meaning which is distressingly vague and variable. My suggestion is that that expression, and what is by its employers apparently taken to be the virtually or even completely synonymous expression 'equality and social justice' can be defined most illuminatingly as referring to what their employers see as constituting an ideal distribution of burdens and benefits, of good things and bad things, among the citizens of a welfare state.

This suggests the reason why Hayek was also wrong to maintain "that the people who habitually employ the phrase (social justice) just use it as an assertion that a claim is justified without giving a reason for it" For anyone asserting that some policy is required by a kind of justice is in fact giving what – if but only if their assertion were true – would constitute the best of reasons. The truth, however, is that social justice as customarily conceived is precisely not a kind of justice.[5]

On the contrary, such 'social' justice essentially involves what, by the standards of plain, old-fashioned, without prefix or suffix, justice must constitute a paradigm case of flagrant injustice; namely, the abstraction under the threat of force (the taxing away) of (some of) what must be presumed to be the justly acquired property of the better off in order to give it (less, of course, some often substantial service charge) to those whose previous just acquisitions or lack of just acquisitions have left them worse off.[6]

Many of those who are concerned to promote social justice as here understood conceal from themselves the force, indeed even the possibility, of this objection by tacitly assuming that the sum of all the incomes received and all the wealth owned within some nation is already the collective property of that nation and hence is available for distribution, free of all morally legitimate prior claims at the discretion of its masters. For instance: the National Economic and Social Council of the Republic of Ireland is by its terms of reference required to "promote social justice", which apparently either involves or is "the fair and equitable distribution of the income and wealth of the nation" (Donnison, 1975).

The crucial truth which is here being overlooked is that the national income', 'Gross Domestic Product','Gross National Product', and so on are all what Gilbert Ryle used to call systematically misleading expressions (Flew, 1951, pp. 11–36). For while "It is of course true to say that in 1938 Britain produced X million tons of coal" this is so "only in the sense in which it is correct to say" such things as "This morning Britain shaved 10 million faces and blew 40 million noses" (Polanyi, 1951, p. 196).

The objection that social justice is not a kind of justice is often countered either by urging that the world would be a better place if the distribution of income and wealth was different from what it actually is or by protesting that this objection is at best trivially verbal. It is easy to agree with the first of these contentions. In my personal ideal world, for instance, successful pop stars would not become multimillionaires. But this is simply irrelevant. For – to employ a useful distinction introduced by William Frankena – it is one thing to *justify* a situation, that is, to show it to be desirable or excusable or in some other way preferable to the available alternatives, but it is quite another thing to *justicize* it, that is, to show it to be not just 'socially' just but plain old-fashioned, without prefix or suffix just (Brandt, 1962, p. 22).[7]

To appreciate why the issue is most emphatically not merely verbal it is sufficient to ask and answer the question why people should be so keen to maintain that their actions or policies or whatever else are indeed (socially) just. It is of course because they want to arrogate to these actions or policies or whatever else the psychological associations which are presently linked with, and the logical implications which are presently carried by, employments of the word 'just'. Very understandably they want thus to see themselves and to be seen by others as occupying the moral high ground, and they want to see their opponents as ex officio callous, selfish and immoral (Sowell, 1995, p. 5 and passim).

Perhaps even more importantly, though this is rarely recognized, they need to equip themselves with what if only it were true, would be a decisive answer to an otherwise properly embarrassing question: 'By what right are you proposing to deploy the forceful machinery of the state in order to impose upon all concerned your own personal or party vision of an ideal society?' For justice is precisely not an expression of individual or group preferences, not such an individual or party vision of an ideal society. To appeal to justice is to appeal to a standard logically independent of all individual and collective interests (Flew 1995). That is why everyone has to allow that what is prescribed by (moral) justice may properly, though not always prudently be enforced by (legal) law. This point was put most decisively by Adam Smith in the penultimate paragraph of Chapter I of Section II of Part II of his other masterpiece (Smith 1759):

The man who barely abstains from violating either the person, or the estate, or the reputation of his neighbours, has, surely, little positive merit. He fulfils, however, all the rules of what is peculiarly called justice, and does everything which his equals can with propriety force him to do, or which they can punish him for not doing.

2. Rawls's Theory of 'Social' Justice

It was again in the Preface to *The Mirage of Social Justice* that Hayek explained why he did not try "to justify my position vis-à-vis a major recent work", namely "John Rawls *A Theory of Justice*." It was "because the differences between us seemed more verbal than substantial" (Hayek, 1976, pp. xii-xiii). This decision was both somewhat surprising and extremely unfortunate. It was surprising since it was explicitly grounded upon a passage from an article Rawls published much earlier, and to which Hayek himself confessed that he could find no satisfactory parallel in the later book. (Ibid., pp. 100 and 183). It was unfortunate, since it ensured that *The Mirage of Social Justice* received far less attention than it should have done, and otherwise would.

It ensured it because, although the book of Rawls is misleadingly entitled *A Theory of Justice*, it in fact deals only – or, some might say, alternatively – with "the principles of social justice", principles which, we are told, "provide a way of assigning rights and duties in the basic institutions of society and define the appropriate distribution of the benefits and burdens of social cooperation" (Rawls, 1972, p. 4). Because this book attempted to satisfy the need for some clear formulation and persuasive rationalization of the putative principles of social justice, it received on its first appearance such a wide and overwhelmingly enthusiastic welcome that it at once became, and has ever since remained, the standard starting point for all subsequent discussion. For instance, in a notably uncritical 'Critical Notice' published in the third 1972 issue of *The New York Review of Books* the lifelong socialist Stuart Hampshire wrote:

I think that this book is the most substantial and interesting contribution to moral philosophy since the war, at least if one thinks only of works written in English. It is a very persuasive book, being very well argued and carefully composed.

It presents, he continued,

a noble, coherent, highly abstract picture of the fair society, as social democrats see it ... This is certainly the model of social justice that has governed the advocacy of R. H. Tawney and Richard Titmuss and that holds the Labour Party together.

This tribute suggests that it was right to define the expression 'social justice' as referring to what its employers "see as constituting an ideal distribution of good things and bad things among the citizens of a welfare state", and right too to identify those employers as what Hayek in his dedication of *The Road to Serfdom* characterized as "the socialists of all parties". Furthermore our suspicion that – to borrow the phrase which General Lee used to describe Union armies – "those people" treat the expressions 'social justice' and 'equality and social justice' as nearly if not entirely synonymous is confirmed when we find that Rawls, after confessing with captivating frankness that "We want to define the original position so that we get the desired solution" (Rawls, 1972, p. 141), then goes on to insist that his social (socialist?) contractors cannot but "acknowledge as the first principle of justice one requiring an equal distribution. Indeed this principle is so obvious that we would expect it to occur to anyone immediately" (Ibid., pp. 150–1).

The preliminary statement of the actual limitations of what Rawls is publishing as *A Theory of Justice* tout simple, and of the scope of what he calls the principles of social justice, is preceded by a trumpet blast:

Justice is the first virtue of social institutions, as truth is of systems of thought ... Each person possesses an inviolability founded on justice that even the welfare of society as a whole cannot over-ride ... Being first virtues of human activities, truth and justice are uncompromising (Ibid., pp. 3–6).

Although justice is acceptable as a morally overriding principle governing all human activities it can scarcely be said to be the first virtue of all social institutions. The members of sports clubs and other similar social institutions certainly ought not to treat each other or anyone else unjustly. But does it even make sense to ask whether football teams are just or unjust; and, even if it did, would any fans consider justice to be the first virtue of the teams which they supported?[7]

The one sort of social institutions of which justice obviously and incontestably is the first virtue is courts of civil and criminal justice. But these institutions, apparently, are in no way relevant to a theory of justice as conceived by Rawls. This failure to recognize their relevance[8] in part explains and is in part explained by his failure to offer any definition of the key word 'justice'.[9] It is indeed only on his five hundred and seventy ninth page that Rawls thinks to explain, but with no suggestion of apology, that he was eager "to leave questions of meaning and definition aside and get on with the task of developing a substantive theory of justice" (Ibid., p. 579).[10]

So what is justice as conceived in, so to speak, its home territory? Among those there who have asked themselves this question there seems, at least until comparatively recently, to have been little disagreement. The central, crucial element in their definitions has always been what in *The Republic* Plato scripted Polemarcus to offer as his first suggestion, namely, "to render to each their due" (331E), a phrase later translated into Latin as S u u m c u i q u e t r i b u e r e. Ulpian was much later to preface this with two further clauses. The version of Ulpian's definition employed in the *Institutes* of Justinian is inscribed on a wall of the library of the Harvard Law School. It is there helpfully Englished as: "To live honourably, not to injure another, to render to each his due."

The expressions 'his due' or, better, 'their due' are here naturally construed as referring to the several deserts and entitlements of different individuals, the deserts primarily under the criminal and the entitlements under the civil law. So why should anyone think that everyone's deserts and entitlements, whether legal or moral, are the same and equal? Why should anyone assume, as so many do, that justice can be identified with equality, and that inequalities are self-evidently evil?

3. Formal or Substantial Equalities?

Someone might respond that, in what is surely the first systematic treatment of distributive justice on record, Aristotle wrote: "If then the unjust is the unequal, the just is the equal – a view that commends itself to all without proof ..."[11] Yes indeed, Artistotle hath certainly said it. But he went on at once to argue that "if the persons are not equal they will not have equal shares."[12]

So his actual conclusion was not a substantial practical prescription but a purely formal principle. It is not that equal shares for all is the imperative of justice. Rather it is that the rules of justice, like all rules, require, not that all cases, but only that all relevantly like cases, should be treated alike. A system of criminal 'justice' requiring that convicted criminals should be treated in all respects in the same way as those judged innocent of any

175

crime would – as Kant might have said had he ever been confronted with a suggestion so absurd – contradict itself.

The same confounding of the formal with the substantial is essential to Rawls's establishment of "the original position so that we get the desired solution" (Rawls, 1972, p. 141); namely, that we should all "acknowledge as the first principle of justice one requiring an equal distribution "(Ibid., p. 151). Rawls adds as his next sentence: "Indeed this principle is so obvious that we would expect it to occur to anyone immediately." No doubt that is what would occur immediately to most people if they had been told that they had been assembled and placed in that "original position" in order to establish "a first principle of justice". But on second thoughts they should realize that the conditions stipulated by Rawls must disqualify them from ruling on the justice of distributions. For his hypothetical contracting parties are hypothesized as lacking all knowledge of the several deserts and entitlements of any of the members of the society for which they are being asked to rule. And without such knowledge they have no business to assert that an equal or indeed any other distribution would be just.

The most, therefore, that they would be in a position to offer is a ruling on the fairness of some distribution among these to them unknown individuals. But even here they could without any knowledge of the recipients contribute only a purely formal principle, that an equal distribution will be fair unless there is good reason to make one which is not equal. Rawls himself characterizes his system as "justice as fairness", and makes that the title of his first chapter. Fairness as justice would be somewhat more appropriate.

For a distribution to be allowed to be truly fair and proper what is distributed must be something which a distributor is entitled to distribute and is actively distributing. In the beginning Rawls asserts that social justice[14] concerns "the basic structure of society, or more exactly, the way in which the major social institutions distribute fundamental rights and duties and determine the division of advantages from social cooperation" (Ibid., p. 7). Here the distributions are clearly passive while the major social institutions are not thought of as agents, even collective agents. But later we are told that "All social values – liberty and opportunity, *income and wealth* ... – are to be distributed equally unless an unequal distribution of any, or all, of these values is to everyone's advantage" (Ibid., p. 62: emphasis added). And "For simplicity" we are required to "assume that the chief primary goods *at the disposition of society* are rights and liberties, powers and opportunities *income and wealth*" (Ibid., p. 62: emphases added).

4. No Deserts and No Not-deserved Entitlements?

Such arguments about the deserts and entitlements of individuals and the differences between them would, surely, carry little weight with Rawls? For although it is, it seems, usually considered that The Veil of Ignorance is drawn in order to secure impartiality, which makes this whole exercise of comprehensive blinkering a dramatization of Hume's colourless appeal to the impartial spectator, the stated primary purpose is quite different, and altogether preposterous. Thus at the beginning, under the Section heading "The Main Idea of the Theory of *Justice*" (Ibid., p. 11: emphasis added), Rawls asserts:

Once we decide to look for a conception of justice that nullifies the accidents of natural endowment and the contingencies of social circumstance as counters in the quest for political and economic advantage we are led to these principles. They express the result of leaving aside those aspects of the social world that seem arbitrary from a moral point of view (Ibid. 'p. 15: emphases added).

The preposterousness is to present this nullification as a first and necessary step towards developing a conception of justice. Certainly, if all possible grounds for any differences in deserts and entitlements are thus to be dismissed as morally irrelevant, then indeed – always allowing that anyone is still to deserve or to be entitled to anything at all – it does become obvious that everyone's deserts and entitlements must be equal. But it is precisely and only upon what individuals individually and severally have done or failed to do, what has and has not happened to them, and so on, that all their several and often very unequal particular deserts and entitlements cannot but be based. It is, therefore, bizarre to dismiss all this as morally irrelevant.

Ultimately Rawls is reluctant to allow that anyone truly either deserves or is entitled to anything at all. If he were right about this then it would carry the ruinous implication that there can be no application for the concept of justice. That "the accidents of natural endowment and the contingencies of social circumstance" are indeed "arbitrary from a moral point of view" Rawls argues on two grounds: first, that these natural endowments are not themselves deserved; and, second, that, in consequence, what they make possible cannot be either itself deserved or a proper basis of desert. The more fundamental notion that anyone might be entitled, or have a moral right, to anything which they had neither earned nor deserved is not entertained at all. As Rawls sees it, the crux is that "the natural distribution of abilities and talents" is the (morally arbitrary) outcome of a "natural lottery"; a conception which surely collapses when pressed by the question

'Who are the individuals to whom diverse collections of genes are thus actively distributed?' Furthermore, Rawls continues, "Even the willingness to make an effort, to try, and so to be deserving in the ordinary sense is itself dependent upon happy family and social circumstances" (Ibid., p. 74).

Notice that Rawls is not saying, what no one should dispute, that natural endowments are neither deserved nor undeserved; and hence that, since neither of these two contrasting notions applies, we need an Aristotle-type three term distinction between deserved (good), undeserved (bad) and not-deserved (neutral). Excellent examples of such not-deserved entitlements are provided by the option rights proclaimed as self-evident in the American Declaration of Independence. Further and perhaps even less controversial examples are provided by everyone's rights to his or her own bodily parts. But since the possibility of not-deserved entitlements appears never to have occurred to Rawls he makes a much stronger claim, carrying an important practical implication. It is, he insists, a matter of principle, the principle of redress, "that undeserved inequalities call for redress; and since inequalities of birth and natural endowment are undeserved, these inequalities are to be somehow compensated for" (Ibid., p. 100).[15] So he takes it from there:

We see then that the difference principle represents, in effect, an agreement to regard the distribution of natural talents as a common asset and to share in the benefits of this distribution whatever it turns out to be. Those who have been favoured by nature, whoever they are, may gain from their good fortune *only* on terms that improve the situation of those who have lost out (Ibid., p. 100: emphasis added).[16]

5. Radically Collectivist Assumptions

If we accept the contention that everyone's natural abilities are to be regarded as a collective asset, then we must surely, by parity of reasoning, also accept that everyone's natural handicaps are to be regarded as a collective burden. This proposal chimes well with the requirement "to assume that the chief primary goods *at the disposition of society* are rights and liberties, powers and opportunities, *income and wealth*" (Ibid., p. 62: emphases added). But either alone, and still more both together, make it astonishing that anyone, and least of all a committed social democrat, should characterize "the Book of Rawls as presenting *The Liberal Theory of Justice* (Barry, 1973).[17]

The assumption that all income and wealth is "at the disposition of society" is an appropriate assumption for extreme socialists labouring to discover the proper pattern for the centrally planned and enforced active distribution of all such goods, in their ideal state. But for anyone who is supposed to be asking whether and how far actual, present passive distributions are just and, where and in so far as they are not, what state-enforced re-distributive transfers are or would be mandated by justice, that assumption is altogether unwarranted and misleading. For it just is the assumption that all those listed "chief primary goods are already "at the disposition of society", that is to say, that they are now freely available for distribution at the absolute discretion of some supreme authority, altogether unhampered by any morally legitimate prior claims to possession.

Those who like J. S. Mill equate social with distributive justice should be made aware that Aristotle, who so far as we know was the first to identify distributive as a kind of justice, defined it in his *Nicomachean Ethics* as the sort which "is exercised in distributions of honour or of wealth or of anything else which is to be divided among those who have a share in the constitution."[18] His conclusion was that this "justice in distributing common property ... when a distribution is made from the common stock ... will follow the same ratio as that between the amounts which the several persons have contributed to the common stock."[19] Throughout, therefore, Aristotle is presupposing the subsistence of private holdings which could not, on any of Aristotle's alternative accounts of the principles of distributive justice, have resulted from previous state distributions.

Failing to heed Plato's warning of the need to pursue enquiries about justice armed with knowledge of what justice is, and failing too sufficiently to distinguish active from passive distributions, Rawls proceeds – without question and, it would seem unwittingly – simply to assume that all those "chief primary goods" are the collectively owned common property of his hypothetical social contractors.[20] For if they are not, then by what right are his hypothetical contractors deciding how to distribute those goods – and exclusively among themselves, at that?

But this enormous assumption is one which cannot be made with regard to any existing non-Communist nation state. Always there are innumerable claims to individual possession which we must defeasibly presume to be legally and morally legitimate. So before anyone has any business to maintain that a different distribution is mandated by justice they have first somehow to defeat these presumptions. Nor, as has already been shown, will it do to argue, however truly, that in an ideal world the distribution would be very different. For what would be true in some ideal world is simply irrelevant to questions about what, in the actual world, are the imperatives of justice.

Notes

1   The original Preface was datelined "Cambridge, December, 1943".

2   As Gerard Radnitzky loves to tell us, the Swedish Social Democrats have preferred to "nationalize people rather than industries"; a preference which was explicitly shared by Adolf Hitler as Leader of the National Socialist German Workers' Party.

3   It was in this sense of 'socialism' that in December 1994 Jacques Delors, in what turned out to be his valedictory address to the European Parliament as President of the European Commission, "claimed to have defeated Reagan and Thatcher by installing socialism as the guiding principle of the European Union (Connolly, 1995, p. 104n; and compare pp. 31–2, 67, and 74–80). Delors had of course been Minister of Finance in an administration implementing a Common Programme agreed by the French Communist and Socialist Parties, and which was strongly socialist in the first sense.

4   I will not resist the temptation to point out that Gaitskell, borrowing the key phrase from Lenin's endorsement of his New Economic Policy (NEP), urged his party to content itself with nationalizing only "the commanding heights of the economy."

5   For further treatment of this contention, see Flew 1981, pp. 804 and Flew 1989, Ch. 6 and 8.

6   In practice in what Anthony de Jasay calls these churning societies the transfers are not by any means always from the better off to the worse off. In the UK the escalating costs of maintaining the welfare state have resulted in formidably rising tax burdens even on those earning average or less than average incomes. See, for instance, Parker 1982, p. 73.

7   "To apply the term 'just' to circumstances other than human actions or the rules governing them" – such as the operation of social institutions or the behaviour of some hypostatized Society – "is a category mistake" (Hayek, 1976, p. 31).

8   The nearest that Rawls comes to recognizing this relevance, and it is not very near, is on the occasion when with no sign of embarrassment he warns readers not to confuse "The principles of justice for institutions [presumably his principles – AF] with the principles which apply to individuals and their actions in particular circumstances" (Rawls, 1971, p. 54). Compare this with the surprised statement of one later writer of a treatise on *Social Justice*: "there appears to be a category of 'private justice' which concerns the dealing of a man with his fellows where he is not acting as a participant in one of the major social institutions" (Miller, 1976, p. 17).

9   "There is in fact a vast hole in his 600 page book which should be occupied by a thorough account of the meanings of these words, which is the only thing which can establish the logical rules which govern moral argument" (Hare, 1973, p. 147). Hare having achieved First Class honours in Litterae Humaniores could not ignore the warning issued by Plato's Socrates in the final sentence of Book I of *The Republic*: "For if I do not know what justice is I am scarcely likely to find out whether it is an excellence, and whether its possessor is happy or not happy" (354C).

10   A similar eagerness inhibited L. T. Hobhouse in his *Elements of Social Justice*, a work widely recommended to students for forty or more years after its first publication. The expression 'social justice' is actually employed only once, and without explanation, on the very first page of the text (Hobhouse, 1922, p. 13).

11   *Nicomachean Ethics*, 1131A 12–14.

12   Ibid. 1131A 23–4.

13   See Note 9, above.

14   It is also worth noting that Mill's employment of the expression 'social justice' is the first recorded by the big *Oxford English Dictionary*. The earliest so far recorded employment of its equivalent in any language is in an Italian book published in 1840 (Hayek, 1976, p. 176). It is argued in Sowell, 1987, pp. 190ff. that the first systematic treatise on what is now called social but what was then called political justice seems to have been an *Enquiry Concerning Political Justice* (Godwin, 1793); a work not noticed in either Rawls, 1971 or Hayek, 1976.

15   It has famously been objected that – absent any such rights, such not-deserved entitlements, to our bodily parts – "An application of the principle of maximizing the position of those worst off might well involve forceable redistribution of bodily parts …" (Nozick, 1974, p. 206).

16   This radically collectivist dog-in-the-manger manifesto is one of many passages which make it impossible to believe that it was his study of *A Theory of Justice* rather than of very different earlier Rawls papers which led Hayek to write: "the differences between us seemed more verbal than substantial" (Hayek, 1978, pp. xii-xiii).

17   This conclusion may be seen as a proposal for the nationalization of people, a project mentioned in Note 2, above.

18   1130B 31–3.

19   1134A 25–9 and 1131B 28–33. For some of the illustrations which Aristotle might have provided, but unfortunately did not, see Flew, 1981, pp. 68–9.

20   This is an assumption which, if it could itself be justicized could justify the behaviour of those whom Gordon Tullock characterizes as
"patriotic egalitarians", people who while scandalized by inequalities
in their own country remain altogether unmoved by even much greater inequalities between that country and others (Tullock, 1995). Not
(Stalin's) socialism, but 'social' justice in one country?

References

Barry, Brian (1973), *The Liberal Theory of Justice*, Oxford University
Press, Oxford.

Brandt, R. B. ed. (1962), *Social Justice*, Prentice-Hall, Englewood Cliffs, N.
J.

Connolly, Bernard (1995), *The Rotten Heart of Europe*, Faber and Faber,
London and Boston.

Donnison, D. V. (1975), *An Approach to Social Policy*, Stationery Office,
Dublin.

Flew, Antony ed. (1951), *Essays in Logic and Language*, First Series, Basil
Blackwell, Oxford.

Flew, Antony (1981), *The Politics of Procrustes: Contradictions of Enforced
Equality*, Temple Smith, London.

Flew, Antony (1989), *Equality in Liberty and Justice*, Routledge, London
and New York.

Flew, Antony (1993), 'Is "Social" Justice a kind of Justice?', *Journal des
Economistes et des Etudes Humaines*. 5, pp. 281–94.

Flew, Antony (1995), 'Responding to Plato's Thrasymachus', *Philosophy*,
70, pp. 442–53.

Godwin, William (1793), *Enquiry Concerning Political Justice*, Toronto
University Press, 1969, Toronto.

Hare, R. M. (1973), 'Critical Notice of A Theory of Justice', *Philosophical
Quarterly*, 23, pp. 144–55 and 241–52.

Hayek, F. A. (1944), *The Road to Serfdom*, Second Edition, 1976 Routledge
and Kegan Paul, London and Henley.

Hayek, F. A. (1976), *The Mirage of Social Justice*, Volume II of *Law, Legislation and Liberty*, Routledge and Kegan Paul, London and Henley.

Hobhouse, L. T. (1922), *Elements of Social Justice*, Allen and Unwin, London.

Nozick, Robert (1974), *Anarchy, State and Utopia*, Oxford, Basil Blackwell.

Parker, Hermione (1982), *The Moral Hazard of Social Benefits: A study of* the impact of social benefits and income tax on incentives to work, Institute for Economic Affairs, London.

Polanyi, Michael (1951), *The Logic of Liberty*, Routledge and Kegan Paul, London.

Rawls, John (1972), *A Theory of Justice*, Harvard University Press and Clarendon, Cambridge Mass and Oxford.

Schumpeter, Joseph (1954), *History of Economic Analysis*, Oxford University Press, New York.

Smith, Adam (1759), The Theory of Moral Sentiments, Liberty Press Edition 1969, Indianapolis.

Sowell, Thomas (1987), *A Conflict of Visions: Ideological Origins of Political Struggles*, William Morrow, New York.

Sowell, Thomas (1995), *The Vision of the Anointed*, Basic Books, New York.

Tullock, Gordon (1995), 'Patriotic Egalitarianism', in Radnitzky, Gerard and Bouillon, Hardy eds. *Values and Social Order*, Vol. II, Avebury, Aldershot, Brookfield, Hong Kong, Singapore and Sydney.

Nothing New Under the Sun: the Disguised Return of Totalitarianism

Roland Baader

While there may be phylogenetic reasons for the tendency of human beings to embrace fundamentalist convictions, to see things in black and white terms and to want to force their opinions on others, it is preposterous to assume there are particular nations with a more or less totalitarian character, as is often done in legends about Germany. It is true that the mental thresholds separating an open, pluralistic social order on the one hand from a closed, fundamentalist or totalitarian society on the other vary from country to country; but that has nothing to do with any innate "national character". For one thing, the very concept of a character shared by all members of a nation makes no sense. The differences between nations are due instead to the duration and intensity of historical experiences, the nature and depth of religious convictions, and the age and strength of democratic traditions. Other factors are wars and other tragedies, forms of government and economic organisation, a society's level of enlightenment, its educational institutions and standards, and its spread of wealth and poverty, to mention but a few.

However, we need to beware of the misconception that the Western phenomenon that parades under the name "Enlightenment" and the political system that calls itself "Democracy" are of and by themselves effective defence mechanisms against any kind of totalitarianism. The opposite is the case. The exaggeration of democratic principles in western democracies leads to totalitarian democracy, which can be just as oppressive and coercive as any dictatorship. This exaggeration says not only that no political decisions must be taken without the support of a majority, but also that anything decided by a majority is right and fair. As F. A. von Hayek has shown, the first statement is correct, the second is not. Nor must we be under any illusions about our achievements in the field of enlightenment. Consider the excesses of which some feminists have proven themselves capable: Advocating changing the Lord's Prayer to "Our Mother, which art in heaven" or justifying abortion on the grounds that "My body is mine" is more totalitarian than our non-judgmental, pluralistic legislative is willing to admit. Even the Enlightenment created myths of its own, including perhaps the myth of its own existence. As Thomas Molnar writes: "There is no reason why human existence today should not flourish in the soil of myths any less than it did in the past. ... We invent new myths from the material available: science, technology, psychology and the struggles of the new titans (social conflicts). People today are even more attached to the new myths than their forbears were to the old ones. They want some justification for the way they are and an explanation of the world" (Molnar, 1995).

One thing is certain: Man in general, regardless of ethnic background, is susceptible to totalitarian temptations in his own socio-economic sphere and to corresponding adaptations on a personal level. Then there are phenomena of mass psychology and power strategy that have been sufficiently explained and publicised in the works of Ortega y Gasset, Elias Canetti and others and need no elaboration here.

We ought, however, to focus on one particular aspect of the problem, in order to better understand the present pernicious trend to newer, less obvious forms of totalitarianism. We could call it the primeval fear of the modern mass society based on technology, division of labour, anonymity and pluralism. Thanks to the works of Friedrich A. von Hayek, Konrad Lorenz, Arnold Gehlen, Irenäus Eibl-Eibesfeldt and others, we know how difficult it is for people to live in two worlds at the same time. On the one hand there is the "warm world" of the face-to-face group, which includes one's family and circle of friends. On the other there is the "cold world" of the anonymous mass society with its division of labour. The thousands of years our ancestors lived in small groups such as hordes, clans and tribes, in which everyone more or less knew everybody else, have far more bearing on the way we are than the few seconds of historical time we have had to internalise the thin layer of civilised patterns of behaviour. To put it another way, our motivational and behavioural structures are virtually the same as those of the stone-age hunters of fifty or a hundred thousand years ago. We have merely managed to plaster a veneer of civilisation over them.

We can express this state of affairs another way: Our primeval fear of modern industrial society is deeply rooted and tremendously strong. From an ideological point of view that means there is great potential for any kind of socialism to hold sway and survive.

There are still people today who cannot understand the worldwide phenomenon of anti-Americanism. They fail to see how the socialist specialists of twentieth century genocide have been able to get away with oppressing and wiping out whole peoples without student or trade union demonstrators so much as raising a single flag in protest, whereas the crack of an American toy torpedo is sufficient to bring outraged crowds to the streets. Our stone-age hunter could probably solve the riddle: Anti-Americanism is at bottom nothing other than anti-capitalism. And anti-capitalism is in turn nothing other than the "natural" primeval hostility of man to a modern industrial society.

In the light of this, let us take a look at the German National Socialist movement. Of course, we have to beware here of over-simplification. Nor must we, when analysing the reasons for the success of the brown brand of socialism, ignore the circumstances preceding and accompanying its development, such as the international economic crisis, mass unemployment, the impoverishing effects of inflation, deflation and currency reform on the middle classes, the Treaty of Versailles and the fear by the middle classes of a communist revolution on the Soviet pattern. However, even more significant, it seems to me, was the little-known fact that National Socialism derived its greatest impetus by harnessing people's archetypal hostility to modern industrial society. The rallying cry of "Blubobrausi" (from "Blut und Boden, Brauchtum und Sitte" – "blood and soil, tradition and custom"), the slogans of the nation as a community and of one nation under one leader, the racist ideology harking back to the prehistoric cohesion of clan and tribe, the mobilisation of the the primitive horde's xenophobia by the focusing of attention on a common enemy (Jewry): all these things were the palaeolithic humus in which the seed of totalitarian violence and mania was able to sprout so readily.

However, that is all history and not the object of this essay. What I am concerned to show is that only a few decades after those terrible events the same forces are again emerging from their prehistoric tombs and fast gaining ground. Socialism, an ideological blanket term for man's primeval fear and hatred of modern capitalist society, which has so far afflicted mankind in its red and brown varieties, is now at work in shades of pink and green.

Let us talk about the green kind first. Who would dispute that the environment needs protection, that nature deserves our respect, that it is our duty to treat the creation with reverence? Of course there is no doubt about that, if only for our own sake and the sake of our children. However, when we consider the political feats of ecological parties and pressure groups and the missionary militancy of the whole movement, we see that we are faced intellectually and psychologically with the same kind of "Blubobrausi" energy and religious mania that has already cast the nations of the earth into the abyss twice this century. The third Trojan horse is being pushed through the gate of the modern industrial city called Capitalism or Civilisation, to conquer and destroy. Green is merely its outward colour, designed to appeal to the mood of the times. Whether its adherents are conscious of the fact or not, the true aim of this fundamentalist *Ersatz*-religion is a return to the supposed idyllic life of archaic society and the extinction of civilisation.

One of the few people to have recognised the problems here is, significantly, not an academic social engineer, but the tax expert of a major German group of companies. Concerning the proposed "environment tax" he recently wrote in the Handelsblatt: "To subsidise the mining of coal and penalise its combustion with a CO_2 levy is the height of absurdity. ... The debate is out of touch with reality. The arguments are irrational, because the topic attracts people for whom the issue of the environment is a romantic substitute for direct social change" (Müller-Dott, 1995).

The supposedly free-thinking members of the middle classes are, as ever, the ones working hardest for their own destruction. Dyed-in-the-wool socialists, Mother Theresa moralists and journalists, federal presidents and political pastors whose favourite role, as Josef Isensee puts it, is to be other people's conscience, have always been at the same time the best victims and deceivers, whenever it was a matter of leading the masses to an enthusiastic suicide.

Perhaps even more amazing than the revival of socialism in green disguise is the success of its pink version. This is more than the "Creeping Socialism" that has been rampant in western welfare states for decades and has paradoxically been flourishing more than ever since the collapse of "hard core" socialism in eastern Europe. In the present context the reference is more to a linguistic shift that the German mass media, with their almost total left-wing bias, have engineered with great success. This shift has revolved around a dual strategy:

(1) The brown breed of socialism that for a while held evil sway is no longer called "socialism" or even "National Socialism", but "fascism", and

(2) the wretched fruits and the ultimate failure of the red brand of socialism in the eastern part of our country are blamed on the human weaknesses of the Stasi (secret police) crooks and their victims, rather than on the system itself.

This dual strategy is directed at the surreptitious purpose not only of leaving socialism unscathed, but of making it look even better than before. On the one hand socialism takes the noble form of anti-fascism. On the other it is portrayed as a good cause that was cruelly sabotaged. The dreadful result of this cunning, diabolical trick is what Gerhard Eiselt has called "the rapid transformation from an anti-totalitarian to an anti-fascist consensus" (Eiselt, 1995). To put it in plain language: All forms of left-wing totalitarianism (including Hitler's nationalist, fascist version of socialism) that have caused cataclysmic catastrophes this century are declared never to have existed or at least not to have been totalitarian. Instead real fascism à la Mussolini and Franco, which though criminal too, was far less so, is made out to be the greatest threat to humanity by being associated with Hitler's brand of socialism. By means of this strategy the media have succeeded in blinding all public and published opinion in our country to wrongdoings on the left of the political spectrum, while making anything slightly to the right of the red-green popular front seem like a brown swamp.

Whereas almost nobody recognises the true character of green politics, the situation is fortunately different in the case of the red masquerade, which a dozen leading lights have long since understood and exposed. Most of them, the classical to radical liberal author freely admits, are more conservative than liberal. As a matter of fact, there are very few "real" liberals left. Special credit is due to the publications by the Hohenheim philosopher Günter Rohrmoser, the Hohenheim political scientist and historian Klaus Hornung, the Bayreuth political scientist Konrad Löw, the journalist Rainer Zitelmann and Josef Isensee, who teaches public law at the University of Bonn, to name but a few (see bibliography). A radical liberal who ought to be mentioned is the Trier philosopher of science Gerard Radnitzky (honoured in this volume), who has recently published a study with the title "Karl R. Popper."

"A sign of the long-term re-orientation of the German democracy," writes Josef Isensee, "is the change from an anti-totalitarian self-concept to an anti-fascist self-image, which has been developing since the cultural revolution of 1968 and has achieved increasing general acceptance since 1990. ... The centre, which in the anti-totalitarian scheme of things was the buttress of the whole system, becomes the precarious right wing within the antifascist framework. It resurfaces in the united anti-fascist front with the left-wing extremism that used to be frowned upon. This left-wing extremism is now the persuasion at the greatest distance from fascism, whereas the former centre, that is, the middle class camp, has been moved dangerously close to it and has to take pains to stay within the tolerance zone. Antifascism is an ideology whose purpose is to rob the middle-class centre of legitimacy. The result of the paradigm shift is that the political system becomes weary of fighting on two fronts. Hostilities cease on the left, to increase on the right. The willingness of the system to defend itself is lopsided" (Isensee, 1995). Gerard Radnitzky sums it up well, when he writes: "The fundamental thesis of Hayek's 'Road to Serfdom' was that the ideologies of the German National Socialist Workers' Party and the Soviet Socialists were both members of the same totalitarian family. This insight is just as relevant today as it was then. For even now the left is trying to cloud this relationship by calling National Socialism 'fascism'" (Radnitzky, 1995).

With regard to the second aspect of the dual strategy mentioned above, it remains to be said that the "grief work" on the demise of real-life socialism/communism in eastern Europe focuses too much on political figures, usually deliberately. There are those who would have us believe that a good theory, or at least the good aspects of a theory, was perverted and disgraced by corrupt leaders and other self-indulgent individuals. However, Stalinism was not a perversion, but a perfection of communism, and the Stasi and their informers were not the betrayers of socialism, but the elite troops of its strategic logic.

Here we have a confirmation of Professor Rohrmoser's perceptive comment, that "political differences in our country revolve around interpretations" (Rohrmoser, 1995).

If we had the room here, it would be an interesting exercise to do a literary analysis to show how the Federal Constitutional Court has jumped on the bandwaggon of the "revaluation of all values". Whether its judgment on the display of crucifixes in Bavarian schools was justified or not, the crucial point is that such revolutionary cultural adjustments can only take place if they are in keeping with the spirit of the times. It cannot have been a coincidence that the German Green Party were calling at the same time for the banning of religious instruction from state schools and that their legal spokesman demanded the abolition of section 166 of the Penal Code, which makes it an offence to malign religious creeds. The former economics minister, Professor Karl Schiller, described this kind of "liberalism" well, when he said (in a different context): "In the course of history, liberalism has appeared in various hues. At times it has focused more on the individual's right to liberty, on the lines of the Enlightenment, at other times it has been more left-wing, that is, to be blunt, Jacobin. ... It is my impression that liberalism is again faced with choosing between the alternatives of individual liberty and radical Jacobinism" (Schiller, 1979).

One thing is clear: The societies of the welfare states are already sick. The state has deprived individuals and families of their responsibility for dealing with the normal risks of life, creating the illusion that responsibility can be collectivised. By destroying responsibility, it has broken the back of liberty. The moral-ethical infrastructure of liberty, rule of law and free enterprise in the western world consists, or rather, used to consist, of that stock of values called "western, Christian virtues." This stock is now depleted. Its place has been taken by the fragile structure of positivist, pluralist law and the self-exploitative pseudo-charity of the redistributionist state, neither of which will be able to stand up to any severe strain. The welfare state democracies have created a crippled system of law that is ever at pains to replace eternal law (which was characteristic of the spirit of the rule of law) with a horrific jumble of cleptocratic, paternalistic ad hoc regulations. When this transmogrification of a legal system now begins to remove the outward symbols of a dying culture, it is only being true to form.

Another observation that ought to be made in this context is that the increasing subversion of language by means of a kind of Orwellian Newspeak is symptomatic of a strange moral schizophrenia that has taken hold of the whole western world. Morality is in and riding high and its guardians deserve to be called Pharisees, like their counterparts two thousand years ago. For what is booming under the flag of the Pharisaic morality of the welfare state is collective morality. However, as morality only has meaning in terms of an individual with responsibility and a conscience of his own, collective morality is a pseudo-concept, a hypocritical substitute for a genuine structure of taboos and values, which have long since been stifled by the overwhelming bear-hug of the do-goody, aunty-knows-best welfare state.

The Newspeak of modern Pharisaism is the terminology of so-called "political correctness", a hypocritical, pussy-footing, mendacious mincing of words. On the other side of the coin, as with all pussy-footing, are cowardly slander, repressed rage and rat-like heel-biting. The somersaults this "anti-fascist" squeaky-clean pathology is capable of can be illustrated from two reports in my regional newspaper: The criminals who participated in a burglary are said to belong to "a minority in the Balkans", while those who took part in another offence against property are described as "three young ladies with long, black, combed-back hair and long, colourful dresses." At this rate the "fascist" *Zigeunerschnitzel* (lit. "gypsy cutlet") will soon disappear from our menus.

The other side of the coin of the collective cerebral flatulence mentioned above is, however, less amusing. The trend that began with the hypocritical outcry over the Jenninger speech and continued with the Constitutional Court ruling on the "soldiers are murderers" statement has now blossomed into a media standard on a level with Goebbels propaganda. The German television audience seems not to notice the macabre way in which people and groups are subjected to rhetorical executions for deviating ever so slightly from the socialist *Zeitgeist*. Freisler's *Volksgerichtshof* would feel honoured. Martyrs are being burnt at the stake in German lands yet again. Only this time the fuel is not wood, but headlines, and the inquisitors are now called presenters and commentators.

Of the many examples that could be quoted, let us look at two. The first concerns a profession that has been greatly affected by the inherent anomalies of the three-quarters socialist German health system, namely the dentists. The dentists have the further disadvantage of not being numerous enough to have much influence at the polls. They are also a prime target for the social-democratic politics of envy, enjoying a higher income than average (*Besserverdienende*). The way our minister of health, who has lived in a planned economy and really ought to know better, treats this hard-working profession makes a mockery of the rule of law and would provide enough material for a horror film of the most gruesome kind. However, I will confine myself to an example that illustrates the repressed rage of the representatives of political correctness. A reporter on a late-night Channel 1 news show begins his commentary by holding a thousand-mark note up to the camera and saying, "This is the certificate dentists like to see most." On the main news the newsreader begins with the sentence, "It seems that the dentists are never satisfied." The average envious German just leans back in his recliner with smug satisfaction, never thinking to wonder when the next pogrom is going to break out, this time against the dentists.

My second and last example is drawn from the sidelines, to show how meticulously left-wing neo-totalitarianism is creeping even into the capillaries of our free society with the intent of poisoning its very roots and removing them without trace. In the city of Münster there is a small Catholic publishing house by the name of Komm-Mit ("Come along"), which for fifty years has put out a monthly youth magazine and a calendar by the same name. Fine, upstanding and refreshing journalism by publisher Günter Stiff and editor Felizitas Küble, who is at once both brilliant and unconventional. But journalism in which words like "God", "prayer", "faith" and "conscience" have their place and descriptions of Michael Jackson's latest sexual antics do not. In other words, you could put this literature in the hands of your eight to eighteen-year-old children, without having to worry about them being made unfit for life in normal society.

Nevertheless, the normality was brought to an abrupt end in the tranquil city of Münster in April 1994, when a Channel 1 documentary claimed to "reveal" that the altar servers' calendar, despite its rich tradition, had "extreme right-wing propaganda" in it. This accusation was based on three main assertions: First, all three verses of the *Deutschlandlied* ("Song of Germany") were printed in one of the calendars. Secondly, the calendar allegedly demanded the restoration of Germany within the borders of the Third Reich. Thirdly, the calendar had supposedly encouraged support for the German Republican Party.

The author of this essay, as already mentioned above, does not consider himself a conservative, but a radical liberal along the lines of American libertarianism. That means he is as far removed from any nationalist feelings as from the furthest star in the Milky Way. However, intellectual honesty demands mention of the fact that all three verses of the Deutsch-landlied were officially declared by Konrad Adenauer in 1952 to be the national anthem, even though only the third verse is used on official oc-casions. Furthermore, even though the German borders as they were in 1937 are still valid in international law, Komm-Mit has never demanded a corresponding revision of frontiers. Lastly, the Komm-Mit calendar has never included any recommendation to the effect that people ought to vote for the Republicans. The accusations against Komm-Mit have since been rejected by the state prosecutor as groundless.

Our concern in this article, however, is to show how effective the me-chanisms of the neo-totalitarian dictatorship of public opinion are. No sooner had the accusations been aired on television than the Catholic news agency KNA added its own voice to the smear campaign, and the German bishops, with the exception of the ever courageous Johannes Dyba, fell head over heels in the rush to distance themselves from the Komm-Mit calendar. When finally the same yellow journalist's Channel 1 morning news programme announced that Claudia Nolte, the minister for youth affairs, had graced the diabolical Stiff publication with an introduction, she was almost hounded out of office. So she penitently declared that she had written her recommendation two years earlier, at a time when she was only familiar with a few harmless extracts from the calendar.

That is not the end of this and other farces on the stage of our much vaunted freedom of opinion (witness the pussy-footing over the concept of "liberation" on the fiftieth anniversary of the end of the Nazi dictatorship). However, it will have to suffice to expose the "spirit" that is blowing through German politics and media since the supposed victory of freedom over eastern totalitarianism.

I would like to close with a discerning statement by Josef Isensee: "Anti-fascism is the last weapon to be deployed from the arsenal of left-wing ideologies, now that everything else they believed, hoped and promised has suffered a crushing defeat at the hands of reality" (p. 15), and add a warning of my own: Unless the much-mentioned middle-class political centre and all people of liberal disposition wake up from the slumber into which tele-vision has lulled them, these ideologues will have their way. They will have their way too as long as those who consider themselves "intellectual" con-tinue to restrict their political reading to the *Spiegel*. They will have their way until the last representative of a truly anti-totalitarian way of thinking has been verbally liquidated. It is very likely that that is what will happen, as indicated not only by the imminent disappearance of the last forlorn remnants of liberalism from the German political scene, but also by the lukewarm attitude of people who consider themselves genuine friends of freedom. The way most people react to the almost total regulation of all spheres of their lives by state institutions is disturbing. They think that things are never as bad as they sound, that one has to compromise out of respect for the "democratic consensus" or that things are much better than they used to be (which in many respects is of course true). One cannot help thinking of the people in Aldous Huxley's "Brave New World", where the enslaved population no longer has to be forced to do anything, because they all love their slavery.

A society like ours, in which individuals no longer take their own decisions or use their income as they see fit, in which they are no longer allowed to have their children educated at the kinds of schools they consider appropriate for them, is, in the words of American author Nelson Hultberg, a society of slaves. "Anyone who justifies such a society," writes Hultberg, "is either of a dictatorial or an obsequious disposition. He either wants to rule or to be ruled" (Hultberg, 1995, p. 10, back-translated from the German). Either attitude, I would like to add, is the raw material of totalitarian dreams and nightmares.

References

Baader, Roland, 1991: *Kreide für den Wolf – Die tödliche Illusion vom besiegten Sozialismus* (Tykve: Böblingen).

Baader, Roland, 1995 (ed.), *Die Enkel des Perikles*, vol. 1 of the series *Freiheitsdenker der Gegenwart* (Resch: Gräfelfing).

Baader, Roland, 1995 (ed.), *Wider die Wohlfahrsdiktatur*, vol. 2 of same series, (Resch: Gräfelfing).

Hornung, Klaus, 1993, *Das totalitäre Zeitalter* (Propyläen: Berlin, Frankfurt).

Hultberg, Nelson, 1995 "Invasion of the Mind Snatchers" in *The Freeman*, vol. 45, no. 1, Jan 1995.

Isensee, Josef, 1995 "Verwerfungen der Demokratie in Deutschland", in *Die politische Meinung*, no. 307 of June 1995, pp. 13–18.

Löw, Konrad, 1993, ... *bis zum Verrat der Freiheit* (Langen Müller: Munich).

Löw, Konrad, 1994 (ed.) *Verratene Treue* (Kölner Universitätsverlag: Cologne).

Molnar, Thomas, 1995, "Die Mythen der Moderne", in *Criticon*, no. 145, Spring, pp. 23–25.

Müller-Dott, Johannes Peter, 1995, "Die Ökosteuer ist eine falsche Zauberformel" in *Handelsblatt*, 21. 06. 95.

Radnitzky, Gerard, 1995, *Karl R. Popper* (Comdok: Sankt Augustin).

Rohrmoser, Günter, 1994, *Der Ernstfall* (Ullstein: Berlin, Frankfurt).

Rohrmoser, Günter, 1995, "Triumphieren wieder die halben Wahrheiten?" in *Mitteilungen der Gesellschaft für Kulturwissenschaft e.V.*, Bietigheim, May.

Schiller, Karl, 1979, "Über den Verfall der Marktwirtschaft zum Lippenbekenntnis" (speech given on the occasion of being awarded the Ludwig Erhard Prize for Economic Journalism on 2. 2. 79). Reprinted in *Orientierungen*, series published by the Ludwig Erhard Foundation, no. 63 of March 1995, pp. 74–76.

Is There a Morality in Redistribution?

Angelo M. Petroni

Defining Redistribution

More than forty years ago, the great French liberal thinker Bertrand de Jouvenel made a distinction between two different notions relating to the very idea of redistribution.

The first is to provide people in need with the "means of subsistence, whether it be a minimum income in days of unemployment or basic medical care for which (they) could not have paid". This notion, for de Jouvenel, is inherent in the very idea of society, and is "a primary manifestation of solidarity".

The second notion of redistribution follows from the idea that "inequality of means between the several members of society is bad in itself and should be more or less radically removed"[1].

Despite the fact that this distinction might appear to many people as a matter of conceptual analysis, without much relevance for the real world, I believe that it stands at the core of the contrast between the liberal view of society and the socialist view in one of its many versions, including the social-democratic one.

The basic difference between the two notions is that the first can be defined in terms of "absolute" level of income (or equivalent goods). In this sense, what constitutes an acceptable level of income will be dependent *only* on the average level of wealth of a country or any other community taken as a reference. On the contrary, the second notion is by essence a *relational* concept. Even in a society where the poorest members earn a million dollars a year there is room for a redistribution of means from the more well-off to the less well-off.

The main ethical *and* political problems for a liberal order are posed by the second notion of redistribution. The main reason is that providing the resources to help the poor does not necessarily imply *systematic* interference in the social orders which are the product of the rules of just conduct that prevail in a free society. More particularly, no idea is implied of "correcting" the results of these orders because they would not correspond to some criteria of "social justice".

In the real world (or rather in real politics) the two notions are almost inextricably intermingled. It is regrettable that even a large part of those who consider themselves as liberal seem to believe that redistribution is a self-evident idea, and that the only difference between a liberal and a social-democratic view of society and politics ultimately rests on the *level* of redistribution. What I shall try to show in my lecture is that this is far from being true, and that the only morally acceptable idea of redistribution is the first sense of the notion, not the second one. Furthermore, I shall try to show that the moral justification of this idea of redistribution does not imply at all that liberals should consider as morally justified the policies that are currently applied in order to help people in need.

Judging Intentions

One of the basic distinctions in the ethical discourse is the difference between judging some actions (for example, some public policies) on the basis of the goodness (or badness) of the *intentions* that moved them, and judging some actions on the basis of the goodness (or badness) of the *consequences* that they produced in the real world.

There are few doubts that all those who favour redistribution are persuaded that their position is morally justified – and, above all, morally superior to any competing position – because redistribution is based on intentions that are moral *par excellence*. They are moved by love of humanity – if not of every single individual; they put altruism before egoism; they consider that all men are to be treated as having equal value, and not the subjects of chance of nature or of birth. (The list could go on forever).

Of course, it would be a matter of mere mob psychology to decide if all those who favour redistribution do so because they are moved by such intentions, or because they are moved by the most anti-ethical sentiment at all: *envy*. But it is perfectly clear that it should not be assumed that the first alternative is the true one. As a matter of fact, since the extraordinary work of Helmut Schoeck it is impossible to ignore the massive biological, psychological, and anthropological evidence which proves that envy *is* the basic motivation that underlies the modern claim for redistribution, or for any of the many means that have been conceived for realising it – such as "steeply progressive income tax (and) confiscatory death duties". Referring to the well-known fact that progressive high-rate income taxes actually yield only a minimal part of the total income (in 1962 in the United States income tax of rates of 75 per cent to 91 per cent yielded only 0.2 per cent of the total revenue), Shoeck remarked that "not even conservative governments, when they succeed a left-wing administration, are able as a rule to do much toward dismantling this step progression. They are too afraid of the envy they suppose this would arise in the electorate (...) To claim 'humanitarian motives', when the true motive is envy (...) is a favourite rhetorical device of politicians today, and has been for at least a hundred and fifty years"[2].

It is impressive to see how far in the public consciousness the confusion has gone between true moral sentiments and sentiments that are all but remote from morality. This concerns also Churches, that should have the task of keeping the principles of morality well-evident to the believers. For example, in the 1985 Report of the Archbishop of Canterbury's Commission on Urban Priority Areas the Parable of the Good Samaritan was taken as the moral basis for endorsing ever rising tax-funding for the redistribution operated by the welfare state. But, as was pointed out by the British philosopher Antony Flew, this was "perverse or perhaps just ignorant ... For the Good Samaritan applied his own bandages with his own hands, and paid the inkeepers from his own purse. His actions manifested a love trascending the demand of the law (of justice)"[3].

Unfortunately, this way of thinking has become the standard view of the majority of the Christian churches in the world, including the Catholic church. They consider that it is a logical consequence of the *moral duty* of any Christian to help his less fortunate fellows that redistribution is compulsorily imposed by the State in order to help these latter. But of course the fact of assuming that the bulk of resources for redistribution has to come from compulsory legislation, and not from voluntary giving, is tantamount to assuming that the moral duty of charity is basically unrecognized by believers. Seen from a historical perspective, this is an unprecedented position in the history of the Christian churches, or at least of the Catholic church. For if anything has characterized the political dimension of the Catholic church this has been its claim to organize charity independently from any State power – and sometimes to have the monopoly on it. The fact that churches are now advocating an ever increasing power of the State in all social matters is likely to have radical consequences on their influence on the morals of people. As has happened in all countries where a pervasive welfare state has been implemented, it is to be expected that this influence will decline sharply.

We do not have to go too far in discussing this matter of the moral goodness of the intentions of redistributionists. The simple reason is that we have today the largest evidence for affirming that redistribution in contemporary societies, its size and its shape, is completely explained by the very logic of the processes of representative democracy. Politicians may well believe, at the bottom of their souls, that they enact redistribution because they follow moral principles. The reality is that redistributing the resources extracted from general taxation towards those social groups who can grant electoral support is the basic mechanism that ensures that politicians in power get their chance to stay there. In turn, politicians who are not in power get their chance to win power from their capacity to persuade a plurality of social groups that they will be the net beneficiaries of alternative redistributional policies. If Machiavelli were alive today, he probably would not write a book entitled *Il Principe* advising political men how to get into power and stay there, but a different book for the very same purpose: *Il Redistributore*.

That this was to be the necessary result of representative democracy with universal franchise was the unpalatable prophecy of Frédéric Bastiat and Vilfredo Pareto – to name only two of the most famous. As a result of the extensive theoretical and empirical research of the school of Public Choice in the last forty years this has almost become a piece of evidence. And common-sense analysis of politics points out in the same direction.

Perhaps some might object that I have an over-pessimistic view of human nature, but I believe that it would be scientifically wrong to look for good intentions to explain human behaviour (the behaviour of politicians, in this case) wherever strict self-interest is a sufficient reason on its own.

Judging Consequences

One does not have to be a follower of an utilitarian view of ethics to believing that the morality of public policies has mainly to be judged on the goodness of one's consequences much more than on the intentions of the politicians who propose and implement them. As Max Weber has taught us, the proper ethical standard that has to be used in evaluating politics is the "Ethics of responsibility" more than the "Ethics of intention".

Redistributional policies, like any others, must therefore be judged as being ethically acceptable or not on the basis of their consequences.

We have here two distinct – albeit concurrent – ways of doing this. On the one hand, we can judge what the consequences are of a value-inspired policy (such as redistribution) on other ethical values. On the other hand, we can evaluate what the consequences of such a policy have been in the real world.

a. Values

Let me start from the first point. It was the common opinion of liberals such as Bastiat, de Tocqueville and Pareto, that redistribution by compulsory legislation (be it "social" legislation, or limitation of freedom of contract of customary law, or economic regulation) would have had the inescapable consequence of basically weakening the sphere of individual freedom for *all* citizens, irrespective of their relative wealth. In this judgement there were nothing that was specific to redistribution. Redistributional legislation was incompatible with liberty because it amounted to the idea of imposing a given *model* to society, no matter whether this model was represented by the preservation of traditional caste priviledges, by the protection of vested economic interests, or by socialist views.

The very idea that liberty was incompatible with any model to be imposed upon society was already well clear to David Hume. In more recent times, it has been revived by the American philosopher Robert Nozick. Assume that one has been able to realize a state of society (a given egalitarian distribution of wealth, say, but also a very *in*egalitarian distribution), and that this happens at time T. But if individuals are let free, it becomes almost inescapable that at moment $T + 1$ the situation will be a different one. As a result of individuals' interaction, some will have more, and some less, than they had at moment T. Irrespective of the differences that exist between individuals in terms of natural gifts, *chance* is a sufficient reason for the model not to be maintained. Preserving the model in the course of time necessarily requires *systematic* interference with individual liberty[4].

The claim of the defenders of so-called "social rights" in the last century was that such rights represented an *extension* of traditional "negative" rights, not a limitation of them. Negative rights (for example, property rights) were based upon individual liberty. Positive rights would ensure that liberty was no longer the priviledge of few. "Liberty for all" was the final result of the implementation of positive rights through social (redistributional) legislation.

Real world experience in this century has been nothing but proof that Bastiat, de Tocqueville and Pareto were right. Redistributional policies have drastically reduced the sphere of liberty for the great majority of citizens. The growth of social legislation has sharply reduced the range and scope of free individual choices. In modern welfare democracies, a great part of education, health, production, even leisure, is today in the hands of the State, not of the citizens. Sweden is the case-school country where the process of redistribution of income and wealth has gone hand in hand with the reduction of the sphere of individual liberty, both for the worst-off and the better-off citizens. But the process is qualitatively the same in all welfare democracies. Redistributionists may possibly claim that the result of redistribution over more than one hundred years has been "Wealth for all". But they definitely cannot claim that redistribution has attained the original ideal of "Liberty for all". The value of liberty has proved to be incompatible with the values expressed by redistribution.

But liberty is not the only value that has been eroded by redistribution. Since liberty is a necessary – albeit not a sufficient – condition for other moral values, the restriction of the sphere of liberty has resulted in the weakening of other values. *Responsibility* is probably the main value that has suffered from the losses of individual liberty. This was a result already predicted – again! – by de Tocqueville, and that has been empirically confirmed by a massive evidence, especially as far as family relationships are concerned. It is intellectually shameful that redistributionists are now more and more advocating "communitarian values" as the "new" basis of the "new" welfare state. By and large, the weakening of the "natural societies" was the aim of the welfare policies. The weakening of the sense of responsibility of the individuals for themselves and their fellows was its necessary consequence.

b. Facts

This bring us naturally to the other side of our question. Redistributionists claim that the morality of their policies rests upon two facts: that redistribution has increased the well-being of the poor, and that it has increased the economic wealth *and* the utility of society. It is hard to see how these statements can bear scrutiny.

Let me start from the first claim. The point at stake here is not the fact that redistribution may have some beneficial effect for the recipients under static conditions. This is obviously true for any recipient, be he poor or wealthy. The real issue is to know whether redistribution aiming at removing "inequality of means among the several members of society" – using the above-quoted definition by de Jouvenel – has really been an effective means of helping the poor not to be poor any more.

Since redistribution has been the basic feature of public policies in all modern democracies, the answer to this question is not self-evident. As almost always happens in the social sciences, we do not have the possibility of varying the conditions in order to isolate one causal element from the other. However, one fact is crucial in this context. Despite the enormous increase in the resources destined to redistribution through the welfare state, poverty *in absolute terms* is still a serious problem in almost all countries.

Redistributionists claim that this is due to the fact that there is not enough welfare state. Social security today absorbs around 30 per cent of GNP of our countries. One may wonder what redistributionists actually mean when they say that there is not enough social expenditure!

The real fact is that redistributional policies have proved to be a very ineffective way of coping with poverty, incomparably less efficient than private charities are.

The fact that all-pervasive redistributional policies have not eradicated poverty comes as no surprise for those who understand why and how redistribution exists in representative democracy. Redistribution derives from the fact that wherever there is a difference in wealth among citizens average income is higher than the income of the median voter. Under these conditions, there will *always* be a majority of voters in favour of redistribution (and progressive taxation), irrespective of the absolute level of wealth. But since the marginal as well as the average rate of taxation and redistribution is determined by the median voter, there is no reason why redistribution should be directed towards the poorest part of the population.

Analysis of the processes of how interests are organized and politically represented reinforces this conclusion, because poor people are less able to organize themselves and direct their votes to specific politicians than almost any other social group. Of course, all this has been well-known for a long time. As George Stigler put it, "Public expenditures are made for the primary benefit of the middle classes, and financed with taxes which are borne in considerable part by the poor and rich"[5].

Let me now come to the second claim, that redistribution has increased the wealth and utility of the "average" citizen. Here again the complexity of the social world makes it difficult to give a simple answer.

On a more theoretical ground, redistribution has traditionally been justified upon the assumption that for any individual the marginal utility of money decreases. The economic welfare of a given society can therefore be increased by forced transfers of wealth from rich to poor, where "rich" and "poor" are defined in relative terms. But in order for redistributive prescriptions (from the wealthy to the poor, of course) to be drawn several other assumptions must hold, including the assumption that utility can have a cardinal measure as to allow interpersonal comparisons of utility. Despite the considerable amount of ingenuity that has been profused (most recently and authoritatively by Mancur Olson), the utilitarian justification of redistribution suffers to the highest degree from the difficulties of the very concept of utilitarianism[6].

What about wealth? For a very long time it was claimed that redistribution would increase *both* the global welfare of a country and the average wealth of citizens. (We do not need here to enter into the details of the different ways in which this "average" can be defined). Assuming the validity of Keynesianism was, of course, an essential ingredient of the first part of the claim. But there is no reason to assume that the claim was *and* is true.

Since economic growth is the result of a variety of factors, it is difficult to isolate the effect of redistribution. Furthermore, it is difficult to calculate in an exact way the real redistributive effects of social security spending and of public spending at large. With sufficient ingenuity, and choosing the "appropriate" time period, it is easy to produce examples which show that a high economic growth is compatible with a high redistribution or on the contrary, that economic growth goes along with low redistribution. Germany in the Fifties and Japan are two cases recently recalled by Olson.

However, some non-anecdotic evidence has become available, largely thanks to the research of the German sociologist Erich Weede. As he said, "By and large results on government revenues and social security spending together support the idea that creeping socialism hurts growth. Whether creeping socialization of the economy is pushed by ideologically committed socialists or by 'conservatives' who prefer the power of administering socialist policies over frustration in conservative or libertarian opposition makes no difference. Deeds rather than words matter"[7].

Rather than econometrics, microeconomic logic and evidence matter here. Redistributive policies affect the production of wealth in different ways.

In the first place, redistributional political coalitions remove resources from the most productive sectors, shifting them toward less productive uses. In the second place, since they guarantee vested interests, they weaken the incentives for the beneficiaries of redistribution to innovate. In the third place, they exert strong pressure against the opening of the national economies to international competition, since international competition makes it much more difficult to enjoy rent-seeking guaranteed by the State. Fourthly, the fiscal policies implied by redistribution disincentivate the most productive members of society from making full use of their abilities.

I believe that this rough outline suffices to show that there is much room for claiming that the existence of redistributional policies possibly has the consequence of decreasing the wealth of nations.

It is interesting to note that the costs of redistribution are largely *hidden* costs. If, and when, redistribution takes the form of a money transfer towards a given social group, it may seem relatively easy to evaluate its cost for the remaining groups. But this does not include the so-called "opportunity costs", namely, the losses deriving from the fact that redistribution and the legislative protection of vested interests prevented the creation of wealth. (One scarcely pauses to reflect that the mere fact of maintaining by legislation a given distribution of wealth is itself a kind of redistribution). As Bastiat would have put it, the advantages of redistribution are well clear for the recipients. But the wealth that was never produced as a result of redistribution is "Ce qu'on ne voit pas". Its destruction affects both the winner and the loser of redistribution.

A similar analysis holds for the question of whether redistribution has improved the average wealth of citizens. In the "Public Choice" analysis of redistribution I mentioned above, the conclusion is that the wealth of the median voter is increased. But this is just a static view. If direct as well as opportunity costs are considered, it becomes questionable whether redistribution has really meant that the middle class in absolute terms is in fact better-off than it would have been if redistributional policies had not become the political backbone of our democracies since the Thirties.

I believe that an important sign of this fact is the changing justification for redistribution. As I have said, the original argument of redistributionists was that redistribution could make the greatest majority of citizens better off than they would have otherwise been. Only very wealthy people needed to be the losers. But today the argument is completely different. Redistributionists now claim – as Paul Samuelson recently did – that redistribution is a good thing *even if* it makes societies globally *less* wealthy. Of course, the reason adduced why redistribution is still a good thing is that the vast majority of people would be better off anyway than in a wealthier society without redistribution[8].

In this way, redistributionists come to recognize that their original and main claim has been refuted. But their second claim rests upon precisely the same assumptions as the first: namely, the same view of the working of the economy, and the same view of human behaviour. There is no reason why they should be right in their emended views.

Beyond Economy

Many socialist and conservative thinkers and politicians seem to have realised that there is something that does not work in redistributional policies. But they believe that the problem lies in the present structure of the welfare state. They believe that the problem is in the ways that have been employed to implement the redistributional ideals. For them, all that is needed are "smart" reforms – for using the adjective mostly loved by the so-called

"Market Socialists" – of the welfare state, with some mix of personal incentives and more extended welfare benefits.

Moreover, they believe that the ideal of redistribution is such a good principle in itself that one should not give too much relevance to the objections that point to the costs that redistributive policies have for the great majority of people.

It is odd to see how redistributionists are defending their ideal without looking at how redistribution is actually effected by legislative processes. Here too we are seeing a remarkable shift. It was one of the primary claims of socialist parties that Parliaments were by definition right when they decided the endless series of statutes that implemented the ideals of redistribution. They were right by definition because parliamentary majorities represented the majority of people, and the majority, in turn, was made up of people in need of redistribution from the better off.

Now, addressing the problems posed by redistributional policies, socialists put the blame on the "greed" of the so-called "Two thirds of the better off" who refuse to take care of the "One third" of the worst off, and use legislation more and more to their own advantage.

The truth is that socialists are seeing what liberals predicted a long time ago. They should not blame the "greed" of the majority of people, but the fact that they overlooked the reality of representative democracy. They have to bear the moral responsibility for the consequences of their views and their political action.

I am afraid that negative consequences in terms of wealth are not the main problem that we are addressing now and we shall have to address in the future as a consequence of the ideals of imposing on society a redistributional model. The main consequences are *political*. Let me try to illustrate this point.

One of the cornerstones of the rise of the constitutional regimes was the principle of the distinction between *law* and *morality*. It was the proper task of the State to provide the legal framework within which individuals could interact and peacefully cooperate. The State had no *ethical* aims. Actually, any idea of an *ethical State* was strictly contradictory with liberalism, while it was the very ideological foundation of absolutism before and the mass dictatorships of this century later on.

The redistributional State is an ethical State. No aspect of human life is left outside its range of action. This must be so if a general model is to be imposed upon society. By definition redistributional legislation is not general legislation and is not *value-neutral*. The imperative of reaching greater and greater equality of means becomes the basic moral criterion for the legitimacy of all public policies. They punish some kinds of behaviour not because they could harm somebody, but because they do not conform to the imperative of equality. As a necessary consequence, any boundaries between the sphere of *private* relationships amongst citizens and the *public* sphere faded away, because the first was made dependent upon the second in order to pursue the imperative of equality.

As I said before, the reality of the political processes of representative democracy has substantially modified the content of redistributional policies with respect to the original socialist ideal. But the negative consequences for liberal democracy did not fade away at all. The separation between the private and the public sphere was Liberalism's main instrument for avoiding *conflict* within society. But the redistributive State is deprived of this instrument. Almost no aspect of the life of citizens is left outside the range of parliamentary majority decisions.

As a consequence, one should not wonder that the political process has become a continuous fight amongst organized interests which try to get their share of the resources collected by the State. And what they get is not a function of their contribution to the well-being of their fellow citizens, but a result of their weight in the distributional game. Under these conditions it is perfectly obvious that those groups that believe they have been the losers of the game feel resentment towards the other groups.

It has always been a major pretence of redistributionists that redistribution was and is the only way for securing peace amongst social groups in the democratic regimes. As they always did in their history, redistributionists confuse the results of capitalism with the results of their own action. It is because capitalism produces such a wealth that the social conflicts that are generated by redistributional policies do not growth to such a point as to become dangerous for the peaceful cooperation of people.

Another consequence is equally obvious. Citizens no longer consider that the State is *above* private interests. Even the limited experience of the common people is sufficient for them to realize that the State – both at national and local level – is not serving the *general interest*, but the private interests of different pressure groups. One may wonder what the consequences will be of this state of affairs upon the *legitimacy* of the democratic regimes. Never has the State been so extended: never – except in war time – has it absorbed such a large part of national wealth. But at the same time it has become obvious even to the common people that the State is increasingly unable to perform its traditional functions effectively. Vital decisions are taken slowly or not taken at all, as is shown by the permanent formation of high budget deficits. There is barely any need to point out that budget deficits are precisely the result of redistributional schemes targeted for electoral support. More than budgets, what are in deficit today are democratic institutions. One wonders whether they will continue to command the loyalty of citizens when the impossibility of further expansions of deficits make clear that the political promises of giving everything to everybody have come to the end.

A Moral Redistribution

There is no theoretical or empirical necessity to assume that most of the negative effects of redistribution that we experience today upon the economy and the State would have been there if redistribution had been intended in the first sense suggested by de Jouvenel. There are two main reasons for this.

In the first place, redistribution in this sense does not imply any of the policies that have been implemented in order to achieve greater equality amongst citizens, not by increasing the level of the bottom but by preventing the top from rising. No obstacles to the creation of wealth have to be implemented.

In the second place, if redistribution is directed exclusively to help people whose income falls below a given level, there is no possible political justification for all those money transfers which go to groups whose income is higher than that level. Despite the fact that there is little redistribution today because of the ideals of equalizing means between citizens, it was these very ideals that prepared the way to redistributional policies. Except for a small elite, anybody might claim to be worse off than somebody else, and advocate his "right" to be the beneficiary of redistribution. Egalitarian ideals have opened the way for the corporativism of today.

What is the moral justification of non equality-seeking redistribution? For strict individualistic liberals the answer is none. Any extension of the functions of the State beyond the protection of individual rights implies that coercion is exerted upon citizens and – even more important – that some of them (those who are the net losers) are treated differently from the others.

More recently, eminent liberal thinkers, such as James Buchanan, have tried to prove that redistribution could be morally justified even under individualistic descriptive and normative assumptions.

The conceptual mechanism that generates redistribution out of individual rights is *contractarianism* or, more simply, a generalization of the theory of insurance. Individuals would freely pay a part of their income to be assured that if they were to be in need they would get a decent income.

Buchanan's position is very attractive. Nevertheless, I am afraid that it fails to prove, under general conditions, that redistribution does not violate individualistic principles[9].

This is not the proper place for entering into technical and somewhat abstract arguments. In my opinion it is difficult to escape the conclusion reached by the late Friedrich von Hayek: "Even the recognition of a claim by every citizen or inhabitant of a country to a certain minimum standard [...] involves [...] the recognition of collective ownership of the resources of the country, which is not compatible with the idea of an open society" – an individualistic society[10].

But perhaps von Hayek went too far. In order to giustify this form of redistribution we do not necessarily have to assume the concept of collective ownership. Redistribution can be justified in the same way that we *morally* justify the power of the State to require its citizens to play their part in case of war or natural catastrophes. Namely, taxation for the purpose of granting people in need a means of subsistence is an evil that is justified by the necessity of avoiding even worse consequences for the totality or the great majority of citizens.

We have here an example of the moral principle that, according to the late Karl Popper, has to inspire all the activities of the State: *negative* utilitarianism, that is to say, *removing* unhappiness without aiming at *promoting* happiness.

There is no need to stress that the difference between these two concepts corresponds almost completely to the difference between the two concepts of redistribution defined by de Jouvenel.

An important asymmetry is demonstrated here. The first concept of redistribution implies the *duty* of citizens to contribute to help the less fortunate members of society. But it does not imply any *right* of these latter to the resources legitimately owned by the first. The political consequences of this asymmetry may be very far-reaching.

Perspectives

Liberal redistribution is not egalitarian redistribution at a lower level. It is a completely different view of man, politics, economy, institutions and ethics.

Is there any chance that our democracies will abandon their present redistributional policies for more liberal alternatives? Any answer to this question is likely to be more similar to a prophecy rather than to a scientific prediction. As Popper said, whether prophecies turn out to be true or false is not a matter of knowledge but of mere luck. Since, in general, I am not a lucky man I prefer not to make any prophecy.

If we had to follow the ideas of such thinkers as de Tocqueville, Pareto and Ortega y Gasset, it is unlikely that the working of future representative democracy with unrestricted franchise will be much different from the present one. And since what they said has found remarkable confirmation in reality, one may well understand the pessimistic feelings of many liberals about the future of *both* liberty and democracy.

However, I believe that opportunities for change have not to be underevaluated. There are several elements that suggest that some of the structural conditions that determined the present situation are changing.

In the first place, the transaction costs of redistributional policies have become so high that even for the median voter these policies becomes less attractive, even from the purely "static" point of view: i.e., without considering the long-run effects of redistribution on the production of wealth.

Secondly, one of the basic mechanisms that makes redistribution attractive to people may no longer be so effective. Redistribution is attractive because there is an *asymmetry* between its costs and its benefits. The costs are spread as uniformly as possible among citizens (or, alternatively, are placed on categories of citizens who have little weight in the political game either because there are too few of them – like the rich – or because they have low organizational capacities – like the poor). On the contrary, benefits are targeted as precisely as possible in order to win electoral support. This would be in itself a sufficient proof that redistributional policies are by essence *anti*-democratic. Their very existence crucially depends upon the fact of concealing to the citizens the relevant information they would need in order to make their own reasoned decisions upon the redistribution they want.

But there is no guarantee that the game of so-called "Fiscal illusion" can go on indefinitely. There is probably a point where the burden of taxation becomes so high that even for the median voter the costs of policies can no longer be made "invisible" by such mechanisms as "Pay-as-you-earn" or "Pay-as-you-go", and many others.

At the same time, one should not underestimate the fact that, after decades, the benefits of redistribution are perceived by people as something which is due from the State anyway. This would reinforce the perceived costs of the high taxation needed for redistributional policies.

In the third place, the unprecedented opening of the economies of our democracies to international trade makes it more and more difficult for governments to maintain redistributional policies that decrease the competitiveness of firms on the world market. It also makes it more difficult to implement confiscatory fiscal policies on the most successful members of society in order to finance redistributional policies.

Of course, these are just a few hints. Liberals do not believe in historical materialism. They know that the economic element is only a component of social and political reality. Ideas matter more than interests, as Keynes and Hayek both agreed. This means that any perspective for a deep change in redistributional policies – and ultimately, in politics itself – will crucially depend upon the sentiments that develop amongst the majority of citizens.

Nobody can tell if these sentiments will be strongly egalitarian *or* corporative, or if people will attach greater importance to the principles of liberty. The reason is that this will largely depend upon the capacity of the different ideological movements and political parties to persuade public opinion, the "Sanior et maior pars" of citizens, as Luigi Einaudi liked to call it.

There is no reason why liberalism should be the loser in this ideological fight. But something new is needed. Liberal intellectuals should leave the rather defensive position they have assumed in the last half century. They should elaborate positive views and projects to persuade the public opinion that a liberal society is a good society for all individuals, and not only for the better off. In turn, liberal parties should cease to act as if they believed that liberalism can survive only as a residual component of political life, or as a rather snobbish imitation of socialist and conservative parties.

There is no reason why the well-educated and prosperous citizens of our democracies should continue to give overwhelming electoral support to socialist and conservative parties. In their private lives people attach an importance to freedom that is probably unprecedented in history, at least at mass level. But at the same time they attach a great importance to protection against material uncertainty.

It is our task to persuade them that liberalism is the only political view that can offer in real world freedom, security and prosperity to all.

Notes

1   See B. de Jouvenel, *The Ethics of Redistribution* (1952), Indianapolis, Liberty*Press*, 1990, pp. 17–22 *passim*.
2   See H. Schoeck, *Envy* (1966), Indianapolis, Liberty*Press*, 1987, pp. 388–9.
3   See A. Flew, 'Liberalismo e socialdemocrazia: la differenza dei principi politici', *Biblioteca della Libertà*, XXVII (1992), n. 118, p. 37.
4   See R. Nozick, *Anarchy, State and Utopia*, New York, Basic Books,

1974, *passim*. For a more detailed analysis see my *Giustizia e conseguenze delle azioni* in A.M. Petroni (ed.), *Giustizia come libertà? Saggi su Nozick*, special issue of *Bibilioteca della liberta*, XX (1984), n. 91.

5   G. Stigler, 'Director's Law of Public Income Redistribution', *The Journal of Law and Economics*, XIII (1970), n.1, p.1.

6   See M. Olson, *A New Approach to the Ethics of Redistribution*, The Manville American Enterprise Lecture, College of Business Administration, University of Notre Dame, 13 February 1986.

7   See E. Weede, 'Democracy, creeping socialism, and ideological socialism', in *Rent-Seeking Societies, Public Choice*, vol. 44, 1984, n. 2, p. 360. The thesis of Olson has best been expressed in his *Logica delle Istituzioni*, Milan, Comunità, 1994, chapter IV.

8   See P. Samuelson, 'My life philosophy', *American Economist*, 1983.

9   On the whole problem see my 'What is right with Hayek's ethical theory', *Revue européenne des sciences sociales*, XXXIII (1995), n. 100.

10 See F.A. von Hayek, *Law, Legislation and Liberty*, London, Routledge and Kegan Paul, 3 vols., 1973, 1976, 1979; vol. 3, pp. 55–56.

Competition Among Systems – An Ordo Liberal View

Gerhard Schwarz

I. Introduction

In Switzerland the vote on joining the European Economic Area (EEA) – whose outcome was clearly negative – has lead to ferocious and highly emotional discussions on all levels of political and intellectual life. It is against this background that the following essay has been written. Many of the arguments may seem outdated or at least already well known for EU citizens. They try, however, to put the Swiss integration policy, which is seen from many critics inside and outside the country as purely isolationist, in a broader perspective. Given the heated debate in Switzerland the arguments are also more often political than economical. The text is based on a speech given in the fall of 1993 in the "Aula" of the University of Zürich[1], in the same place where Winston Churchill has given his famous speech to the young people of Europe "Let Europe arise".

The starting point of the article is the conviction, that, in order to continue to live in a free economy and in a free society, it is indispensable to subject possessions and conditions that have become dear to so many to critical scrutiny. This seems the only way to acquire the inner freedom that is necessary to shape a better, more liberal future – liberal of course meant in the European sense. It is in this light that the idea of competition between systems is to be understood, which can be applied to traditional nation states, and thus to Switzerland, just as it can be applied to larger-scale unions. Against this background it becomes clear, that the question for member states and potential new members like Switzerland should not be Integration, yes or no? but What kind of integration?

Regrettably enough the EU is suffering greatly from the lack of sufficiently clear-cut guidelines, since from the very beginning there was a clash of two model systems, one advocating free trade, the other focusing on an emerging state:[2] in its history, the EC was alternately bitten by an evolutionist and by a constructivist dog. Both models aim at integration. One is represented by liberal personalities such as, formerly, Ludwig Erhard and Wilhelm Röpke – who contributed towards the fact that initially, competition between systems in Europe experienced a substantial increase thanks to the EC – or the majority of today's German-speaking economists and, naturally, also Margaret Thatcher. The other model, the constructivist model, was originally represented by Walter Hallstein and in more recent times not least by the Christian Democrat Helmut Kohl and the socialists François Mitterand and Jacques Delors. It is this constructivism and the faith in feasibility which put freedom in jeopardy – not the centralism of Brussels, which is a pet target in debates characterised by soundbites.

II. Competition between Systems

1. Introduction

What is meant by the evolutionist approach, and thus with competition between systems, can best be illustrated with a small historical reminiscence. Voltaire, the great 18th century champion of the Enlightenment, had several places of residence and was thus able to protect himself against the reach of governmental power. His French residence, the small castle of Ferney, was immediately adjacent to Switzerland. This enabled him to escape to Switzerland – where he had another residence – in a matter of minutes whenever the French state wanted to get hold of him. If, however, the Calvinist authorities in Switzerland had designs on him, he fled to Ferney. Voltaire's entire existence as a spirit of the Enlightenment was thus crucially dependent on the fact that there was no single state in Europe, but several states, and that it was possible to move from one jurisdiction to another – and vice versa.[3]

This brief excursion into the realm of history shows quite graphically what competition between systems is all about. It will be evident that nowadays, years after the collapse of socialism, the term does not refer to the old antagonism between capitalism and communism, even though this antagonism still exists and will continue to exist, quite contrary to the unrealistic triumphalism of the liberal idea that found expression in the thesis of the end of history. Meanwhile, Francis Fukuyama has fortunately restated his theory – whose success may not least have been the result of its pronounced one-sidedness – in somewhat more relative terms, and perceives a challenge for the Western world primarily in the emerging South-East Asian region.[4] Today, we undoubtedly live in a more liberal century than Voltaire. We have not, however, reached the end of history, and for this reason there should and there will continue to be dissenters, deviationists, mavericks and innovative spirits – also in the societal sphere. To protect such people's right to freedom, competition among systems is likely to be a much more effective instrument than provisions of interior policy and constitutional safeguards.

What is touched upon, then, by competition between systems is the rivalry between political entities – no matter whether they are nations or cantons, member states or communities – which basically may well be committed to the same or at least to similar values, for the mobile production factors of labour, capital and knowledge. If the Swiss Canton of Zug has succeeded in drawing in countless firms from at home and abroad by means of an attractive fiscal legislation, then this is nothing other than competition between systems. However, this is of course not just a matter of taxation but equally extends to legal, social, education and monetary systems, to name but a few, so that in more comprehensive terms, one could also speak of competition between jurisdictions. The rivalry does not take place between companies but between governments. Customers or demanders are the production factors, and the supply is constituted by the policy mix and thus, finally, by the quality of the location. For competition between systems to function at all, it is absolutely indispensable to have a completely free movement of persons and capital. As soon as such free movement is restricted, competition will no longer fully function. This is precisely what characterises today's reality. Although competition between systems exists, it only does so to a limited extent. Competition between systems may be an economically inspired approach, but since the economy can and must never be an end in itself, the goal is not economic in nature, but is the protection of freedom. People should not live in conditions that have been decreed or are fatalistically endured; rather, they should be able to choose their societal and economic conditions themselves. For as economic competition turns the customer into a king, political competition should turn the citizen into a king. This is the raison d'être of competition. With respect to the EC – or the EU – this is tantamount to the replacement of erstwhile bloody rivalry between nations by a bloodless competition between nations – concurrent with the rejection of the monopoly of a superstate sui generis.

2. The Country-of-Origin Principle

Yet how should this competition between systems function in detail? Possibly the most convincing approach in this context has been provided by the EU itself – not by the Commission, however, but by the Court of Justice: the famous, often quoted Cassis-de-Dijon ruling. With the example of this well-known French fruit liqueur, it declares the principle of the mutual recognition of national rules and standards. According to the country-of-origin principle, national rulings within the EU should generally be recognised as being of equal value. If this approach is followed up consistently, it still remains possible – to put it simply – to decree specific national standards, but those must not turn into a non-tariff barrier for foreign suppliers; the market must be accessible. Thus the Cassis-de-Dijon ruling basically states that discrimination against domestic producers may be admissible while discrimination against foreign producers is not. Germany, say, is entitled to order its own brewers to adhere to the so-called law of purity but must not impede the import of beers that have been brewed according to other methods. So much for the basic idea of this so simple and so liberal ruling.

3. Federalism and Subsidiarity – Related Terms

The notions of subsidiarity and federalism (meaning a system of government in which power is divided between a central authority and constituent political unities) are related to the idea of competition between systems. They are frequently even lumped together with competition between systems and, indeed, they overlap it to a great extent. To be sure, they set somewhat different accents. However, all three concepts aim to decentralise the power of the state geographically; they aim to distribute power.

3.1. Federalism

It is a fundamental feature of federalism that first, citizens belong to several state levels at once, second, each of these levels fulfils certain functions autonomously, third, the central level ensures cohesion, and fourth, the member states participate in the formulation of political objectives at the highest level. Thus a federalist state consists of a mix of centralised and decentralised elements, and this mix may take various shapes and guises.[5] The idea of federalism tends to aim at a national distribution of power and competence among the member states of a federation, whereas competition between systems tends to focus on the rivalry between existing nation states. When we look at the EU, both terms naturally almost merge. Nonetheless, Daniel Thürer is probably right when he states that many Swiss feel that the EU's legal system has a tendency to run counter to federalism since it is not inspired by a federalist philosophy or ethic. Jacques Delors' famous reply to a question in the European parliament to the effect that the word federalism did not appear in the EC foundation treaties nor in any later amendments, and that it was not the Commission's job to interpret an expression unknown to Community law, naturally reinforces such feelings.[6]

3.2. Subsidiarity

Susidiarity, a principle which is liberal as such but, in terms of the history of ideas, has primarily been propagated by the social teachings of the Catholic church, places an emphasis on small units.[7] Undoubtedly, competition between jurisdictions will increase in proportion to the extent to which the lowest levels, that of communities and federal member states, are granted authority to regulate; yet competition between systems can also function between large-scale nation states. Accordingly, such competition is not only constituted by the element of smallness. Conversely, bureaucracy is easier to control in one single small unit than in bigger organisations, but it is only the existence of several geographically distributed bodies at the same level that allows for comparisons and thus provides additional possibilities of control.[8] Subsidiarity has long become a hackneyed phrase that can virtually mean what anyone wants it to mean. The fact that the Maastricht Treaty explicitly takes up this principle may be regarded as progress, yet only if it is interpreted in a liberal sense – for which, however, there is no guarantee. Rather, it must be suspected that – as so often in the history of the EC – subsidiarity has been taken as a formula wide enough to unite the ideas of no fewer than twelve member states under one umbrella while being sufficiently open-ended to leave members in the hope that they will be able to interpret and apply it according to their own individual predilections.[9] Thus the establishment of the principle of subsidiarity in the EU is unlikely to provide a safeguard against excessive state centralism, at least for the time being. If article 3(2) of the EC Treaty states that the Community would only be able to become active – apart from a list of exclusive competencies that is too long in any case – if and when the objectives envisaged at the level of member states could not be sufficiently attained and, owing to their scope and effects, were therefore more likely to be attained at Community level, then this formulation is only of little use as an abutment against centralist tendencies. (It is therefore not a matter of pure chance, either, if Horst Friedrich Wünsche, an economist conversant with Ludwid Erhard, maintains that the latter would have been sceptical about the subsidiarity rule.[10])

To begin with – as Wernhard Möschel[11] points out – this rule is juristically modified by the mere fact that it rivals principles which run counter to it but are also established in the EC and Union Treaties: cohesion, for instance, and solidarity, but also the social chapter of the Treaty of Maastricht. More crucial, however, is the rule of delegation, i.e. the question as to the onus of proof and the allocation of competence. The answers to this question will be one thing if the smallest political units are a priori regarded as autonomous and thus as competent, so that any transfer of functions to a higher level is authorised by them alone, on the grounds of qualified arguments, and they will be quite a different thing if the highest level decides that communities, cantons or countries are not able to cope and must therefore be relieved of certain competencies and functions.

Even if the onus of proof were properly distributed from a liberal perspective, it still remains a question of one's view of the world and of people whether or not to diagnose that a lower level is unable to cope and needs help. That means: Even an interpretation of the principle of subsidiarity which is formally correct from a liberal point of view will thus not automatically preclude the tendency towards more state power and more centralisation: it will not do so whenever individual communities at any level do not want it to for ideological or other motives. Finally, one can always find sufficiently good reasons for an escape into the higher instance.[12]

III. The ex-ante Harmonisation

In comparison with the aforementioned ideas committed to decentralisation and competition, in the EC the tendencies towards a policy of harmonisation were always stronger. This meant an extremely laborious path to an attunement of ideas at a central level. In the long run competition, too, breeds a tendency towards harmonisation, but in a process evolving out of the markets. Here, however, what is meant is a harmonisation decreed from above, on the basis of lengthy political negotiations about the adaptation of laws, rules and taxation. This type of policy might well have been even more pronounced if the unanimity rule and the so-called democracy deficit of the EU had not acted as a brake.[13] There is no reason, then, for indulging in any illusions: within the framework of the EC, more democracy does not necessarily mean a better safeguard of individual freedom at all.

1. The Attraction of Standardisation

The attraction of harmonisation is primarily based on four factors: first – and this has been done ever since the Enlightenment – an antagonism is construed between unitarian-rational and pluralist-intuitive tendencies, with the former taking precedence over the latter. If, for instance, Descartes thought that Sparta had become such a flourishing body politic because its laws had been invented by one single individual and because, at the same time, all these laws had been aimed at one single goal with logical consistency, then it is probably such thoughts that have given rise to the idea of uniformity as the driving force of progress. Second, it is envy, regrettably an all too human trait, that has always been pushing for standardisation. Third, the costs and drawbacks of harmonisation are much more difficult to ascertain and quantify than those of diversity. Fourth, harmonisation is often appreciated from a static perspective. And with a given state of knowledge, the coercion to reform, which for many countries is a consequence of harmonisation, may indeed appear to be quite reasonable. This appearance is deceptive, however, to the extent to which even here and now, the harmonised standards may well constitute a regression in comparison with the previously applicable standards – or part of them. Since, as we all know, political processes do not run according to objective considerations alone but invariably contain a political *do ut des*, it is even possible that the worst or the second worst solution may win the day. Why, then, not rather leave the existing diversity in place? Above all else, however, harmonisation is questionable from a dynamic viewpoint because it reduces the compulsion or motivation constantly to produce new answers abreast of the times. Even if harmonisation should lead to the best solution for today, it will still not provide a suitable basis that serves to look for, and find, the best solutions for tomorrow and the day after tomorrow.

Ultimately, ex-ante harmonisation degenerates into a political cartel; it protects government from competition. Governments need not make efforts to look for better laws because their competitors have exactly the same. At the same time, harmonisation also tends to satisfy the cartellistic temptations evinced by entrepreneurs: just like any cartel attempts to do, it restricts the number of parameters that play a role in competition. If bottle sizes are standardised and safety standards imposed for the whole of Europe *ex officio*, then competition and thus the permanent search for the best solution in this field will no longer be able to come into play.

2. Arguments for Standardisation

Three arguments in particular have entered the lists in defence of standardisation and harmonisation.

2.1. *Excessive Transaction Costs?*

The most frequent economic justification is that of inefficiency and high transaction costs of differing legal systems, currencies, etc., i.e. the argument of the costs of non-Europe. What a traveller through Europe may sometimes experience as nuisance, and sometimes as a perfectly fascinating change – different currencies, languages, shopping hours, highway codes, etc. – may indeed turn into a genuine encumbrance for companies active in Europe and worldwide. Diverging patterns of conduct, as well as the coercion to adapt products partially to local conditions – which reduces economies of scale – and to protect oneself against exchange losses, often cause companies considerable costs. This consideration provides the basis for the ardour of those who would like to harmonise any possible obstacle to a free single market out of harm's way. However, the opinion, which prevailed in the founding years of the EU and has been a hallmark of Commission rhetoric ever since[14], i.e. the idea, that the number of people is proportionate to prosperity and that the size of the single market is thus automatically an economic advantage, is most questionable. This has not only been proved by many recent studies[15], but may be ascertained by one single glance at the globe. Small states such as Hong Kong, Singapore or Taiwan, but also Switzerland, Sweden or the Netherlands, have achieved national prosperity because their small sizes force them to face international competition. In small countries, economic freedom is practically a natural constitutional standard.[16] The success of small countries is based on the openness which they are forced to display, whereas big nations or political entities regularly succumb to the temptation of protectionism. Added to this, the wholesale enthusiasm induced by the market size to be achieved by means of harmonisation always makes people forget that, from an ORDO point of view, what should be pursued is harmonised liberalisation and not harmonised regulation; however, most harmonisers neglect this aspect in an unpardonable manner.[17]

2.2. *Equal Rights for All*

A further argument in favour of harmonisation and thus against competition between systems propounds that successful competition in any given market is only possible if the same legal standards apply throughout. This extremely problematical claim can be refuted with one single glance at the world market. Equally questionable is the argument – mostly voiced in the same breath –, that different legal systems lead towards different burdens of cost for competing companies. This observation may be correct, but international – and thus also European – division of labour is based not only on differences in productivity, but precisely also on differences in costs, which range from labour costs to environmental costs, from capital costs to taxation. Certainly every company that operates in a country with high overall costs will find itself under pressure in the course of time – as will that country itself – but this is a good thing since it encourages the competition between systems which harmonisation prevents everywhere.

The demand for equal rights for all is closely related to the idea that the sphere of political influence must be congruent with the sphere of economic activities. For precisely this reason, the liberals of the 19th century were not precursors of federalism at all even then. They wanted to establish a larger economic space, the large space of free movement, and for this purpose preferred, or at least readily accepted, a certain centralisation of state power.[18] Then as now, it is overlooked in this context that market integration and political integration, often mentioned in one single breath, constitute an antagonism. Market integration multiplies the number of demanders and suppliers – no matter whether this concerns goods, services, capital, or labour – and thus leads to an expansion and intensification of economic competition. Conversely, political integration leads to an assimilation of policies by means of agreements or to a centralisation of decision-making, i.e. to a curtailment of political competition.[19]

3. Does Decentralisation equal Nationalism?

Possibly the weightiest argument for standardisation and thus against competition between systems is not economic or genuinely liberal in nature, but of a political and moral bent. It states that only through harmonisation can a revival be prevented of that nationalism which brought so many wars and so much misery to Europe and which has been rearing its ugly head again in the southeast of the continent for far too long. This must no doubt be taken seriously. Looked at in broad daylight, however, the reproach is wide of the mark. It must be said in advance that first, nationalism per se is neither good nor bad and that the terms "nation" and "nation state" must not be too closely linked with the notion of bad, xenophobic nationalism[20], that second, the concern for the greatest possible decentralisation of political power must not be equated with nationalism, and that third, a plea for competition between countries is far from postulating an ethnically homogeneous nation state. Above all, however, competition need not necessarily be destructive and warlike – nor, to be sure, need it generally be less of a safeguard for peace than a European superpower capable of acting, or than the United States of Europe which is sometimes invoked in romantic exaggeration.

On the one hand, people look for identity within the framework of a nation state. This need not lead to excessive nationalism; on the contrary: an attempt to more or less abandon the nation state to a superordinate entity at a forced pace may have extremely counterproductive effects. This was pointed out by Irenäus Eibl-Eibesfeldt, who based this statement on numerous studies conducted all over the world, and who was then immediately labelled a fascistoid on this account. He asked the question as to why diversity resists even the greatest opposition with such stubborn tenacity, and provided the following answer: because life uses diversity to ensure its survival. At a biological level, life incessantly makes use of mutation and gene combinations to create variants, subspecies and species which face their environments and either sink or swim. With human beings, this occurs through the diversity of cultures and races. Every group of people who characterises themselves through their own customs, ideologies and thus through objectives, social techniques and economic systems constitutes an experiment within the stream of life and thus becomes, as it were, one of the spearheads of evolution. Diversity, not standardisation is a principle of life. It survives with the help of mechanisms of demarcation. These include a wide variety of patterns of keeping one's distance, of territoriality, the we-group behaviour characteristic of many higher mammals, and xenophobia.[21] Eibl-Eibesfeldt thus regards it as important that an integration process should encourage diversity rather than repress it; the open society in Popper's sense of the term on the one hand, and demarcation on the other, do not form a pair of opposites for him. Conversely, a forced levelling-out of differences reduces the width of adaptation, is basically anti-evolutionary, and reinforces fear and mistrust.

On the other hand, it is perfectly conceivable that a large number of small and medium-sized, not excessively powerful nations are more conducive to world peace than a world with three, four or five strong blocs, among them the EU. For one thing must not be overlooked: in spite of Salvador de Madariaga's warning[22] that Europe is no nation, the EU now runs the risk of developing into a copy of a 19th century nation state on a higher level, including the numerous nation state symbols ranging from the national anthem to the flag, from national citizenship to the single currency. To this extent, the EU, despite its legal system sui generis, is by no means so innovative as is often claimed. Above all, the emphasis on its peace-keeping function is based on a Eurocentric point of view: an integration by means of harmonisation and a levelling-out of differences may in future prevent the conflicts inside Europe that have created such a great amount of trouble over the centuries. However, in view of the American and Asian challenges which must apparently be faced, and in view of the concomitant demand that Europe must gain political and military weight to match its economic potential, this is not apt to give rise to confidence alone. In any case, it would be geopolitically fatal to accord the new Euronationalism a more elevated moral dignity per se than is accorded to the patriotism of traditional European nation states.[23]

IV. Of the Benefits of Competition

How do these arguments in favour of harmonisation from above contrast with the advantages of competition between systems and thus largely also with the advantages of federalism, subsidiarity and small states? There are mainly four arguments in favour of competition among systems: knowledge, limitation of errors, power and incentives. If understood properly, they make clear that a lack of diversity causes costs, too – even though they are difficult to assess – the costs of non-diversity[24].

1. Competition: a Process of Discovery

Before anything else, a characteristic of competition must be mentioned which economic theory had not even recognised for a long time before it was moved into the foreground by Friedrich August von Hayek: competition is a process of discovery. After all, no one knows in advance which regulations, taxes and government performances will prove to be the best for any participants in the market, for individual members states, or for the EU. Competition between different systems makes it possible in each case for the best to win through.[25] For this reason it is erroneous to assume that competition between systems opposes a harmonisation of national regulations. Indeed, it even leads quite clearly to such an assimilation, but from the bottom up, not from the top down with decrees and political negotiations. The adaptation process is left to the market to ensure that harmonisation will take place precisely to the extent to which demanders wish. Undoubtedly, such a procedure requires more time than a dictate from above. Nowhere, however, is a process of testing and correcting, of experimenting and constant search for innovations so desirable than in the fields of society and politics. A state or a confederation which wants to ensure its survival will remain open to the uncoordinated and contradictory elements of competition even if it is totally convinced that it has found the one and only true solution for the time being, and even if this rather runs contrary to Helvetic or Germanic perfectionism. For standardisation ends all too easily in averageness, in the morass of mediocrity.

In recent times, a number of historians and social philosophers[26] have begun to sing the praises of diversity in Europe. They have used this diversity as a basis for their explanation of why it was precisely here that technical and economic developments experienced such an acceleration, and not in China, which had for a long time been far ahead in the field of technology. The most prominent of these historians-economists is probably Douglass North[27]. According to his theory of economic development, capitalism was able to evolve in Europe because it was only here that the possibility of the mobility of capital and the risk of losing valuable human capital was operative as a mighty deterrent against the confiscatory machinations of the rulers who were then in power. The secret of success was the diversity that is a prerequisite of evolutionary competition. This led to the taming of Leviathan, to respect for private property, to growth and prosperity. Thus it was Europe's very good fortune that there was no central power.[28] However, the list of champions of diversity reaches much further back into history,[29] as far back as Aristotle and Plato, who despite a strong ideological antagonism agreed that a sound political life was only possible in manageable forms of state of the size of a Greek polis; this list further includes Justus Möser and Johann Gottfried Herder; it includes Montesquieu, who analysed the almost naturally given small size of the European states as the cause of the great urge towards freedom; it includes Rousseau and – in Switzerland – Johannes von Müller and Jakob Burckhardt. All of these not only paid tribute to life in a small state but also to pluralism and to competition between small-scaled political entities.

2. The Limitation of Errors

Closely linked with the characteristic of competition as discovery process is a further advantage, namely the limitation of errors. This is one of the most important arguments in favour of a decentralisation of decision-making, be it in companies, be it in government and society. Both corporate management and politics are in a permanent stage of experiment, and wrong decisions are bound to be as numerous as right ones. In addition, their effects are not symmetrical: if big states make a big mess of things, to put it somewhat casually, this may be disastrous for the whole world and cannot simply be compensated for by big acts of charity. It is therefore an advantage that the Swedish welfare state remained confined to Sweden, and that the French wave of nationalisation in the early 1980s remained confined to France, and that both were able to act as a model – but above all as deterrent – from there. By the opposite token it is as well an advantage that only in Switzerland it took so long for women to get the right to vote, and that only there people stubbornly retain a school system that ties women to hearth and home, and that other countries are permanently showing the Swiss how they could perform better – at least in the fields mentioned. Competition between systems is almost naturally tantamount to a limitation of damage inflicted by false decisions, and it is therefore also more open to experiments; at the same time this does not at all mean that the best solution will not prevail in time – only that the time for it is not ripe everywhere at the same time. In contrast to this, the harmonisers' constructivist approach shows exuberant optimism: it aims to introduce and implement the momentarily best solution everywhere, i.e. in the whole of Europe. In doing so, the harmonisers erroneously assume that it is immediately evident what the best solution is, or that in any case the number of right decisions is greater than the number of errors.

3. Proximity to the Citizen

A further aspect of competition between systems is the a higher degree of compliance with the preferences of the citizens. Evidently, pan-European laws and standards that have only been backed by a small majority are unsatisfactory for virtually the other half of the population. The more that is regulated at subordinate regional level instead of at central level – the less, at any rate, that is standardised – the fairer the chance of being able to satisfy major parts of the population. This is because competition between systems ensures that only those policies can be instituted which are accepted by the population of individual member states or cantons. If a standardised solution is imposed, however, whole regions may be steamrollered. Moreover, a decentralised structure basically helps minorities, including ideological ones, to obtain more rights. The proverbial parish-pump horizon, thus also has its good sides.

A better consideration of the individual preferences has also something to do with the distance between the level of decision-making and the level of effects. Proximity to the citizen is a modern slogan, although it is not that modern, after all, if we consider that Jakob Burckhardt once wrote in his "Weltgeschichtliche Betrachtungen": "The small state exists so that there is a corner in the world where the greatest possible quota of inhabitants are citizens in the full sense of the term."[30] Of course the objection may be raised that a central government is also capable of drawing up differing regulations, but, to quote another great Swiss, Benjamin Constant, such laws are made at a place which is so far distant from the place of their application that serious and frequent errors are inevitable as a consequence of this distance.[31] The further the decision-making level is removed from social and economic reality, the further removed from reality will be the decisions. For this reason, standardised rules and regulations for so many nations and for various hundred million people must be restricted to a minimum if opportunities of choice, options and practical solutions are not to be precluded and welfare thus diminished.

Ultimately, competition also means more power for the individual, more sovereignty for citizens. Full civic sovereignty like consumer sovereignty is only possible with competition, i.e. only if citizens do not merely possess the right to cast their votes but are also able to vote with their feet and bank accounts. Albert O. Hirschman has expressed this in the formula of "exit and voice".[32] After all, ballot papers do not enable citizens to elect the government of their choice. That decision is taken by the majority, and an individual's vote is virtually devoid of any influence. The possibility of emigration, however, lends citizens additional weight, since it is perfectly sufficient that a threat of emigration looms over a government to discipline this government to a certain extent.[33] The numerousness and the proximity of countries in Europe increases this competitive pressure. Even so, no migration wave the length and breadth of the continent need be expected since the readiness to migrate across barriers of language and religion undoubtedly has its emotional limits.[34] As it is also more profitable to be informed in smaller units, either in order to exert influence or, possibly, to emigrate, the federalist concept of competition between systems is also likely to lead to a stronger political commitment on the part of citizens.[35]

4. The Pressure to Liberalise

Finally, from a liberal point of view, the most important advantage of competition between systems is the fact that it maintains a high pressure to preserve a liberal order or – in countries where this pressure is not very highly developed, like present-day Switzerland – that it increases this pressure. We all know in our heart of hearts that when all is said and done, genuine liberalisation in a democracy is usually only possible in the wake of wars and crises. It takes an earthquake to break up power and interest structures that have been cemented throughout long phases of prosperity.

There is only one exception to this rule: open borders – tariff- and non-tariff-wise – which expose national systems to competitive pressure and thus force them to adapt and to imitate successful problem solutions such as low taxation, a stable currency, an efficient educational system or a good constitution. Rather than as a consequence of the Eurosclerosis cliché or of a genuine will to political union, it was probably the challenge presented by deregulation efforts in the USA or the will to performance displayed in South-East Asia that prompted the EC to prescribe itself the biggest liberalisation programme of the century – provided it is carried out consistently. If the states have to compete for companies and inhabitants, this will restrict their opportunities to lead individuals by their noses. This is the fascination exerted on liberals by competition between systems.[36] There may well be only one way left to come to grips with the wildly sprawling intervention and welfare state of the late 20th century: exposing it to unharmonised competition.[37] This would fight at its very roots the vice of the modern good-turn democracy to distribute all kind of pleasantnesses – as opposed to necessities – although performance does not allow for it, and then to draw a bill of exchange on the future. Also, competition between systems would hardly permit political bodies to disregard economic principles known to every private household for such a long time and to try to balance expenditure and revenue only after it is almost to late. Competition with other countries would probably reveal the wrong turn taken by budget policy much sooner, and the threat of emigration would force the government much more strongly to promise only social policies for which the financial resources are in fact available.

Such a restriction of the scope of the state is by no means improper since it is carried out for the benefit of civic freedom. While a democracy prevents a government from ruling against the majority, competition between systems prevents a majority from exploiting a minority, from fleecing its economic élite or from imposing undue burdens on certain professions or regions. In this respect, democracy and competition between systems complement each other. One principle postulates majority power, the other is opposed to this power being set up as an absolute, and protects minorities. Incidentally, this idea that Leviathan could be successfully tamed by a government system that would decentralise power has already been aired by Alexander Hamilton, John Jay and James Madison, in their famous The Federalist Papers.[38]

Additional support for the liberal rejuvenation cure would be provided by the fact that in an open competition between systems, interest groups from the business sector would also make urgent and massive demands for less regulation and lower taxation – that is to say, whenever competitors abroad are less heavily regulated and taxed. As long as all competitors share the same burden – as is the case under decreed harmonisation – state-imposed encumbrance is mostly regarded as less aggravating, and the motivation to contradict is therefore likely to be weaker.[39] Anyone who considers a framework of liberal conditions to be an ethical concern above and beyond demand and supply, will no doubt welcome this support on the part of trade and industry even if it is solely based on competitive deliberations. Another effect, however, must not be overestimated. In his work *The Rise and Decline of Nations*, which has already become a classic, Mancur Olson claims that one dynamising impulse of an opening of borders consists in the fact that those interest groups which have contributed towards a restraint on individual competition are now confronted with an economic area that by far exceeds their political sphere of influence. Such an opening of borders would weaken them.[40] It may be argued, however, that this effect will be transitional in nature since interest groups quickly adapt to new conditions, forming international alliances, opening up offices in Brussels, etc.

In fact governments, too, should show an interest in learning something about the viability of their interventionism. In this respect, votes cast with feet and bank accounts are more expressive than the ballot box. Nevertheless, it is hardly surprising that competition between systems has not found a great number of followers among politicians so far, since this competition does not only tend to limit state power but fosters also an inequality and diversity which, to quote Constant once more, contains the seed of resistance which government power only tolerates unwillingly and seeks to uproot as quickly as possible.[41] Each law that has been standardised throughout Europe reassures politicians since it ensures that no other country will be able to raise its appeal by possibly more liberal legislation and thus attract capital and people. In this manner, harmonisation degenerates into a welfare-state cartel that protects governments from making any efforts.[42]

5. Competition for Everything?

Now, a liking for competition between systems has nothing at all to do with gullibly wanting to subject everyone and everything to competition. It is of extraordinary importance to ask the right question here, namely the question as to what absolutely must be regulated together in Europe, and not the question as to what can be regulated together.[43] Although some liberals (e.g. in Germany Radnitzky) voice the pronounced opinion that only an open system with competition in all spheres would be able to guarantee respect for private law,[44] yet the predominant view is that even a Europe based on the model of competition between systems would require certain common rules of play.

The majority of those who advocate a more loosely structured Europe, too, do not want to renege on the idea of a single market with a common foreign trade policy, the protection of competition through a central authority, and a constitutional community based on the rule of law and on democracy.[45] If such a community really only regulated what was objectively required – certain health provisions, say – and if apart from that the Cassis-de-Dijon principle would be applied, this would exercise a substantial pressure on governments to liberalise. Such impulses cannot be expected, however, from a proposed Council Directive running to more than 100 pages, to harmonise the legal provisions of member states concerning "the roll bar with two pillars mounted behind the driving seats of narrow gauge traction vehicles with pneumatic tyres" (in short: provisions concerning roll bars of small tractors), from a proposed directive to fix minimum standards for the keeping of animals in zoos, or from European standards for drinking water quality, to name but a few examples. A liberal community concentrating on essential issues could also regulate principles of a common foreign and security policy. Conversely, in any spheres where cross-border effects appear, such as jurisprudence, home affairs and environmental policy, common solutions are not strictly necessary; in such instances, preference should be given to cooperation. In 1980 Jacques Delors prophesied that in ten years 80 per cent of economic and possibly also fiscal and social legislation would be of Community origin. Even if this may have been exaggerated it is still sufficiently frightening.

The fact that any further-reaching harmonisation is unnecessary, indeed even harmful, can be briefly illustrated with the help of three examples:
1. Monetary policy: Instead of the single currency aimed at by "Maastricht", it would be enough to admit all EU currencies as legal tender in all EU member states without any discrimination; the weakest currencies, which would not survive on the strength of their quality but only because they are protected from competition by dint of being a nation-state relic, would soon be squeezed out. Three or four European currencies of some significance would be likely to survive. The advocates of the Euro might well get their money's worth in such a case: if a European central bank issued an Euro in competition with existing currencies, it would succeed if this currency were at least as stable and popular as, say, the German mark or the French franc – which, incidentally, owe their strength to competition between systems and not only to the independence of a central bank or similar institutional arrangements. Thus the European currency would have

to prove its worth; if it managed to do so, it would not have to be imposed on any country. Rather, citizens would voluntarily and gradually use it to replace the national currency that had been dear to them.[46] Failing to arrive at such a solution the great harmonisers will turn into terrible simplifiers.

2. Social security: The obstinate attempt to standardise working hours, Sunday rest hours, overtime, night-shift work, maternity leave, pensionable age, wages, ancillary wage costs, etc., or at least to approximate them to each other ex ante, is one of the most dangerous tendencies of EU policy. For one thing, an undifferentiated upward adaptation of the security systems is plainly unaffordable, and for another, any such development is at the expense of the poor countries, whose greatest hope for prosperity consists in keeping costs low, working more and taking fewer holidays, etc.[47] Only if the national social security systems are exposed to a geographical competition is there a chance that social covetousness will be curtailed by economic reality in good time. Regrettably the undesirable trend of European integration in the field of social security has, apart from agricultural policy, progressed furthest without any effective countermodel being proposed.[48]

3. Taxes: The conditio sine qua non of genuine competition is a competition of prices. If taxes are regarded as the price to pay for government goods and services, then their harmonisation would equal a massive restraint of competition. It would ascertainably lead to a neglect of individual preferences. Additionally, an optimum supply of public goods and services can only be expected if those who benefit from it also finance it. This principle of fiscal equivalence is, of course, massively violated by any transfer payments from one region or one country to another, even though it may shroud itself in the euphemism of cohesion – for instance, if the EU finances more than half the costs of Athens' underground train system. In view of the transaction costs caused by differing indirect taxes, the plea can occasionally be heard that only direct taxation should be exposed to competition between systems.[49] Yet even if those costs were indeed as high as is claimed, a free single market would in any case force countries with high VAT rates to revise these downward since otherwise purchases in foreign countries would become rampant. This proves that a competition between systems leads to an assimilation at a low level, whereas an ex-ante harmonisation allows for higher taxation.

This is precisely what many critics reproach competition between systems for. They are frightened that the state would be exposed to ruinous rivalry and thus no longer able to sustain an optimum supply. However, Josef Schumpeter – and later primarily Charles Tiebout, who is the originator of the idea of competition between systems – pointed out that the mobile factors of production draw a net balance.[50] High direct taxes and regulations are perfectly possible, provided they are offset by government goods and services that are correspondingly appreciated. Also, fiscal competition by no means prevents redistribution, as is occasionally claimed.[51] As long as such a redistribution produces the public good of social stability and cohesion, the account may be perfectly balanced. Thus empirical surveys reveal that redistribution is not less pronounced in Switzerland than, say, in Germany, despite the fiscal competition between the cantons.[52]

V. Conclusion

In Switzerland, the liberals of the 19th century wanted the whole of the country as one economic area, and they proceeded from the assumption that the extension of state power and of the economic area ought to be largely identical.[53] At the same time they wanted as small as possible an influence of the state on the individual – then, as at all times; the central power was supposed to partially provide the means to overcome local state power. Also today many liberals – in Switzerland and elsewhere – are fascinated by the idea of participating in a large area, the single market, even though this market is incomparably much larger than it was Switzerland at that time. These liberals are also in favour of free movement inside this area, which in terms of population is only second to China and India, and they hope that a superordinate level like the one the EU is providing is able to push forward the deregulations and economic reforms which national governments sometimes seem unable to bring about. As more than a century ago the higher EU level is supposed to serve as an instrument for the removal of excessive state power at national level. So far, so good.

However, many of today's liberals think further than this. They discern – not least on the basis of the national experience of a trend towards ever more state power in the capitals – that a danger of power concentration and of everything-but-liberal policies is also lying in wait at the level of the EU. In order to counter this danger for individual freedom, prosperity and progress, modern liberals back competition between systems, they back federalism, and they back genuine subsidiarity. They do not consider it sufficient if integration and a single market secure competition in the economic sphere for such banal objects as cars, deep-frozen food or dishwashers to do more justice to individual requirements.[54] They also want this consideration shown towards individual preferences in relation with more important things – societal matters, rules of living together, collective decision-making; they want to achieve this through competition between systems, which at the same time should clamp down on the tendency towards ever increasing state power.

From a liberal point of view therefore every effort must be made to ensure that the EU will not only commit itself to competition on the markets for goods and services but will also expose the jurisdictions of its member states and of lower levels to competition instead of uniting them in a harmonisation cartel. This is why the idea of establishing all this in an EU constitution of liberty is perfectly sensible.[55] This is in complete accordance with ordo-liberal ideas. The more such a constitution attempts to create a Europe that displays inward and outward openness, the more this would do justice to the objectives of the liberals among the founding fathers of the EC. To the same extent, the EU would also recover the partially diminished acceptance of its citizens. And to the same extent it might, above all, succeed in securing freedom and peace and in putting a stop to creeping socialisation. For the time being, however, the latter is moving forward with great alacrity – both in Switzerland and in the EU.

Notes

1 Schwarz, 1994, pp. 59.
2 Cf. Röpke, 1966, p. 44.
3 The story is taken from Wieland / Hoffmann, 1989, p. 34.
4 Cf. Fukuyama, 1993, p. 58.
5 Cf. Blöchlinger / Frey, 1992, p. 518. Cf. also Bütler, 1993, for the topicality of Swiss federalism and its lessons for Europe.
6 Cf. Thürer, 1993, p. 16. The question was Lord O'Hagan's, 1992.
7 Possibly the most significant philosopher of smallness is Leopold Kohr. Cf., for instance, Kohr, 1941. However, cf. also the arguments from the natural science end of the spectrum by Haldane, 1956, and Thomspon, 1956.
8 Cf. Kirchgässner / Pommerehne, 1993, p. 17.
9 Cf. CEPR, 1993. This report supplies a wealth of information and valuable representations of the issue although it is a typical product of double-handed economics (on the one hand, on the other hand) and thus argues only partially in favour of competition between systems.
10 Cf. Wünsche, 1993, p. 36.
11 Cf. Möschel, 1993, pp. 32f., and CEPR, 1993, p.XVI and pp. 5.
12 Nef, 1992, p. 688.
13 Cf. Baumberger, 1992, p. 7.
14 Watrin, 1993, p. 187.

15 Cf. Jones, 1991; Weede, 1991, and Raico, 1993. However, the thought was already expressed by Montesquieu.
16 Cf. Giersch, 1991.
17 Cf. Baumberger, 1992, p. 3.
18 Cf. Weizsäcker, 1987, p. 220.
19 Cf. Kammler, 1992, and Blöchlinger / Frey, 1992, p. 545.
20 Cf., for instance, Schauer, 1993, and Goble, 1993, who both plead for a differentiated view of nationalist tendencies.
21 Eibl-Eibesfeldt, 1992, p. 319.
22 de Madariaga, 1959, p. 264.
23 Cf. Habermann, 1993a, p. 3.
24 Cf., in particular, Baumberger, 1992, especially pp. 4.
25 Cf. Frankfurter Institut für wirtschaftspolitische Forschung, 1992, pp. 40f.
26 Cf., for instance, Jones, 1991; Weede, 1991, and Raico, 1993.
27 Cf., in particular, North, Robert, 1973, and North, 1993, for a brief survey.
28 Radnitzky, 1991, p. 142, argues along the same lines.
29 Habermann, 1993b, p. 2., has a more detailed look at the ideational histories of small countries. It is to him and to Kaltenbrunner, 1979, that I owe numerous pointers.
30 Burckhardt, 1963, p. 34.
31 Constant, 1942, p. 53.
32 Hirschmann, 1974.
33 Cf., for instance, Prosi, 1993, p. 9.
34 Cf. Weizsäcker, 1987, p. 223.
35 Cf. Eichenberger, 1993, p. 10.
36 Cf. Weizsäcker, 1987, p. 220.
37 Baumberger, 1992, p. 4, argues along the same lines.
38 Cf. Kramnick, 1987.
39 Cf. Eichenberger, 1993, p. 11.
40 Cf. Olson, 1991.
41 Constant, 1942, p. 47.
42 Cf. Baumberger, 1992, pp. 3f.
43 Cf. ASU, 1993, p. 15.
44 Radnitzky, 1991, is one of the advocates of such a view.
45 Cf. Möschel, 1993, p. 36.
46 For this view, cf. also Berthold, 1993, p. 38, for instance, who says: Ultimately, the ordo-political differences of opinion in this important question boil down to whom we consider more likely to be capable of imposing discipline on the decision-makers of monetary policy: the

market mechanisms, which depend on intensive competition in the currency markets, or the government coordination mechanism, which wants to avoid inflation risks in Europe by means of a strict regulation of the European monetary monopolist. Since in free market economies, the onus of proof is always on those who want to take interventionist action, a monetary union should not be entered into in the conditions prevailing at present.

47 This was also pointed out by Margaret Thatcher in her 1991 Zurich address (p. 13).

48 Cf. ASU, 1993, p. 37. CEPR, 1993, also criticises the social chapter of the Maastricht Treaty as being in clear contradiction to the principle of subsidiarity.

49 Cf. Kirchgässner / Pommerehne, 1993, pp. 17., and Wünsche, 1993, p. 34.

50 Cf. Stephan Sinn, 1992, p. 184, and the literature referred to there.

51 Cf., for instance, Hans-Werner Sinn, 1990.

52 Cf. Kirchgässner / Pommerehne, 1993, p. 20, but also p. 12.

53 Cf. Weizsäcker, 1987, p. 220.

54 Cf., for instance, Blöchlinger / Frey, 1992, p. 545.

55 Cf., for instance, the conference of the Friedrich-Naumann Foundation, 1992, and the draft of the European Constitutional Group, 1993.

References

Arbeitsgemeinschaft Selbständiger Unternehmer (ASU), 1993, *Für ein Europa des Wettbewerbs. Ein ordnungspolitisches Leitbild*, Bonn.

Baumberger, Jörg Peter, 1992, *Kosten und Nutzen der Diversität*, mimeo, St. Gallen.

Berthold, Norbert, 1993, 'Europa nach Maastricht – Die Skepsis bleibt', in: *Aus Politik und Zeitgeschichte*, Vol. 28, 9 July, pp. 29.

Blöchlinger, Hansjörg / Frey, René L., 'Der schweizerische Föderalismus: Ein Modell für den institutionellen Aufbau der Europäischen Union?', in: *Aussenwirtschaft*, 47th year, No. IV, pp. 515.

Burckhardt, Jakob, 1963, *Weltgeschichtliche Betrachtungen*, Stuttgart.

Bütler, Hugo, 1993, 'Ist der schweizerische Föderalismus noch zeitgemäss?', in: Linder, Willy (ed.), *Föderalismus – Mittel der Konfliktbewältigung*, Zurich, pp. 69.

CEPR, 1993, *Making Sense of Subsidiarity: How Much Centralization for Europe?*, *Monitoring European Integration*, No. 4, London.

Constant, Benjamin, 1942, *Über die Gewalt. Vom Geist der Eroberung und von der Anmassung der Macht* (translated from the French 1814 original and edited by Hans Zbinden), Berne.

Eibl-Eibesfeldt, Irenäus, 1992, *Und grün des Lebens goldener Baum. Erfahrungen eines Naturforschers*, Cologne.

Eichenberger, Reiner, 1993, 'Neue Perspektiven für die ökonomische Theorie des Föderalismus', contribution to Cost A7: *Workshop on Democratic Rules for the Future Europe, 4–6 Nov.*, mimeo, unpublished.

European Constitutional Group, 1993, A European Constitutional Settlement, draft for a conference in Frankfurt on 24 September, mimeo.

Frankfurter Institut für wirtschaftspolitische Forschung, 1992, *Einheit und Vielfalt in Europa. Für weniger Harmonisierung und Zentralisierung*, Bad Homburg.

Friedrich-Naumann Foundation, 1992, *A Constitution of Liberty or the New Leviathan? The market and the Constitution of a United Europe – Liberal Think Tank Thinking Ahead*, results of an international conference in Königswinter, mimeo.

Fukuyama, Frances, 1993, contribution to the 4th Symposium of the Informedia Foundation (ed.), *Was nun – Was gibt uns Halt?, Ideen zwischen Sicherheit und Chaos*, Cologne, pp. 54.

Giersch, Herbert, 1991, 'Grosse Chance for kleine Länder. Im Wettbewerb der Standorte entscheiden Weltoffenheit, Privatrechtsordnung und der Rang der individuellen Entscheidungsfreiheit', in: *Frankfurter Allgemeine Zeitung*, No. 300, p. 13.

Goble, Paul A., 1993, *A new Age of Nationalism*, written version of an address delivered at the Wolfsberg Conference.

Habermann, Gerd, 1993a, 'Für ein Europa des Wettbewerbs', in: *Forum. Vortragsreihe des Instituts der deutschen Wirtschaft*, Cologne, 43rd year, No. 23.

Habermann, Gerd, 1993b, 'Der bürgernahe Staat: Eine Jahrtausende alte Forderung', in: *Orientierungen zur Wirtschafts- und Gesellschaftspolitik*, No. 56, June, pp. 2.

Hirschman, Albert O., 1974, *Abwanderung und Widerspruch*, Tübingen.

Haldane, J.B.S., 1956, 'On being the right size', in: Newman, J.R. ed., *The World of Mathematics*, Vol. II, New York, pp. 952.

Jones, Eric L., 1981, *The European Miracle*, New York

Kaltenbrunner, Klaus ed., 1979, *Lob des Kleinstaates*, Freiburg / Basel / Vienna.

Kammler, Hans, 1992, 'Ein Markt und viele Staaten. Auch die Politik braucht den Wettbewerb', in: *Frankfurter Allgemeine Zeitung*, No. 302, 30 December, p. 24.

Kirchgässner, Gebhard / Pommerehne, Werner W., 'Tax Harmonization and Tax Competition in the European Community: Lessons from Switzerland', contribution to Cost A7: *Workshop on Democratic Rules for the Future Europe, 4–6 Nov.*, mimeo, unpublished.

Kohr, Leopold, 1941, 'Disunion now. A Plea for a Society Based Upon Small Autonomous Units', in: *The Commonweal*, 26 September.

Kramnick, I. ed., 1987, *The Federalist Papers*, Middlesex.

de Madariaga, Salvador, 1959, *Von der Angst zur Freiheit*, Berne / Stuttgart / Vienna.

Möschel, Wernhard, 1993, 'Eine Verfassungskonzeption für die Europäische Union', in: Gröner, Helmut / Schüller, Alfred eds., *Die europäische Integration als ordnungspolitische Aufgabe*, Stuttgart / Jena / New York, pp. 21.

Nef, Robert, 1992, 'Subsidiarität – Prinzip für alles', in: *Schweizer Monatshefte*, 72nd year, No. 9, pp. 683.

North, Douglass, 1993, 'Die Bedeutung von Konkurrenz, Nachahmung und Werten beim Aufstieg der westlichen Welt. Wirtschaftshistorische Streiflichter auf die Quellen des Wachstums', in: *Neue Zürcher Zeitung*, 25/26 Sept., No. 223, p. 83.

O'Hagan, Lord, 1992, 'Written question No. 1146/92 to the Commission of the European Communities', in: *Journal Officiel des Communautés*, 11 May, 92/C 285/58.

Olson, Mancur, 1991, *Aufstieg und Niedergang von Nationen*, 2nd ed., Tübingen.

Prosi, Gerhard, 1993, *Die Demokratie in der Rationalitätenfalle – Finanzpolitik im Schatten einer zunehmenden Staatsverschuldung*, address before the Hamburgische Landesbank, 12 March, mimeo.

Radnitzky, Gerard, 1991, 'Towards a Europe of Free Societies: Evolutionary Competition or Constructivist Design', in: *Ordo. Jahrbuch für die Ordnung von Wirtschaft und Gesellschaft*, Vol. 42, pp. 139.

Raico, Ralph, 1993, 'The Meaning of the European Miracle', in: *Reflexionen*, No. 30, July, pp. 15.

Röpke, Wilhelm, 1966, 'Nation und Weltwirtschaft', in: *Ordo. Jahrbuch für die Ordnung von Wirtschaft und Gesellschaft*, Vol. 17, pp. 37.

Schauer, Hans, 1993, *Europa der Vernunft. Kritische Anmerkungen nach Maastricht*, Bonn.

Schwarz, Gerhard, 1994, 'Wettbewerb der Systeme. Eine ordnungspolitische Sicht', in: Schweizerisches Institut für Auslandforschung (ed.), *Europäische Antagonismen*, Chur / Zürich.

Sinn, Stefan, 1992, 'The Taming of Leviathan: Competition among Governments', in: *Constitutional Political Economy*, Vol. 3, No. 2, pp. 177.

Sinn, Hans-Werner, 1990, 'The Limits to Competition between Economic Regimes', *Empirica* 17, pp. 3.

Thatcher, Margaret, 1991, *The Real Questions Facing Europe in the 1990s.*

Tiebout, Charles M., 1956, 'A pure theory of local expenditures', in *Journal of Political Economy*, Vol. 74, October, pp. 416.

Thompson, D'Arcy Wentworth, 1956, 'On Magnitude', in: Newman, J.R. ed., *The World of Mathematics*, Vol. II, New York, pp. 1007.

Thürer, Daniel, 1993, 'Das schweizerische Nein zum europäischen Wirtschaftsraum: Versuch einer konstruktiven Interpretation', *Zentrum für europäisches Wirtschaftsrecht – Vorträge und Berichte*, No. 26, Bonn.

Watrin, Christian, 1993, 'Europas ungeklärte Ordnungsfrage', in: Glatzel, Norbert / Kleindienst, Eugen eds., *Die personale Struktur des gesellschaftlichen Lebens. Festschrift for Anton Rausch*, Berlin, pp. 169.

Weede, Erich, 1991, *Wirtschaft, Staat und Gesellschaft*, Tübingen.

von Weizsäcker, C. Christian, 1987, 'Föderalismus als Verjüngungskur', in: Buhofer, Heinz ed., *Liberalismus als Verjüngungskur. Freiheit und Selbstverantwortung*, Zurich / Wiesbaden, pp. 217.

Wieland, Bernhard / Hoffmann, Johannes, 1989, 'Binnenmarkt Europa – falsche und richtige Wege', in: *Neue Zürcher Zeitung*, 29/30 July, No. 174.

Wünsche, Horst-Friedrich, 1993, 'Europapolitik: Visionen und neue Konstellationen', in: *Orientierungen zur Wirtschafts- und Gesellschaftspolitik*, No. 57, October, pp. 32.

Competition Among Systems as a Defence of Liberty

Manfred E. Streit

1. Introduction

At a symposium organized to celebrate the 80th birthday of the late Sir Karl Popper, in May 1983, Gerard Radnitzky ventured the hypothesis that one of the preconditions for an open society is the institutionalization of criticism. Furthermore he pointed to two forms of such criticism: (1) In a democratic system criticism can take the form of voting a government out of office. (2) A second form and – according to him – the ideal case would be a competition among systems and governments in attracting citizens (Popper, Lorenz 1985, 112f.) Using Hirschman's terms, Radnitzky stressed that "exit" could, like "voice", be an effective instrument in criticizing governments and in defending liberty. In the meantime, the reception of studies like those of Berman (1983), Jones (1987) and North (1990) has stimulated the discussion of this form of "exit".

Like other proposals which aim at the taming of Leviathan, competition among systems (CS) requires the assent of the very Leviathan. In other words, CS depends on rules (legislation) including a hand-tying of governments to prevent them from interfering when the disciplining effects of competition make themselves felt.

The Treaty establishing the European Economic Community is an interesting case in point. It involves a basic decision of the signatory states to open up among themselves to an extent which goes way beyond their commitments to GATT and now to the WTO. However, this was only gradually realized as a consequence of the rulings of the European Court of Justice. Furthermore, the basic arrangement is particularly far-reaching in view of the aforementioned hand-tying. The provisions of the Treaty have to be considered as rules of a level higher up than those of the member states themselves. As a consequence, citizens of the member states can refer directly to the rules of the Treaty whenever they believe that they are restricted in their freedom of action by their own governments to an extent which is incompatible with the provisions of the Treaty.

In the present analysis, the Rome Treaty will be used to illustrate the rule dependency and the corresponding limitations of CS (part 4). However first, this rather complex form of competition and its general effects will be examined (parts 2 and 3). The final part of the analysis will be devoted to a phenomenon which can be interpreted as a spontaneous process of substituting formal rules of national private law for informal ones. As a process of decentralized rule formation, it is tolerated and partly supported by national jurisdictions. I am referring to the modern form of Law Merchant (lex mercatoria) and its specific enforcement procedures.

2. Elements of the Competitive Process

CS is a process in which elements of economic and political competition interact in a rather complex way.[1] The process of interaction is – like its two constituting forms of competition – channelled by rules. The rules define the possibilities of the private agents to choose between territorial systems of formal and informal institutions. The range of opportunities to choose is defined by the degree of openness of the systems considered. Furthermore the openness depends – as already mentioned – on rules which effectively prevent governments from interfering with border-crossing activities of citizens when the disciplining effects of CS make themselves felt. Originally, the discussion of CS centred around international factor movements. To allocate mobile factors in a specific country necessarily implies that their further use is subjected to the corresponding territorial private and public law or to specific legislation on resources owned by foreign nationals.

Differences in territorial law can be among those factors which influence decisions on locating mobile resources. Adam Smith (1776/1981 vol. 2, 848f.) already discussed the potential influence of differences of profits after tax on international capital flows. Thereby he was much more cautious in his evaluation of the intensity of the resulting fiscal competition than some authors in the more recent discussion (cf. Streit 1995, 120ff.) appear to be. Extending the reasoning beyond fiscal dimensions, it can be argued, that transnational allocation of mobile factors always implies an institutional arbitrage. Whether differences between institutional arrangements have been decisive, is an empirical question. In addition it may well be that concrete cases of institutional arbitrage (e.g. international direct investments) form part of competitive strategies of enterprises operating on an international scale. Political actors as suppliers of institutional arrangements may either observe such factor movements and interpret them as a result of a choice of systems by private agents, or their attention will be drawn to it through "voice" by those – particularly owners of immobile factors – who are negatively affected by this kind of "exit". CS would become effective in the country considered, if political actors were induced to revise their institutional supply in order to improve the attraction of their constituency for mobile factors.

Besides mobile factors, a second channel of transmission exists in the process of CS. A choice of systems also becomes possible, if economic agents can choose between products and services which originate from different regulation regimes. This requires that foreign regulations are considered by national regulatory agencies as equivalent to domestic ones. In terms of the Common or Internal Market of the European Union (EU), this amounts to introducing the country of origin principle as opposed to the country of destination principle. Under these conditions, "exit" means importing goods and services which are influenced in their characteristics by deviating regulations. This time, regulation induced changes in trade flows can provoke competitive action by the domestic political suppliers of institutions (regulation). "Voice", calling for action by domestic political suppliers of institutions (regulation) may come either from economic agents producing import substitutes or from their pressure groups, respectively. However, "exit" is also a possible response. Given the domestic regulatory regime, it may be promising to import competing firms to relocate their activities internationally. As already indicated, CS in the sense of regulatory competition is a key issue of the Internal Market Programme of the EU.

Whereas regulation has attracted much attention in the discussion of trade flows and CS, private law as a set of formal (external) institutions has hardly been touched upon. This is quite remarkable because border-crossing transactions necessarily require a choice of private law systems. Furthermore, these transactions draw on complementary informal (internal) institutions like customs of trade and general conditions of sale. In other words, trade also implies exit at least for one party in a transaction "exit" with regard in the domestic system of external and internal institutions. This "exit" may be induced by expected differences in transaction costs accruing from the use of domestic institutions. Another factor affecting the choice could be the extent to which domestic, dispositive private law is affected by compulsory public law due to legislation which is typical for welfare states.

Already this brief presentation of CS by considering primarily the perspective of private actors should demonstrate that many aspects of this phenomenon require further theoretical and empirical clarification. This holds true e.g. for the question to what extent international factor movements can be attributed to differences in institutional arrangements. The same applies to the presumed relationship between border-crossing trade flows and differences in regulation. Equally, the choice of private law systems is far from being over-researched.

Furthermore, the perspective of political actors and their behaviour in the CS requires analytical attention. Explanatory difficulties arise in particular when exploring the interface between the economic and the political processes which form parts of the phenomenon. The difficulties can be summarized by posing the following questions: How are (negative) changes in the performance of the domestic economy perceived and explained by political actors, by pressure groups and by the electorate? Which kind of political response is signalled by "voice«? Which reactions are to be expected when taking into account political competition within a country? Employing the conventional economics of politics, political competitors would have to substantiate the following abstract answer (cf. S. Sinn 1992, 180): In case they are in government, they have to win sufficient support to become re-elected. To achieve this, they have to make sure that the positive reactions of the electorate on the provision of new institutions and the preservation of old distributive privileges (rents) are not overcompensated by negative reactions resulting from losses of prosperity which, in turn, are due to e.g. the "exit" of investors (capital) or to reduced inflows of productive resources. To substantiate this answer, a host of knowledge problems has to be overcome. If these problems were easily solvable, political entrepreneurs would become rather dull economizers, akin to the entrepreneur compatible with the conventional economic theory of the firm.

3. Effects of Competition

Drawing on an understanding of competition as it was developed by Hayek and by the Austrian School and applying it – adequately – to competition among systems, two basic propositions appear to be feasible:
- CS is a procedure allowing private competitors to test the expediency of available institutional arrangements. At the same time it induces political competitors to develop more attractive institutional innovations.
- CS is initiated as a consequence of actual and potential substitution of institutional arrangements by private competitors. This, in turn, has a

controlling effect on political competitors as suppliers of old and new institutional arrangements.

The first proposition – CS as a discovery procedure – takes into account the constitutional lack of knowledge of all actors. In this case, institutions have to be considered as fallible "hypotheses" (Mussler, Wohlgemuth 1995, 17ff.) with regard to the order of human interaction. As such, they are permanently tested and their relative expediency can be found out as soon as it is possible for private agents to choose among different institutional arrangements. The choice of owners of mobile resources and of buyers of differently regulated products is also a judgement on the capacity of these arrangements to contribute to the solution of societal problems. It also has to be born in mind that neither the political competitors as institutional suppliers nor the private competitors as institutional demanders know the most expedient solution. Furthermore, the problem-solving capacity of "institutional hypotheses" is altering with the change of conditions under which they are supposed to apply.

The first proposition draws on the possibility of institutional demanders to discover more suitable solutions as soon as they are able to choose among institutional offers. Comparable to economic competition processes, their choice can initiate an adaptive response by the suppliers; they may imitate those institutional arrangements which turn out to be more attractive in the process of border-crossing competition. However, such a response could be inadequate because the individual institutions form part of a grown system which has its own requirements of consistency and which relies on stabilizing traditions. This may be an additional reason for political suppliers to search for a competitive response consisting of institutional innovations within the domestic system. Taken together, the possible competitive reactions can be interpreted as a decentralized procedure to adjust and develop institutional arrangements.

To consider CS as a discovery procedure has analytical consequences which differ significantly from those obtained in the discussion based on neoclassical economic theory. In this case, for example, regulatory competition on the European Internal Market is far from leading necessarily to a "harmonization from below". Like economic competition, CS may turn out to be an innovative and hence evolutionary process and not an adaptive process converging to the most expedient regulatory system available at any one time. Hence it would be wrong to consider regulatory competition merely as a superior means to achieving harmonization. It would not simply be an attractive alternative to "ex-ante harmonization" as some studies (e.g. Siebert 1990) suggest. In addition, it is possible to conceive that diverging regulations may survive competition simply because those affected by the regulation of products do have diverging preferences with regard to the degree to which common regulatory objectives are to be achieved.

The second proposition identifies CS as a controlling device. As such, it is based on two arguments. The first refers to the possibility that institutional demanders assess the discovered supply with regard to its problem solving capacity, including their constraining effects. It is their personal judgement which may possibly lead to "exit". This, in turn, has a controlling effect on the supply of institutions. The second argument does not refer to the problem solving capacity of institutions but to the controlling effect of CS on the use of political power. The better the chances for the private actors to withdraw their mobile resources (property rights) from the sphere of influence of one group of institutional suppliers (national governments, jurisdictions) and to employ them in the sphere of competing suppliers, the more reduced is the political power to which those actors are exposed. This is basically Radnitzky's argument which is mentioned at the beginning. It reflects the hope which liberal economists and philosophers put into CS: within its limits, it could inhibit the political encroachment on liberty which is typical of the development of welfare states and which produces the "institutional sclerosis" (Olson 1982) and its detrimental effects on individual prosperity.

4. Limits of Competition Among Systems

CS is limited by exogenous and endogenous factors. Exogenous are the politically determined rules which define the legal scope of this type of competition. Endogenous limits result from the competitive process as such and from the properties of institutions exposed to CS.

4.1. Exogenous Limits: the Case of the European Union

Like economic and political competition, CS is a rule dependent process. Rules which are exogenous to it determine the scope of freedom to compete. The basic rules are simple but politically demanding. CS requires, that the so-called four basic freedoms (free trade in goods and in services, free choice of location and free movement of capital) are guaranteed and that they are protected against private and political restraints of competition.

With regard to European integration in general and to the Internal Market in particular, it was already a core objective of the Rome Treaty to establish the four basic freedoms and to protect the resulting freedom to compete against restraints. The basic freedoms became "constitutionalized"

(Mestmäcker 1994, 272ff.) by the ruling of the European Court of Justice: the obligation of the Community to establish the basic freedoms was transformed into individual rights of citizens of the Community which could be claimed in court. According to this interpretation, the basic freedoms define economic spheres of action which cannot be infringed upon by the member states. These spheres can be used by the citizens in the Common Market according to their economic requirements within the framework of private law (e.g. Behrens 1992, 147).

As to restraints of competition, the Treaty provided a legal basis to protect competition against private restraints as far as trade between member states would be affected. The same holds true for distortions of competition by member states. However, the possibility that Community action itself may lead to distortions of competition and consequently should also be considered as bound by the Treaty, has not attracted sufficient attention, e.g. by the Court of Justice. Furthermore a closer examination of the Treaty of Maastricht clearly shows that this problem has become more pressing than ever before. The common objectives which have been added to those of the Treaty of Rome and the provisions which set out the corresponding tasks of the EU almost inevitably imply conflicts with the principle of undistorted competition as soon as the Commission tries to fulfill these tasks (cf. Streit, Mussler 1994). In addition, the self-commitment of the Community to liberalize the economic relations with non-member countries and to foster in this way competition, including CS, is far from being realized. The complaints about a "Fortress Europe" appear to be justified (cf. Streit, Voigt 1991).

Basically, the legal framework of the Community provided conditions for CS. However, further institutional requirements have to be taken into account when assessing the scope for CS within the Community:

(1) CS is possible to the extent in which the competence of rule setting remains with the member states. The widening of those legal areas which are handed over to the Community (Union) necessarily reduces the potential influence of CS. The erosion of the "principle of limited individual competences" (e.g. von der Groeben, Mestmäcker 1974) laid down in articles 2 and 3 of the EC-Treaty cannot be discussed here. However, this erosion leads to the question, to what extent it is indispensable to have a unification of legal and administrative rules. There appears to be widespread prejudice in favour of unification. It is rather uncritically assumed that a unified legal framework represents a value on its own and that because unification leads to optimal results it is worth promoting it. If the propositions presented in the previous sections are correct, such a position is clearly untenable.

(2) CS must be enforced by applying Community law. To start with, it has to be recognized that the consequences of the already mentioned constitutionalization of the basic freedoms were far from being obvious when the Treaty was signed. In a wider sense, the contracting parties had to decide behind a veil of ignorance. (cf. Mestmäcker 1993b, 24). The domain of Community law with regard to these freedoms had to be identified by the European Court of Justice in the process of its rulings. This process cannot be presented here. With regard to trade in goods and the corresponding regulations, the decisions "Dassonville" of 1974 and "Cassis de Dijon" of 1979 have to be considered as cornerstones. Taken together, these two rulings reduced significantly the leeway for national regulation and favoured correspondingly freer trade. This was possible by imposing the principle of origin with regard to regulation. On the other hand, exceptions from the free access to the markets were granted within reasonable limits in order to cater for differences in the intensity with which the member states pursued the commonly accepted objectives of regulation.

The principle of origin required the mutual recognition of national laws, regulations and administrative provisions. This can be achieved in two ways. Products originating in other member states can be explicitly exempted from national regulations or it can be decided that these regulations will not be applied as far as these products are concerned. However, experience with the two procedures is not very satisfactory (cf. Tigges 1991; Winkler 1995). Even if mutual recognition is provided, new trade barriers can be erected, for example, by asking for a specific labelling of products originating from other member states which, in turn, may involve, for example, additional packaging costs. In this case complaints regarding a violation of mutual recognition have to be assessed individually by the courts. The same holds true for the refusal of recognition with the argument of "major needs" according to article 36 of the EC-Treaty. From an economic point of view this means that the enforcement of the principle of origin may be a major source of transaction costs for suppliers from other member states.

The aforementioned difficulties illustrate a general enforcement problem regarding basic freedoms. It is always possible, that an opening up by removing restraints of trade in goods and services, of capital movements and of migration will be revised by introducing grey area measures and by misusing negotiated exemptions. However in the case of the EU, it is possible to challenge those violations in court, although to private agents, this may turn out to be quite costly and time-consuming. As far as the Commission as "the guardian of the Treaties" is concerned, it has considerable discretion in deciding whether to take action in those cases which it either discovered itself or which were brought to its attention. It is also at its discretion to decide on the specific procedure in pursuing cases. Ultimately, much is left to negotiations between the Commission and the governments of the member states. Hence, even in the specific case of the EU with its rules superior to those of the member states and a jurisdiction with overruling powers, there are remarkable external limits for regulatory competition as an important part of CS. These limits can be plausibly explained by applying the political economy of protection and the economic theory of bureaucracy (e.g. Winkler 1995).

4.2. Endogenous Limits

Endogenously, the adaptive and innovative impact of CS is limited by the process itself and by properties of those institutions exposed to it. Limits of the process itself can be traced to preconditions and to the functioning of economic and political competition as well as to the way in which the two partial processes are linked in the case of CS. This is not sufficiently taken into account when considering a significant part of the discussion of CS. Simple answers on the questions raised in part 2 are only possible (1) if the knowledge problem which private and political actors have to face is underestimated, (2) if economic competition is merely modelled as an adaptation to objectively given "data" and not as a discovery procedure based on subjective knowledge, and (3) if political competition is modelled like adaptive economic competition, following the logic of equilibrium analysis. Under these conditions the interaction between the two partial processes hardly poses any serious analytical problems.[2]

The range of simple answers is defined by two extreme cases which were well received in the political discussion: (1) CS as a case of perfect institutional arbitrage leading to the selection of the "best" available institutional arrangement and allowing it to be interpreted as an "ex-post harmonization". (2) Failure of competition, leading to "ruinous" results in the sense of a "race to the bottom", ending up with "zero regulation".[3] However, as soon as the extreme assumption regarding knowledge and mobility are dropped and the analogy between economic and political competition is abandoned, the analytical picture changes significantly. What seems to be justified then is a moderate optimism regarding the positive effects of CS which have been set out in part 3.

The second category of endogenous limits of CS results from differences in flexibility and exchangeability of institutions. In terms of institutional economics the differences refer to structural compatibility (consistency) and path-dependency of institutions. These endogenous limits are of qualitative nature. In their reference to the structure of the institutions forming a system (compatibility) and their historical dimension (path-dependency) they are hardly accessible for a conventional economic analysis. Conventional modelling makes it necessary to reduce qualitative differences to objective differences of costs and of benefits.

Structural compatibility (consistency) of institutions may be illustrated by two examples. An opening up for regulatory competition in the construction of houses etc. in Germany by exempting products from other member states of the EU from the domestic regulations would probably be largely ineffective if the complementary provisions related to fire protection remained in force. The second example refers to indirect taxation within the EU. The example can also serve to demonstrate that structural compatibility equally applies to harmonization. It turned out to be very difficult to harmonize the rates of indirect taxation (value-added tax) within the EU because this tax forms part of a structure of taxation which differs widely among the member states. This holds particularly true for the proportion of direct and indirect taxation. With regard to CS and considered in isolation, it appears plausible to assume, that differences in individual elements of taxation only induce institutional arbitrage if they are not compensated by other elements in the tax structure.

Path-dependency means persistence of, in our case, formal or external institutions. Persistence grows out of their use over longer periods of time. It is the consequence of individual learning and of network effects. Individual learning can be based on reflection but also on unreflective imitation. The latter is already to some extent related to network effects. These effects occur when the use of institutions is spreading within a population. The more individuals familiarize themselves with institutions, the easier their interaction will be which draws on them. This, in turn, tends to lower the level of transaction costs. The persistence is probably the larger, the more external institutions are related to internal institutions by complementarities.[4]

Considering CS, its flexibility requirements regarding institutions are clearly in conflict with the property of persistence. Persistence is required if institutions should serve their purpose, i.e. to give guidance to individual behaviour and, as a consequence, stabilize expectations in interactions. Taking this into account, institutional flexibility would be counterproductive in reducing the problem of constitutional ignorance. This holds at least true as long as path-dependency does not block a move to another path which suggests itself in view of changes in the societal conditions (e.g. Adams 1994, 524ff.).

Setting aside the last-mentioned case, it can be asked which external institutions are particularly exposed to CS. The answer is related to political attempts to achieve concrete, mainly distributional results by public law and by manipulations of private law. To the extent in which these institutional changes imply discriminations by applying only to specific persons and cases, they represent an invitation to institutional arbitrage. Their persistence in the process of CS is lower than the one which can be expected from general, open (abstract) and certain – i.e. universal – rules.

As a result, it can be assumed that a considerable part of the production of laws, regulations and administrative provisions by welfare states is particularly exposed to CS. Waves of deregulation, reactions on adverse capital movements due to taxation of capital revenues, competitive changes of the taxation of enterprises are at the same time symptoms of an active use of these external institutions in the CS. Furthermore, within the public debate on international competitiveness, attention is drawn to manipulations of the freedom to contract (e.g. discriminatory conditions of notice), distortions of competition due to sectoral subsidization and cost pressure resulting from an excessive expansion of social security systems. However, it would be a clear overstatement to expect that CS would bring about a total erosion of discriminatory (redistributive) welfare state arrangements. This is clearly prevented when taking into account the endogenous limits of CS which can be traced to the process itself.[5]

The intermediate result of the analysis of CS can be summarized as follows: (1) CS is a suitable procedure to discover institutional innovations and to allow a control of political suppliers of institutional arrangements by demanders through potential or real "exit" in the sense of a withdrawal of mobile resources (property rights). (2) Even if CS as a complex interrelationship between economic and political competition is made feasible by corresponding external rules, there are endogenous limits of this process which can be traced to the process as such and to properties of the institutions which form a system. (3) These endogenous limits provide reasons to expect that primarily those institutions are exposed to CS which are the typical result of the institutional production of welfare states.

5. Freedom of Contract and Evolution of Rules: Lex Mercatoria

Regarding suitable procedures to discover institutional innovations and to select the expedient ones in a process of institutional change, one layer of institutions and their change hardly receives attention although it is of extreme importance to border-crossing transactions. I am referring to the modern form of lex mercatoria and its specific enforcement procedures.[6] This system of rules is the unintended outcome of a competitive search for uniform rules governing border-crossing trade. The system represents a spontaneous order in the sense of Ferguson and Hayek. The emergence and the enforcement of these institutional arrangements as well as their development as a system are the result of human action but not of human design.

The modern form of lex mercatoria comprises of standardized contracts and provisions, customs of trade, behavioural codices of international organizations and general principles which can also be found in formal private law. Some formal institutions like the 1980 Vienna Convention on Law of Commerce have also to be included. The dispute settlement is primarily the task of private arbitration tribunals. The rules of the lex mercatoria are dominating border-crossing trade to an extent, which – already in 1930 – was described by one of the founders of the Freiburg School of law and economics, Grossmann-Doerth, as follows: "To oversea trade national dispositive law is but a piece of printed paper, not more." (quoted according to Dasser, 1989, 9; own translation).

From an institutional economic perspective the lex mercatoria reflects a reaction on the fact, that border-crossing transactions are carried out by autonomous private actors operating from different systems of territorial law. They are transactions between strangers when considering legal systems (Schmidtchen 1990, 64). In this case special enforcement problems arise, the solution of which causes transaction costs. Contractual claims against strangers to the system of the claimant cannot be legally assessed in a straightforward manner and eventually executed because the other party is subjected to a foreign jurisdiction. Even if it is possible to refer to an agreement of legal redress, enforcement problems can occur because of a conflict between different traditions of private law. Although international private law (IPL) has been developed as a formal instrument to decide which national private law applies in cases of border-crossing transactions (collision norms), one has to take into account that every state has its own IPL. As a consequence, private actors are still confronted with the territorial law when carrying out border-crossing transactions (cf. Schmidtchen 1995).

It is possible to interpret the reaction of private agents on this legal uncertainty from the perspective of CS. To a considerable extent the territorial private law was substituted for uniform rules of the lex mercatoria. The successful substitution of formal for informal institutions governing border-crossing transactions can be explained by the following conjectures:

(1) In the case of those transactions which are typically based on the lex mercatoria, the probability is quite high, that the partners in these transactions will meet again. As a consequence, reputation becomes an important factor in delimiting the transaction dilemma (problem of defection). Hence

the private agents are less dependent upon the comprehensive but transaction-cost-intensive protection of the formal private law which also includes additional constraints of contractual design. Reputation may also help to explain, why conflicts are settled and possibly enforced by one of the private arbitration tribunals. In probably less than 10% of all cases brought before private arbitration tribunals public courts serve as courts of last instance.[7] This does not exclude the possibility, that the success of the substitution of formal for informal institutions in border-crossing trade is at least partly founded on the fact, that this substitution is not only tolerated but positively supported by the states as providers of courts of last instance. This support and the related possibility of surveillance of private arbitration tribunals with regard to their jurisdictional competence does vary between states.

(2) The lex mercatoria corresponds to the demand for internationally uniform rules in order to reduce transaction costs. However, the result is not a narrow set of standardized rules. The rules of the modern form of lex mercatoria vary according to the practical requirements of specific transactions and trades. A further characteristic is that these rules are adjusted with little friction to changing conditions (for example techniques of transport and of communication). "These rules do not emerge from the drawing table of a centrally planning legislator. They rather emerge on the spot, i.e. in the different corners and niches of international commerce where a practical need for its creation – and its change – makes itself felt" (Kötz 1992, 216; own translation). In comparison with the lex mercatoria, the unification or harmonization of law by legislators is the product of a cumbersome political process of compromising.

(3) International arbitration is characterized by intensive locational competition. This may well lower transaction costs. Furthermore it does not seem to lead to a "competition in laxity". As major instruments of competition serve the statutes and procedures of arbitration as well as the reputation of the arbitrators and their fees. Formal law is drawn into this competitive process because its quality becomes decisive as soon as public courts are acting as last instances regarding settlement as well as enforcement. As a consequence, competitive responses by legislators are observable although the rôle of public courts is limited by the efforts of the private parties to avoid the elaborate stages of appeal which characterize formal jurisdiction.

With regard to CS, the reflections on the lex mercatoria can be summarized to the effect, that this is an example allowing us to show that the search for uniform rules and the competition for their improvement are not mutually exclusive. It is also an example for the capacity of private agents to organize their affairs autonomously. Admittedly, those involved in border-crossing transactions are not representative of their societies. However, they are not the only ones who are able to prove that the tutelage of the welfare state is far from being necessarily the most preferable solution to societal problems.

Notes

1   In sections 2 and 3, extensive use is made of a recent study (Streit, Mussler 1995).
2   For a thorough analysis of these analytical issues from a Hayekian point of view see Wohlgemuth (1995).
3   How sensitive analytical results are with regard to informational assumptions can already be demonstrated when varying these assumptions within conventional models of asymmetric information. In this case, multiple equilibria as a special form of indeterminateness emerge (e.g. Leland 1979). If one tried to tackle innovations, the framework of conventional modelling would definitely break down.
4   For an analysis of the various types of institutions, their path-dependency and for potential relationships between external and internal institutions cf. Kiwit, Voigt (1995) and Kiwit (1995).
5   Hence arguments brought forward against CS, suggesting the end of any social policy (e.g. H. W. Sinn 1990) appear to be overstatements. A thorough discussion and criticism of this kind of reasoning and of corresponding policy proposals, related to the EU, has been provided by the Council of Scientific Advisors to the German Federal Ministry of Economics (Wissenschaftlicher Beirat beim Bundesministerium für Wirtschaft 1994).
6   A thorough analysis of the modern form of lex mercatoria and the international arbitration tribunals has been provided by Dasser (1989) and Berger (1993). For a summarizing presentation, including the discussion of the enforcement problem, and an evaluation from the point of view of transaction costs cf. Voigt (1992, 175 pp.). An evolutionary approach to Law Merchant has been provided by Benson (1995, 115; cf. also the references).
7   The empirical evidence regarding this issue is scarce because of the confidentiality of the arbitration procedures.

References

Adams, M. (1994), 'Rechte und Normen als Standards', in: M. Tietzel (ed.), *Ökonomik der Standardisierung – Homo Oeconomicus* XI (3), Acedo, 501–552

Behrens, P. (1992), 'Die Konvergenz der wirtschaftlichen Freiheiten im europäischen Gemeinschaftsrecht', *Europarecht* 27, 145–162

Benson, B. L. (1995), 'The Evolution of Values and Institutions in a Free Society: The Underpinnings of a Market Economy', in: G. Radnitzky, H. Bouillon (eds.): *Values and the Social Order*, Vol. 1, Aldershot etc.: Avebury, 87–125

Berger, K. P. (1993), *International Economic Arbitration*, Deventer, Kluwer

Berman, H.-G. (1983), *Law and Revolution – The Formation of Western Legal Tradition*, Cambridge (Ma), London: Harvard University Press

Dasser, F. (1989), *Internationale Schiedsgerichte und lex mercatoria*, Zürich, Schulthess

Jones, E. J. (1987), *The European Miracle*, Cambridge: Cambridge University Press

Kiwit, D. (1995), *Path-dependence in Technological and Institutional Change – Some Criticism and Suggestions*, Jena: Max-Planck-Institute for Research into Economic systems, Discussionpaper 10/95

Kiwit, D. / S. Voigt (1995), 'Überlegungen zum institutionellen Wandel unter Berücksichtigung des Verhältnisses interner und externer Institutionen', in: *Ordo* 46, 117–147.

Kötz, H. (1992), 'Alternativen zur legislatorischen Rechtsvereinheitlichung', *Rabels Zeitschrift für ausländisches und internationales Privatrecht* 56, 215–218

Leland, A. E. (1979), 'Quacks, Lemons, and Licensing: A Theory of Minimum Quality Standards', *Journal of Political Economy* 87, 1328–1346

Mestmäcker, E.-J. (1993a), 'Der Kampf ums Recht in der offenen Gesellschaft', in: (by the author), *Recht in der offenen Gesellschaft*, Baden-Baden: Nomos, 11–25

Mestmäcker, E.-J. (1993b), "Rom oder Maastricht?" in (by the author), *Macht in der offenen Gesellschaft*, Baden-Baden: Nomos–618–624

Mestmäcker, E.-J. (1994a), 'Zur Wirtschaftsverfassung in der Europäischen Union'; in: R.H. Hasse u.a (eds.), *Ordnung in Freiheit*, Stuttgart u.a.: Gustav Fischer, 263–292

Mussler, W. / M. Wohlgemuth (1995), 'Institutionen im Wettbewerb – Ordnungstheoretische Anmerkungen zum Systemwettbewerb in Europa', in: P. Oberender, M. E. Streit (eds.), *Europas Arbeitsmärkte im Integrationsprozeß*, Contributiones Jenenses Vol. 1, Baden-Baden: Nomos, 9–45

North, D. C. (1990), *Institutions, Institutional Change and Economic Performance*, Cambridge: Cambridge University Press

Olson, M. (1982), *The Rise and Decline of Nations – Economic Growth, Stagflation, and Social Rigidities*, New Haven / London: Yale University Press

Popper, K. R., K. Lorenz (1985, 1993), *Die Zukunft ist offen*, München: Pieper, 5th edition

Schmidtchen, D. (1990), 'Neue Institutionenökonomik Internationaler Transaktionen', in: U. Schlieper und D. Schmidtchen (eds.): *Makro, Geld und Institutionen*; Tübingen: Mohr, 57–84

Schmidtchen, D. (1995), 'Territorialität des Rechts, Internationales Privatrecht und die privatautonome Regelung internationaler Sachverhalte: Grundlagen eines interdisziplinären Forschungsprogramms', *Rabels Zeitschrift für ausländisches und internationales Privatrecht* 59, 56–112

Siebert, H. (1990), 'The Harmonization Issue in Europe: Prior Agreement or a Competitive Process?', in: by the same author (eds.), *The Completion of the Internal Market*, Tübingen: Mohr, 53–75

Sinn, H.-W. (1994), 'How Much Europe? Subsidiarity, Centralization and Fiscal Competition', *Scottish Journal of Political Economy* 41, 85–107

Sinn, S. (1992), 'The Taming of Leviathan: Competition Among Governments', *Constitutional Political Economy* 3, 177–196

Smith, A. (1776/1981): *An Inquiry into the Nature and Causes of the Wealth of Nations*, Indianapolis: Liberty Press

Streit, M. E. (1995), 'Dimensionen des Wettbewerbs – Systemwandel aus ordnungsökonomischer Sicht', *Zeitschrift für Wirtschaftspolitik* 44, 113–134

Streit, M. E. / S. Voigt (1991), 'Die Handelspolitik der Europäischen Gemeinschaft aus weltwirtschaftlicher Perspektive', *Hamburger Jahrbuch für Wirtschafts- und Gesellschaftspolitik* 36, 193–219

Streit, M. E. / W. Mussler (1994) 'The Economic Constitution of the European Community – From "Rome" to "Maastricht"', *Constitutional Political Economy* 5, 319–353

Streit, M. E. / W. Mussler (1995), 'Wettbewerb der Systeme und das Binnenmarktprogramm der Europäischen Union', in: L. Gerken (ed): *Europa zwischen Ordnungswettbewerb und Harmonisierung – Europäische Ordnungspolitik im Zeichen der Subsidiarität*, Berlin, Heidelberg, New York: Springer, 75–107

Tigges, U. (1991), *Zur Aktualität nichttarifärer Handelshemmnisse im europäischen Binnenmarkt*, Baden-Baden: Nomos

v. d. Groeben H. / E.-J. Mestmäcker (eds.) (1974), *Verfassung oder Technokratie für Europa*, Frankfurt: Fischer Athenäum

Winkler, T. D. (1995), 'Wo kein Kläger, da kein Richter – Die Verwirklichung der gegenseitigen Anerkennung von Produktregulierungen in der Europäischen Union', Jena: Max-Planck-Institute for Research into Economic Sytems, *Discussionpaper* 7/95

Wissenschaftlicher Beirat beim Bundesministerium für Wirtschaft (1994), *Ordnungspolitische Orientierung für die Europäische Union*, BMWi Dokumentation 356, Bonn

Wohlgemuth, M. (1995), 'Economic and Political Competition in Neoclassical and Evolutionary Perspective', *Constitutional Political Economy* 6, 71–96

The Austrian School – Its Significance for the Transformation Process

Václav Klaus

Austrian economics has provided ideas which are extraordinarily valuable for solving the problems of the transformation from communist systems to a free society and a free market order, one of the most pressing tasks of our era. Many of my recent lectures and writings have been devoted to the logic and economics of the transformation process (1992, 1993a, 1993b, 1994c). In this essay the focus has been narrowed-to some remarks on the importance of the Austrian School for mastering that process.

Let me state right from the beginning that, in spite of the isolation in which we lived in the former communist states, many of us had long discovered Austrian economics, and its thinking has been influential over decades. Sometimes we have the impression that we have taken an interest in its thoughts to even a greater extent than did our Western colleagues living in a simpler and more pleasant world. What has attracted us in a fundamental way was the School's consistent methodological individualism (combined with the subjectivist value theory) as well as its consistent systematic (and therefore also complex) world view resulting from its methodological stance. The methodology of Austrian Economics offered us surprising and convincing insights into the social order and the economy of that difficult period. Thus I concentrate on those contributions of Austrian Economics that have particularly influenced us economists of East-Central Europe and Eastern Europe.

In my opinion, the most important contribution of Austrian Economics consisted in its clear-cut proof that the "communist episode" in our country and in many other parts of the world did not come about by accident. On the contrary. It was the result of a process lasting for decades and was rooted in the world of ideas, namely of those ideas which the Austrian School so admirably described and interpreted. This was and is the School's singular historical contribution.

All this, of course, does not concern merely communism and its past. Rather it constitutes a general analysis of present society and its development through the decades. The communism we have come to know is "merely" (in the technical sense of the word) an extreme expression of the socialist mind-set, which existed and exists in every country with a long-standing tradition of political democracy and market order. Hence this theme comprises so much. If, in the world of ideas we look for a contrast to socialist doctrines of all kinds, we can scarcely find a more perfect contrast than the thoughts of the Austrian School. And this holds from its very beginning.

When in 1871 *Carl Menger*, the founder of the School, published his book *Grundsätze der Volkswirtschaftslehre*, it constituted a veritable milestone. He shattered the then dominant classical orthodoxy (or what Jevons called the Ricardo-Mill economics). That doctrine landed in a dead-end, in particular owing to its false conception of the economy as a system determined solely by physical parameters – by the scope and structure of the resources of production. Very likely it is thanks to our personal experience that we appear to see more readily and clearly than our Western colleagues that from this "physicalist" world view there is but a small step to socialist ideas on centralization of the resources of production and on centrally-steered distribution of their yield.

Menger had a vision of the economy that was completely different. In his view the economic process begins with the consumers' subjective evaluation of the utility of goods and services and continues, via the transformation of that utility in the market process, to a concrete way of utilizing the resources of production. In this way Menger introduces causal chains that are completely different from those used in the classical orthodoxy. In that body of doctrines the whole process starts with the use of the resources of production, and the consumers' role is reduced to passively consuming the "values" created without his participation. Among all the pioneers of modern economics Menger understood perhaps better than anybody else the real meaning of the creation of values (in the economic sense) and of wealth. He understood that wealth does not merely have a physical dimension, but is determined by human preferences, i.e., by subjective choice.

This insight enabled Menger to dissolve the boundary between the world of goods and the world of the resources of production and thereby to invalidate the artificial boundary between the subjective world of preferences and the physical world of resources. In this way he created a unified and universal image of the economy that was based upon the principle of subjective value. Not without good reason J. A. Schumpeter labeled Menger's vision a 'stroke of genius'.

Of no lesser stature as a representative of the School was Menger's successor *Eugen von Böhm-Bawerk*, who was born in Brno (Brünn), Moravia. His extraordinary abilities manifest themselves in his special talent to integrate theory and practice. His activity as Minister of Finance absorbed most of his energy (among other things he prepared the principal reform of the Austro-Hungarian fiscal system). As a theoretician he succeeded in creating a comprehensive and important ouevre. It became a lasting part of world economics and contributed to the formation of modern economic theory. His involvement in the duties of his office, combined with a certain reluctance to employ mathematics in economics (a reluctance which appears fairly typical of the whole Austrian School), prevented him from developing his theoretical work to formal perfection. This, however, does not diminish the depth of his thinking or the originality of his work, which reached its apogee in his book *Kapital und Kapitalzins*. It constitutes a refutation of the Ricardo-Marx's theory of distribution, which is based on the labor theory of value and the conception of the exploitation of labor through capital. Böhm-Bawerk's elucidating commentary to the foundations of capital and interest became indispensable building stones of distribution theory and an inspiration to the advancement of modern economics. There can be no doubt that Böhm-Bawerk's work was a highly important impulse also for students of economics in a communist country.

Even today we cannot tell how long the errors of Ricardo-Marxian labor theory of value would have survived, if Böhm-Bawerk's book *Zum Schluß des Marx'schen Systems* had not been published. It brilliantly and convincingly showed the contradiction between the first and third part of *Das Kapital*.

It comes as no surprise that Böhm-Bawerk was one of the authors who were most frequently banned in communist countries. Of course, this holds even more for the authors of the succeeding generations of the Austrian School.

Examining the work of the economists of the Austrian School in the 20th century we clearly recognize that it was they who had undertaken the enormously important task of exposing the contradictions and the artificiality of socialist doctrines. This was shown with particular clarity in the thirties, in the famous economic calculation debate, the dispute about rationality of economic calculation in socialism. That dispute constitutes not only an important step in the development of economic thinking as such; at the same time it gave a powerful impetus to the further development of the unique Austrian School.

It was *Ludwig von Mises* and *Friedrich August von Hayek* who showed that it is impossible in principle for an economic central agency to replace or even to handle the many millions of human decisions and to provide a substitute for the role of the entrepreneur as a searching, discovering and innovating subject. Mises no longer conceptualized the entrepreneur as a mechanical "computer" (the neo-classical view supported by Lionel Robbins's definition of economics), as operating with given resources and, excluding anything else, rationally calculating how to allocate the available resources between competing ends. In real life, the entrepreneur is a creative, active and activating force. Driven by the profit motive he discovers gaps in the market and fills them with his creativity, imagination, and innovative capacity. It is not the case that he adjusts to some end-state of an "equilibrium" which is given as an exogeneous factor; on the contrary, he changes those end-states through his entrepreneurial activity. Mises convincingly showed that it is not "human design", but "human action" that operates as the creative and inspiring force in the society and the economy. And it is no accident that another fellow-country man from *Moravia*,[1] *Joseph Alois Schumpeter* (born in Triesch), nowadays finds so many followers in the Czech Republic.[2]

It was Hayek (cf. 1993c) who understood that there can be no way, no method for centralizing the knowledge necessary for economic calculation and the ensuing decision making, because the relevant pieces of knowledge have necessarily the character of dispersed knowledge, which can in principle be handled only by individuals. Only the individual "knowledge-holder" is capable of making efficient use of it. This insight of the Austrian School played the key role in our leaving behind all illusions about good and less good varieties of socialism. In particular Hayek's seminal paper in the *American Economic Review* of 1945[3] was considered to be basic to "Austrian" thinking.

The economists of the Austrian School understood better than all others how delusive it is to think that it might be possible for a central agency to model the general economic equilibrium and to compute it. Thanks to these insights we have in the Czech Republic never toyed with hybrid systems and "Third Ways" of various design.

However, the relevance of the Austrian School for us did not end with the adoption of its arguments for the rejection of communism and central planning. It was not less important for the rational conception of transformation strategy and last but not least also for our daily life during the transformation phase, in which the Czech Republic now definitely finds itself (1994a).

For the transformation – for the systemic change – from 1990 to 1993 Mises's and Hayek's distinction between "human design" and "human action" was decisive. From the very beginning I was convinced that the need of a clear vision of the type of society we wish to live in is basically different from the need of a detailed, technocratic, constructivistic and reformatory "blue-print" that would enable an enlightened mind to plan and steer the transformation process step by step. Constructivism and "social engineering" are the pride of certain intellectuals and the expression of their efforts to guide human life. Other intellectuals – the Austrian School and in particular Hayek – have finally cured us of that conceit. We have been able to see with our own eyes that the transformation of a society as complex as the Czech Republic requires a complex combination of governmental intentions and the spontaneity inherent in human action (cf. my 1994a). Here too Hayek's ideas on "spontaneous order" are absolutely indispensable.

In times of radical systemic change the tasks of the political and economic center are of course more extensive than in a stabilized market order. Hypothetically considered, the center could play a completely passive role. However, in that case the transition from one system to another will take disproportionally long time and the transformation costs will be high. These costs have to be paid by those participating in the transformation process, and that means by the ordinary citizens. (Unfortunately, there are no others who could shoulder those costs instead of the citizens, which is something that many people both at home and in other countries are not willing to understand.) However, the center can also play an active and constructive role. This will shorten the transition period, and the costs for the citizens will be correspondingly lower.

This procedure was exactly that carried through in the Czech Republic. Our state had and still has "solely" the ambition to organize the systemic change – and not to organize economic life.

Therefore, we proceeded in the following way:
- Fundamental change of property rights – privatization;
- deregulation and liberalization of markets – in particular through liberalization of prices and foreign trade;
- abolishing state paternalism – radical elimination of subsidies of all kinds;
- macroeconomic stabilization, sound fiscal and monetary policies (at least balanced budget) and independence of the central bank.

We have in principle rejected the idea that the state should, besides restructuring the system, also take on the task of restructuring individual firms by means of government action (or by means of other agencies like, e.g., the German type of "Treuhandanstalt") (1994b) . The reason is that the state or the agency to which it may delegate that task can never know better than the real owner what should be restructured and how it should be done – this is the lesson we have learnt from the Austrian School. Our privatization concentrated on a consistent change of property relations, and we never attempted to issue governmental directions on the modernization of individual firms – an abstinence which has provoked and is provoking criticism from certain quarters.

I am convinced that all of the above reflections, including our conception of the role and the scope of the state, apply as well to standard systems of west-European style. When today – in the context of the European dialogue, or more accurately speaking, in the dialogue about Europe – we enter into a dispute with the proponents of "industrial policy", or of the newly-conceptualized trade policy or environmental policy, it is as if the socialist calculation-debate of the thirties would flare up again. The advocates of microeconomic governmental activity, who propose the selective use of tariffs or taxes and there recommend price subsidies, endowments or licenses, all use a "new-old" argumentation. Asked about the rationality and effectiveness of such policies they argue in ways that are basically similar to those used by Oskar Lange or Abba Lerner in the thirties. We can answer them best if we take as our point of departure the ideas and arguments of Mises and Hayek.

The same holds with respect to the contemporary discussion about social policy, about the welfare state or about state paternalism.

The Austrian School not only won the "Socialism Dispute", but, in my opinion, it also won the famous "Methodology Dispute". Therefore we should not omit to mention its importance for the methodology of all social sciences. Methodological individualism and the subjectivist value theory of the Austrian School guarantee a solid theoretical foundation for these disciplines. It can be demonstrated what false social-constructivistic and statist visions of social order result from the rejection of these basic insights, or from a half-hearted regard for them.

Hence, in this connection we must not forget Hayek's deep and penetrating analysis of the nature and the roots of socialism, an analysis which goes beyond pure economics and which deals with the phenomenon of socialism in all its societal and historical complexity. The road to socialism – for Hayek "The Road to Serfdom" – is embarked on when the role of the individual and the spontaneous, creative force of the market process is put into question. Socialists of all colors have in common the craving to suppress individual liberty and correspondingly to augment the role and the power of the state – at the cost of the individual. They yearn for planning and regulating the life of others hoping that their future place will be in those regulating institutions. Hayek's exposure of their tendencies and striving as well as his warning against them is today as topical as ever. It is precisely this legacy of the Austrian School which we have kept in mind and which we will not forget.

References

Klaus, V. (1992), *Dismantling Socialism: A Preliminary Report*, Prague, Top Agency.

Klaus, V. (1993a), *Ten Commandements of Systemic Reform*. Occasional Papers No. 43, Washington, DC, Group of Thirty.

Klaus, V. (1993b), "Interplay of political and economic factors in the transformation of post-communist countries", *The Mont Pèlerin Society Newsletter*, December 1993.

Klaus, V. (1993c), "Žijeme v Hayekově době" (We live in the Hayekian era), in Rok – málo či mnoho v dějinách země (A year too little or too much in the country's history). Prague, Repro-media

Klaus, V. (1994a), "Systemic change: The delicate mixture of intentions and spontaneity. (Luncheon address at the Mont Pèlerin Society General Meeting in Cannes 1994), *Cato Journal* 14:171–177.

Klaus, V. (1994b), Privatization Experience: The Czech Case. (Lecture at the Conference of the International Chamber of Commerce, Cancún). Prague, COWI.

Klaus, V. (1994c), *Rebirth of a Country: Five Years After*. Prague, Ringier CR.

Economic Dynamism: Lessons From German Experience

Herbert Giersch

I. Introductory Remarks

While I unduly hesitated to accept the invitation to give such an address,[1] I was too venturesome and quick to formulate the topic. In an entrepreneurial mood, I committed myself with dynamism, before really knowing what I would be able to produce. Let me therefore begin with four clarifications and qualifications, to lower the level of expectations.

First: I take dynamism to mean spontaneous growth with technological progress in a modern capitalist economy.

Second: This field is probably not yet over-researched. So, I do hope that we can still make use of "lessons". By lessons I mean impressionistic conclusions, admittedly mixed with subjective elements; they are derived from personal experience and professional observations. Critics may take these lessons as mere hypotheses – surely as hypotheses in search of evidence, even of contradicting evidence.

Third: The main field of my professional observations is the German economy, but viewed and widely framed – in the context of an increasing liberalisation of world trade and an increasing globalisation of production.

Fourth: Though insights which may turn out to be pretty subjective do not constitute hard science, we should not ignore them altogether, not even for reasons of scientific dignity. A narrow focus would make economics much less attractive; it might prevent us economists from submitting sensible contributions to the contemporary economic policy debate. In this context, I conjecture that it is better to be controversially productive than to run into the trap of sterile perfectionism.

II. Thirty Propositions to Think About

Having said this, I dare to submit the following propositions. They are fairly general to begin with and will become more specific when their number approaches twenty-five.

(i) Economic dynamism arises from intensive evolutionary competition, i.e. from competition in the exploitation of new (and hence risky) opportunities. Such competition is comparable to a race the outcome of which is not determined and cannot be foreseen nor predicted. This implies almost by definition: Conditions must be such that it is impossible to pick the winner. In the global economy, this condition tends to be fulfilled, given the fact that more and more countries succeed in catching-up and in approaching the technological frontier. The world economy has now several centers of excellence. The game, in its outcome, is becoming more and more undetermined, the future more and more open. Governments, by still trying to pick the winner in advance, may believe to push ahead. But as they actually interfere to offer protection, they are likely to give rise to moral hazard and to impair rather than foster the competitive spirit – except in the business of lobbying for government subsidies. If we had more government control over investment, and less openness towards the future, we would probably have to expect less economic dynamism. This leads to a proposition of historical dimensions: The globalisation of innovative competition is likely to enhance the world economy's growth prospect, as it probably has done in the last fifty years, when the unfolding of a multipolar world economy with a liberal trade order made us forget the stagnation thesis of the 1930s. (But consider also point xxviii and the possibility that there will be more control of investment and innovation – for reasons of environmental protection – on a national and international scale, which is likely to temper dynamism and to limit economic growth.)

(ii) There can hardly be too large a number of entrepreneurs participating in the race. Dynamism thus depends on openness in the horizontal dimension, i.e. on easy entry – for the young and for all sorts of non-conformists, including foreigners as owners of financial and human capital. On this account, dynamism can be enhanced by progressing towards a less constrained economy. The constraints to be removed may include bureaucratic regulations, cartel arrangements and restrictive business practices, impediments to imports and to foreign investments. Post-war Germany greatly benefited from the influx of enterprising refugees from the East, i.e. from Germany's former territories and from the G. D. R., but also from entrepreneurial people among the guest workers. The reform countries of Central and Eastern Europe would be well advised to let foreign investment and entrepreneurship come in freely and for this purpose move fairly quickly to full currency convertibility on capital account.

(iii) Horizontal openness also involves tolerance towards immigrant labour. There is, however, one qualification to be added. The condition is that immigration must not severely impair cultural values that are economically efficient. Such values include personal safety, property rights, loyalty under the law, trustworthiness, compliance with contracts and similar features of business ethics. They are factors of production which help to save transaction costs. In a sense, they are valuable club-goods. Immigrants will have to contribute to their maintenance and preservation in order to be readily accepted as equals.

(iv) Tolerance towards foreigners and foreign capital is related to another requirement for economic dynamism. I mean the suppression of envy. Envy gives rise to xenophobia, but also to quests for redistributive taxation. Instead, envy should be turned into a motive power for efforts to catch up with one's neighbours. The apppropriate means is moral suasion. Moreover, excessive envy can be tempered by demonstrating that individuals can expect positive externalities from other people's success. The individual must learn to trust that, in some way, he or she will benefit from the neighbour's achievements directly or through the price mechanism. The poor in the neighbourhood of the rich can and often will be absolutely better off than the poor in the neighbourhood of the poor. It is true that housing rents are higher where people benefit from saving of transportation costs, but prospering agglomerations offer increasing income and sales opportunities for suppliers of local goods and services, including services for the rich. These opportuinities can help to transform envy into effort and to make people aware that they participate in a positive sum game. Such an interpretation of economic life is essential for creating a social atmosphere that is progressive and free of distributive quarrels and conflicts. I believe to have observed such an atmosphere during the period of postwar reconstruction in West Germany. Ludwig Erhard spoke of "Wealth for all".

(v) In the same vein, there is reason for attributing a positive social value to tolerance vis-à-vis winners of all sorts. Those who are sufficiently lucky, eager and skilful to win should be free to keep much of the gain for their own disposition. In a competitive environment, they will anyhow devote much of it to investment. If marginal income taxes are high, the expected gains (before tax) must be correspondingly larger – for the same excitement to be aroused. Even if gaining profits was attributed to sheer luck – as in a lottery – profits would still be useful like lottery gains as they induce people to participate in the game. The huge profit has an exciting influence; it makes many people move or run faster. Non-pecuniary prizes may be a substitute, but not a perfect one: The Nobel Prize owes its high reputation at least partially to the large sum of money attached to it.

(vi) As a main proposition I submit that dynamism goes along with inequality. The reasoning is as follows: There is a given distribution of talents; if people are completely free to use them – within the legal constraints imposed to protect private property rights – there will quickly be a maximum of activities in a wide division of labour limited only by transportation costs and communication costs. Activities may be constrained, to be sure, by abstract rules of conduct as they have emerged in a Lamarckian process of evolution, but as long as these rules remain abstract and non-discriminatory they will merely lower the overall motivation level and will not affect the distribution of outcomes and incomes which is essentially determined by differences in talents and tastes. Only specific interferences in the market – designed to suppress the activities of the talented achievers – and outright measures to redistribute incomes from the achievers to the non-achievers (and losers) will produce more equality. Such discriminatory interferences require coercion that will reduce dynamism. There is only one redistributive device that is likely not to impair economic dynamism: It is the taxation of pure talent. Yet pure talent cannot be assessed indepently of the person's will to develop it. Like beauty it would quickly disappear from this world if it became a tax base. A metaphor may help to understand a complex system of interdependence. Imagine a traffic congestion on the road, e.g. in the face of a railway barrier. When the road is closed, all cars waiting in the queue are equal at speed zero. The distances between them are minimal. The drivers' talents and the cars' motive power and brakes do not matter. But once the barrier is lifted and the traffic is deregulated, the cars soon move at different speed, with varying distances between them. Compared to the orderly queue before, the acceleration that follows liberalisation looks like chaos. People not accustomed to the complexities of freedom and inequality will be irritated. The greater the average speed, the greater will be the dispersion. At full average speed, the inequality will reach its maximum, the "cohesion" its minimum. A speed limit will appear sensible. It will limit the dispersion together with the average speed. If fixed low enough, the speed limit will transform a competitive crowd into a slow convoy; and the convoy will stop once a single car happens to break down. In this sense, dynamism and equality are surely at odds with each other.

(vii) Globalisation which promotes world-wide dynamism increases inequality in the advanced countries as well as in newly industrialising economies. In advanced countries, globalisation depresses the incomes of unskilled workers. In the less advanced poorer countries it is entrepreneurs and skilled workers who see their income opportunities improved. This is a trade-off between equality and progress (or growth). As a dynamic trade-off I consider it to be more relevant for economic policy than the static trade-off between "equality and efficiency" that is the subject of Arthur Okun's celebrated 1975 book (published by the Brookings Institution). Okun's perspective was neo-classical rather than Schumpeterian. The evolutionary perspective I prefer is less focused on factor endowments and on an efficient factor allocation and more concentrated on factor augmentation, i.e. on saving and investment, on the formation of human capital, on the process of innovation and on the growth of knowledge. Inequality may be indispensible in a system of incentives for such factor augmentation and hence for an acceleration of economic growth in present circumstances.

(viii) In an evolutionary perspective, competition is not so much a mechanism for factor allocation but a growth race. Even more important, competition is a process of discovery (Hayek) which enables us to find out what we did not, and could not, know before. The knowledge that counts is the knowledge that will be considered useful in the future. It is the future that determines the evaluation. Time will show and appreciate what is useful; and time will depreciate what is becoming obsolete under the impact of new knowledge. Only a society that is forward looking in this sense and is prepared to welcome new discoveries as potentially useful, will fully test and effectively expand its dynamic properties. A precondition is full freedom of thought and research mixed with a minimum of protection for old values as it seems necessary to conserve the stability that even an evolutionary society needs. What is mostly required is optimism – technological and environmental optimism in particular. I consider this in tune with Popper who is reported to have said: "Optimism is duty".

(ix) The outcome of dynamic competition may often be some form of co-operation. I mean first of all the co-operation that evolves within the pattern of a deepening division of labour. People want to make use of their comparative advantages once they have discovered their relative strength and weakness in a competitive and stormy process of trial and error. They want to specialise and thus to deepen their knowledge and expertise in the division of labour. They are likely to pursue the path of learning by doing. And they have some interest to cultivate their complementary relations with customers and suppliers for improved (factorial) terms of trade – undisturbed by elements of substitution and competition. Competitive self-organisation thus leads to co-operation. Such competition for subsequent co-operation may be called "co-opetition", more specifically: co-opetition in time.

(x) Co-opetition in time – as a general notion – may also be useful for describing the two distinct phases of the business cycle.

There is tough competition in periods of recession when efforts are concentrated on cutting costs, improving the product mix, and searching for new markets. Sclerotic firms go bankrupt, new combinations and alliances are being formed. People speak of a crisis because the future appears most uncertain and can hardly be ascertained by extrapolating past trends. The market co-ordination through price signals seems to have broken down. Relative prices seem to change too fast.

These competitive irritations disappear in the course of the new upswing when price and cost competition give way to output expansion and when the fruits of the new division of labour among firms show up in increased company profits. Such output dynamism resembles co-operation and cartel-like behaviour, but it is really nothing else than the period of harvest following the time of competitive sowing and intensive cultivation.

Our national accounts ignore this as they focus on output, thus creating the illusion that the recession is merely a slowdown, a temporary stagnation or decline. In actual fact, there are, of course, such mini-recessions. But we also recognize deeper structural declines, perhaps once in a decade. They serve as phases of restructuring or preparation for the spurt of economic development that is bound to come afterwards. The unemployment that arises in such structural recessions under the impact of globalisation is likely to persist, if the labour market – including the wage system – is as inflexible and sclerotic as in Europe, not prepared to accept what appear to be the new inequalities.

(xi) Co-opetition in time has its parallel in space and geography: You observe how centralised production plants cater for dispersed markets; you see hierarchically organised firms having horizontal relations with customers and suppliers for "just in time delivery"; you notice office districts in central cities bringing together people who commute from and to their homes in surrounding rural areas. Most nuclear families cultivate reciprocal altruism within a narrow realm and have less intimate relationships with more distant relatives, friends, or anonymous markets. And small teams share their knowledge internally and simultaneously take part in extensive research networks world-wide. The point to be made in this context is that the centre or nucleus or team serves as the locus of creation, while the surrounding area and the periphery are the field of application, testing, and marketing. The nucleus is a kind of volcano, a powerhouse for the dynamism of the spatial economy. Look at Stanford and Silicon Valley, at MIT and Route 128 near Boston! Or consider how a few chemical research centres in Germany gave birth and nutrition to the chemical industry at the River Rhine!

(xii) Central places are in competition with each other – just as families and firms, teams and universities compete with their likes. We call this locational competition. It includes competition among jurisdictions and political systems, among institutions and fiscal authorities. The ultimate objective in each case is excellence – for a better standing, a better living or mere survival. What these central places are competing for in locational competition is mobile resources such as physical capital or human capital, including technological knowledge. These factors of production are hoped to contribute to raising the income of local residents and to broadening the local tax base for lower tax rates or for better public services. Locational competition will deserve more attention among scholars than it has attracted in the past. It is most likely to bring competitive pressure to bear on national and regional governments and on local communities. More civil servants will have to study business administration.

(xiii) The driving force behind locational competition is the increase in the world-wide mobility of capital and human capital, including embodied and disembodied knowledge. Globalisation, as a step towards openness, may be considered to have followed from liberalisation, a policy mistake in the judgement of some observers. On this policy interpretation, the change appears quite reversible. But there are deeper causes: The decline of transportation costs and, perhaps more important, the decline of long-distance communication costs. This process towards openness brought down east European socialism and is likely to prevent the re-emergence of closed systems for a long time to come. "Fortress Europe", e.g. will turn out to have been an anachronistic conception or ideological monster.

(xiv) The lowering of communication costs is greatly increasing the size of the market for ideas. From decade to decade tens and hundreds of million of more people are becoming part of Western civilisation. The talent pool, on which the centres of research have to rely in recruiting personnel, is becoming larger and larger. From this I draw the heroic conclusion that the process of knowledge creation will accelerate. The same will hold for the stream of inventions and innovations. What technical progress did gain from Japan's integration into the progressive world order appears to me immense. A repetition can be expected from China and India becoming an integral part of the world economy.

(xv) This acceleration is likely to raise the demand for investible funds relative to the supply of savings and thus to drive up the real rate of interest. Financial analysts and fund managers please listen! You will have to learn (or re-learn) the lesson that the real rate of interest is the price of time (rather than of liquidity) and that time is becoming short in supply when the growth of knowledge accelerates.

(xvi) The tendency for the rate of interest to rise under such conditions may create disorientation or irritation in designing monetary policy. What is the tolerable inflation rate when the basket of goods and services used as a yardstick improves in quality rather than in quantity and contains more and more services which have no physical property to dissociate from their nominal value when one wants to identify their contribution to price inflation? And if one does not know today's true inflation rate, how can one formulate substantive views on the inflation rate expected by the bond market to find out what today's real rate of interest really is? What is, and what will be, the true rate of productivity advance to be used for judging wage increases if output mainly consists of intangible services? How much should I deduct from the official inflation rate in order to take account of the additional flow of information and knowledge that comes to me in exchange for what I pay to the print media and the electronic media?

Should it become more and more difficult to answer such questions, we may have to give up price level stability as a goal of monetary policy and use a more simple yardstick. Perhaps, we may have to tie money again to the price of gold.

(xvii) If capital is scarce and affords a high price, "the" wage rate as the price for complementary labour will have to be relatively low – low in line with the abundance of labour, of unskilled labour especially. In the years to come, wages in Europe will have to lag behind the advance of labour productivity until the pool of structurally unemployed labour has been exhausted.

(xviii) An important lesson can be learnt from comparing the West German employment miracle of the 1950s with the labour market failure in East Germany in the present decade. In both cases there was domestic liberalisation, the removal of import controls, substantial aid from outside, and a stable monetary policy. The main difference – apart from the restoration of property rights in ex-Soviet East Germany – was in wage policy. Wage moderation in West Germany, in the first experiment, led to the miraculous return to full employment in the late 1950s. This is in stark contrast to the wage explosion in the name of equality that accompanied East Germany's social unification with the West in the 1990s. That explosion made much of the capital stock economically obsolete as if it had been physically destroyed. The remedy is now expected to come from investment subsidies. Reduced investment costs are to compensate for excessive labour costs, as if capital were abundant and labour were the scarce factor. The outcome can only be excess capital deepening, a waste of capital in a process of jobless growth. We will also observe excessive commuting within Germany from East to West and will witness the emergence of a dual economy in Germany's new territories. Compared to a scenario with undistored factor prices, East Germany will require more aid, will gain less from trade and will need more time for wholly catching up with the West and with its own long-run development potential.

(xix) Wage moderation in West Germany in the post-war period was partly due to the mystery of continuous gains from trade. These gains from trade were the result of a favourable export mix – with a high income elasticity of demand – and of fast income growth in industrial countries. And " ... wage policy allowed firms to keep their terms of trade gains for investment purposes" (Giersch, Paqué, Schmieding, 1992, p. 72). The explanation for this mystery is sheer ignorance. Until late 1964, when the newly created German Council of Economic Experts submitted its first report, hardly anybody was aware of the fact that terms of trade gains (losses) raised (depressed) the potential for wage increases in the same way as the increase (decline) of physical productivity that used to be in the centre of the wage policy discussion. The terms of trade gains thus accrued to exporters and importers and were mostly invested for further growth when post-war Germany became an integral part of the expanding world economy. It was a positive feedback at the expense of income equality.

(xx) Another factor contributing to wage moderation was Ludwig Erhard's mode of moral suasion. In contrast to modern monetarist views, he held wage setting responsible for inflation (rather than for employment) thus mobilising the public's fear of inflation in his fight against excessive wage claims. In the same vein, business was persuaded to expand volumes at constant prices. Thus, a kind of decency – in contrast to greed – became the moral characteristics of what is being labelled the "Social Market Economy".

(xxi) We can also speak of a "morally repressed inflation" to indicate the existence of a macro-economic disequilibrium, a disquilibrium that was associated with the undervaluation of the D-Mark from the beginning to the end of the 1960s. This disequilibium produced high growth rates, especially in 1968 and 1969, similar to the rates achieved in the 1950s. The disequilibrium had its parallel in an excess demand for labour which induced an inflow of guest workers who were flexible and mobile. Thanks to this imported flexibility, West Germany enjoyed an absence of structural unemployment despite structural change. The labour market disequilibrium also induced employers to unfold search activities and to engage in labour hoarding, notably for training workers on the job. The market thus made private enterprise to bring about what would otherwise have been public labour market policies. The labour market performed smoothly, and firms in search of labour often invested in backward regions with pockets of unemployment.

(xxii) This disequilibrium system not only attracted immigrant workers for faster GDP growth; it was also accompanied by a balance of payments disequilibrium of the following sort: German capital exports were too low to match the current account surplus, not to mention the inflow of speculative short-term funds that looked for revaluation gains. Pulling-in even more guest workers and using more resources for a faster growth of the capital stock might have stabilised the economy on a steep growth path, though only for a couple of years and perhaps at the expense of growth in countries at the periphery of Western Europe. This alternative was not considered as a policy option. Instead, the twin disequilibria led to a currency revaluation and a wage explosion (at the end of the decade). Nevertheless, it is still worth considering the twin disequilibria as a possible growth strategy in the game of locational competition. How – and how long – can domestic labour and land underprice themselves in order to make domestic locations more attractive for mobile capital and for complementary immigrant labour? How can domestic resources be kept undervalued for faster growth in world-wide competition?

(xxiii) The West German case of growth acceleration raises the question as to what kind of exchange rate would be suitable for speeding up economic growth in less developed countries. My conclusion boils down to the following advice: Have an exchange rate sufficiently undervalued in terms of production costs for traditional goods (Heckscher-Ohlin goods) so that domestic exporters gain market shares in expanding world markets. If this goes along with an import of capital and a deficit in the balance of payments on current account, please do not get worried: The capital inflow is needed to build up production facilities for a fast growth of exports. And consider that foreign capital would not come in without a high profitability of investment for export production. In that case you are not living beyond your means; instead, you merely invest in excess of domestic savings. The deficit in your current balance of payments testifies to your locational advantages in a world economy with a global capital market. And you test the country's potential for real growth. The country may be under-industrialised, given its catching-up potential, its labour force or its raw material deposits; or the country can count on an excess supply of potential entrepreneurship. If entrepreneurship happens to be in short supply, you may pull in entrepreneurs – together with foreign capital – in the form of foreign direct investment. If such complementarities are not perceived as strong enough to warrant the inflow of long-term capital, the deficit on current account will come under criticism. The answer then is to reduce domestic absorption by fiscal austerity. This will release resources for exports and/or depress the flow of imports. A quick reaction of the trade balance will show you (and convice the IMF) that the deficit in the balance of payments does not represent a fundamental disequilibrium. The criterion for an ex ante judgement is whether the deficit is small enough in relation – not to exports – but to the rate of growth of exports. With fast export growth, the inflow of capital can be taken to enhance export capacity rather than consumption.

(xxiv) Promoting the inflow of capital will certainly be criticised as being a patent case of Beggar-thy-Neighbour policies. The answer to this in a sense is yes; but in this broad sense one could denounce almost all supply side policies unless they had been sanctioned before in consultations, in harmonisation efforts, or in other cartel-like arrangements euphemistically called co-operation. Using a more objective language, we better call such supply-side measures competitive behaviour in the context of locational competition – thereby admitting that competition in this field is bound to be imperfect or oligopolistic and may harm others unless these others also make themselves more attractive to internationally mobile resources. My advice towards an undervaluation of domestic resources as a means of attracting foreign resources is exactly what we have to conceive as being the essence of locational competition. Should all countries happen to follow such a strategy, there would of course be less to gain for any single one. But an overall acceleration of growth world-wide would result as a free good benefiting all.

(xxv) The best policy to attract forward looking resources from abroad is to grant them freedom from coercion, including guaranteed property rights, unlimited out-migration, and fair taxation in return for the supply of public goods, in short: a policy of openness. Such a policy may benefit capital and other mobile resources in the short run. In the long run it will be to the (absolute) advantage of immobile domestic resources, notably land and labour, thanks to a leaner government and to a more efficient use of capital, including human capital and knowledge.

(xxvi) Acceleration will be followed by deceleration once the economy's potential and driving force have been exhausted. In the medium run, i.e. after several business cycles, one may say in very general terms: Deceleration is likely to occur when the politicians' time horizon is shortening, when people's time preference is markedly increasing, when impatience becomes characteristic of the public's mood. We observed this in Germany in the early 1970s. In general it appears that deceleration is around the corner

– when people resent new knowledge and innovation and the costs of adjustment to structural change;
– when the demand for economic security expands at the cost of entrepre-

neurship and competition;
- when the demand for equality leads to wage pressures and a profit
  squeeze, to a compression of the vertical wage spread, and to a more
  progressive tax system; and
- when government and bureaucracy pervade and regulate the market system, perhaps under the pressure of special interest groups, so that the
  economic system becomes more and more sclerotic.

(xxvii) Such deceleration can be postponed for a while if it is possible to
exploit a stock of money illusion. This is what government tried in Germany in the 1970s (after the explosion of wages and oil prices) under the
slogan "Five percent inflation is better than five percent unemployment".
The inflationary "trick" behind this is a compression of real interest rates
under the impact of unanticipated inflation. This compression of the costs
of capital serves the purpose of compensating firms for excessive wage
costs. Such a twist of the two decisive factor prices, however, leads to a
serious distortion of the growth process; it leads to excessive capital deepening and – after a while – to a capital shortage in the sense that the
capital stock contains very capital intensive jobs, but necessarily too few of
them (Giersch 1983).

(xxviii) The most popular reason suggested for a deceleration of growth
is a shortage of natural resources. While the fast growth of the world
economy in the third quarter of this century can be interpreted as the
march into an oil-intensive society, the slowdown of growth in the 1970s is
often associated with the oil price explosions of 1973 and 1979. Whether
the Club of Rome was right or wrong in its 1972 predictions is not the
point in this context; but a major change in relative resource prices is bound
to indicate the need for a re-direction of economic activity, including R &
D. This cannot but result in less output growth, if growth is measured on
the basis of past – rather than current – relative values. But our statistics
might show more growth, perhaps even an acceleration, if we could and
would properly assess the gains in utility that we derive from the computer.

(xxix) Since the oil price shocks, world economic growth seems to have
taken a new direction: It has turned into a move towards the information
society where the communication of ideas and knowledge will become even
more important relative to the transformation and transportation of materials. The growth of knowledge does not seem to have any limits at all,
but it will be very difficult to subject it to any form of precise measurement
(though there are people who believe that science is measurement – and
little more or nothing else). And how will we evaluate – other than by its
cost – the progress we will believe to make in approaching or ascertaining
the truth in such fields as cosmology, astronomy, medicine, history and

271

even economics? Will the impossibility of disentangling quantity elements and price changes, and thus real growth and inflation, ultimately mean the end of economic growth as a topic of interest to the public?

(xxx) As a central field of economic dynamics, economic growth may soon be replaced by structural change. Let me mention two reasons. The first one is that growth goes along with structural change, almost inevitably. The second point is that structural change often tends to harm as many inhabitants and voters as it benefits. Insurance against harmful changes will then play an increasing role in public policy. The fundamental conflict between social values will then not be growth versus equality, but progress versus security. The ghost of protectionism is raising its head. We will have to find intelligent responses.

III. Concluding Remarks

Socialism lost the competitive race between socio-economic systems mainly for its lack of freedom in the market of ideas and knowledge. Social democracy surely has a role to play in the competition among beliefs to the extent that it takes care of those who can gain from greater equality. But once the equality issue fades into the background and the security aspect dominates the concerns of people, it appears that there remains little difference between social democracy and conservatism – conservatism in the European sense of conserving traditional values and structures against the forces of innovation and structural change. Individuals will then have to choose
– between halting or promoting progress,
– between technological pessimism or evolutionary optimism.

As for myself, I have several times come out in favour of long-run optimism. We will be able to solve the problems that we create just as mankind has done in the past. I feel happy that I happen to live in this century rather than in any previous period, and I feel sorry that I will not be able to observe the dynamism to be expected from the growth of knowledge in the future. These are admittedly very personal judgements but they seem to be quite in order and pertinent in a broad, though impressionistic and very preliminary, assessment of economic dynamism before an audience with an evolutionary mind.

Note

1 This essay, originally an address given at the Schumpeter Society in 1994, was first published in: Ernst Helmstätter, Marl Perlman (eds.), 'Behavorial Norms, Technical Progress an Economic Dynamics', in: *Studies in Schumpeterian Economis*, The University of Michigan Press, Ann Arbor 1966. – The editor kindly gave his permission to reprint it here.

References

Giersch, Herbert, 1983, 'Socialist elements as limits to economic growth', in Herbert Giersch, 1991, *The World Economy in Perspective: Essays on International Trade and European Integration*, pp. 247–259, Brookfield, VT, Edward Elgar.

Giersch, Herbert; Paqué, Karl-Heinz; Schmieding, Holger, 1992 *The Fading Miracle: Four Decades of Market Economy in Germany*, revised and updated 1994, Cambridge, Cambridge University Press.

Hayek, Friedrich A. von, 1968, *Der Wettbewerb als Entdeckungsverfahren*, Kieler Vorträge NF 56, Kiel, Institute of World Economics.

Popper, Karl R., 1994, *Alles Leben ist Problemlösen*, Munich, Piper.

Down with the Bishops?

Lord Harris of High Cross

I don't know if the organisers of this lecture[1] are insured against damage from acts of God. But I thank the audience for braving the risk of thunderbolts from on high in retaliation for my chastisement of all those turbulent priests in the Anglican communion. As a struggling member of the Church of England, I should perhaps take no pleasure in challenging its more vocal leaders. Yet as a professional economist, I regard their lofty, self-righteous rejection of the liberal market economy as not only wrongheaded, but damaging to all of us and potentially self-destructive to themselves.

Their most consistent criticisms are variously directed at such prominent features of capitalism as competitive enterprise, profit-seeking, the multinational corporation, and individual responsibility. They take for granted the wondrous multiplication of output which has transformed human material welfare in both West and East – indeed wherever dispersed enterprise has been given its head – and has done so despite the dramatic explosion of the population in the two centuries since the Rev. Thomas Malthus proved such progress was impossible.

Not for the Bishops daily prayers of thanks, nor even grudging acknowledgement, that the success of competitive markets has not merely 'trickled down' but positively cascaded to transform the luxuries of yesterday's privileged minorities into the conventional necessaries of today's masses. They never pause to ask what other system in history or across the contemporary world can boast such success in the annihilation of disease, squalor, hunger, ignorance and destitution, which was the lot of almost all mankind in the 18 centuries following the birth of Christ. Instead, they appear to curse their deformed caricature of capitalism at its worst for what they regard as its two central failures which they describe in the question-begging terms of 'poverty' and 'inequality.' On each they are damnably careless and casual in both definition and measurement.

Thus on poverty, they relish to paint the darkest picture. In Britain they echo the wild claims of the poverty lobby which repeatedly bids for the headlines in claiming that about one-third of the population is living 'in or on the margins of poverty.' Closer inspection reveals that the last precise estimate in 1985 was 29 per cent, of which only 5 per cent were below the level of Income Support which is the state payment available unconditionally to keep people out of poverty. Another 12 per cent were shown to be exactly *on* the Income Support level, that is to be out of poverty. And the remaining 12 per cent had less than 40 per cent *more* than the Income Support level which the Child Poverty Action Group tautologically define as 'on the margins of poverty'. Thus the headline total of 'one in three Britons in poverty' dissolves into 5 per cent below the poverty line. None of these statistics allow for the tendency known to all scrupulous students for people submitting to a means test to understate their income, for example from family and black economy, and to overstate their outgoings, for example on rent and dependants.

Comparisons over time are distorted by the contemporary convention of measuring poverty by the elastic yardstick of a relative, rather than an absolute, standard. In this way, successive increases in the real level of Income Support show 'poverty' continuing, if not rising, for ever. This optical illusion is exploited in a recent poverty lobby symposium entitled unambiguously *The Growing Divide*. After acknowledging that Income Support *rose* between 1978 (i.e., pre-Thatcher) and 1987 by 5 per cent more than prices, one author complains that average personal disposable income rose by 14 per cent more than inflation. He concludes that by comparison 'benefit levels have *fallen* considerably'. In this way, *more* is advertised as *less*, as a prelude to indicting the Thatcher Government for 'grotesque inequalities' which prove Britain is 'rapidly losing its claim to be a civilised society'.

If we turn to so-called inequalities of income and wealth, the methodology is no more scrupulous. First I must enter a semantic objection against the conventional use of the world 'inequality', which implies the unnatural departure from the norm of equality. We would not discuss our fellow men, much less our womenfolk, in terms of their 'inequality' of height, girth, good looks, or speed, with the implication that tall, slim, handsome or fast people should be deprived of such 'unfair' advantages.

When we examine recent claims in Britain that differences in wealth can be summed up for popular consumption by the statistic that 10 per cent of the population own 70 per cent of the nation's wealth, we find the figures are equally phoney. Without digging too deeply into admittedly complex statistics and categories, we can rely on a detailed study published in 1975 by the Institute of Economic Affairs under the title: *How much Inequality?* The authors worked over the official data derived largely from estates assessed for death duties, and showed how they failed to take account of the widely dispersed wealth of millions of under-recorded estates below the exemption limit, omitted the shared ownership of public assets, the imputed capital value enjoyed by the tenants of subsidised rented homes, and the universal entitlement to state pensions, and, more important, ignored the shared benefit of family wealth by wives, children and other dependants. Thus the biased estimates assumed that 24 million adults owned nothing at all in 1970!

The IEA study concluded that after allowance for such distortions, a truer summary than '10 per cent owns 70 per cent' might be nearer the '10 per cent owns 30 per cent' which would reflect differences in wealth from savings accumulated by older people through their lifetime, even if incomes and inheritance were equal. To take a simple analogy, suppose the average height of all Australians, irrespective of age, worked out at four and a half feet, would we be agitated to be told that, say 20 per cent were below this meaningless average height? Are Bishops not capable of grasping such a natural phenomenon, or would they join a public outcry about stunted lives and inequality of physique?

The exaggerated emotional and political clap-trap about so-called inequalities in the *distribution* of income pay no regard to even the most obvious differences in what might be called inequalities in the *generation* of income. I strongly believe we all need constantly reminding that even our least favoured neighbours should be respected, if not positively loved, as of equal moral worth, not only in the sight of God, but we must hope in the sight of their parents, children, family and friends. Differences of income or wealth are not meant to reflect intrinsic human valuations. A higher rate of wages, interest, or profit arising from a competitive market serves at once as an incentive to increased labour, saving, or investment, and a measure of their contribution to the social product as valued by the preferences of the sovereign consumer.

If Bishops and others wish their criticism of market outcomes to be taken seriously, they must show a glimmer of understanding about how the liberal economy operates.They might start from one of the prime wonders of God's creation that individuals, even in the same family, differ so widely in their physical, psychological, intellectual, and temperamental endowments. Such inborn 'inequalities', which we usually call 'differences', are further multiplied by variations in education, training, experience and personal avocation. The central question for serious social philosophers in a free society is how can countless millions of people with such diverse talents be brought together in voluntary cooperation to supply most effectively their own and one another's requirements. In short, how can unequal natural endowments be harnessed for the public good?

In his crowning work, *The Fatal Conceit,* Hayek argues that the case for market economy does not depend on value judgements or ideology, as was commonly supposed in the pre-Gorbachev era. Instead, it rests on the further *fact* that man's finite knowledge falls short of the infinite complexity of the physical creation. The extent of human ignorance and uncertainty is compounded by ceaseless changes in production, techniques, resources, invention and consumer preference. Accordingly, if society is to make the fullest use of scarce and changing human and material resources, we have to draw on as much as possible of the detailed, fragmentary, even contradictory information which is dispersed among millions of people. This assorted knowledge cannot be fully known to any group of central planners, let alone a bench of bishops. The miracle of the market is that, without a directing intelligence, it shapes an extensive international division of labor and brings about a spontaneous order which, in a favourite phrase of Hayek, is 'the result of human action but not of human design'.

The paradox that markets yield order while, as Gorbachev acknowledges, central planning leads ultimately to chaos, follows from the role of market prices as signals that guide the actions of producers and consumers so as to bring supply and demand everywhere towards equilibrium. Even Gorbachev has now come round to the view that output will not match demand unless wage and salary differentials are more closely related to productive performance.

But if rewards for work are to be determined by unequal payment through markets for labor, how can we measure this productive performance? Again, Gorbachev has mocked output that fulfils the plan but does not supply even the meat, bread, clothes, accommodation that people want, let alone their more sophisticated preferences. Indeed, he is increasingly sounding like Adam Smith who declared in *The Wealth of Nations* that 'Consumption is the sole end and purpose of all production'.

From such elementary requirements for an effective economic system follows the logic of market pricing for competitive production to meet consumer choice. It would take volumes to deck out that skeleton in full raiment. We would have to expound the indispensable role of government, not least in protecting private property rights, imposing the rule of law against force and fraud, and providing other services which markets either cannot supply, or cannot do so economically.

But Gorbachev's confessions have made it easier to assert that the system variously described as liberal capitalism, economic freedom, market economy, or private (competitive) enterprise has no rival in the multiplication and spreading of wealth. It is fashionable for the poverty lobby to mock the 'trickle-down' effect of prosperity in elevating the poor. Yet how otherwise can they explain why their chosen standard of poverty is above the average earnings os such well-endowed socialist regimes as the USSR? The transformation of standards of living, conditions of work and prospects for leisure over the past century or more has sprung from the process of innovation, investment and competitive production of which dispersed initiative has proved, without doubt, the most powerful stimulus known to man.

Writing as one who has increasingly come to believe in the primacy of moral values over 'economic salvation', I no longer advocate competitive markets exclusively as helping us resolve the central economic conundrum of how and what to produce. Even more important, the market alone allows maximum freedom for individuals to make their own choices and keep the reins of their mortal and immortal destinies so far as possible in their own hands. Christian critics have too easily taken for granted the twin boons of material progress and spiritual freedom conferred by liberal capitalism. They ignore the lesson that the churches have historically been most severely controlled and persecuted in countries that lack the dispersed initiative and private property rights which are the cornerstone of a market economy.

They are too ready to appeal for state intervention, and gloss over the unalluring reality that government necessarily involves force. Hayek's ideal set out in *The Constitution of Liberty* is the limitation of state power so as to minimise that coercion which occurs where 'one man's actions are made to serve another man's will, not for his own but for the other's purpose'.

Despite the rhetoric of party politicians, the choice for government is not between collectivism and *laissez-faire*. The strongest adherents of market economy acknowledge an indisputable role for strong (not big) government. Markets cannot work in a vacuum. It cannot be too often repeated that they require a framework of law to protect person and property, specify standards, enforce contracts, police monopoly and check pollution. Competing producers catering for consumer choice are not appropriate to supply 'public goods' like national defence, street lighting or a social safety net. There is a growing 'market' in charity, despite the 'crowding out' effect of the providential state. Thus people still supply personal services or cash (encouraged by tax concessions) to satisfy the needs of others who cannot help themselves. But until private philanthropy is stronger, few economic liberals deny an essential role for state finance to support social services so long as they are administered in ways that will do least damage to the incentive for able-bodied recipients to support themselves and their families.

To hear some Bishops denouncing Mrs Thatcher, you could be forgiven for believing that since 1979 the conservatives had been fully engaged in dismantling state services. A sharply contrasting picture is presented by the last audited national accounts for 1988. The figures show that what is blandly called 'public expenditure', which I would describe more graphically as politically-controlled spending, amounted to 175,000 million pounds, which was 44 per cent of a total national income around 400,000 million pounds.

This outlay was equal to more than 3,000 pounds a year for every man, woman and child in the United Kingdom or, on a more homely scale, an average of 240 pounds *a week* for a family of four. Social services alone accounted for 100,000 million pounds (averaging 140 pounds a week), made up of over 22,000 million pounds on state education, 23,000 million pounds on the health service and a massive 54,000 million pounds on social security. Since 1979 each of these lines of spending has increased significantly in real terms after generous allowance for the inflation of prices.

Is it not remarkable that this massive and mounting outlay under the sacred banner of the welfare state, absorbing one quarter of the total value of rising national output, appears to satisfy no-one, neither teachers, parents, doctors, patients, ancillaries, pensioners, nor poverty lobbies? The most obvious explanation is that social spending is not effectively managed. Instead of being directed scrupulously and selectively at the declining minority in need, this largesse is sprayed indiscriminately in 'free' services or social benefits for everyone in the name of universalism. It was a Bishop in the House of Lords who most vividly expressed the fallacy which this wasteful policy embodies:

'The image of strong, independent citizens who do not need help from the resources of others is feasible for only a *very few privileged people* ... Today the great *majority of people* and I include myself depend upon the social wage to maintain the quality of life.'

Here is the most naive expression of the fantasy of a universal free lunch. I seriously question whether it is forgivable, even for an unworldly Bishop, to confuse counsels by preaching the self-evident falsehood that the welfare state could enable (nearly) everyone to live better at someone else's expense? The plain truth is that the cost of universal benefits is so high that they require finance by taxes falling on millions of people with incomes well below the Bishops' favoured poverty line. Most people pay their own way in welfare through general taxation. Indeed, they pay through the nose, but indirectly and are thereby deprived of consumer sovereignty over the bureaucratic suppliers of education and health care.

Economic textbooks have much to say about theoretical imperfections of the market. But the practical failures of government are far more pervasive and less corrigible. Books have been written about the inefficiency and outright waste of resources inseparable from government provision of monopoly service like education or medical care without charge or choice for the conscripted consumer. If politicians defer to elitist sentiment in perpetuating this economic abomination of zero pricing, literally a free-for-all, they must not be surprised that large additional expenditures continue to fall short of unpriced expectations. More recently American students of social policy like Charles Murray have pointed to accumulating evidence that today's more generous social benefits have the cruelly perverse effect of undermining self-help by prolonging, deepening and extending dependency and voluntary unemployment. For able-bodied claimants, including heads of 'single-parent' families, the social benefits intended to keep them out of poverty, at the same time exert an *unintended* disincentive to striving harder for training, mobility and employment as more fulfilling routes to self-support, self-respect and self-fulfilment.

Economic analysis can point to dozens of similar examples where well-intentioned government policies have perversely led to deplorable results. As with welfare, the reason is that politicians take a narrow and short-term view which overlooks the full effects on human action of distorting price or income incentives. The classic example has long been rent control which protected sitting tenants only by excluding others, often more deserving, and (unintentionally) destroyed the incentive for landlords to keep property in good repair, much less build additional houses to rent at a loss.

Equally disastrous has been the effect under the Common Agricultural Policy of raising food prices in the interests of less efficient farmers which (unintentionally) induces higher production, costly surpluses, and the closing of markets to cheaper produce from poorer farmers in Africa and the West Indies, as well as the abudant supplies of wheat, meat, and dairy produce from Australia and New Zealand. The opposite policy by many African governments of fixing farm prices too low, in the short-term interests of urban consumers, has everywhere led to the (unintended) consequence of discouraging peasant production and condemning millions to chronic deprivation, periodic starvation and lingering death. No less malignant have been government and trade union policies to raise minimum wages which have (unintentionally) increased unemployment, and then provoked monetary expansion which, in turn, has unleashed inflation.

In all such cases, governments of both advanced and backward countries may claim to have been moved by only the best of intentions. But because their expendiencies have depended on suppressing market forces, they have finished up distorting production, discouraging enterprise, destroying wealth and retarding economic welfare. Without a grasp of the linkage between prices and supply and demand, even benign intentions are not proof against malignant results.

Widespread misunderstanding and mistrust of market pricing are not the only explanation of so much misdirected political travail. The economic analysis of democratic politcs teaches us that politicians may escape the profit motive only to fall foul of the 'vote motive'. The American school of 'public choice', led by Nobel Laureate James Buchanan and Gordon Tullock, points to the systematic corruption of public policy from the process whereby sectional interest groups offer to trade their electoral support in exchange for subsidies, protection, or other favours. Competition in the political market can no longer be presumed to promote the elusive 'public interest'. So long as political parties have unlimited power to promise people more than they could earn in a competitive market, farmers, trade unions, professions, owner occupiers, tenants, pensioners and other lobbies are not slow to push their claims for sectional privileges.

Furthermore, since concentrated producers, whether capital or labour, can be organised more effectively than scattered customers, policies are likely to favour the producer interest in higher prices and restricted output, over the consumer interest in cheapness and plenty. The chief novelty of Thatcherism has been to confront such pressures by resisting union and professional special pleading, by reducing subsidies, deregulating markets and sharpening competition. The success of such policies can be measured by the reversal of economic decline and the record increases of productivity, output and income since 1979. But ten years has not proved long enough to reverse over half a century of creeping collectivism. There is still a long way to go in removing restrictions on competitive markets that continue to hamper mobility and adjustment in response to new opportunities, for example in the European market, and to meet the growing challenge from Japan and the newly industrialised economies of the East.

Yet all the opposition parties confronting Mrs Thatcher's radical reforming Government are already back at the old game of promising less bracing routes to easier times for (almost) everyone. Against this sombre background, I conclude that the priestly disposition to join in calling upon the 'state' to promise short-term, soft options for deep-seated economic problems is one of the most dispiriting forms of idolatry in my lifetime. They should ponder Adam Smith's warning against 'that insidious and crafty animal, vulgarly called a statesman or politician, whose counsels are directed by the momentary fluctuation of affairs'.

It is commonplace that people sharing similar if not identical aims, whether in social policy or other spheres of human action, may conscientiously differ sharply about the best way of achieving their shared purposes. From some acquaintance with Church spokesmen and Labor as well as Conservative leaders, I have no doubt that most serious disagreements on policy are about means rather than ends. Would it not anyway be more charitable, especially for Christians, to assume that scholars on both sides of the argument are equally concerned to eradicate such scourges as poverty, homelessness and unemployment? On social isses where sentiment often prevails over disciplined reason, it would hardly be remarkable for Bishops among others to adopt a preference for the socialist ideal, even if collectivism has not invariably worked very well in practice. What is surely inadmissible is for them to proclaim their chosen method *blessed* and to denounce the way of the market, which is conscientiously preferred by other Christians and which has proved the chief engine of economic and social progress.

To judge by the tendency of socialists to boast of superior compassion, a large part of the explanation is that they persist in assessing the merits of alternative approaches by their professed motives rather than their practical outcomes. At the heart of this widespread emotional distaste for the competitive market is its reliance on the supposedly narrow motive of individual self-interest, which in political debate is too easily equated with greed and single-minded selfishness. The case for the prosecution is too well-known to require further elaboration. In the time that remains I shall offer ten reasons why this charge should be earnestly reconsidered, if not rejected outright, by those who truly wish to understand the case for the defence. At the outset we must dig deeper into the setting in which self-interest is assumed to operate.

As founder of modern political economy in *An Enquiry into the Nature and Causes of the Wealth of Nations*, Adam Smith asserts that 'the principle from which public and national as well as private opulence is originally derived' is nothing more nor less than what he called:

'The uniform, constant and uninterrupted effort of every man to better his condition ...'

As though anticipating the poor performance of our post-war dalliance with collectivism, Smith declared that this principle, which might be described in more homely terms as self-improvement:

'is frequently powerful enough to maintain the natural progress of things towards improvement, in spite both of extravagance of government and of the greatest errors of administration.'

Indeed he continues:

'Like the unknown principle of animal life, it frequently restores health and vigour to the constitution, in spite not only of the disease, but of the absurd prescriptions of the doctor.'

My first plea is that the classical economists never denied that most people are capable of acting from compassion or altruism, which Adam

Smith calls 'benevolence' and Alfred Marshall 'chivalry'. We may thank the Lord that, despite the undoubted strengh of original sin, most of us do not exclusively seek to maximise our incomes or wealth. But might not Bishops acknowledge that they also act from mixed motives? Or would they blame their own falls from grace on the market, like the fat man in the restaurant who curses the waiter for his own obesity?

Before the famous *Wealth of Nations* (1776), Smith wrote the little known *Theory of Moral Sentiments* (1759) in which he denounces as sternly as any Bishop the man who 'devotes himself for ever to the pursuit of wealth and greatness'. More positively, he emphasises our need for 'love, friendship and gratitude' and dwells on the promptings of conscience as the 'impartial spectator' or 'the great inmate of the breast, the great judge and arbiter of conduct'. For Smith as moral philosopher, 'The perfection of human nature 'would require us 'to restrain our selfish, and to indulge our benevolent, affections'. As a practical Scot, however, he concludes, not without reverence:

'... the care of the universal happiness of all rational and sensible beings is the business of God and not of man. To man is allotted a much humbler department, but one much more suitable to the weakness of his powers and the narrowness of his comprehension – the care of his own happiness, of that of his family, his country: that he is occupied in contemplating the more sublime can never be an excuse for neglecting the more humble department ...'

It is clear that Smith is far from lauding the motive which critics dismiss as material self-interest. Insofar as he offers a moral, *normative* view of 'what ought to be', he puts love well above self-love. But as a practical, *positive* statement of 'what is', he concludes that the most consistently powerful incentive to action is the everday human effort to better our condition. Alfred Marshall had much the same distinction in mind when he talked of the necessity to harness the strongest, not only the highest, motive to the promotion of economic progress.

My second witness for the market is Hayek whose extensive writings have demonstrated the indispensable role of the incentives of price and profit (and loss) as impersonal signals to guide consumers, workers, investors and entrepreneurs in the daily progress of economising scarce resources. We may wish it were otherwise. Our instinctive preferences may be for the face-to-face relationships of simpler, local communities in which co-operation and sharing could soften personal dealings. In *The Fatal Conceit*, Hayek explains how the emergence of a complex modern economy – what he calls 'the extended order' required and reinforces a society based on individualism. competition, private property, and more remote, 'faceless' dealings. The trouble is that the Christian social critique reflects the ideal of behaviour appropriate to more intimate groupings of smaller-scale, static, pre-industrial – in a word, primitive – communities.

This modern dilemma was illustrated by David Sheppard, Bishop of Liverpool, who remains a better cricketer than economist. On page 136 of his *Bias to the Poor*, he blaimed capitalists for closing firms 'which happen to be operating in areas from which the market has shifted away'. Yet on page 219, he defends Bishops for closing churches 'in areas where the population has drastically reduced'. His alibi turns out to be an unwitting confession of guilt or humbug for the earlier criticism of capitalism:

If we keep too many church buildings, we trap small congregations into putting all their energies into maintaining the buildings and justifying their existence by running Church organisations to use them.

Adam Smith would agree; so would Mrs Thatcher. If you substitute 'coal mines' or 'steel mills' for 'churches', you have a complete vindication for the closure of uneconomic plants.

Bishops, like entrepreneurs and ordinary families, have to be guided by financial calculations in deciding the most effective disposition of limited resources. On precisely the same principle, prices in the form of income differentials which the Left find so offensive, are necessary to guide the local, national and international division of labour.

Another jolly example dates back to 1947 when British planning was suffering one of its periodic crisis, Mr Clement Attlee as Prime Minister of the Labour Government appealed to the nation in a radio broadcast as follows:

'Ask yourself whether you are doing the kind of work which the nation needs in view of the shortage of labour. Your job may bring you in more money but be quite useless to the community.'

One of our rare economic jesters, George Schwartz, pictured the chaos if people had tried to act on that advice by every worker unilaterally deciding what job is more useful to his fellows. Mr Schwartz hinted that the resignations might best start with the civil servants responsible for economic planning! A third affidavit for the market can be stated in seven words: voluntary exchange yields benefits to both parties. Buyer and seller both derive what economists call 'gains from trade'. So long as competition prevails, we can only 'better our condition' by serving others through supplying something for which they choose to pay. In short, as Milton Friedman has said, to do well, you have to do good. Henry Ford may have sought riches, but he ended up enriching society far more. Let critics ponder the concept of a cheap millionaire.

My fourth claim emerges when we contemplate the opposite to voluntary exchange. The distinctive feature of collectivism is coercing others to behave in ways the government decrees. We cannot avoid overriding individual choice for public goods, including national defence, law enforcement and standards of purity, safety, environment, weights and measures. Pushed beyond such essential services, consumer choice is frustrated with no guarantee of countervailing public benefit. If individual self-advancement is transmuted by Adam Smith's 'invisible hand' of competition into increased output, state coercion of production, consumption and exchange is often perverted into decreased supplies as we have argued in nationalisation, rent control, agricultural price-fixing and other policies where results mock the best intentions. Even if competition were not in Hayek's phrase 'The optimum discovery procedure', it would merit our allegiance as the best guarantor of individual liberty against the stealthy encroachment of the state.

Fifth argument against involving government in activities better left to the market, is that it diverts over-worked politicians from tasks only they can discharge but so often neglect, like avoiding inflation, enforcing the law, policing competition and helping people who through physical or mental handicap cannot unaided 'better their own condition'. The familiar result is that the most persistent difficulties arise in the over-extended public sector where a wag has complained that political 'solutions' are the cause of most of the problems.

A sixth reckoning is that for the generality of goods and services the market is a more democratic instrument than the ballot box. It has been likened by Lord Robbins to a perpetual referendum in which the consumer votes every day with his pounds and dollars for the precise, distinctive array he prefers from a wide variety of competing supplies at published prices. He, or more often she, can always change his mind! Furthermore, the market is neutral. It will offer whatever consumers want, from prayer books and communion wine to pornography and hard liquor, unless the law forbids it. Unlike the political market, the consumer does not need to demonstrate, nor to secure a majority vote to get what he wants. In contrast to the ballot box where 51 per cent or less prevail over the rest, and racial or other minorities may be voted down, the market gives proportional representation to customers and is colour blind in employing unfavoured groups with appropriate qualifications.

The seventh consideration is that by calling on government, we do nothing to transmute human conduct or to subdue self-interest. We simply transfer the same self-seeking propensities in human nature to the political plane where their scope for abuse is far more corrupting of public morality as well as damaging to freedom and economic progress. At every election I have observed since 1945, the Labour Party has certainly not shunned the most blatant, calculating appeal to naked, short-term self-interest of pensioners, parents, tenants, trade unionists, welfare beneficiaries and most other sizeable lobbies, with the bill to be paid by a conveniently small minority of higher tax-payers with 'the broadest backs' and not too many votes.

An eighth argument for the market based on dispersed initiative and power is that it sets narrow limits to the evil that bad men can perpetrate. Keynes, who was no uncritical champion of the free economy, said almost the last word with his warning:

'... dangerous human proclivities can be canalised into comparatively harmless channels by the existence of opportunities for money-making and private wealth, which if they cannot be satisfied in this way may find their outlet in cruelty, the reckless pursuit of personal power and authority, and other forms of self-aggrandisement ...

It is better that a man should tyrannise over his bank balance than over his fellow citizens ...'

My post-script would be that people who tyrannise over their fellow citizens seldom neglect to attend to their personal bank balances, as so many African socialist leaders have demonstrated.

A ninth argument is that socialist policies which purport to protect the poor from the insecurity of the market, disable them from doing what they could to help themselves and their families. It must have taken rare courage for the British Labour MP and professing Christian, Frank Field, to agree that the plight of single-parent families has been intensified by the incentives which social benefits and housing priority now give for abandoned or unmarried mothers to continue depending on state support. A market solution would seek to strengthen the positive incentives for responsible parenthood and self-support by requiring contributions from the fathers of abandoned children, developing child-minding facilities and making it easier and more accepted for mothers to take suitable employment. A truly compassionate policy towards the able-bodied poor would rely less on doling out unconditional benefits and more on tackling the personal handicaps and deficiencies, including education, training and motivation, which inhibit self-support.

My final testimony for the market is that it provides our best, if not our only hope, or eradicating the causes of poverty in Britain and around the world, without risk to freedom and other values. Whatever lip-service collectivist Bishops pay to the necessity for wealth-creation, there is little dispute that their dominant obsession is with the redistribution of existing income and wealth which their social(ist) policies would be likely to reduce. If we look back in history, or around the contemporary world of

Eastern Europe, Africa and South America, we may more easily conclude that the most effective war against poverty is being fought nor from the pulpits, or party platforms, but on the advancing frontiers of modern technology powered by dispersed initiative, competitive innovation, bold risk-taking and high enterprise.

So let the debate continue with less intimidatory denunciation of the market and its upholders. Perhaps one or two Bishops might even break ranks and give a lead in celebrating next Rogation Sunday the remarkable social advance which economic freedom has enabled frail, fallen men to achieve in fulfilling God's command in Genesis: 'Be fruitful, and multiply, and replenish the earth, and subdue it ...' Bishops may even take heart from the increasing acceptance that the pollution of our natural environment can most quickly be remedied by deploying part of the wealth that men's enterprise has multiplied and shaping market incentives to reward production that sustains our natural environment and to penalise both public and private enterprise that does it harm.

My title 'Down with the Bishops?' is not therefore a prelude to a new call for the dissolution of the cathedrals or the burning of heretics. It is a sober warning against their destructive assault on liberal capitalism which is the best shield imperfect man has devised against poverty, tyranny and inhumanity. Let Bishops stick more to prayer and fasting and less to politics and sniping. For if they were to help bring down our free economic institutions, they risk bringing themselves down to the cellars from which the Church in Eastern Europe is only now hesitantly emerging.

Note

1   Latham Memorial Lecture 1989, in: *Quadrant* January – February 1990, Sydney; originally published under the title, *Down with the Bishops? Reflections on the dangerous economic delusions of leading spokesmen for the Church of England.*

Ideas and the Future of Liberty

Antonio Martino

The subject of my paper[1] is the role of ideas in the fight for liberty. It's a broad subject, and I shall try to limit myself, following the old principle that a talk, like a miniskirt, should be short enough to attract attention, and long enough to cover the argument.

I am convinced that the case for liberty is today better understood than in, let's say, the last fifty years. To show this, all that's needed is to look at the prevailing intellectual climate in the 1940s. In 1947, at the first meeting of The Mont Pelerin Society Hayek remarked that his goal was that of putting together *"a group of people who are in agreement on fundamentals, and among whom certain basic conceptions are not questioned at every step."* His evaluation of the number of such people, however, was pessimistic: *"the number of those who in any one country agree on what seems to me the basic liberal principles (is) small,"* especially if compared with the "very big" task it faced.[2]

One could also quote a remark made by Schumpeter in 1949 on the effectiveness of the Society in its infancy. After having listed a series of socialist principles, which, as a result of the *"disintegration of capitalist society,"* were being *"taken for granted by the business class ... and by the large number of economists who feel themselves to be opposed to (one hundred per cent) socialism,"* he added: *"I believe that there is a mountain in Switzerland on which congresses of economists have been held which express disapproval of all or most of these things (e.g. socialist policies). But these anathemata have not even provoked attack."*[3]

We believers in freedom have come down from that mountain, but have we made any progress since then?

On the question of freedom's future, opinions have always differed widely. Schumpeter himself was, as we all know, very pessimistic. At the time of the foundation of the Society, he wrote: *"Can capitalism survive? No. I do not think it can. (...) [T]he actual and prospective performance of the capitalist system is such (...) that its very success undermines the social institutions which protect it, and 'inevitably' creates conditions in which it will not be able to live and which strongly point to socialism as the heir apparent."*[4]

The pessimism has continued to flourish until recently. For example, I remember that at the MPS meeting in Hillsdale in 1975, a prominent member of the Mont Pèlerin Society was convinced that England would become a dictatorship in five years. Though many on the British left would probably say that his prediction was confirmed by Mrs. Thatcher's rule, most of us would conclude that this kind of pessimism proved to be excessive; and today, while socialism seems to be fading away, capitalism is alive and there seems to be a widespread revival of faith in the free enterprise system.

Indeed, in political rhetoric we have many reasons for being at least moderately optimistic in our evaluation of current trends. Political rhetoric has been changing fast in many countries, including, for example, the People's Republic of Italy. Thirty two years ago, at the time of the 1963 general political elections, statism was the consensus of the overwhelming majority of politicians of almost all political parties. Those of us who dared to challenge the prevailing wisdom – based on deficit spending, national economic planning, nationalization, and direct government intervention – were labeled reactionaries and simply ignored by the new mandarins.[5] Today things have changed drastically. Let me say a few words about my country.

In 1993, confronted with a collapsing political system, frightening financial disarray, confiscatory taxation, and the real danger of a recession, Italians thought that all of the country's problems could be cured by a change in the electoral system. In a referendum held in April 1993 some 83% of voters indicated that they wanted to move from proportional representation (PR) to a majoritarian system. In haste, a new electoral law was approved, which replaced PR with a mixed system – 75% of senators and deputies would be elected on a "first pass the post" basis, the remaining 25% on a bizarre version of proportional representation.

Elections were held on March 27–28, 1994, with two contestants. On the one hand, there was the Left, led by the Pds (the Democratic Party of the Left, heir of the old Italian Communist Party), and a large and mixed assortment of groups, which included parties as diverse as the unreconstructed communists, the greens, what was left of the Italian Socialist Party, left leaning Catholics, and so forth. On the other, an alliance led by Silvio Berlusconi, a successful entrepreneur and TV tycoon. He had convinced a few academics, including myself, that a new political movement had to be formed with the aim of creating an alternative to the left. A spontaneous movement began to form, and, in a matter of weeks, the movement, "Forza Italia" (Come on Italy!), started to gather momentum. Forza Italia (FI) succeeded in assembling a coalition with the conservative

National Alliance in the South and the "Northern League" in the North, so that together they could provide an alternative to the Left. That alliance won the elections on what was probably the most radical free market program ever presented in Europe.

The program of Forza Italia included, among other things, a ceiling on taxation and the enforcement of a balanced budget amendment, the reform of the income tax with the adoption of a single rate system, fiscal federalism on the lines of "reverse revenue sharing" (all taxing authority would reside in local governments, which would be required to give the central government some proportion of the tax revenue they raise), privatization, school vouchers, the dismantling of the national health system and its replacement with a private insurance system, with means-tested health vouchers for the needy, and so forth. It sounds familiar, doesn't it?

I have elsewhere dealt with the fate of the Berlusconi government[6] and I shall not repeat that sad story now. The point I wish to stress is that the political debate preceding the elections of March 27–28 was entirely centered on our proposals. Liberal ideas were carrying the day. And today some of those very ideas, in a somewhat diluted form, are being imitated by the leader of the Pds, Massimo D'Alema. Plagiarism is the highest form of flattery! But, let's go back to the more general theme.

Statements in support of economic freedom are being made by political leaders of different parties almost everywhere, and a comparable change can be observed both in the academic world and in public opinion. Isn't it tempting to conclude that we've been winning? In answering that question, we must first of all be aware of the danger of historicism and be skeptical of what Karl Popper sarcastically called the belief in the "Inexorable Laws of Historical Destiny." Our question, however, does not necessarily entail a fatalistic attitude towards history. It's a very important question, and, if we can specify its meaning exactly, it deserves to be asked.

The first problem is that of specifying the time interval under observation: over which time span are we making our comparison? This is a universal problem. In the words of a scientist: *"When people ask me whether the climate is getting warmer or colder, I generally answer 'yes.' It all depends on over what time scale we average. If the time scale is a few months, then the answer in the spring would of course be 'warmer' and in the fall 'colder.'"*[7] The intellectual climate is now more favorable to the cause of freedom than it was 25 years ago, but, does this mean that it is more favorable than it was, let us say, 10, 50, or 100 years ago?

What I mean is that there is the danger of mistaking a temporary lapse in the historical process for a radical change of direction. Schumpeter was well aware of this, when he warned: *"The transformation of social orders into one another is an incessant process but, in itself, a very slow one. To an observer who studies a moderate span of 'quiet' time, it may well seem as if the social framework he beholds did not change at all. Moreover, the process often suffers setbacks which, considered by themselves, may suggest to him the presence of an opposite tendency."* (Schumpeter 1949, p. 419)

Let me stress that at this point I am concerned with the intellectual climate, not with actual policy. We are all painfully aware that drastic changes in rhetoric do not necessarily translate themselves into changes in policy. It is important, therefore, to separate the two and maybe ask ourselves under what conditions a change in the intellectual climate results in a change in policy.

From the perspective of the ideological confrontation, I am convinced that we live in one of the happiest times in the contemporary history of mankind. It seems to me that never before has the case for freedom been more thoroughly analyzed and better understood.

I realize that this is a strong statement. There is an inevitable distortion on our perspectives produced by chronological selection. Few people who are great thinkers in the eyes of their contemporaries stand the test of time and are still considered great by future generations. As a result, we are often lead to believe that there are more great scholars among our contemporaries than there were in the past. However, even if we allow for this distortion, it seems still true to me that a very large number of the great liberal thinkers of all times belong to this century. Furthermore, even though ideas always have parents, in the sense that their origin can be traced back to past achievements, the case for freedom as presented by today's thinkers is more consistently argued and better supported than ever before. Finally, more people are aware of the importance of freedom on a theoretical level today than at any other time in the past 50 or 100 years.

Let me illustrate. I think we all agree that the gravest threat to freedom comes from government, private threats are easier to deal with.[8] The growth of government and the resulting danger to freedom have two major sources. The first is the pressure coming from interest groups trying to secure political rents or to be sheltered from competition. This threat is more formidable because, as Adam Smith pointed out[9], the collusion of private and political interests is favored by the structure of political incentives.

The second source of government growth has been socialism and its faith in the benevolence of government, what Frank Knight called "the essential content of socialism," which he thus defined: "It is imagined that the state, i.e. the government, conceived in the abstract as a benevolent and all-powerful agency – *essentially as God rather than realistically as a group of politicians – could order economic affairs rightly without generating new evils or incurring serious social costs; that humanity would with approximate unanimity approve and like the result; that no other serious problems would remain; and, finally, that everybody – or nearly everybody, apart, perhaps, from a few criminally recalcitrants – would 'live happily ever after.'"*[10]

At the intellectual level, both of these sources of government growth have been subject to extensive critical scrutiny, and the underlying interplay of interests has been exposed. As a result, it's much more difficult today to enlarge the scope of government in the name of the "public good." We now have extensive empirical evidence that regulation often ends up serving the interests of the regulated producers, thus providing a good illustration of Adam Smith's view on the "mean rapacity and monopolizing spirit" of merchants and manufacturers.

Even more important, we have seen a dramatic shift of opinion away from the myth of the benevolent government in the past two decades. That shift has largely resulted from viewing government as a group of politicians rather than as a mythical, abstract entity. The sobering effect of the economics of politics on the intellectual climate has somewhat tempered the mystique of government as the problem solver, leading Jim Buchanan to conclude: *"I can be very pessimistic when I look at many aspects of our current economic policy and as I contemplate post-Reagan political economy. But I am optimistic when I compare the discussion and dialogue in the 1980s with that which might have taken place in the '60s or even the late '70s. Ideas do indeed have consequences, the fatal conceit has been exposed, and the romantic notion will not return. Camelot will not return."*[11]

The economics of politics and the economics of regulation are only two examples of our intellectual victories. Liberalism has faced the challenge of Marxism, Fascism, "Welfarism," and Keynesianism, and it has won: except for a few desperate, hopeless fanatics, no one believes in central planning, nationalization, wage and price controls or incomes policy, deficit spending, inflationary growth, protectionism, the superiority of public health care, and all the assorted paraphernalia of excuses for bigger government that were so overwhelmingly popular only a generation ago.

An interesting question arises at this point: must the intellectual change be credited to the work of prominent liberal thinkers in general, and economists in particular, or has it been the product of circumstances? Having had the great fortune of doing graduate work at the University of Chicago in the second half of the 1960s, I tend to attribute great importance to the work of liberal scholars in general and economists in particular. However, as far as economists are concerned, George Stigler has always been convinced that, as a profession, they are not terribly relevant.

In a 1959 paper[12], he asserted that "Economists are subject to the coercion of the ruling ideologies of their times," which would suggest that their output has little, if any, impact in shaping those ideologies. But, he adds: "I believe that the economics profession has been basically more conservative than the educated classes generally." (p. 54–55). However, he has often repeated that "economists exert a minor and scarcely detectable influence on the societies in which they live," (p. 63), and "[t]he main lesson I draw from our experience as preachers is that we are well received in the measure that we preach what the society wishes to hear." (p. 13)[13]

On this point I tend to agree with Keynes: the views of economists are probably less important than he thought, but, as his own influence confirms, they are far from having a minor impact on society. Probably, a compromise between the two positions can be found in the view that economists influence society only when circumstances are "right," when their theories are not in sharp contrast with the organized interests of powerful pressure groups.

As far as our question is concerned, there is no doubt that the popularity of liberal ideas has been reinforced by the failure of statism and the desire to find an alternative. But, it's equally true that without the revolutionary contribution of liberal thinkers, both the analysis of "government failure" and the alternative to its problems would not have existed.

That, however, is the intellectual part of the story. In terms of actual policy, things are totally different. While the rhetoric has changed dramatically, policies have not always changed much. No one advocates a Socialist system, but when it comes to policy, the organized action of pressure groups inevitably leads to more government intervention.

Each one of us nowadays seems to favor market discipline and competition in general, that is for everybody else, but when it comes to his own interests he does not refrain from trying to use the democratic political process to extract political or monopolistic rents. We demand economy and efficiency from the suppliers of the goods and services we buy, but we like to have as high a pay as possible and we don't mind being sheltered from competition in what we produce. To some extent we are all guilty of this kind of schizophrenic behavior: I am normally very vocal in my opposition to the growth of government spending, but don't count on me to oppose increased spending on university professors' salaries! The same is true, for example, in the field of trade restrictions: people who support free international trade in principle, that is for everybody else, often argue that their industry is a special case deserving some kind of protection.

It may very well be that we devote more energy to promote our interests as beneficiaries of political favors than we do to promote increased reliance on market processes for society in general. This is simply a variation on an old theme: we like high prices for the product we sell, and low prices for the products we buy. But, our interest as producers of some good or service is greater than our interest as consumers of goods and services produced by others, and, as a result, we spend more efforts to keep the price of our product high than we do to keep other prices low. Or, we devote more resources to increase government intervention on our own behalf than we do to reduce government intervention in favor of others. This can explain why, if we compare the size of government's interference in our lives today – in our times of great liberal rhetoric – with what it was 25 or even 15 years ago, we must conclude that in most countries we are much worse off now than we were then.[14] Regardless of what measure one chooses, government has grown very rapidly in the past quarter century, and this is true, although to a different extent, of almost all Western countries.

It may very well be that what we are witnessing is an illustration of the Friedmans' cycle, the view that: *"a major change in social and economic policy is preceded by a shift in intellectual opinion (...) At first it will have little effect on social and economic policy. After a lag, sometimes of decades, an intellectual tide "taken at its flood" will spread at first gradually, then more rapidly, to the public at large and through the public's pressures on government will affect the course of economic, social, and political policy. As the tide in events reaches its flood, the intellectual tide starts to ebb ... "* (pp. 455–456)[15] On another occasion, however, Milton Friedman has explained that: *"it takes a long time. And I emphasize that the reversal in the climate of opinion is one thing; the reversal of policies is a very different matter. The real change in the intellectual climate didn't start until the late forties or early fifties. So you really don't expect it to be fully implemented until something like the year 2000."* (p. 7)[16]

Maybe so. I often tend to agree with Professor Friedman and I certainly hope that he is right on this issue. But how do we know that this is the case? Couldn't the present intellectual climate, as Schumpeter would say, be one of those *"setbacks which, considered by themselves, may suggest (...) the presence of an opposite tendency."*? Couldn't the present climate favorable to freedom be a temporary exception in history's course?

The obvious answer to these questions, of course, is that we do not know. There are no "inexorable laws of historical destiny," no deterministic trends in either intellectual climate or policy. There is no such thing as victory (or defeat for that matter), a state of affairs which, once attained, will forever be maintained. The struggle for freedom is a "natural," inescapable component of life. We can successfully meet the challenges of our time and score a temporary "victory," but new problems will soon come up, as new ways of hindering our personal liberties are discovered or old ones are resurrected.

The disappointing change in policy, furthermore, is to a large extent due to the limitations of our intellectual successes. For example, we haven't produced a workable, realistic plan or blueprint for dismantling the existing statist structure. The few instances in which there has been success in demolishing the socialist framework are remarkable in that there was (and there still is) no previous, generally accepted formula for neutralizing the entrenched interests which resist any change in the *status quo*.

Our present successes are especially vulnerable in that they have generally consisted in a change of policy w i t h i n a g i v e n , u n c h a n g e d s e t o f r u l e s , rather than in a Constitutional change of rules. Constitutional arrangements are not eternal, but, if correctly devised, they certainly possess greater durability than do policy changes within given rules. Again, this is one of our intellectual weaknesses. For example, we all agree on the desirability of replacing discretionary policy with a monetary Constitution. However, when it comes to the s p e c i f i c t y p e of monetary Constitution, our opinions widely differ: some favor a fixed monetary rule, others want a gold standard, or competing currencies, or a variety of different remedies, and the same is true of a fiscal Constitution. The wide discrepancy of views in our camp reduces the likelihood of significant success. That's why we have no a priori reason for being complacent, satisfied with the present state of affairs. We a r e n o t w i n n i n g .

I would like to end, however, on a moderately optimistic conclusion. First of all, if it is true that we are not winning in the sense that we don't have generally accepted (acceptable) Constitutional solutions for the major problems of our times, it is also true that they are losing: the statist recipes once so popular are totally discredited, so that our opponents don't know what to suggest.

But there is another reason for being optimistic. Like Churchill at the time of World War II, we can base our confidence in the future on their mistakes. The cumulative effect of decades of socialism has produced a state of near-bankruptcy which makes further expansions of government interference almost impossible. Statism is both intellectually and financially bankrupt: it has a past, albeit an inglorious one, but it has no future.[17] Under these circumstances, it is difficult to imagine any further growth in the size of government.

Maybe, the change of rhetoric is not to be credited to our intellectual victories, being only a reflection of the simple arithmetic of government bankruptcy. In any case, if present trends continue, instead of capitalism being killed by its success, as Schumpeter maintained, we shall see socialism destroyed by its failures. Definitely, these are glorious days for us reactionaries!

Notes

1   What follows draws on my lecture "Are We Winning?," The Mont Pelerin Society, Christchurch, New Zealand 1989.
2   F. A. Hayek, "Opening Address to a Conference at Mont Pelerin," *Studies in Philosophy, Politics and Economics* (1967), Simon and Schuster, 1969, pp. 148–159.
3   Joseph A. Schumpeter, "The March into Socialism," 1949, reprinted in *Capitalism, Socialism and Democracy,* Third edition, Harper Torchbooks, The University Library, Harper & Row, Publishers, New York 1950, pp. 415–425.
4   J. A. Schumpeter, *Capitalism, Socialism and Democracy,* cit., p. 61.
5   See my article "The Leaning Tower of Statism," *Reason,* February 1989, p. 46.
6   "Antidisestablishmentarianism Italian Style," *National Review,* February 20, 1995, p. 32.
7   S. Fred Singer, "My Adventures in the Ozone Layer," *National Review,* June 30, 1989, p. 36.
8   This was Adam Smith's view: "The capricious ambition of kings and ministers has not, during the present and the preceding century, been more fatal to the repose of Europe, than the impertinent jealousy of merchants and manufacturers. The violence and injustice of the rulers of mankind is an ancient evil, for which, I am afraid, the nature of human affairs can scarce admit a remedy. But the mean rapacity, the monopolizing spirit of merchants and manufacturers (...) may very easily be prevented from disturbing the tranquility of any body but themselves." *The Wealth of Nations* (1776), The Modern Library, New York 1937, p. 460.
9   "The member of parliament who supports every proposal for strengthening this monopoly, is sure to acquire not only the reputation of understanding trade, but great popularity and influence with an order of men whose numbers and wealth render them of great importance. If he opposes them, on the contrary, and still more if he has authority to be able to thwart them, neither the most acknowledged probity, nor the highest rank, nor the greatest public services, can protect him from the most infamous abuse and detraction, from personal insults, nor sometimes from real danger, arising from the insolent outrage of furious and disappointed monopolists." (Smith, 1776, p. 438).

10   Frank H. Knight, "Socialism: The Nature of the Problem," *Ethics*, Vol. 50 (1940), pp. 253–289, reprinted in *Freedom & Reform, Essays in Economics and Social Philosophy* (1947), Liberty Press, Indianapolis 1982, pp. 154–193. The quote is from p. 159.

11   J. M. Buchanan, "Camelot Will Not Return," *Reason*, January 1989, p. 37.

12   G. J. Stigler, "The Politics of Political Economists," *The Quarterly Journal of Economics*, Vol. LXXIII (November, 1959), reprinted in *Essays in the History of Economics*, The University of Chicago Press, 1965, pp. 51–65.

13   G. J. Stigler, *The Economist as Preacher*, Basil Blackwell, Oxford: 1982.

14   If one looks at Italy, for example, where, as previously mentioned, the change in rhetoric has been substantial, there is no doubt that statists of all parties have had a go at it: from 1960 to 1993, government spending has increased 120 times in nominal terms, 653 percent in real terms, and it has gone from less than one third of gross domestic product (32.7%) to well over one half (58.6%). Despite the fact that revenue has increased by leaps and bounds, the deficit has exploded: from 382 billion lire in 1960 to 153,138 billions in 1993, i.e. from 1.4% to 9.8% of gdp. In real terms total public debt outstanding has gone from US $87.3 billion in 1960 (40% of gdp) to almost US $1.1 trillion in 1993 (120% of gdp). Similar conclusions can be reached with respect to all possible indicators of individual freedom.

15   Milton & Rose Friedman, "The Tide in the Affairs of Men," in *Thinking About America, The United States in the 1990's*, Annelise Anderson and Dennis L. Bark eds., Hoover Institution, Stanford University 1988, pp. 455–468.

16   "An Interview with Milton Friedman," by Peter Brimelow, in *Fraser Forum*, July 1989, pp. 4–20.

17   Take Italy, for example. Interest payments on government debt amount to almost 21% of total public sector spending, or 73% of total income tax revenue. Taxation on labor income in all its forms has reached unbearable proportions: net take-home pay is only 54.8% of labor costs, and the tax protest front now includes organized business and labor. All of this while the failure of government is underscored by the tremendous success of private delivery of mail, private health insurance, private police protection, private schools, etc.

What do Liberals Have to Say About the Future of International and Inter-ethnic Relations?

Victoria Curzon Price

In the small but rapidly growing family of scholars concerned with the preservation of liberty, Professor Radnitzky stands out as being a philosopher whom even a mere economist can (sometimes) understand. It is also reassuring to find that scholars from any different academic disciplines are struggling with the same issue. Although we come from different horizons, we recognize each other instantly because we stand on the shoulders of the same giants. One of the giants we share is F. A. von Hayek, who devoted much of his life to the question of liberty, its origins, its implications and how to preserve it.

In this contribution to the Festschrift prepared for Professor Radnitzky, I shall try to address the question of whether we can preserve liberty in a world composed of many sovereign states, none of whose leaders are even faintly inspired by liberal thought.

Now that the Cold War is over, may the world look forward to a prolonged era of peace and prosperity, during which mankind will develop and explore the many benefits of Popper's 'Great Society' and finally fulfil the undoubted promise of its intelligence, creativity and ingenuity? Or will the whole adventure self-destruct, in terrible armed conflict, as it has in the past?

Contemporary liberal thinkers, I find, tend to shy away from such questions. They are much concerned with the conditions for human flourishing, for creating a just and free society, but they 'stop at the frontier', so to speak. For fear of appearing naive, they are perhaps unwilling to repeat the boundless optimism of 18th and 19th century liberal thinkers, who believed that laissez-faire and free trade led to peace.

Apart from the general proposition that the State should be very small and limited to a few essential tasks, leaving adult individuals free to make most choices for themselves, today's liberals do not address the question of inter-State relations directly. They agree that defence against foreign aggression is one of the admissible functions of the State, but I have yet to see a *contemporary* liberal interpretation of the limits of State action at its borders, and the teachings of previous generations tend to be forgotten (although a recently published collection of essays, edited by Edmund A. Opitz and entitled *Leviathan at War* (Opitz, 1995), should make such amnesia less plausible).

For instance, there are people who believe strongly in de-regulation, tax-cutting, privatization and the like, but who are deeply suspicious of cultivating close economic or cultural links with alien societies and cultures, and who will advocate protection against foreign competition (Goldsmith, 1993) or strict controls on immigration (Brimelow, 1995). Does the phrase 'defence against foreign aggression' (one of the permissible tasks of the State) include protectionism and obstacles against foreign immigration, or does the phrase refer only to *military* response to *armed* aggression? A broad definition of the phrase opens the door to much more State action than a narrow one, and allows people to call themselves liberals whom others might consider dangerous interventionists. Wherever one places oneself on this scale, it is an issue worthy of debate.

This short essay is not intended to explore exhaustively the entire international dimension of liberalism, but only to derive some ideas on this score from the general body of liberal thinking. The original paper on which this essay is based was presented to the 1994 General Meeting of the Mont Pèlerin Society, a symposium devoted to the comemoration of its late President, Friedrich A. von Hayek. During this symposium I realized that although Hayek never explicitly addressed the problem of international relations, his division of social 'order' into the *extended order*, on the one hand and the *restricted order*, on the other, could be reinterpreted to cast light on the question of inter-State relations. The following essay is the outcome of this insight.

Part I discusses Hayek's *extended order*, how it comes into existence, what its advantages and drawbacks are as compared with the *restricted order*, how it survives (or not) over time, and the nature of its link to freedom. In particular, we discuss the rise and fall of civilizations, the process of cultural evolution and 'discovery' of socially effective institutions. This leads us to Part ll, entitled 'The extended order, nationalism and the sovereign state', where, with additional reference to the writings of Ludwig von Mises and Wilhelm Röpke, we make two interconnected observations: (1) at the level of international relations, only limited states can be peaceful states and (2), at the level of inter-ethnic relations *within* states, the same is true: peaceful relations *may* develop between different ethnic groups, but only on a market basis – economic planning leads to conflict.

There is therefore complete coherence between liberal thinking and the nightwatchman state on the one hand, and peaceful and prosperous international relations on the other. The trouble is that the converse is also true: a bloated state leads to international conflict, perhaps to war. To remind ourselves of this is to add urgency to the liberal agenda, for failure to convince our fellows of the benefits of laissez-faire will lead, in the end, not only to loss of liberty and lower material standards of living, already bad enough in themselves, but also, inevitably, one day – to war. And modern warfare is surely something which is worth avoiding.

The Extended Order and Liberty

1. The Extended Order

By way of introduction, let me start with some of Hayek's definitions of the *extended order*. This is the term Hayek finally came to prefer, since he used it in *The Fatal Conceit* (Hayek, 1988), his last major work. But in *Law, Legislation and Liberty* (Hayek, 1973,1976,1979) we find the terms 'Great Society' and 'Open Society' used in the same sense. The term 'extended order' is perhaps to be preferred because it can be used in contradistinction to the 'restricted order' of the small horde or tribe (the contrast between the two being the central issue in *The Fatal Conceit*. But the idea that two different kinds of rules prevail simultaneously in society, the one related to the 'self-generating or spontaneous order' (the 'Great Society' or extended order) and the other to 'organization' (the restricted order of the small group) is already present in *Law, Legislation and Liberty* (Hayek, 1973, p. 2). However, it is in *The Fatal Conceit* that we find these concepts coming into sharp focus.

The Great or Open Society is one 'where millions of men interact' (Hayek, 1973, p. 14). It constitutes a *spontaneous order (order* because within it men can 'form correct expectations, or at least expectations which have a good chance of proving correct' (Hayek, 1973, p. 36)) and *spontaneous* because it is 'the product of the action of many men but ... not the result of human design' (Hayek, 1973, p. 37). It is the product of *cultural evolution*, spanning thousands of years, during which certain groups of men developed *morals*: 'rules of human conduct that gradually evolved especially those dealing with several property, honesty, contract, exchange, trade, competition, gain and privacy' (Hayek, 1988, p. 12). These morals or *traditions* survived the process of cultural evolution because they allowed the groups of men that happened to practise them to prosper through trade and peaceful exchange. Like the Great Society they make possible, these traditions are also the product of human action but not of human design, along with language, law, the market system, private property and so forth. The Great Society, or the extended order, is thus the outcome of many spontaneous sub-orders, all of which contribute to the very complex whole.

These *morals* or *traditions* are non-instinctive rules. In fact they place constraints on the *instinctive rules* that govern the behaviour in the small group (especially 'instincts of solidarity and altruism – instincts applying to the members of one's own group but not to others' (Hayek, 1988, p. 12)). Aggressiveness towards outsiders, cooperation rather than competition within the group, determination of common ends by an acknowledged chief or group of recognized wise men or agreement on a unitary purpose (Hayek, 1988, p. 15) – these are some of the characteristics of the small roving band, which permitted our primitive ancestors to survive and which today characterize their modern counterparts, such as firms, football clubs, the army, the Church, political parties, or the State itself.

It is Hayek's contention that our *morals or non-instinctive rules*, in placing constraints on these *instinctive* rules based on such comforting notions as solidarity, harmony, altruism and commun unitary purpose (which are much older and which have a strong hold on our emotions), are thereby much disliked (Hayek, 1988, p. 13). But it is these non-instinctive rules and traditions which allow us to escape from the confines of the cosy group, develop peaceful trade with other groups and become wealthy. Clearly, feelings of solidarity, harmony and altruism cannot be genuinely felt beyond the confines of a very small group, so relations between strangers must be organized on a different basis. Or to put the problem more starkly, the inevitable counterpart of strong feelings of intra-group solidarity are strong feelings of non-solidarity with the rest of humanity.

Indeed, in the absence of non-instinctive rules and morals permitting trade, relations *between* different, small, tight-knit bands would quickly become conflictual and aggressive. Von Mises points out, for instance, that:

'nature does not generate peace and good will. The characteristic mark of the 'state of nature' is irreconcilable conflict ... The means of subsistence are scarce and do not grant survival to all ... The source of the conflicts is always the fact that each man's portion curtails the portions of all other men. This is a dilemma that does not allow of any peaceful solution.' (von Mises, p. 669)

And Mises concludes: 'What makes friendly relations between human beings possible is the higher productivity of the division of labor. It removes the natural conflict of interests' (idem) – but he does not tell us how we get from here to there. It is Hayek's contribution to point out that humanity discovers by trial and error to adopt *noninstinctive rules* which permit trade based on trade and specialisation. So societies may occasionally escape from the sterile zero-sum game of conflict and aggression, and enjoy the positive-sum game of trade and specialisation – but only if they 'learn' the *non-instinctive rules* of this new game.

For instance, a moral or religious obligation to treat strangers well is an example of what Hayek means by a *non-instinctive* rule. Thus, societies may learn by experience that it is, generally, a 'good' rule (leading to order rather than chaos), but it does not come naturally – to rob or kill the stranger is the first, instinctive reaction. To this day, xenophobia is an *instinctive* sentiment, constantly breaking through the thin verneer of acquired civilized behaviour ...

Instinctive and non-instinctive rules therefore apply, respectively, to the restricted and to the extended orders of human existence. They are complementary to one another, and both are needed. But *they must not be mixed up*. As Hayek puts it:

'If we were to apply the unmodified, uncurbed, rules of the micro-cosmos (i.e. of the small band or troop, or of, say, our families) to the macro-cosmos (our wider civilisation), as our instincts and sentimental yearnings often make us wish to do, *we would destroy it*. Yet if we were always to apply the rules of the extended order to our more intimate groupings, *we would crush them*.' (Hayek, 1988, p. 18, italics in the original).

Hayek continues with this warning:

'Yet despite the advantages attending our limited ability to live simultaneously within *two* orders of rules, and to distinguish between them, it is anything but easy to do either. Indeed, our instincts often threaten to topple the whole edifice' (idem).

Thus, in *The Fatal Conceit* Hayek interprets the modern Welfare State („soft socialism') as an attempt to apply the rules of the micro-cosmos (solidarity, altruism, generosity) to society as a whole, with disastrous consequences for liberty and material efficiency.

More to the purpose of this essay, however, we can find far less innocent applications of the rules of the micro-cosmos to the macro-cosmos, to fan the flames of nationalism (always referred to as patriotism), to encourage xenophobia (national preference comes quite naturally ...) and to develop an artificial sense of 'belonging' to a very large tribe indeed. 'Motherland', 'fatherland', 'brotherhood' are all terms borrowed from the micro-cosmos of the family and press-ganged into the service of the State, eager to create an *Ersatz*-family on a macro-scale. The more successful are our fearless leaders in this enterprise, the more power they may enjoy from mobilizing the enthusiasm of the masses, all the keener for financial (and other) sacrifices in the name of the parent-nation. Having fanned the flames of nationalism, however, how does one nation maintain peaceful relations with others? The answer is – it cannot. As Ayn Rand puts it: 'If men want to oppose war, it is *statism* that they must oppose. So long as they hold the tribal notion that the individual is sacrificial fodder for the collective, that some men have the right to rule others by force, and that some (any) alleged 'good' can justify it – there can be no peace *within* a nation and no peace among nations.' (cited from Opitz, 1995)

In its capacity for mischief, this mixing of the rules of the micro and the macro-cosmos is at least as great as that pointed to by Hayek with regard to the Welfare State. But whereas the unbridled development the Welfare State threatens individual liberty through over-taxation and over-regulation, the encouragement of nationalism leads at the very least to economic loss through protectionism, and at the worst, to armed conflict and loss of life. As we shall see, however, the two are linked, for the Welfare State is likely to become nationalistic and belligerent in its mature phase.

2. The Advantages of the Extended Order

This is a subject with which we are all familiar, but it is worth repeating the basic Hayekian point that it is *knowledge* (and its opposite, 'the fundamental fact of man's unavoidable ignorance' (Hayek, 1960, p. 22)) that is the central issue in organizing peaceful and prosperous human societies. In the small, roving band, knowledge of the chief and the best hunters is all that can be applied to solving the problems of daily survival of the group (the same is incidentally true of the modern corporation and other hierarchical communities). But the extended order coordinates and puts to good use the knowledge scattered among millions (today, billions) of individuals through the intermediary of the market order. This mysterious and misunderstood property of the extended order makes it infinitely more capable of serving man's material needs than the restricted order.

Readers will be familiar with the many passages in which Hayek describes this order, but I particularly like this one, which could be entitled 'Ode to Ignorance':

'We are led ... to do things by circumstances of which we are largely unaware and which produce results that we do not intend. In our economic activities we do not know the needs which we satisfy or the sources of the things which we get. Almost all of us serve people whom we do not know, and even of whose existence we are ignorant; and we in turn constantly live on the services of other people of whom we know nothing. All this is possible because we stand in a great framework of institutions and traditions – economic, legal and moral – into which we fit ourselves by obeying certain rules of conduct that we never made, and which we have never understood ...' (Hayek, 1988, p. 14).

Or again:

'It is through the mutually adjusted efforts of many people that more knowledge is utilized than any one individual possesses ... that more achievements are made possible than any single mind can foresee. It is because freedom means the renunciation of direct control of individual efforts that a free society can make use of so much more knowledge than the mind of the wisest ruler could comprehend.' (Hayek, 1960, p. 31)

The restricted order can only solve simple, local problems, on the basis of very limited information. It can never be as efficient as the extended order in solving complex problems. This is why societies which tried to replace the market order by central commands have failed so miserably, and why societies which today place serious obstacles in the path of the market order deprive themselves of the full extent of its information-processing capacity, and succeed mainly in impoverishing themselves.

The problem of *ignorance* is all the more acute in that mankind must constantly adapt to changing and unknown circumstances. Not only does the extended order serve an infinite number of diverse, individual ends, but both the ends, and above all the means of achieving those ends, are changing constantly. The extended order takes this all in its stride, suggesting to free individuals the courses of action which at all times will use the most abundant resources in order to meet the most urgent needs with the most appropriate technology.

The extended order accomplishes the dual feat of coordinating dispersed knowledge, and generating new knowledge in order to permit adaptation to changing circumstances, through an interlocking system of non-instinctive rules and institutions (spontaneous sub-orders in their own right), which were mentioned above, namely *rules dealing with several property, honesty, contract, exchange, trade, competition, gain and privacy*. Within this set of institutions, there is one of overriding importance: that of private or 'several' property. Without private property there can be no concept of what is mine and what is thine, of honesty, of exchange, of privacy, of loss or gain. But more important still, without private property there can be no liberty.

Thus we learn that 'several property is the heart of the morals of any advanced civilization ... it is also inseparable from individual freedom' (Hayek, 1988, p. 30). On the other hand, common property is the mark of the restricted order.

The cornerstone upon which the extended order rests is therefore liberty, defined by Hayek quite simply as 'independence of the arbitrary will of another' (Hayek, 1960, p. 12). Combined with the institution of several property, liberty becomes 'a person's right to dispose over a recognised private domain, thus allowing individuals to develop a dense network of commercial relations among different communities' (Hayek, 1988, p. 29).

3. Why People Might Fear the Extended Order

But as important as *allowing* individuals to trade with others, liberty virtually *compels* them to act to improve their own lot in the light of their own knowledge specific to time and circumstance, because inaction, laziness, or an irresponsible attitude to others is very quickly sanctioned by loss of status and income. It is this feature of the extended order which is so disliked, and attracts people to the safety and cosiness of the clan. Personal failure in the restricted order is not possible, since members of the clan are not individually responsible for the outcomes of their actions. Their role is to obey orders and submit to the clan's common purpose. On the other hand, personal failure in the extended order is not only possible, it is a necessary part of it. In order for new information to be developed, for the process of discovery by trial and error to work, mistakes have to be made, individuals have to take risks and suffer failure.

Some people find that this form of existence is uncongenial and alienating; as Hayek reminds us 'many people are afraid of liberty' (Hayek, 1960, p. 72). In fact, as he warns us already in *The Road to Serfdom*, 'only few will resist the temptation of safety at the price of freedom' (Hayek, 1944, (1946 ed), p. 67).

To summarize, the extended order is based on individual liberty and yields wealth and insecurity as by-products, while the restricted order is based on coercion and yields security and poverty as inevitable side-effects. Misunderstanding of the problem of ignorance, (especially by constructivist rationalists – Hayek, 1973, pp. 8–34) leads people to believe that they can, *at the level of society as a whole*, enjoy simultaneously the security of the small clan or group and the wealth generated by freedom in the extended order. They believe that material abundance can just as well be obtained by intelligent planning, regulation and redistribution, as by the process of discovery through markets. This myth has, one hopes, been laid to rest by the disastrous results of Soviet economic planning. But a more subtle myth subsists: people believe that they can choose between a bit more security (and a bit less freedom) on the one hand, and a bit less material wealth on the other. What is the point of so much freedom, they cry, if we are so stressed out that we cannot enjoy it? So they are prepared to give up a *small part* of their freedom (i.e. pay heavy taxes for 'social security'). But as liberals know (and as people are gradually beginning to realise as they see their promised pensions disappearing down a fathomless black hole) these trade-offs do not really exist. As Mises puts it bluntly: 'The choice is between capitalism and chaos' (Mises, p. 676).

It would be naïve to believe that most people value freedom intrinsically. They value the wealth it produces, and consider freedom at best an added virtue and at worst a heavy burden to bear. This is why they are so easily persuaded to abandon freedom. Even today, when nobody advocates any more the abolition of private property or the adoption of centralized economic planning, the sum total of wealth and income redistribution by taxation and regulation in advanced 'western' countries is such that we are no more than half-owners of our work-effort or of our homes. So we must not be surprised to learn that we are only half-free and only half as prosperous as we thought we could be. In Misian terms, we appear to prefer chaos to capitalism.

This brings us to the question, raised earlier, of the relationship between the extended order and liberty.

4. The Spread of the Extended Order Despite Its Enemies: Hayek's Theory of Cultural Evolution

Hayek sets the beginning of his extended order many thousands of years before the development of freedom. The extended order developed over a long period of time 'taking perhaps hundreds of thousands of years' (Hayek, 1988, p. 16). The market order (a sub-set of the extended order) appears 'comparatively late': between five thousand (Hayek, 1988, p. 60) and eight thousand years ago (Hayek, 1960, p. 40). It is the discovery of the market order which permits our nomadic ancestors to settle down, develop agriculture, build cities and religions, experiment with tyrannies, monarchies and democracies, invent courts, judges and secret police forces, discover refrigerators and atom bombs, wage war on each other and, in a word, become 'civilized'.

Liberty, on the other hand, 'can hardly be traced back farther than the England of the seventeenth century' (Hayek, 1960, p. 162). Furthermore, it is so fragile a plant that Hayek devotes the rest of his life to the question of the preservation of a society of free men in our times.

In fact, it is clear from Hayek's account of the evolutionary process which takes us from 'the small horde to the organized tribe, the still larger groups of clans and the other successive steps towards the Great Society'

(Hayek, 1976, p. 42) that liberty flourishes from time to time, but is always crushed in the end: 'over and over again, powerful governments so badly damaged spontaneous improvement that the process of cultural evolution was brought to an early demise' (Hayek, 1988, p. 44). Historians fail to teach us much about this evolutionary process because they tend to concentrate on the period in which the civilization under discussion is already in decline, that is when a highly organized state is already in existence. This is when the civilization, in appearance, is at its most glorious, when great monuments are built and great wars waged. But in fact it is already dying for lack of liberty:

'Nothing is more misleading, then, than the conventional formulae of historians who represent the achievement of a powerful state as the culmination of cultural evolution: it as often marked its end. In this respect students of early history were overly impressed and greatly misled by monuments and documents left by the holders of political power, whereas the true builders of the extended order, who as often as not created the wealth that made the monuments possible, left less tangible and ostentatious testimonies to their achievement' (Hayek, 1988, p. 33).

It seems therefore that there are (brief) periods when liberty flourishes and when the foundations of a spontaneous, extended order are laid. But the very wealth that is thus made possible is then used to feed governments that will in the end swallow up freedom – and much of the wealth as well. In the meantime, another tribe or clan will (by learning, imitation or sheer chance) be experimenting with institutions, stumble across liberty and start to prosper. Thus do civilizations succeed one another, setting in motion the far greater process of human cultural evolution, which mankind has been caught up in for 'perhaps hundreds of thousands of years' (Hayek, 1988, p. 16).

The story of human civilizations, according to my understanding of Hayek, is thus rather like that of a three-stage rocket: freedom constitutes the first stage; wealth and statism the second; and decline (due to unfreedom) the third. Freedom is needed to start the process, but the trouble is that the extended order (stage two – roughly where we are now in western Europe) can manage without it for quite some time before decline and weakness sets in. The decay comes from within, although the final push to extinction will often appear to come from without, as happened with both the Greek and Roman civilizations.

Mises is so convinced of markets' intrinsic superiority that he asserts that 'No foreign aggressor can destroy capitalist civilization if it does not destroy itself' (Mises, p. 667) but 'Man is free in the sense that he must daily choose anew between policies that lead to success and those that lead to disaster, social disintegration, and barbarism' (Mises, p. 193). So capitalism (Mises' term for the extended order) can be destroyed, but only from within.

This may be splitting hairs, but I find this too simple, too optimistic. Today, thanks to the ease of communication and immitation between societies, the story of human evolution is complicated and accelerated by the fact that unfree societies can skip stage one and become rich and powerful enough to crush peaceful, fairly free societies (at stages one or two) – indeed have done so in the past and came within a whisker of doing so on a world scale three times during the course of this century.

Although Hayek's life spanned two world wars and one cold war, and although a great deal of human history can be written in terms of armed conflict, genocide and brutal government, he does not mention these as part of the process of evolution. Nor does he discuss problems of international relations, except indirectly. His vision of cultural evolution leading to the Great Society is basically peaceful and optimistic. Liberty wins out in the end because it is more efficient than oppression. For his part, on this issue, Mises asserts bluntly: 'Where capitalistic entrepreneurship is allowed to function freely, the fighting forces will always be so well equipped that the biggest armies of the backward peoples will be no match for them' (Mises, p. 667).

Hayek's is a gentler vision. Human cultural evolution does not proceed like biological natural selection (inherited characteristics of individuals becoming dominant through a brutal Darwinian struggle for survival) but through 'selection by imitation (by individuals and groups) of successful institutions and habits ... what emerges is ideas and skills – in short, the whole cultural inheritance which is passed on by learning and imitation' (Hayek, 1960, p. 59). The process of selection of successful institutions and habits seems essentially peaceful (learning and imitation), rather than conflictual. In the *Fatal Conceit*, for instance, Hayek develops the theme that 'increase of particular populations following particular rules, led to the selection of those practices whose dominance has become the cause of further multiplication' (Hayek, 1988, p. 131). He does not seem to consider the possibility that rival populations might wage war on each other, or that the more 'successful' group might crush or enslave the less successful by means less than moral.

This is because Hayek is interested in developing the broad, long-term picture. Over a period of thousands of years one can reasonably expect the 'successful institutions' of human social organization to prevail (and this time-scale is *fast* by the standards of biological evolution). But on the scale of an individual's lifetime, or of a few human generations, who knows where we may be on the countless cycles of trial and error that we must go through before we *learn* to build less unfree societies? The process is not linear (Hayek, 1988, p. 20). Which is why one can be, as I think Hayek was, a long-term optimist but a short-term pessimist. In the short run, liberty, however 'successful' in principle, may self-destruct or be destroyed from outside.

The fundamental question for our generation, therefore, is whether the institutions of liberty which emerged in England at the end of the seventeenth century, which have since spread somewhat over the globe and which according to Hayek are currently at risk (Hayek, 1973, p. 6–7), will be engulfed by institutions and countries inimical to freedom, or whether they can be saved for future generations. And the reason why this is an issue at all is because ,*success', in terms of material wealth based on market order, can occur without full freedom* – not as well as within a free market order, of course, but well enough to get by, to pose a challenge to freer societies.

Liberty is composed of many sub-elements: the right to own property; legal status as a protected member of the community; immunity from arbitrary arrest; the right to work at whatever one desires to do; right to movement according to one's choice (Hayek, 1960, p. 20), the right of free speech, etc.

We can conclude from this list that liberty is a complex spontaneous sub-order, composed of several elements which together guarantee 'independence of the arbitrary will of another' (Hayek, 1960, p. 12). But this list is not complete, because it is static. It may perhaps define the minimum essential conditions of liberty at a point in time, *but it does not protect liberty over time from internal or external aggression.* And one must admit that the gradual, democratic, but inexorable expansion of the State, especially in Western Europe, has already eaten up so much freedom that few people today are prepared to experiment with new ideas and play the role of the entrepreneur, with the result that the whole process of joining means to diverse individual ends in ever more inventive ways is slowing down.

Starting from the other end of the spectrum, there are undemocratic, unfree societies which (because they like the idea of material wealth which a free society produces) have begun, by imitation, to experiment with some elements of liberty. It is such a condition of semi-liberty which explains why unfree societies, like Singapore or China, can be quite successful economically. For instance, fairly secure private property rights, and conditional immunity from arbitrary arrest (just make money, pay your taxes and keep out of politics) seem to be sufficient to produce impressive rates of economic growth. Of course, this rapid economic development would be impossible without the pre-existing extended order (to be practical, the dense network of world trade, investment, capital and technology flows), which itself could not have started without liberty. But this network having been started, unfree societies can plug into it, and grow rich – and agressive – from it. After all, Iraq came uncomfortably close to building an atomic bomb and the capacity to deliver it.

Let us listen to Hayek on this subject.

'That even countries or groups which do not possess freedom can profit from many of its fruits is one of the reasons why the importance of freedom is not better understood. For many parts of the world the advance of civilization has long been a derived affair, and, with modern communications, such countries need not lag very far behind, though most of the innovations may originate elsewhere ... so long as somebody else provides most of the new knowledge and does most of the experimenting ...' (Hayek, 1960, p. 47).

There is a paradox here, for at this point in the history of our civilization we can see autocratic, unfree societies growing fast and *soi-disant* free societies stagnating. How is this so? Is Mises wrong when he asserts: 'the searching mind of the capitalistic world will always have a head start on the peoples who merely copy and imitate clumsily' (Mises, p. 667)? Or are 'Asian values' (*The Economist* May 28th 1994, pp. 13–14) (rejection of individualism and democracy, respect for authority, family ties, hard work and thrift – all values of the restricted order, it should be noted) superior to ours? Will they win the evolutionary contest, as the former Prime Minister of Singapore, Mr. Lee Kwan Yew, does not cease to warn us?

As Hayek already foresaw as early as 1960:

'Regardless of whether from some higher point of view our civilization is really better or not, we must recognize that its material results are demanded by practically all who have come to know them. Those people may not wish to adopt our entire civilization, but they certainly want to be able to pick and choose from it whatever suits them ...' (Hayek, 1960, p. 51).

The answer to the paradox pointed out above is, I believe, not that the 'new mix' of Asian values is in fact superior to freedom as a mode of social organisation, but simply that we, too, are picking and choosing from what Mises refers to as 'capitalism'. Since we have succumbed to the Hayekian 'Fatal Conceit' that we can *construct* a better society by partially rejecting the morals and traditions of the extended order, by modifying the rules of the market system, and partially replacing them by those of the restricted order, we must not be surprised that we live today in a jungle of laws and regulations which deprive us of much of our liberty and, thereby, most of our wealthcreating capacities. The taunts that the West is decadent are unfortunately well taken. Freedom has yet to be practised on a large enough scale or for a long enough time for its benefits to become apparent.

Whether the emerging civilizations of modern Asia represent real progress on the road to liberty or merely partial parasitic development, remains to be seen.

The Extended Order, Nationalism and Sovereign States

1. The Extended Order and the Sovereign State

I have already alluded to the fact that Hayek has little to say about international relations, war and peace. In a telling passage in the *Constitution of Liberty* he tells us why:

'There are many parts of government activity which are of the highest importance for the preservation of a free society but which we cannot examine satisfactorily here ... we shall have to leave aside the whole complex of problems which arise from international relations – not only because any serious attempt to consider these issues would unduly expand this book but also because an adequate treatment would require philosophical foundations other than those we have been able to provide. Satisfactory solutions to these problems will probably not be found as long as we have to accept as the ultimate units of international order the historically given entities known as sovereign nations ... only makeshift solutions to problems of international relations seem possible so long as we have yet to learn how to limit the powers of all government effectively and how to divide these powers between the tiers of authority ...' (Hayek, 1960, p. 263).

In its ideal state, the extended order based on non-instinctive rules dealing with 'several property, honesty, contract, exchange, trade, competition, gain and privacy' (Hayek, 1988, p. 12) guarantees peaceful relationships between individuals based on voluntary exchange. But the fact that humanity is organized into 'historically given entities known as sovereign nations' tarnishes this idealized vision of the 'Great Society'. While *inside* certain favoured nations an acceptable extended order may flourish, protected by limited government (coercion ... 'cannot be altogether avoided because the only way to prevent it is by the threat of coercion' – idem, p. 21), an extended order *between* sovereign nations cannot be guaranteed because the 'moral foundations for a rule of law on an international scale seem to be completely lacking still' (idem, p. 263).

Hayek's solution is to 'limit the powers of all government effectively' (the programme set forth in the last volume of *Law, Legislation and Liberty,* in effect leaving *individuals* to conduct 'international' relations on the basis of voluntary exchange. But in practice we are far from this ideal, and in itself it would only set the stage for 'a rule of law on an international scale'. These limited governments would have to bind themselves legally to respect the principles of the extended order. But how to believe them?

Wilhelm Röpke, in *International integration and disintegration* (Röpke, 1942), considers the whole problem in greater detail, but reaches much the same conclusion. He says that 'an intensive economic intercourse, which involves a wide scale of division of labour' requires 'a framework of institutions and of a strong legal order, and behind them, there must be a generally observed and undisputed code of moral norms and principles of behaviour' (idem, p. 72). Otherwise, people would not accept the implications of the international division of labour, namely, economic dependence. He in effect agrees with Hayek that the 'rule of law on an international scale' is needed to underpin extensive international trade and globalization of economic relations, and deplores its absence.

Among the most important generally observed principles, according to Röpke, is that 'economic affairs should be free from political direction' and that there should be 'a thorough separation between the spheres of the government and the economy' (Röpke, 1959, p. 75). If this rule is respected as a guide for domestic policy by a group of States, then inter-State relations will tend to be peaceful and harmonious, since international economic affairs will be determined by individuals acting according to the rules of the game of free exchange, accepted by all internally, and therefore acceptable to all externally. The 'surface for international conflict' will be reduced in direct proportion to the de-politization of economic affairs on the domestic level. This is the same as saying that international economic order reposes, necessarily, on domestic economic order, or (in an ultimate sense) that only limited states can be peaceful states.

Conversely, if the State sets the domestic price of milk (for instance), then international trade in milk necessarily involves the State and the suspicion is that decisions will not be taken according to the rules of the game of free exchange. The seeds of conflict are laid, because the outcome of the process of exchange is tainted with politics (‚unfairness'). Hence the Röpkerian conclusion that state intervention on the domestic level leads to a break-down of international 'order', that no number of international conventions, conferences, or diplomatic effort can put right.

Mises reaches the same conclusion via a slightly different route. He notes that 'irreconcilable conflicts of biological competition (arise from) the fact that all people by and large strive after the same things' (Mises, p. 669), but that this source of conflict, in a free society, is transformed into harmony of interests thanks to specialisation and trade. 'The fact that my fellow man wants to acquire shoes as I do, does not make it harder for me to get shoes, but easier' (Mises, p. 670). In a market economy no conflicts exist between the interests of buyers and sellers – only disadvantages caused by inadequate foresight (p. 661). Trade is always advantageous both for the buyer and the seller, and foreign trade differs from domestic trade only in so far as goods and services are exchanged beyond the borders (p. 662). In a free trade world, 'frontiers are drawn on the maps, but they do not hinder anybody from the pursuit of what he thinks will make him more prosperous. No individual is interested in the expansion of the size of his nation's territory, as he cannot derive any gain from such an aggrandizement. Conquest does not pay and war becomes obsolete.' (p. 681).

In conclusion, according to Mises:

'Aggressive nationalism is the necessary derivation of the policies of interventionism and national planning. While laissez-faire eliminates the causes of international conflict, government interference with business and socialism create conflicts for which no peaceful solution can be found' (Mises, p. 819).

Combining these various converging strands of thought, we conclude that an Extended Order containing several sovereign states is only possible if (a) they accept the Rule of Law among themselves and (b) if they are themselves minimum, or limited states. Conversely, where will nationalism and statism lead us?

These reflections on the principles that underlie orderly (or, respectively, disorderly) international relations help us to understand and interpret contemporary events. For instance, it should come as no surprise that the older industrialized countries, deeply engaged as they are in the Welfare State and 'soft socialism', should be endlessly inventive when it comes to new forms of protectionism. The growing tax burdens which individuals are forced to bear to finance the Welfare State make it increasingly unattractive to make the effort to remain competitive internationally – hence calls for protection. Nor should we expect any real change in behaviour as a result of the adoption of the Final Act of the Uruguay Round and the conversion of GATT into the World Trade Organisation (WTO), since nothing has changed *internally*. Unless I am much mistaken, the older industrialized countries are *moving away from the conditions of international economic order*, despite the apparent success of the Uruguay Round.

On the other hand, dozens of developing countries, not to speak of the countries 'in transition' of Central and Eastern Europe, the ex-USSR and China, have abandoned the ideology of a totally state-dominated economy. Compared with the recent past, they are *moving towards the conditions of international economic order*. Hence their interest in joining the WTO,

313

although many of their governments are probably unaware of the full implications of applying the rules. Out of this group of countries may emerge one which is truly liberal, in the sense of operating a democratic, nightwatchman state. But many will stop far short of this ideal, falling into the hands of power-hungry groups and clans, who will hi-jack the resources of semi-liberal economies and who will justify it all in terms of nation-building, mystical needs of the mother (or father) land, necessary sacrifice in the light of external dangers, etc.

A Hayekian Extended Order containing hundreds of night-watchman sovereign states is still far beyond our grasp, but a half-order exists, and surprisingly, even in this imperfect state it is massively dynamic. We saw earlier that it has permitted poor, unfree societies to become rich (and perhaps freer) and richer, freer societies to become richer still (but perhaps less free). In the absence of armed conflict, the international half-order has already accelerated the process of institutional competition between societies beyond all recognition. And herein lies a genuine ray of hope: while the motivation for sovereign states to adopt institutions which have been tested elsewhere and found 'successful' may be basely materialistic, if the Hayekian view of the evolution of human societies is correct, governments will have to include freedom in the recipe, or they will lose out in the race for wealth – not slowly and imperceptibly over generations, but quickly and obviously to all. In more everyday terms, international competition is gradually forcing our over-extended governments to privatize state industry, cut taxes and de-regulate in order to keep up with dragons of various size and nationality. Does it matter that their development is 'a derived affair'? That they are un-free societies by our standards? No. It matters only that they reveal our own shortcomings to ourselves, on the basis of which we may, or may not, take appropriate action.

On the whole, however, I tend to view the international arena, composed of some 200 sovereign states, as a power-sharing cartel which certainly tends to break down in armed conflict from time time, but whose members – the political elites in each country – would never knowlingly share power with the people they govern. The nightwatchman state has to emerge by accidental, unplanned competition, or not at all.

2. Why Nationalism, War, Ethnic Conflict?

Economic nationalism, while undesirable, only reduces people's incomes. Unfortunately, as we know all too well, much worse manifestations of aggressive nationalism can occur, leading to armed conflict and loss of life. Even more upsetting, the term 'ethnic cleansing' has taken on a new, contemporary meaning. We are indeed far removed from Hayek's extended order, where millions of people interact anonymously with one another through the peaceful process of market exchange. But this does not invalidate his analysis. Quite the contrary, it gives us a tool for understanding some of the more deplorable and inexplicable manifestations of human behaviour.

Take for instance virulent *nationalism*. As Hayek himself acknowledges, 'the ultimate units of international order' are sovereign nations. But how have these units come into being? Hayek unfortunately does not tell us in detail, because he is more interested in how the rules of the extended order came into being. But the two are inextricably linked. Thus 'such new rules would spread not because men understood that they were more effective, or could calculate that they would lead to expansion, but simply because they enabled those groups practising them to procreate more successfully *and to include outsiders.*' (Hayek, 1988, p. 16, emphasis added)

It is this process of 'including outsiders' which concerns us here.

Without going back into the history of nation-building the world over, we can perhaps agree that today's nation-state is the modern heir of the small horde or tribe which *used* to be the 'ultimate unit' of social organization. After all, what are our proud nation-states but the result of one tribe absorbing another? We know from our history books that the process of absorbtion was often painful and violent, and entailed the suppression (cultural if not physical) of many weaker tribes.

Here I beg to differ somewhat from Hayek, for I fear that in the practical struggle for power and dominance, many of the characteristics of the restricted order would prove of more immediate benefit than those of the extended order (which, although they would provide wealth in the long run, might not mobilize the group for battle in the short run). If so, we should not be surprised if we observe occasions when the nation-state takes on, or tries to develop, many of the characteristics of the restricted order: respect for leaders, not to say cult of leadership, solidarity among members of the group, not to say suppression of individual freedom in the name of group interests, cultivation of xenophobia, not to say outright hostility towards foreigners, etc. Hayek himself refers to 'the propensity of instinctive mass action (which) remains one of several beastly characteristics that man has retained' (Hayek, 1988, p. 17). Nor have we 'shed our heritage from the face-to-face troop' (idem).

Establishment of strong, dominant nations is impossible unless formerly absorbed tribes have lost most of their previous identity, which is why today's 'successful' nations are fairly mono-cultural and mono-lingual, with some noted exceptions nevertheless. Even today, although one can speak of the Welsh nation, or the Basque nation, they do not possess 'sovereignty'. They still possess a linguistic and cultural identity, but their laws and the coercive power of government are exercized by dominant 'nations' (the French, the English, the Castillians). The latter, in order to survive in the perpetual struggle with other tribes, have all done their best to suppress the linguistic and cultural identities of diverse peoples which used to be contained within their political borders. Suppression of individualism, it must be remembered, is a characteristic of the restricted order. Since the French, the English and the Castillians are today's heirs of long-past primitive tribes, one cannot deny the success of the strategy – for themselves.

Another strategy exists, but it has seldom been used, and on the whole has proved less successful in the long run – with one exception. I refer here to tribes which coexist within a federation, where cultural and linguistic diversity is not suppressed, where the various tribes agree to submit to the rule of law, where the extended order prevails in inter-tribal relationships, rather than simple power-relationships. Switzerland is the longest-lasting and most successful example of such a nation-state. But is it perhaps the only one? Other examples of multi-cultural political entities are either breaking up, or have already done so, or show signs of great strain. Are they doomed to failure?

Let us try to use the Hayekian explanation of how human societies work to interpret recent events in Central and Eastern Europe.

After decades of communism, state planning, and the negation of market processes, people within the sphere of influence of the Soviet Union were deprived of one of the main methods of building a network of human relations outside the family – the development of friendships as a result of voluntary exchange. Quite the contrary, contacts outside the immediate *entourage* would tend to be conflictual, or at best hierarchical, often based on fear and mutual suspicion, given the nature of the system. Since the extended order was destroyed, the only thing that remained was to build on the restricted order of the family or small group. But this must have been problematic: families, after all, were small and shrinking and Stalin in fact did his best to destroy them. The 'new man' did not need such an outdated institution. Mao took much the same view ...

Since human beings cannot survive without any friendly order at all, I would guess that people began to organize themselves according to certain common interests or characteristics: chess, bridge, opera – but also on liguistic, cultural and ethnic principles, which are the oldest, most instinctive and most atavistic of organizing principles, since they hark back to our long heritage of the roving band or tribe. It is of course in the last of these that communism turns out to have been at its most pernicious. For it not only destroyed the basis for peaceful exchange *between* groups, it reinforced, quite artifically, the restricted orders *within* these groups. And the dark side of the values of the restricted order are aggression towards outsiders, the feeling that contact with non-members is a negative-sum game. Nor did these sentiments need reinforcing, for it has taken tens, if not hundreds of thousands of years to overcome our tribal aggressivity, and develop the beginnings of a Great Society. Thus, long before the collapse of the Soviet system, one saw the emergence of 'the Georgian Mafia', or the 'Uzbek Mafia', within a great Empire which had claimed to have solved 'the nationalities problem'.

And now that there has been a complete breakdown of even the hierarchical, fearbased system, nothing remains in terms of social organization except the relative security of the linguistic-cultural-ethnic group, based on the principles of the restricted order. Add to this the sheer poverty which results from a complete breakdown of spontaneous trade based on specialisation and property rights, long before the oh-so subtle and sophisticated method of exchange has taken root, and it becomes obvious that grabbing land, goods and chattles from another linguistic-cultural-ethnic group is the best method of survival. One wonders how it is possible for people of different cultural backgrounds, who have lived peacefully together for generations, even intermarrying, can suddenly start killing each other in the most brutal way, but looked at in terms of Hayek's extended and restricted orders, the wonder is that ex-Yugoslavia is, so far, the only instance of prolonged armed conflict in the ex-Soviet sphere of influence. (During the short period of a few months that it has taken to write, re-write and revise this essay, however, I must now add the many recurring and irrepressible armed conflicts that have become endemic to Russia's southern borders).

If the breakdown of multi-cultural political entities in Central and Eastern Europe and the ex-USSR seems to have been induced, in part, by the nature of the communist experiment, then there is still hope for the Spanish, Belgian and Canadian experiments, not to speak of the general west-European experiment in multi-tribal political organization, which of course is at its very beginning. If successful, it will be only the second instance (after Switzerland) in history, of various tribes submitting jointly and voluntarily to the rule of law and organizing relations among themselves on the basis of the extended order. But to be successful, they need to prune back the State.

Conclusion

The extended order, or Great Society, holds out the promise of a better, freer life for mankind. But the process by which humanity might, perhaps, approach this ideal is fraught with obstacles. Among the most dangerous are those which are created endogenously by the Great Society itself: Hayek was most concerned with the 'scientific error' by which men believed that they could replace the spontaneous extended order by a rational order of their own creation. But since the collapse of the USSR (which attempted the most complete experimentation to date of this false idea) this, it seems to me, is no longer the greatest danger. Rather, it is the Great Society's very own genius for creating wealth, which inevitably seems to attract power-grabbers. Wealthy societies can afford to create great governments, great armies, great parasitic castes, vastly oppressive political systems, and have often destroyed themselves, or progressed, by waging war on each other. How can we stop this endless cycle repeating itself?

A more peaceful, prosperous method of human organization is at our fingertips. The long process of selection of successful human institutions by learning and imitation must necessarily also include the instinctive rejection of obviously false solutions to problems by most people. Modern warfare is surely one such false solution. But can we discover the right solutions? One can place little faith in 'constructed' solutions, like constitutions or international organizations, and none at all in 'rational' responses. But information and competition on a global scale, such as we have today, may prove enough to keep freedom alive, keep the State within reasonable bounds and keep the military within safe bounds. It is a slender hope, the only one we have.

References

Peter Brimelow (1995), *Alien Nation*, Random House.
Jimmy Goldsmith (1993), *Lepiège*, Fixot (Hachette).
F. A. von Hayek (1944), *The Road to Serfdom*, Routledge & Sons.
– (1960), *The Constitution of Liberty*, Routledge & Kegal Paul.
– (1973, 1976, 1979): *Law, Legislation and Liberty*, Routledge.
– (1988), *The Fatal Conceit*, Routledge.
Ludwig von Mises (1949), *Human Action*, W. Hodge & Co.
Edmund A. Opitz (1995), *Leviathan at War*, FEE
Wilhelm Röpke (1942), *International Economic Disintegration*, W. Hodge & Co.
– (1959), *International Order and Economic Integration*, D. Reidel, Dordrecht-Holland.

Civilized Ants

Gordon Tullock

Holdobler and Wilson on pape 215 of their *Ants* have a map of a powerful nation in Switzerland. The biologists would call it a super colony. It has about 2 million workers, about 500 queens, and at certain times of the year a considerable number of males. In general, these ants are not closely related to each other. The last may surprise you because inclusive fitness, in which you help your relatives, has been widely used to explain the existence of such social structures among ants and their close relatives to the bees and wasps.

These insects have a peculiar method of reproduction. Formerly, this was thought to mean that an infertile worker was more closely related to the other infertile workers than to the queen or to any off-spring if the worker happened to have them.

For a considerable period of time this was thought to be the basic explanation of this social structure, but there are two problems. In the first place, more than half of all ants have more than one queen, and this particular nest has some 500. Secondly, the individual ant queens are apparently fertilized by a number of males on their mating flight so that the peculiar method of reproduction used in the hymenoptera does not guarantee a close relationship.

Holdobler and Wilson, in their *Ants* have a table which shows the relationship as measured by comparisons of DNA, of ants in a given nest. With super-colonies, it is down around 1 percent or less. It is likely that we are related to each other by less than that 1 percent, but not a lot less. Of course, even if the ants were closely related that would not solve the problem of how they arrange their coordination. It would give them a motive, but not a method.

How then do the ants develop this cooperative operation. I should pause here briefly and say that the ants are not the only ones. Not only are there social bees and wasps, but totally unrelated other animals and plants do the same thing. Aspens are examples as are, essentially, wild raspberries. There is one mammal, the mole rat, and the slime molds, in which individual cells, although not closely related, engage in complex cooperative behavior. The ants have microscopic brains, in the literal sense, but surely the brains of the slime mold cells are even less.

This does not exhaust the number of such cooperating organisms. There are social spiders, which I do not understand, those bazaar creatures called ectoprots, and almost all members of the coelentrata, a group which includes the jelly fish.

The termites are an older and, in my opinion higher, example of social insect. All of these obtain a high level of cooperation without either command or trading. How do they do it?

Let us consider our ant nation a little more carefully. Not only is their level of coordination quite high, but they are able to adapt to changing circumstances. They don't carry in their brains a hereditary complete map of the new nest for example, as is I suppose obvious from looking at the map. There are a number of main nests and then subsidiary nests. There are other even smaller nests which are occupied only part of the year, and even »camps« which are merely shelters where ants can spend the night in security if they are to far from the main structure of nests.

Nor is the whole thing unable to adjust to changing circumstance. Suppose that you take a shovel and begin digging into the nest. The ants will rearrange their labor activities very sharply. Some ants will begin taking the eggs and grubs down to deeper levels, others will begin repairing damage, while others will take guard positions to protect the nests against intruders. All of this must occur at the same time as the routine activity of the nest. They must continue getting food, moving it to the nest, particularly to the ants engaged in repairing the damaged nest, etc. What has happened is that there is a fairly radical change in the number of ants in each activity, and there are further radical changes in exactly where they are undertaking the activity.

To repeat, I am not going argue that all of this is perfectly efficient. I would not even argue that Los Angeles responded to the earthquake in a perfectly efficient way. But it is true that it would be very hard for us to argue that the response of Los Angeles to its most recent earthquake was more efficient than what we would observe in an ants nest which is similarly disturbed.

All of this is not the only thing which we should say. As another example, the ants themselves, although it seems hard to say this about such a small insect, actually do have a high living standard. Turning again to Holdobler and Wilson, they show a table with life expectancies of various ants determined empirically. There are not many worker ants in the table, mainly it is queens, but there are a number of worker ants species shown in which the workers live more than a year. This is most remarkable for such a small insect, particularly granted the fact that the winters are harsh in many of the areas where they live. Ants normally have, for such a small insect, a rather safe life. Much of their time is spent inside the guarded tunnels of their nests, and when they are out they are rarely very distant from other ants. When they are attacked they release a chemical which acts as an alarm call, and other ants congregate to get into the fight. Under the circumstances few of the predators who are small enough so they might want to eat an individual ant are also big enough so that they can defend themselves against a number of ants. Hence the individual ant is fairly safe from predation.

In addition to that they normally have what can only be described as a varied diet. Ants who are out collecting food will collect all kinds of food, including certain vegetable products, honey, meat (mainly pieces of insects), etc.. It is brought back into the nest and shared among the ants. It would be coincidence if any given ant received on any given day the same mix as another, but over time it should more or less average out.

Further, some of the ants actually engage in agricultural activities. The eta which I found in my back garden when I moved into my home in Tucson, strips trees of leaves, takes them down into their nest, chews them up into a fine mulch, and then raises fungus on them. The fungus provides their food. They have fairly big colonies although the individual ants aren't very big and are a major pest in some areas. There are also quite a number of ants that keep livestock in the form of aphids which excrete a honey like substance which the ants eat.

All of this is inherited behavior basically, but the inheritance cannot be a detailed precise pattern. Their brain is literally microscopic and the number of hereditary instructions which it can hold must be limited. How a limited set of instructions can develop the elaborate structure we see here is the problem I propose to address. But first it is necessary to deal with a few other problems.

The nests are connected by roads which are almost straight, and well maintained to make it easier for the ants to get from one place to another. The dotted lines are what would be the ant equivalent of our dirt tracks. If they turn out to be useful they will be converted into the ant equivalent of a paved road. You will note a pattern of these is obviously adapted to the local situation, and could not possibly have been inherited.

Some of the nests have been abandoned, I would hypothesize that in the history of this super colony it started up there and expanded. There are still areas where they are expanding.

321

No where on this map are there places where this community comes in contact with another community of the same type ant. When they do actual wars are sometimes fought and fixed boundaries between the nests may eventually develop.

Our particular ant I am going to call a wood ant, but it should be pointed out that rather similar ants and rather similar nests are found throughout the temperate woodland area. Different species of ants occupy what is apparently a very prosperous niche for ants in different parts of the world, but they all have very much the same pattern of behavior. Presumably once again, the woodlands provide a niche which this particular type of social organization is efficient in exploiting.

They are capable of adapting to not only different types of terrain, but a sudden abrupt changes in the environment. At any given time, the ants are engaged in a fairly elaborate division of labor with some of them taking care of the queen and the eggs, feeding and cleaning the grubs and pupae. Others are repairing the nest, or engaging in road building or road repairs, and a very large number of them are out seeking food.

This particular ant is in the hunting and gathering stage of society, but there are other ants that engage in agriculture or livestock raising.

Conditions change, and the number of ants needed for each of these activities vary. The ants make adjustments to these changes. To repeat, I am not alleging that these adjustments are perfectly efficient no more than I would say that a human society adjusts perfectly efficiently to something like the Los Angeles earthquake. Still, many types of changes, a severe rain storm for example, require significant adjustments.

How do they make these adjustments. Firstly, there is no sign of polit-buro giving orders to everyone. In those ants where there is only one queen, or for example a bee's nest, there is no doubt that the queen releases certain chemicals that do have some effect on the behavior of the other bees or ants. The workers also release chemicals which have some effect on her. But if there is only one queen, then could say to some extent, that there is a little central control by way of these chemicals. In our case, with the 500 that argument will not be made. Indeed that is the reason I chose this species.

It should be said that in case of the termites, they can replace royal pairs. The termites have a king and a queen and they can be replaced by auxiliary reproductives if they die. This, once again indicates that it is not centrally controlled. The bees, if the queen die and they realize it quickly enough, can replace the queen. Again, it is evidence that it is not truthfully centrally controlled.

When we think of coordination, we normally think of either some kind of hierarchical control, which is missing in the non-human social species, or market. There are some slight signs of market structure among the social insects. An ant out on the fringes of civilization who is collecting food will return towards the nest, and if she runs into a porter ant will transfer her food to the porter ant and will go back to hunt for more food herself. The porter ant will take it in, and eventually it gets to workers who have nothing to do with the food collecting.

By observation, the ant which will receive the food intercepts the one with food in its crop and taps its antenna briefly before the transfer. I suppose it could be argued that this gives the other ant utility, which it repays with food. This seems to be an extremely strained line of argument. Certainly, there is no other action which could be called a trade in the ant colony. The general outcome is what we would expect if there were a formal market in food that comes in from the outside areas, the nest is repaired, roads are straightened, etc., and the whole thing functions, but there is no sign of a trade.

There is one place among the social insects in which there is something that looks like a trade. Some of the wasps bring food to their larva, and the larva then exudes a drop of honey fluid which the wasp consumes. This is a trade, but when as occasionally happens, the wasp doesn't find any food and comes in empty, it obviously expects that it will receive the drop of honey anyway, and may roughly treat the larva if it doesn't. I don't think this is a very good example of a trade, but it is close as we can get in the non-human social species.

I take it we must begin by agreeing that these small animals have some fairly strong heritary constraints on their behavior, and constraints lead them to behave in a cooperative way. The question is the structure of such constraints. To repeat, they cannot be such things as building a tunnel of certain dimensions, or go get food of a certain type, etc., because different ants who appear to be identical do different things. Secondly, they change their behavior when the circumstances change.

It would be possible for the genes to arrange that a certain percentage are heritarily driven to repair the nest, another percentage to get food, etc. This would mean that they could not adjust to changes in circumstance which would require a shift in the number in each of those occupations. Since they do make such shifts it is obvious this is not the way it is done.

The second method might be to create a cast of supervisory ants that command and then give more complicated hereditary instructions to those. This would have the same problem but in addition there doesn't seem to be any clear cut evidence that such a thing does exist.[1] In any event such a supervisory class would also require an explanation of how it makes decisions as to how many supervisors go to one area, and how many to another, and how they are shifted in grades of urgency.

To repeat what I have said, ants do succeed in solving these problems and so do all of the other social species which I have referred to. It is to my explanation of how the problem is solved that the rest of this paper will be devoted. The reader may not like it, and if he doesn't I suggest that he produce a better one.

I assume that the ants have inheritance preference structure, which is rather like a preference structure we think most human beings have. Many preferences for a lot things like food, well repaired nests, seeing to it that the eggs and grubs are taken of, and feeding the queen. The ants »satisfaction« from one more unit of labor devoted to each one of these depends upon its present state. The better the state of any one of these »goods,« the less satisfaction can be derived from a unit of labor devoted to it. Equation 1, $S = \sqrt{A} + \sqrt{B-C}$, shows a function with these characteristics.

Of course there are many other equations that have similar characteristics. I make no argument for this particular one, but the general structure I think is sound. The reader will note I put in a »C« at the end and this is to indicate that the ant is repelled by having too many other ants engaged in the same activity. This is necessary for mechanical reason since the number of ants working on any given activity can be large enough so that they get in each others way.

This would explain why ants respond to changes in the environment, whether this change in environment is the man with the shovel breaking the nests or simply that the total population of ants has increased and they must expand outward. A similar set of preferences could, of course, explain the behaviour of non-social insects too. Thus far, I have not explained why this particular set of preferences would lead to highly coordinated efficient activity. Let us leave that temporarily aside.

There is some evidence that animals do have preference functions of the sort we are dealing with. Battalio and Kagel have demonstrated conclusively that mice and pigeons have declining margin utility, and respond much like human beings do to mixed incentives. They can and do make choices between the different foods and decide how much they will work for each one.

Rapport has done somewhat the same with a small microscopic animal called the rotifer. He shows that it has a normal shaped indifference curve between two types of food, except that this being a very simple animal with almost nothing in the way of a nervous structure, the indifference curve is a set of straight lines instead of a genuine curve. Presumably, if we made careful enough measurements we would find that our difference curves are also a series of straight lines, although the straight lines would be extremely short and the number would immense.

This assumption of indifference curves not a very radical one, nor is my equation being in terms of states of the world not production possibilities. The ants want to maximize the satisfaction they get and put their labor into whatever will make the largest contribution to that end. Thus, if a tunnel is damaged, the satisfaction from an hour of different types of labor is changed. More value is derived by work on the tunnel than on, say, food collection.

This leads the an ant to change its occupation, which in turn makes food a little less scarce and hence increases the satisfaction another ant can get from food collection. In theory all of this could lead to a formal equilibrium, in practice it has reasonably good results. This outcome, however, requires a particular, hereditary, pattern of preferences.

I have put in C or congestion as a negative function. This insure that the number of ants at any given building site is not enough so that they get into each others way. Again, this is not surprising.

Note, that this kind of very simple preference function would not require a very large number of the brain cells. Since the ants don't have a very large number of brain cells this is fortunate. The slime mold cells[2] engage in cooperative activity without nerves of any sort, and apparently there are other mechanical methods of getting such cooperation. Of course, there are the plants which cooperate and the lichens which have cooperation between members of two different Phyla.[3]

What I have said so far would imply that the individual ant could make choices among different activities, but would not choose one particular kind of activity if there was too much congestion of other ants there. In connection with this last item it might well be that the individual ant was willing to put up with much more congestion when serving the queen than when out hunting in the forest. Indeed, when hunting or seeking for food the ants apparently act as if they don't want to get completely separated from the others. As mentioned above, the ants are extremely small animal, and the reason they are relatively immune to predation is simply that normally there are a number of them, and if you attack one of them the others will come to its rescue. If an individual ant can, by the mechanism, I have just given select whatever it is going to do among a number of different activities, this doesn't produce a society. Indeed, one would assume that non-social insects also have the same kind of preference function I have given above, and that preference function does not lead to social action.[4]

As we have said, the preference function is probably hereditary in any case, and for a social activity the preference function has to be so organized that the ant prefers to do things which contribute to the well being of the nest.

We have an outstanding example of entities behaving in this way in the form of the cells which make up your, or any other, body. These cells engage in activity which improve the life expectancy of the body as a whole, and not their own. Skin cells for example commit suicide every day in the millions. There is no difficulty in explaining this, and if we wish we can say it is an example of inclusive fitness arguments because these are all clones of each other. It is only by protecting the body as a whole they can they have "descendants" in the next generation.

Social insects or ants are not as extreme as this because as I said before they are not closely related. Nevertheless, somewhat the same phenomea exists, and apparently the wood ants in the niche which they have carved out for themselves are efficient enough so that very large numbers of them can be supported. It can only be explained on the grounds that their behavior pattern or the preference function which I have given above is one which leads to cooperation and efficient cooperation.

This in a way is that aversion of biologists until very recently, group selection. I was an enthusiast for individual selection and thought that the *selfish gene* was not only wonderful popularization but a genuine advance in biological science. In other words, I did not believe in group selection.

A number of developments including discovery that there wasn't much relationship among ants, but also other things have led me to realize that group selection is the only way of explaining some phenomena.[5] Still I think the group selection is, to put it mildly an inelegant expedient. But until we find something better we are stuck with it. If any of my readers can explain these things by individual selection, I think he should immediately put his explanation in writing and send it in to the biological journals.

How then does this group selection work? At the simplest level we could say that if any individual ant behaved in a way which was contrary to survival of the nest, it had the wrong preference function built into it genetically, the nests would die and hence the ant with these inferior genes would die with it. Since the worker ants do not actually reproduce this would mean that the queen who had the genes, and who had produced that particular worker ant would also die. Thus the group would be selected out by the individual ant being selected out. It would be an odd case of individual selection by way of group selection.

No doubt it wouldn't necessarily have to be a single ant. If one of our 500 queens was producing ants that did not cooperate and this was a large enough phenomena, there would be an extinction of the nest from a large number of non-cooperative workers rather than from one.

We now turn to some recent, and in my opinion not wonderful good observations. It is now pretty clear from observation not all bees in a bee-hive are equally industrious . It seems likely that the same is true of ants, although it is a little hard to tell ants apart. Thus it would appear that some of the workers in both the bee and the ant specie carry genes that tell them to take it at least a little bit easy. Obviously the ants nest could not survive as there were too many of these, and if they took too much leisure.

Before dealing further with that, let me consider another problem, parasites. The ants, a very successful specie, have almost as many parasites as that other successful specie, the human being. Human parasites, if we leave out rats and mice,[6] are bacterial or virus. In the case of the ants probably there are also lots of fungus, etc. that are parasitic on them, but the parasites I would like to talk about are other insects, particularly beetles.

There are a number of other insects that are capable of entering the ants nest without much opposition, and indeed may well be fed by the ants. There is one beetle that persuades the ants to carry it down to the nursery where it proceeds to lay eggs which develop grubs which eat ant grubs. The ants take no protective measures against this.

The problem parasites case face is the necessity of avoiding exterminating the host. The parasite, like say black death, which kills its host, is far less successful than any one of the probably four or five thousand parasitic bacteria species that you have in your body which we tolerate and do not cause us any great damage.[7]

In other words, a parasite, if it is to be successful, should try to keep its host alive, or at least keep a lot of its hosts alive. The parasites which cause the destruction of the host will produce fewer descendants in the next generation than those that don't.

Those ants that have been carefully studied all have some kind of population control. The beetle that I mentioned previously whose larva eat the ants larva, is an interesting case. The beetle larva eventually form pupae and the ants treat them like their own pupae. Fortunately for the future generation of both ants and the beetle, this kills the beetle. The only pupae that survive are those few ones where the ants have been careless. If they don't "properly" care for this pupa which they mistake for an ant pupa, it may survive. Thus both species continue in existence.

It is clear that without this apparent mistake in the design of the beetle, it would cease to exist because it would destroy all of its hosts. Thus we have what we may call a optimal level of predation. The beetle remains alive and flourishing by just the right amount destruction of ant pupae. How it gets selected for this amount is a little complicated, and I don't think any biologist really knows, but all biologists are fully accustomed to complicated interactions betweens plants and animals of this sort.

The ant within the ant nest that doesn't work very hard raises exactly the same problem. Suppose a queen, or for that matter a drone who inseminates a queen with genes that produce lazy ants. We know from experience that ant nests can operate with a number of non-ant parasites in them, and presumably a number of lazy bum ants can also be tolerated. If there are too many the ant nests die and they die. I should add here there is no evidence that such queens or male drones would have any particular advantage in starting or getting into an ants nest as opposed to the ones with more industrious genes.

I regard this as a rather shaky explanation as I regard all group selection models as shaky. The advantage it has is that it does explain. If we can find a better explanation, I would be happy.

In any event, we observe these really quite large and successful organizations of social insects, and for that matter a few social mammals and plants. Do they tell us anything much about human society? I think the answer is no, but there is one thing that I can think of that they do tell us about human society.

If all of the ants have the kind of preference function that I have described then each ant responds to its environment according to its own preference function. Its response changes the environment for other ants, and they then respond to this new environment. Thus the coordinating function is a combination of the preference function of the ants and the environment. The environment is very important.

I think that human beings have this same characteristic. Eldon Dvorak changed all of our environments by holding a meeting in Vancouver. We are all now changing each others environment at least a little bit, and the result, we hope, is a coordinated advance in human knowledge.

This is a slightly different way of looking at human society which I derived from the study of non-human societies. It clearly doesn't do very much in the way of offering advice on what we should do in the future. E. O. Wilson has been accused[8] of believing we should study baboons in order to live like baboons. Clearly this is a mistake, but we may learn certain very general aspects of society by studying radically different ones.

Notes

1   Long ago I read a book by Ivan Sanderson, a famous observational biologist, in which he implied that the eta ants did indeed have a supervisory class. I like his work, particularly from the standpoint of entertainment, but I think he was wrong here.

2   There is another type of slime mold in which even the cell walls dissolve so that it is the cell constituents which cooperate.

3   The biologists have dealt with this by creating a "form phylum" for these particular cooperative groups of individual entities from different phyla.

4   There are a great many insects that tend to completely ignore the members of their specie, in others there are very minor coordination. A swarm of male gnats waiting for the passing of a female is an example. There are others where they actually attack, spiders for example. So far, the preference function I have given the social insect is not particularly suited for society, but the clue is that the arguments within the social structure are different from those within the preference structure of a spider.

5   See my "The Economics of [very] Primitive Societies", *Journal of Social and Biological Structures*, Vol. 13, No. 2 (1990), pp. 151–162.

6   And dogs and cats which human beings like, but don't seem to make any other contribution.

7   This is called commensalism, i.e., eating at the same table. It is probable that it reduces our efficiency a little bit, but not significantly.

8   Unjustly.

A Dog's Choice:
Which Constitution Is the Best?

Detmar Doering

'*A bitch about to have puppies asked another bitch to let her deposit her litter in the other's kennel, for which she easily got permission. Later on, when the owner asked for her kennel back again, the other dog resorted to supplications, asking but a brief stay till the puppies were strong enough for her to take with her. When this time also had expired the owner began to insist more stoutly on the return of her sleeping quarters. "If," said the tenant, "you can prove yourself a match for me and my brood I'll move out".*[1]

Phaedrus, has handed down to us this story under the title '*Canis Parturiens*' in one of his *Fables*[2]. Even though ancient fables are more likely to be found in a childrens book than in a *Festschrift* for one of the most eminent (and definitely grown-up!) epistemologists of our times, Phaedrus's lines may nevertheless be a good choice on this occasion. For two reasons:

Firstly, it is a story about dogs. Professor *Radnitzky*, a most passionate dog lover,[3] certainly would object if none of the essays written in honour of his life and work would mention the faithful and loyal canides which are not only considered to be his own best friends but also that of man in general.

Secondly, although some of the dogs portrayed here are not quite as cute as we may wish them to be, they teach us humans a very useful lesson for us humans. This lesson is a libertarian lesson about government – a political lesson.

A Political Problem ...

To the student of ancient civilization the political character of Phaedrus's fable may not be immediately apparent. In fact, the fable was almost certainly meant to be about private morality. It was supposed to be an appeal to the virtue of practical prudence as the supreme virtue that – in the words of *Edmund Burke* – ought to be the 'not only the first in rank of the virtues', but 'the director, the regulator, the standard of them all' (Burke, 1975, p. 81). In this fable the virtues of generosity and compassion have been imprudently extended by one dog to another. The consequence was that they were misused and exploited by that other dog.

To the modern reader, however, the political implications must be quite clear even if they were not intended by the author. To him the fable would be an allegory on the *welfare state* and the entrenchment of interest groups within the political process. If we look around we see governments that have been generous and compassionate to those they thought to be in need. Now even a moderate suggestion to cut down some of the amount given away for that purpose, is dismissed as 'politically impossible' and as leading to political turmoil and destabilisation – even if the original need does no longer exist. Is there a better explanation for the deeper causes of budget deficits in countries all over the world?

The Lockean Contract: A Naive but Useful View

In Phaedrus's times[4] most readers – if they had specifically thought about it at all – would have imagined a quite different connection between the fable and politics. They would have thought that governments were created in order to prevent events like the one described in the fable. The protection of the property rights of the dog that owns the kennel would have been considered the main end of all government. The property-owning bitch of the fable certainly would have expected government to do something about the invasion of her property rights. Even a modern dog probably would believe in government being a help for enforcing legitimate property rights – although it may already have doubts whether this would not end in a long legal battle over the issue if such government action would involve hardships for the 'poor' invaders.

The afore-mentioned view of government is almost archetypically presented in the writings of *John Locke*, who claimed that government is the product of a contract concluded between individuals in order to protect their 'civil interests', which consist of 'life, liberty, health, and indolency of body; and the possession of outward things, such as money, lands, houses, furniture, and the like' (Locke, 1957, p.12). Replace the word 'houses' with 'kennels' and Locke's philosophy could be instantly applied to the land of dogs where *Phaedrus's* story once happened. This view of government could be called the *naive view*, although political philosophy has stuck to its basic notions with almost canine loyalty until the days of *Robert Nozick's Anarchy, State and Utopia* (1974). Its *naivité* does not consist in its being absolutely wrong. In contrast to what some radical libertarians claim, governments do sometimes protect property rights. They may not do it well, and they may not be originally constituted for that purpose, but they nevertheless do.

The reason why the idea of a Lockean contract may be considered naive is purely practical one. One problem is that the Lockean state cannot fulfill its moral imperatives if only because it has to be financed by taxation. Taxation, in contrast to the commercial purchase of services, implies the collectivisation of funds. Funds that were once under individual control are now subject to collective decisions. There cannot be a 'contract' with respect to taxation as we know it,[5] because there is no necessary connection between what an individual pays and what he receives for his payment. The *Federal Chancellor's* office is better protected by the police than the house of most other citizens. This does not necessarily mean that he pays more taxes than others. In fact, nobody can really tell whether he gets what he has paid for, because only the free market could guarantee that. But let us leave this problem aside. In our case it is useful to keep in mind that the starting point of our argument – a dog deprived of its property rights – does belong to the realm of fables. We can, therefore, safely conclude that the creatures that inhabit the land of fables are immaterial that they have no material needs and demands going beyond those that have been explicitly alloted to them by *Phaedrus*. Hence they have – so far! – not bothered about money or taxation.

Yet, there is another practical problem. Can individuals form a government by contract, where no one tries to invade the rights of others? Maybe we would see the formation of a government with the opposite purpose instead. Why not? Why should there be no interest groups that form a coalition in order to do so? In fact, there may be great rewards waiting for them, because the contract would be about the establishment of a monopoly of power. When a government has been installed the means for the exploitation of others are enormously increased. In the light of this view a Lockean contract would only become what it ought to be if there were no specific interests or interest groups.[6] In the real world a paradox would become apparent. A constitutional arrangement that is supposed to check the activities of politicians will inevitably be set up by those very politicians. *Anthony de Jasay* once has remarked ironically that the search for an constitutional arrangement under this normative assumption would be a search for 'an institution or a rule – or a body to interpret it – that is representative yet stands above interests, decisive yet benign, conflictual yet unanimous, square yet round ...' (Jasay, 1993, p. 87).

For the sake of simplicity, in our case the dogs not only are immaterial but also without any prehistory. They do not exist and have never existed outside the short period of life covered by Phaedrus's fable. In this they resemble Rawls's imaginary individuals under the 'veil of ignorance'. Hence no long grown special interests exist in this world.

The question is, what constitution or form of government would the dogs rationally choose if they were the opportunity to establish a government in order to prevent such unfortunate occurences as the one described by Phaedrus? No doubt, that as rational creatures, which they are, they would find the Lockean theory of rights a naive, but still very useful tool, to set the standard for assessing all forms of government. Even if they knew that they were pursuing an ideal that is practically unattainable, they could enjoy the task. The question, which of the basic types of government was most likely to meet that standard, would be intriguing to creatures of the classical world. Aristotle, Polybius and Cicero had treated the question extensively in their works. And it also had an enormous impact on early modern thinkers like Machiavelli or Montesquieu, who in their works copiously referred to the classical distinction between monarchy, aristocracy, democracy and mixed constitution. They would regret that in recent times the question has gone somewhat out of fashion.

Anarchy: Caught in a Paradox?

After having observed the experiences of 'dog's best friend' – man! – Phaedrus's dogs may have come to the conclusion that the whole idea of government is bound to fail. On first sight this view would be supported also by theoretical arguments. If the right to self-ownership is to be preserved, the state – a territorial monopolist in violence – is the greatest possible threat to it. In fact, it can not be upheld at all without invading these rights. The American political scientist *R.J. Rummel* in his book *Death by Government* has estimated that in our century governments have killed 169,198,000 human beings by genocide (Rummel 1995, p. 1). This figure ultimately proves the 'naive' liberal view wrong, that the state as an institution is the protector of the individual against aggression. No potential aggressor, from which the state is supposed to protect us, could have done so much harm.

Therefore the dogs' first choice could be anarchy. It would be a very unclassical choice, to be sure. Most ancient classical philosophers would have abhorred the very idea. The dogs perhaps would have found some encouragement in the fact that those ancient philosophers who sympathised with anarchist ideas were closer to their species than most other humans. The *Cynics*, at least, had borrowed their name from them – κύων is, as we know, the Greek word for *dog*. The Cynics disregard for governmental authority was proverbial.[7]

But could anarchy solve the problem? Let us go back to the original situation. In the fable there is nothing to suggest that the usurpation of property described here did not occur in a state of anarchy. Otherwise the police might have solved the problem easily. In fact, the fable gives us a very good account of the possible deficits and practical problems of anarchy. Libertarian anarchists usually argue that 'protective agencies' will soon evolve in the market. They claim that these private services would deal with the situation far more effectively than any non-market structure. Would they? Under anarchism the defense forces would be agents of the customers. They would reflect their values. In the given case there are two competing sets of values – one that respects property and another that does not. The latter one may still have 'positive' values (the communitarian values of the family, for instance). In a world of anarchy the more powerful 'organisation' will be the winner. In our case, where a 'family-run' organisation has already been established, the outcome, however, would be extremely unsatisfactory. Both sides, of course, could agree on a neutral third agent to mediate in the conflict. But why should the stronger party agree to this procedure? The only reason to do so would be if they could be coerced to accept it. Then, of course, we have something like a state or government standing above all interest groups and being the ultimate source of power.

Thus we may be faced with a paradox. The rise of coercive power structures may be inevitable. There is, of course, no guarantee whether all of them share the believe in unalienable rights. In fact, they may soon turn out to be nothing but governments in disguise. Some more skeptical anarchist theorists like *Mike Gunderloy*, therefore, have dared to ask whether an anarchist order could be stable at all: 'How can we assert that the anarchist society will just endure, when no other society seems to do so? What sort of mechanisms do we have in mind to keep it from changing too far?' (Gunderloy, 1991, p. 14).

These questions have to be answered before anarchy could become a viable solution. There is great danger, that under anarchy the rapacious dog with her puppies continue to occupy someone else's kennel. Maybe that someday we will be able to solve this basic structural problem of anarchism. If so, then it would be the ultimate solution of all our social problems. Until then, however, we should allow the dogs to look around for possible alternatives.

Democracy – An Experiment that Failed?

Some of the contemporaries of Phaedrus's dogs undoubtedly would have given an answer to the paradoxes of anarchy. Their answer would have been: Democracy.

If, as we have seen, a neutral coercive agent as a last contract enforcer above all other agents may become necessary as contractarians claim, it would be wise to avoid one obvious risk. The government thus established should be really neutral. It must not reflect the 'special interest' of any person or group. The dogs are well familiar with *Franz Oppenheimer's* theory that all governments owe their existence to conquest. They have read in his writings that states inevitably replace peaceful 'economic means' of wealth creation with coercive 'political' ones (Oppenheimer, 1929, p. 10f.).

To avoid this the 'neutral' agency must somehow express the common interest of all dogs. The argument for democracy therefore was, that the 'people' should be sovereign. If, as it is most likely the case in larger territorial states, the people as such cannot exercise their power, this should be done by delegates. The access to such offices should be open to everyone and subject to election.

No doubt the spirit of democracy – from the *American War of Independence* to the *British Free-Trade Movement* of the mid–19th century – has done a lot to put an end to many governments based on coerced privilege. On first sight also the theoretical argument in favour of democracy seems to be a sound one. The principle that a majority should stand behind political decisions seems to exclude 'special interests' of a too particularist nature from dominating others.

However, the hope that this would be the case proved to be overoptimistic. John Locke, the ardent advocate of individual rights, thought that (constitutional) democracy was the best way to limit government properly. Instead of being limited by democracy government, however, expanded under democracy to an extent unknown hitherto. Although the redistributive processes that violate individual rights are carried out more peacefully (an advantage that should not be underestimated!), the extent of this elimination has already taken frightening proportions. Two figures from Germany may suffice to illustrate this. The *Handelsblatt*, 14 December 1995, noted the public debts had passed the two trillion Mark mark (= 2,000,000,000,000 DM). The debt would grow at a rate of 3,935 DM per second.

What went wrong? *Public-Choice* economists have provided the answer. Politicians in a democracy are just as much 'utility maximizers' as everyone else. In order to get reelected they have to satisfy the demands of interest groups of all sort. They all may count. In a democracy noone can be kept away from the political process – or democracy would cease to be democracy. Accordingly the number of special interest group with access to the political process is virtually unlimited. The story has been told more than often, and should not be repeated here. The democratic state has become what the great French liberal economist *Frédéric Bastiat* had, as early as 1850, predicted: 'The state is a fictitious entity where everyone tries to live at the expense of everyone else' (Bastiat 1862). It is most likely that under a democratic government no justice would be done to the dog deprived of its property. The fact that the rapacious bitch has a stronger and (given the time she lived in the kennel) more deeply entrenched 'interest group' behind her will secure this. At best a compromise (probably a compensation at the expense of a third party or the taxpayer in general) would be tried, where no compromise is legitimate. 'Social justice' ('Oh, the poor little puppies must not be chased out into the cold ...') would be introduced as an argument to legitimize the infringement of property rights.

This leaves the dogs, who are still studying humanity's triumphs and failures, in a dilemma. They know that in a democracy all incentives affecting politicians and political institutions will work against the rights of the individual. On the other hand, the principal argument of individual rights appears allow nothing but democracy – provided we must have a state. Private clubs can exclude whoever they like from their decision making processes. Coercive public monopolies must not be exclusive. There can be no rational natural rights argument in order to give some people the exclusive access to political domination over others. This would be an additional argument in favour of anarchy, where everything would be private. Then, of course, the above-mentioned problems would arise again.

The dogs are confronted with a dilemma where they have to decide which principle has to be sacrificed: Should they allow the political processes further to run amuck for the sake of preserving democratic rights of access to the public sector, or, should they sacrifice democracy in favor a less rent-seeking society?

Lenin on a Throne? The Strange Case of Libertarian Monarchism

The more daring minds, the top-dogs, would take the latter option. After all, good libertarians must regard private liberty and private property as far more valuable than access to the political sphere.

In recent years we have seen a strange phenonomen arising at the fringe of the libertarian community: The revival of monarchism.

Since the democratic experiment has led to over-government, over-taxation, over-regulation and ever-growing budget deficits it is argued, that we should return to the traditional wisdom of the ancients. Autocratic government has become fashionable again. Even *Professor Radnitzky* seems to have turned to this idea recently (Radnitzky 1993).

There are two lines of arguments used in defense of this position. They both are founded upon the ideas of 'private property' and of 'time horizon'. They are both clustered around the notion of a 'private ownership of government' (Hoppe 1995, p. 96).

The first ' extreme' argument is, or seems to be (since the proponents of libertarian monarchism are always very vague in their definitions), that the monarch 'literally owns the entire country within its borders' (Hoppe, 1995/25, p. 2). Therefore he 'will tend to have a systematically longer planning horizon, i.e. his degree of time preference will be lower, and accordingly, his degree of economic exploitation will tend to be less than that of a ⟨public⟩ government's care-taker' (Hoppe, 1995, p. 95).

All this would, as *Hans-Hermann Hoppe* has argued, enable monarchs to pursue a more reasonable immigration policy. Whereas (as Hoppe correctly observes) under the present democratic welfare state 'free immigration' in reality is 'forced integration', the private owner would have a private choice about whom he 'lets in'. He can even do, what under a 'publicly-owned government' would be discrimination, i.e. he can select certain immigrant groups (religious, ethnic, or whatever). He could even expel people he does not like from the country. It would be in principle the same if I were saying, that I do not want to see a Roman Catholic or Swiss-born gardener in my private garden. Who, then, would be legitimized to force me to accept one in my garden?

There is, however, a fundamental flaw in this argument. The private property in this case would not be 'government' (i.e. the political machinery, such as legislation or jurisdiction), but the whole land. Monarchy would, then, still be 'a territorial monopolist of compulsion' (p. 94). Taken to the extreme, it would mean the loss of the individual's right to self-ownership and property for everybody except the monarch. No libertarian could possibly accept this. It seems that some libertarians have forgotten their great mentor, *Murray Rothbard*, who in his great unfinished work on the history of economic thought wrote an appraisal of *Claude Joly's* book of 1653 *Receuil de maximes veritables*. Joly, he argued, had wisely rejected *Louis XIV.'s* 'new notion that the king is rightly the master – in fact the owner – of the persons and property of all the inhabitants of France' (Rothbard, 1995, p. 257). This rejection, Rothbard concluded, was based on sound libertarian doctrine.

Moreover, a monarchy that owns everything – land and people – will cease to be private. All foreign trade would be a matter of intergovernmental negotiation. Somehow the whole argument seems to resemble *Lenin's* idea that a country could be run like a factory. We now know how well a country works that is run 'privately' by the supervising committee of a shareholder's company called 'Communist Party'. We should also note that the age of monarchies was not an age of successful wealth creation – except perhaps for the monarchs. Monarchism always found mercantilism to be the economic system appropriate for its purposes. *Gordon Tullock* observed that the 'granting of monopolies' is as much a feature of monarchy as is the appearance of 'friends of the ruler' whose 'enterprise is to 'court' the ruler in hopes of getting ... special privileges' (Tullock, 1994, p. 141).

One could – much less extremely – interpret the idea of 'private ownership of government' in a different light. 'Privately-owned government', then, would mean that certain governmental competences are exclusively in the monarch's hand and others not. This was the case in most medieval monarchies. This, of course, presupposes something like a constitutional settlement. It explains why governments were so much smaller in the old days. It cannot be explained in terms of the monarch owning the whole land. On the contrary, medieval monarchs – especially the German emperor – hardly owned anything. This is the reason why their 'government' could be restrained by pre-existing laws. The exclusive owner of the kingdom could have overthrown them at his pleasure (otherwise he would not be the owner).

Also the idea of a privately-owned government having a wider 'time horizon' presupposes that monarchs can not be 'blackmailed' by special interest groups. The fact, however, is that they, too, are dependent on such interest groups. *David Hume* once observed in one of his *Essays* that even an absolute ruler has to act in a way to keep his 'mamalukes or praetorian bands' (Hume, 1985, p. 32f.) satisfied.

It is likely that in a monarchy of dogs the land would be full of kennels ursurped by praetorian guard dogs. It is very likely that the dogs would object to this. Hence, the task is not de-democratisation by re-monarchisation, but de-politicization. The idea of 'privately owned government', however, is not completely useless. It may lead the dogs to a very different line of inquiry.

A Step into the Right Direction: Aristocracy

It would not be surprising if Phaedrus's dogs would turn to aristocracy as a subject of examination. First of all they would thereby follow the line of classical Aristotelian thought. Secondly, they would not completely abandon the idea of 'privately-owned government'. The notion of 'privateness', they may feel, is always superior to that of 'public affairs'. Everything 'public' has a tendency to destroy private liberty.

But why, they will ask, should a 'privately-owned government' necessarily mean a territoral monopoly? This *mono*polisation is what *mon*archy is all about. Why do we need a monopoly at all? The advocates of the superiority of monarchy over democracy seem to have reduced the whole question to the phenonomen of social time preference. This alone does not help much. It was monarchy, not democracy, that laid the basis for the monopolisation and centralisation of power. By reducing everything to the 'time preference'-argument, they (deliberately?) tend to ignore the difference between monarchy other forms of 'privately owned government' – or they dismiss it as irrelevant. It is, however, not. Aristocratic government has several principal advantages over monarchy. The ownership of government is limited to some bits and pieces. It is a truly limited government. To be sure, we are speaking of privileges, but these privileges are – ideally – not the accidental offspring of political 'log-rolling' processes as they are in a democracy. They are unalienable property rights. They can not be abolished by a simple majority decision. If, as in most cases they did, aristocrats within a territory form central political institutions, these institutions included very effective checks to power. The most illustrative case was the Polish constitution. Until the late 18th century the *Sejm* (the aristocratic legislative assembly) recognised the principle of the *liberum veto*. This meant that a decision had to be unanimously. One single member could block the decision ad infinitum. The limitation of government was so effective that even complete political immobility and chaos was accepted as a possible consequence.

Moreover, an aristocratic system is less vulnerable than a monarchy to personal incompetence. It is, by contrast, a collective, where the insanity of one ruler can be effectively counteracted. In fact, aristocracies usually tend to develop moral codes – the *mos maiorum* – that help to discipline its members. Prudence, i.e. political farsightedness (as a consequence of 'private ownership of government'), is the keystone of this code.

The destruction of the aristocratic limitations on government by monarchy (again: not by democracy!) in the 16./17. century laid the foundations of modern 'big government'. The first bancruptcy of government (overtaxation and overspending combined) was the French monarchy in 1789. It also was the European monarchy that came closest to a regime where the monarch 'literally owns the entire country within its borders'. Monarchy, by its nature, could only establish herself by destroying the 'private governments' of the aristocracy. In their search for the best possible constitution the dogs will keep this in mind. The theoretical examination of the more decentralized structure of aristocratic government certainly had made some impact on them. But can they do better?

Mixed Government: The Classical Solution

The heritage of aristocratic government consists of the idea of decentralization and robust constitutional checks on power by the force of non-monopolistic 'privately-owned governments' in the strictes sense. For the mass of the people it nevertheless does not necessarily mean freedom. Just a generation before Phaedrus brought his famous dogs into their fictitious existence, Cicero, although a friend of aristocratic virtues, remarked that 'in optimatium dominatu vix particeps libertatis potest ess multitudo' (Cicero, 1932, p. 130) – under the domination of the optimates the multitude hardly has a share in liberty. Those who have no part in 'private' government are in a less advantageous position with respect to the safety of their property rights than those who have. It may not be always expedient, but the aristocratic ruler may treat his subjects (not citizens!) as property as well. After all slavery often was seen as compatible with and profitable for aristocratic rulers.[8] Aristocrats were always able to ursurp your 'kennels' for reasons of expediency. This tendency would be reinforced by the fact that the moral code of aristocratic rulers usually tends to be centred around politics. Aristocrats form a 'political class' in the strictest sense. This goes along with a strictly 'anti-commercial' ethos. Trade and production (except agriculture) are usually viewed with contempt. Therefore economic liberties usually were not held in esteem by aristocratic regimes. Free Trade in the 19th century, for instance, was adopted against the explicit will of the aristocracy by rather democratic popular movements like the *Anti Corn Law League* in England. Slowly but surely the merits of democracy begin to be appreciated again. Democracy may not be the best method as the sole basis for checking exploitative political processes in the long run, but as a means of self-defense it is still the best thing we have. This idea is also confirmed by history. It was a democratic force that made American Independence possible after 1776; it was democratic force, that brought down the Soviet Empire. Seen as defensive rights, democratic rights can be bulwarks of liberty. In Switzerland all new taxes have to face a plebiscite. Compare the Swiss level of taxation with that of Germany, where there are no such Plebiscites – then you will learn to appreciate the idea of democracy very soon. Thus, all the basic types of constitution – democracy, monarchy, aristocracy – both have their defects and merits. The classical solution, therefore, was to combine the advantages and to avoid the disadavantages of all three of them. The name of the solution was: Mixed Constitution. In fact, almost all the examples named by libertarian monarchists as the 'good monarchies' of the past were mixed constitutions. Hardly any of these, for example, allowed the king the right to tax. This right was always reserved to some kind of parliamentary assembly. No king was the exclusive owner of government, land or people. Here lay the true reason for the restraint of government. Once monarchy had destroyed these restraints (and became exclusive owner of government) government went out of control. The examples for republican government mentioned by the same writers (Venice, Switzerland etc.) (Hoppe, 1995, p. 100), by the way, were also typically mixed constitutions. When we speak of pre-modern times as an era of small government, we speak not of an era of monarchies, republics (in fact most monarchies understood themselves as republics!) or whatever. We speak of an era of mixed constitutions!

Within the environment of mixed government constitutional mechanisms could work fairly well. The problem of modern democratic government is, that sovereignty and the checks and balances against that sovereignity are both derived from the same source – i.e. popular sovereignity. The thief and the policeman are, so to say, one and the same person. In a mixed constitution this is not the case. Some parts of governmental power may belong to a people's community, some to a monarch, and some to a nobilty. None of them owes his part of the sovereignity (his piece of ownership) to the other. It, then, will be increasingly difficult for one top-dog to ursurp someone else's kennel without meeting staunch resistance.

The Modern Way: Pluralism and Decentralisation

The decision now is quite clear. Assuming that we need a state (which is always the second-best of all solutions), it has to be founded on the idea of mixed constitution. This was also the idea that the vast majority of political theorists before the 19th century advocated. No doubt, that the dogs of

Phaedrus's fable would have chosen it as the best way to defend themselves against the violation of their rights.

Humans today are, however, in a different situation. We do have a pre-history, since we are not imagined by a writer of fables. The option of a truly mixed constitution for us does not really exist anymore. The constitutional restraints imposed on or democratic governments have not turned out to be a very effective substitute. There is, in all probability, no way back in restoring the missing parts, i.e. monarchy and aristocracy. This is no reason for a sentimental or nostalgic look backwards into the past. We do not have to mourn for them, because as such they were nothing that the majority of the people ever benefitted from. The modern age of democracy, despite its shortcomings, has proved to be the age of prosperity and (relative) freedom for the mass of the people. Who, but a romantic ignorant could wish to return to the times of feudal bondage? Not even the argument that the tax rate was lower in these days would convince anyone. We should be happy with the delegitimization of any government that can be delegitimized. We should never try to to relegitimize – in particular if nobody can explain how we can do this. That is the road to progress.

This does not mean that we should dismiss other forms of government if they can get somehow accepted by their people. In Latin America, South East Asia and Eastern Europe we have witnessed odd combinations of democratic and autocratic government, which proved to be very efficient. We should be – as much is possible – open to a pluralism in governments. More promising is the attempt to decentralize governments by all means. The smaller a political entity is, the closer together the 'two hearts in everyone's breast' will be. In our modern world almost all are both *taxpayers* and *tax-eaters*. The difference between the exploiters and the exploited has been blurred by the democratic political machinery. The more distant government is, the more apparent is this, because the individual then is very apt to shift over burdens to an anonymous 'society'. *Margaret Thatcher* was right, when in 1987 she said: 'There is no such thing as society'.[9] However, most people – the tax-eater in all of us – will find the fiction of a society very convenient. This will be an obstacle against every decentralizer will have to fight hard. But the fight is worth to be fought. In a smaller political community the shifting over of burdens to 'society' is more difficult, because society has been replaced by real flesh-and-blood people. They know when you exploit them, you know when they exploit you. The smaller the state, the more 'public government' will resemble 'private government' – even if it is (with good reasons) democratic. Small communities do not tend themselves to adopt the absurd idea of 'autarky'; they cannot afford to be protectionist. In a comparative study on economic freedom in various countries of the world economists recently discovered, that smaller states tend to allow more economic freedom and hence to become more prosperous (Gwartney/Lawson/Block 1995). One may hope that this economic tendency is the herald of a political tendency (for once one hopes that *Marx* was right, when he said that political conditions always follow the economic ones).

Whatever the outcome may be, even under a decentralised government there is no guarantee that our liberty will be save in the long run. But, as *Professor Radnitzky* would insist to say most doggedly: ' ... there is no such guarantee in any system' (Radnitzky, 1993, p. 40).

Notes

1 Phaedrus, lt./eng., transl. by B.E. Perry, Cambridge, Mass./London 1975, p. 215 (Loeb)
   For the classicists among us, who love the works of ancient literature in their original language, the Latin words are as follows:
   Canis parturiens cum rogasset alteram
   ut fetum in eius tugurio deponeret,
   facile impetravit. dein reposcenti locum
   preces admonuit, tempus exorans breve,
   dum firmiores catulos posset ducere.
   hoc quoque consumpto flagitari validius
   cubile coepit. 'Si mihi et turbae meae
   par' inquit 'esse potueris, cedam loco.' (ibid., p. 214)
2 Fable no. 19 of *Book I*, to put it more precisely.
3 This essay, therefore, is not only dedicated to Prof. Radnitzky, but also to *Olga*, his poodle.
4 Gaius Iulius Phaedrus, who lived in the 1st century A.D. under the reign of Augustus, knew what the violation of the right to self-ownership meant. He came to Rome as a slave from Thracia. He was freed by the Emperor at a time when he had already become well-known for his *Fables*.
5 The only exception that can be imagined would be a scheme of voluntary taxation. This idea was proposed by *Auberon Herbert* in the late 19th century. Since no modern government has adopted this idea we can leave it aside here.
6 In order to rescue the contract theory some authors (e.g. *John Rawls* in his *Theory of Justice*) proposed that the partners to the social contract should imagine that they were acting under the 'veil of igno-

rance'. But why should they do so? If there is a substantial chance that certain interests can instrumentalise the contract for their (in reality very well-known) purpose they would be extremely irrational if they did not make use of this chance, indeed!

7   Of course, we do not know much about the political ideas of the *Cynics*. George H. Sabine, *A History of Political Theory*, 3rd ed., London/Toronto/Sydney/Wellington 1951, p. 127 (Harrap) says that we only vaguely know that 'the political theory of the Cynics was utopian' and advocated 'perhaps anarchy'.

8   Some libertarians of the excentric kind defend the view that privately owned slaves are treated better than government owned. Therefore they could turn out to work efficiently and profitable as well. This view may be right (and probably is). Nevertheless, there can be no economic argument justifying slavery. Even if slavery were profitable it still would be a violation of the individual's right to self-ownership.

9   For an extremely able defense of this saying by Margaret Thatcher, see: Samuel Brittan, 'There is no such Thing as Society; in: Samuel Brittan, *Capitalism with a Human Face*, Aldershot 1995 p. 85ff (Edward Elgar Publishing).

References

Frédéric Bastiat, *Oeuvres Complètes de Frédéric Bastiat*, 7 Vols., 2nd ed., Paris 1862ff (Guillaumin).

Samuel Brittan, 'There is no such Thing as Society'; in: Samuel Brittan, *Capitalism with a Human Face*, Aldershot 1995 (Edward Elgar Publishing), p. 85ff.

Edmund Burke, An Appeal from the New to the Old Whigs; in: Edmund Burke, *The Works. Twelve Volumes in Six*, Reprint of the Edition: London 1887, Hildesheim 1975 (Bohn Edition).

Cicero, *De Re Publica*, ed. K. Büchner, Zürich 1952 (Artemis Verlag).

Mike Gunderloy, 'Closing the Gaps: Challenges for the Anarchist Movement', in: Mike Gunderloy/Michael Ziesing, *Anarchy and the End of History*, Rensselaer 1991 (Factsheet Five), p. 12ff.

James Gwartney/Robert Lawson/Walter Block, *Economic Freedom of the World 1975–1995*, Vancouver 1995 (Fraser Institute/Liberales Institut/Cato Institute et. al.).

Hans-Hermann Hoppe, 'Free Immigration or Forced Integration', in: *Chronicles*, July 1995/25 (Rockford Institute), p. 1ff.

Hans-Hermann Hoppe, 'The Political Economy of Monarchy and Democracy, and the Idea of a Natural Order', in: *Journal of Libertarian Studies*, Vol. 11, No. 2, 1995 (Center for Libertarian Studies), p. 94ff.

David Hume, *Essays, Moral, Political and Literary*, ed. E.F. Miller, Indianapolis 1985 (Liberty Fund).

Anthony de Jasay, 'Is Limited Government Possible?', in: Gerard Radnitzky/Hardy Bouillon (ed.), *Government: Servant or Master?*, Atlanta/Amsterdam 1993 (Rodopi), p. 73ff.

John Locke, *Ein Brief über Toleranz/A Letter Concerning Toleration*, ed. J. Ebbinghaus, Hamburg 1957 (Felix Meiner Verlag).

Franz Oppenheimer, *Der Staat*, 3rd ed., Jena 1929, (Gustav Fischer Verlag).

Phaedrus, lt./eng., transl. by B.E. Perry, Cambridge, Mass./London 1975 (Loeb).

Gerard Radnitzky, 'Private Rights Against Public Power: The Comtemporary Conflict', in: Gerard Radnitzky/Hardy Bouillon, *Government: Servant or Master?*, Atlanta/Amsterdam 1993 (Rodopi), p. 40ff.

Gerard Radnitzky/Hardy Bouillon, *Government: Servant or Master?*, Atlanta/Amsterdam 1993 (Rodopi).

Murray N. Rothbard, *An Austrian Perspective on the History of Economic Thought*, Vol. 1: *Economic Thought before Adam Smith*, Aldershot 1995 (Edward Elgar Publishing).

Rudolph J. Rummel, *Death by Government*, 2nd printing, New Brunswick 1995 (Transaction Publishers).

George H. Sabine, *A History of Political Theory*, 3rd ed., London/Toronto/Sydney/ Wellington 1951 (Harrap).

Gordon Tullock, 'Industrial Organisation and Rent Seeking in Dictatorships', in: Gordon Tullock, *On the Trail of Homo Economicus*, ed. by G.L. Brady/R.D. Tollison, Fairfax 1994, (George Mason University Press), p. 141ff.

Abstracts

Chapter I

Walter Block: Libertarian perspective on political economy

The Author sets out the basic premises of libertarianism, and applies them to issues such as socialism, capitalism, unionism, free trade, pay equity, minimum wages, underdeveloped countries and pollution. He views it important that this be done, since if we are to discuss this philosophy, we do well to have a clear account of it before us. In that way, whether we accept it or not, we shall not have to fear talking at cross purposes; we will at least all be undertaking a dialogue on the same issue. Perhaps we shall only achieve informed disagreement, but this is a far better result than misunderstanding, the condition that plagues much of dialogue on economic questions.

Gerd Habermann: Liberalism and the libertarians

While it is true that minimal-state liberals and radical libertarians like Rothbard and David Friedman share common ground in some important respects, the two schools diverge on several fundamental issues, in particular the question of the legitimacy and efficiency of state-controlled monopolies. Their respective arguments and premises differ (natural law/utilitarian/evolutionist premises). Minimal state liberals and radical libertarians also disagree on certain practical questions. The arguments and counter-arguments of this exciting debate are examined in detail, including the link to the 'communitarian' movement. In conclusion, the Author draws some inferences from the viewpoint of a minimal state liberal.

Hans-Hermann Hoppe: On the law and economics of socialism and desocialization

The paper first briefly restates and explains the legal principles of pure socialism and the reasons for its economic failure. In its central second part it addresses the question of how to de-socialize. Based on economic insights of Ludwig von Mises and ethical insights of his most important student, Murray N. Rothbard, a proposal for a strategy of 'pure de-socialization' and its ethical and economic rationale are offered.

Hardy Bouillon: Defining libertarian liberty

Telling libertarians from liberals requires a clear conception of liberty, and hence a precise definition of individual freedom. Otherwise we end in a purely gradual distinction which cannot but be arbitrary. The definition of individual freedom by Hayek is used as an example to illustrate this consequence. Moreover, traditional definitions of individual freedom suffer under the problem of circularity. The paper attempts an original, sufficiently clear, and non-self-contradictory definition of individual freedom which avoids the circularity problem. It does so by introducing the term of costs and via distinguishing two different kinds of decision, i. e. meta-decision and object-decision.

Arthur Seldon: Libertarians and the rule of law

The essay addresses a liberal conception that experienced discredit in the past, the rule of law. It is argued that as long as government confined itself to the supply of goods and services that could not be generated by private agreements in the open market, the writ of government – the rule of law – was accepted and respected. It argues further that the rule of law has been weakened by the over-ambitions of the political process taught by socialist thinkers and has been discredited by democratic government during the last two centuries. The paper proposes to recall the liberal reverence for the rule of law in Jeffersonian spirit.

Louis De Alessi: Value, economic efficiency, and rules: Some implicit biases against individual liberty

The failure to separate normative from positive economics continues to bedevil economists, yielding analyses and policy recommendations that are value-loaded and biased against individual liberty and open markets.

In particular, mainstream economists who compare alternative rules (and institutions) routinely introduce assumptions about economic efficiency and the state of the world that disregard individual values. First, analysts typically define economic efficiency in terms of some ideal state, implicitly choosing some social welfare function as a benchmark. Pareto and other social welfare criteria inherently are value-loaded. Second, analysts assume that values can be measured objectively by outside observers, thereby ignoring individuals' subjective (personal-use) values. Third, analysts frequently assume antecedent conditions that are empirically false – for example, that all individuals have identical preferences – and fail to specify rules of correspondence for key theoretical terms. Fourth, analysts compare institutions on the basis of equilibrium conditions that are seldom reached. In a world of change, the process of adjustment may be much more important.

Although current notions of economic efficiency seem to provide scientific, objective criteria for comparing rules, in practice they mask normative criteria that favour rules limiting individual liberty and open markets. At best, economics offers a theoretical framework for analyzing the consequences of changes in circumstances and for examining the interaction and congruence of alternative rules with various ethical norms.

Hans F. Sennholz: The Böhm-Bawerkian foundation of the Interest Theory

The essay is an historical analysis of the importance of Böhm-Bawerk's contribution to economic theory. Böhm-Bawerk's magnus opus, *Kapital und Kapitalzins*, ushered in the Austrian School and helped it gain the ascendancy over classical economic theory. Elaborating on Menger's seminal contribution, it presented an intertemporal theory of value and distribution in which time plays a crucial role. This theory together with its famous application to the doctrines of Marx not only influenced the subsequent development of economic thought but also made Austrian economists the main critic and adversary of socialism. Until today numerous attempts have been made to reformulate Böhm-Bawerk's theory in such a way that it would suit many purposes.

In question of income, the differences of theory are as great today as they were a century ago. And as before, the Austrian body of thought not only provides a logical foundation for a consistent explanation of interest income but also offers the rationale for a system of ethics that sustains the private property order against its numerous critics.

Chapter II

Anthony de Jasay: The bitter medicine of freedom

The main contemporary threat to freedom is no longer foreign oppression or totalitarian rule, but the political decision mechanism or social choice rule that greatly facilitates some groups within society obtaining advantages at the expense of the rest. The essay reviews certain current concepts of freedom and finds that they lack precise content, conceal tradeoffs and costs, and involve no onerous commitments. They accommodate, rather than hinder, the intrusion of social into the domain of individual choice.

Freedom, properly conceived, is inseparable from responsibility for oneself and insecurity of existence. In this sense, it is bitter medicine.

Antony Flew: Social democracy and the myth of social justice

In the Preface to *Law, Legislation and Liberty, The Mirage of Social Justice*, Hayek confessed that he had "come to feel strongly that the greatest service I can still render to my fellow men would be that I can make speakers and writers thoroughly ashamed ... to employ the term 'social justice'". Writing as he was twenty or more years ago Hayek seems not to have seen, and perhaps could not have seen, that 'social' justice was becoming the ideal of 'the socialists of all parties', to whom he dedicated *The Road to Serfdom*.

The purpose of the present paper is to show how completely John Rawls and some others who have tried to provide a systematic rationale for the application of this expression have not even attempted either to meet what should have been the most obvious objections or to offer any justification for their enormous socialist assumptions. Rawls ignores the objection that "social" justice is precisely not a kind of justice, since it essentially involves taking under the threat of force (through taxation) the justly acquired property of some in order to transfer it to others who have not been unjustly deprived of it.

Roland Baader: Nothing new under the sun:
The disguised return of totalitarianism

Neither the democratic method nor the tradition of enlightenment are capable to repulse the latent threat of political totalitarianism. On the contrary, both are degenerated in form and supported by hostility to technology and fear of civilisation, phylogenetically innate to homo sapiens. Both build a mixture of intellectual humus for totalitarian developments. The ecological movement, with its growing and expanding acceptance by the populace, might serve as an instance.

After the collapse of East-block socialism, the disavowed Left by using the 'fascism' trick succeeded in delegitimising the Center and making it blind against left totalitarianism. Mainly destroyed by the collectivism of creeping socialism in the welfare state, the 'moral infrastructure of freedom' is losing its function as bulwark against these mass-psychological manipulations. Hypocritical ethics, named political correctness, does its share to silence the last warning voices. Contemporary examples show how far creeping totalitarianism, tightly connected with creeping socialism, thrived in Germany.

Angelo M. Petroni: Is there a morality in redistribution?

Following Bertrand de Jouvenel, this essay distinguishes between two notions of redistribution. The first is to provide people in need with the means of subsistence, whether it be a minimum income in days of unemployment or basic medical care for which they could not have paid. The second notion of redistribution follows from the idea that inequalities of means between the several members of society is bad in itself and should be more or less radically removed. The basic difference between the two notions is that the first can be defined in terms of 'absolute' level of income. These two concepts of redistribution have been confused ever since. On both, liberal values and facts, only the first concept of redistribution can be moral. It implies the *duty* of citizens to contribute to help the less fortunate members of society. But it does not imply any right of these latter to resources legitimately owned by the first.

Gerhard Schwarz: Competition among systems – an ordo liberal view

The article shows what the idea of competition among systems or governments means – specially regarding the European Union. It contrasts the arguments for ex-ante-harmonisation with those in favour of competition. Among the latter are 'competition as a discovery process', the 'limitation of mistakes', the 'pressure to deregulate and to liberalise' and 'taking the will and needs of the people seriously'.

Manfred E. Streit: Competition among systems as a defence of liberty

Like other proposals which aim at the taming of Leviathan, competition among systems (CS) requires the assent of the very Leviathan. In other words, CS depends on rules (legislation) including a hand-tying of governments to prevent them from interfering when the disciplining effects of competition make themselves felt.

The treaty establishing the European Economic Community is an interesting case in point. It involves a basic decision of the signatory states to open up among themselves to an extent which goes way beyond their commitments to GATT and now to the WTO. However, this was only gradually realized as a consequence of the rulings of the European Court of Justice. Furthermore, the basic arrangement is particularly far-reaching in view of the aforementioned hand-tying. The provisions of the Treaty have to be considered as rules of a level higher up than those of the member states themselves. As a consequence, citizens of the member states can refer directly to the rules of the Treaty whenever they believe, that they are restricted in their freedom of action by their own governments to an extent which is incompatible with the provisions of the Treaty.

In the present analysis, the Rome Treaty will be used to illustrate the rule dependency and the corresponding limitations of CS (part 4). However first, this rather complex form of competition and its general effects will be examined (parts 2 and 3). The final part of the analysis will be devoted to a phenomenon which can be interpreted as a spontaneous process of substituting formal rules of national private law for informal ones. As a process of decentralized rule formation, it is tolerated and partly supported by national jurisdictions. I am referring to the modern form of Law Merchant (lex mercatoria) and its specific enforcement procedures.

Chapter III

Václav Klaus: The Austrian school – Its significance for the transformation process

Austrian Economics has provided ideas which are extraordinarily valuable for solving the problems of the transformation from communist systems to a free society and a free market order.

In spite of the isolation in which intellectuals lived in the former communist states, many of them had long discovered Austrian Economics, and its thinking has been influential over decades. Sometimes they have the impression that they have taken an interest in its thoughts to even a greater extent than did their Western colleagues living in a simpler and more pleasant world. The attraction of Austrian Economics in a fundamental way was the School's consistent methodological individualism (combined with the subjectivist value theory) as well as its consistent systematic (and therefore also complex) world view resulting from its methodoligical stance. The methodology of Austrian Economics offers surprising and convincing insights into the social order and the economy of the communist period. The most important contribution of Austrian Economics consisted in its clear-cut proof that the 'communist episode' in Czechia and many other parts of the world did not come about by accident. On the contrary. It was the result of a process lasting for decades and was rooted in the world of ideas, namely of those ideas which the Austrian School so admirably described and interpreted. This was and is the School's singular historical contribution.

Herbert Giersch: Economic dynamism: Lessons from German experience

This article was originally written as an address for the opening session of the 1994 congress of the international Schumpeter Society in Münster/Westfalia. In thirty propositions which are fairly general to begin with, but become more specific towards the end, it draws general lessons from West Germany's postwar economic development as observed and interpreted by the author.

The basic tenor is a plea for openness, entrepreneurship and flexibility in global evolutionary competition. It rests on a strong belief in the virtues of self-disciplined individualism. Competition is likely to prevail among firms, locations, institutions, and governments though it simultaneously calls for more intense cooperation within the competing units.

Lord Harris of High Cross: Down with the bishops?

The essay attacks the lofty and self-righteous rejection of the liberal market by leading spokesmen for the Church of England. It reveals fundamental misunderstandings of the functioning of the market as well as scrupulous methodologies, such as distortions of comparisons by the contemporary convention of measuring poverty by the elastic yardstick of a relative, rather than an absolute, standard. In this way, successive increases in the real level of Income Support show 'poverty' continuing, if not rising, for ever. It also lays bare such misnomers as 'inequality' which implies the unnatural departure from the norm of equality. The essay is a sober warning against the destructive assault on liberal capitalism which is the best shield against poverty, tyranny and inhumanity that imperfect man can have. It recommends bishops to stick more to prayer and fasting and less to politics and sniping.

Antonio Martino: Ideas and the future of liberty

The subject is the role of ideas in the fight for liberty. It is argued that the case for liberty is today better understood than in the last fifty years. The Author examines the intellectual climate of the last 50 odd years. Pessimism on the future of liberty, as expressed in the late 1940s by Joseph Schumpeter, flourished until recently. Reflecting on the free market program of the alliance that won elections of 1993 in Italy and reflecting on views of Buchanan, Stigler and Friedman, the Author discovers a shift to optimism that is supported by the discredited statist recipes and the cumulative effect of decades of socialism that has produced a state of near-bankruptcy which makes further expansions of government interference almost impossible.

Victoria Curzon Price: What do liberals have to say about the future of international and inter-ethnic relations?

Part I discusses Hayek's *extended order*, how it comes into existence, what its advantages and drawbacks are as compared with the *restricted order*, how it survives (or not) over time, and the nature of its links to freedom. In particular, we discuss the rise and fall of civilizations, the process of cultural evolution and 'discovery' of socially effective institutions. This leads to Part II, where, with additional reference to the writings of Ludwig von Mises and Wilhelm Röpke, we make two interconnected observations: (1) at the level of international relations, only limited states can be peaceful states and (2), at the level of inter-ethnic relations *within* states, the same is true: peaceful relations *may* develop between different ethnic groups, but only on a market basis – economic planning leads to conflict. There is therefore complete coherence between liberal thinking and the night-watchman state on the one hand, and peaceful and prosperous international relations on the other. The trouble is that the converse is also true: a bloated state leads to international conflict, perhaps to war.

We then use what we have learned to cast light on two very different issues in contemporary international relations. What interpretation should we put on the "successful" conclusion of the Uruguay Round? And how are we to account for ethnic conflict (sometimes bitterly armed) in the sphere of influence of the ex-USSR? That two such different issues can be clarified by reference to the same theory is an indication of its interpretative power. We conclude that a peaceful and prosperous Extended Order is tantalizingly close, but that we must rely on the unplanned process of competition to bring it about.

Gordon Tullock: Civilized ants

Some ant nests are extremely large, and many of the ants are not closely related. Nevertheless, they engage in complex coordinated economic behaviour. This is done without either a market or a governmental hierarchy. The point of this paper is to explain how they are able to obtain coordination in complex tasks without either of the two basic mechanisms used by human beings for coordination. It would appear that something like a very simple preference function with declining margin utility, and a selection of particular arguments in it permits an explanation of this behaviour.

Detmar Doering: A dog's choice: Which constitution is the best?

The paper interprets *Phaedrus'* fable *Canis Parturiens* as an example of the entrenchment of interest groups in a given political system, of violation of property rights, and of the difficulties to withdraw privileges once given. The paper, then, analyses the possibility of a theory of government that really does protect property rights against the aspirations of political/economic interest groups. It demonstrates that even the most sophisticated theory of this kind, the Lockean contract theory, does not succeed to formulate such a theory.

In the light of these views the various constitutional forms of government (anarchy; aristocracy; monarchy, democracy) are analysed in respect to how close they approach to this unattainable ideal. The paper proposes an approach that lays more stress on decentralisation than on the idea of specific forms of government. The smaller the units the more it will be likely that the basis of government is consent, not plunder by government. This would allow even more democratisation and make alternatives that per se violate rights (like monarchy/aristocracy) less likely, although such alternatives may still legitimately exist. Competition among small governments in a confederate environment could prove to be the best way to avoid the problem described in Phaedrus' fable.

Authors

Louis De Alessi* is Professor of Economics at the University of Miami, Florida. He has held tenure appointments at the Duke University and George Washington University and several visiting appointments at universities in Italy, Germany and the U.S.A. He wrote numerous articles in journals and books. His recent publications include "Efficiency criteria for optimal laws: Objective standards or value judgements?" *Constitutional Political Economy* (1992), "Reputation and the efficiency of legal rules: An application to breach and product liability laws" *Cato Journal* (1994).

Roland Baader is a German economist. After some 20 odd years being an enterpriser, he became an independent author. He wrote several articles on political economics and money. Among his books are *Anlage 2000* (1987), *Gold: Letzte Rettung …?* (1988), *Kreide für den Wolf* (1991), *Die Euro-Katastrophe – Für Europas Vielfalt – Gegen Brüssels Einfalt* (1993). He is editor of *Die Enkel des Perikles* (1995), and *Wider die Wohlfahrtsdiktatur* (1995).

Walter Block* is a member of the faculty of the Economics Department of the College of the Holy Cross in Worcester, Mass., and Adjunct Scholar at the Fraser, Cato and Mises Institutes. He has edited several books including *Breaking the Shackles: The Economics of Deregulation* (1991) and authored several others, among them: *Defending the Undefendable* (1976), *Focus on Employment Equity* (1985), *The U.S. Bishops and Their Critics* (1986), and *The Lexicon of Economic Thought* (1988). Together with James Gwartney and Robert Lawson he authored *Economic Freedom of the World: 1975–1995* (1996).

Hardy Bouillon* is "Privatdozent" of Political Philosophy at the University of Trier, Germany. He has authored a monograph on Hayek and numerous articles. He is editor (together with Gerard Radnitzky) of *Universities in the Service of Truth and Utility* (1991), *Government: Servant or Master?* (1993), *Values and the Social Order*, 2 vol. (1995). His latest book, *Freiheit, Liberalismus und Wohlfahrtsstaat* (1996) is on the relation between freedom and the welfare state.

Victoria Curzon Price* is Professor of Economics at the University of Geneva and Director of the Institut Européen de l'Université de Gèneve.

She authored many articles and books. Among her publications are *The Management of Trade Relations in the GATT* (1976), *Unemployment and Other Non-Work Issues* (1982) *Industrial Policies in the European Community* (1982), *Free Trade Areas, the European Experience: What Lessons for Canadian-US Trade Liberalisation?* (1987), *1992: Europe's Last Chance? From Common Market to Single Market* (1988).

Detmar Doering is Deputy Director of the Liberales Institut (Liberty Institute) of the Friedrich Naumann Foundation in Bonn, Germany. He has published numerous articles in journals and daily newspapers. He authored *Kräfte des Wandels* (with Lieselotte Stockhausen-Doering) (1990) and *Die Wiederkehr der Klugheit: Edmund Burke und das Augustan Age* (1990). He edited *Kleines Lesebuch über den Liberalismus* (1992, translated into nine languages) and together with Fritz Fliszar he is editor of *Freiheit: Die unbequeme Idee* (1995).

Antony Flew, Emeritus Professor of Philosophy, University of Reading, and Distinguished Research Fellow, Social Philosophy and Policy Center, Bowling Green State University, Ohio (1983–91). Among the more relevant publications are *Crime or Disease?* (1973), *Thinking about Thinking* (1975), *Sociology, Equality and Education* (1976), *A Rational Animal* (1978), *The Policies of Procrustes* (1981), *Darwinian Evolution* (1984), *David Hume: Philosopher of Moral Science* (1986), *Agency and Necessity* (with Godfrey Vesey, 1987), *Power to the Parents. Revising Educational Decline* (1987), *Equality in Liberty and Justice* (1989) and *Thinking about Social Thinking* (1992, 2nd edition,).

Herbert Giersch*, former President of the Kiel Institute of World Economics, is Professor Emeritus of Economics at the University of Kiel. He received many awards (among them Ludwig Erhard Award, Paolo Baffi International Prize for Economics, Prognos Award), three honorary doctorates, and several fellowships. He published extensively in international journals. Among his recent publications are *The World Economy in Perspective. Essays on International Trade and European Integration* (1991), *The Fading Miracle. Four Decades of Market Economy in Gemany* (1992, with K.-H. Paqué and H. Schmieding, 2nd rev. ed 1994), *Openness for Prosperity. Essays in World Economics* (1993), *Marktwirtschaftliche Perspektiven für Europa* (1993).

Gerd Habermann is Scientific Director of the *Unternehmerinstitut* (UNI e.V.) in Bonn, Germany, a newly established free-market think tank connected with the *Arbeitsgemeinschaft Selbständiger Unternehmer* (ASU), a free-trade organisation of entrepreneurs. Since 1978 he has been lecturer in political philosophy at Bonn University. He published numerous articles in scientific periodicals and authored *Antibürokratie* (1980, with Jochen Lö-ser) and *Der Wohlfahrtsstaat – Geschichte eines Irrwegs* (1994).

Ralph Harris* is a Founder President of the London Institute of Economic Affairs of which he was General Director from its creation in 1957 until nominal retirement in 1987. In 1979 Margaret Thatcher made him a life peer as Lord Harris of High Cross and he sits (occasionally) in the House of Lords as a cross-bencher (independent). In active retirement, he works for free trade non-federal Europe. He has written and lectured widely on the theory and practice of classical liberal economics. He is author of *Advertising in a Free Society* (1959, with Arthur Seldon), *Welfare Without the State* (1987) and *Beyond the Welfare State* (1988), and he is a non-Executive director of Times Newspaper.

Hans-Herrmann Hoppe is Professor of Economics at the University of Nevada, Las Vegas, Senior Fellow of the Ludwig von Mises Institute, Auburn University, and co-editor of the *Review of Austrian Economics* and the *Journal of Libertarian Studies*. He is author of *Handeln und Erkennen* (1976), *Kritik der kausalwissenschaftlichen Sozialforschung* (1983), *Eigentum, Anarchie und Staat* (1987), *A Theory of Socialism and Capitalism* (1989), *The Economics and Ethics of Private Property* (1993), *Economic Science and the Austrian Method* (1995), and numerous articles on philosophy, economics and the social sciences.

Anthony de Jasay*, a former Oxford economics don and Paris investment banker, is now an independent scholar living in France.

His recent published work includes *The State* (1985), *Social Contract, Free Ride: A Study of the Public Goods Problem* (1989), *Choice, Contract, Consent: A Restatement of Liberalism* (1991), and *Before Resorting to Politics* (1996). His books have also been published in French, German and Spanish.

Václav Klaus*, first non-communist Czech Minister of Finance and a Founder Member of the Civic Democratic Party, is Prime Minister of the Czech Republic since 1992. His most recent publications are *A Road to Market Economy* (1991), *Tomorrow's Challenge* (1991), *Economic Theory and Economic Reform* (1991), *I do not like Catastrophic Scenaries* (1991), *Dismantling Socialism: A Road to Market Economy II* (1992), *Why am I a*

Conservative? (1992), *The Year – How much is it in the History of the Country?* (1993), *The Czech Way* (1994), and *Rebirth of a Country* (1994).

Antonio Martino*, former Professor of Economics and Dean of the Faculty of Political Science, Free University (LUISS) of Rome, taught at several Italian Universities. He was Italian Minister of Foreign Affairs (May 1994–January 1995) and is now President of the Italian Group, Inter-Parliamentary Union (since February 1995). He published ten books and over 150 articles. His recent publications include *Constraining Inflationary Government* (1982), *Noi e il fisco, La Crescita della fiscalità arbitraria: cause, conseguenze, rimedi* (1987), *Milton Friedman* (1994), *Lezioni di economia politica II* (1994), *Antonio Martino: La rivolta liberale, Fisco, ruolo dello Stato, occupazione e politica estera* (1994), and *Fatti e cronache della politica estera italiana, maggio-dicembre 1994* (1994).

Angelo M. Petroni* is Professor of Philosophy of Science at the University of Bologna and held appointments at several Italian and foreign universities, including the University of Sorbonne, Paris. He is Director of the Centro Luigi Einaudi in Turin, Editor of *Biblioteca della libertà*, the main liberal journal published in Italy, and a member of the scientific board of the Fondazione Einaudi in Rome. He published extensively in the fields of philosophy of natural and social sciences, as well as on political philosophy. Amongst his publications: *K.R. Popper: Il pensiero politico* (1981) and *I modelli, l'invenzione e la conferma* (1990).

Gerhard Schwarz* is one of the economic editors of the Swiss daily newspaper *Neue Zürcher Zeitung* since 1987. Since 1989 he is also lecturing at the University of Zurich on economic systems. His books (as author or editor) include *Ausländische Direktinvestitionen und Entwicklung* (1980), *Wo Regeln bremsen. Deregulierung und Privatisierung im Vormarsch* (1988), *Das Soziale der Marktwirtschaft* (1990), *and Schweizerische Wirtschaftspolitik im internationalen Wettbewerb* (author: Peter Moser, 1991).

Arthur Seldon, CBE*, former Tutor in Economics at the University of London, is a Founder President of the London Institute of Economic Affairs. He is author of *Hire Purchase in a Free Society* (1958), *Advertising in a Free Society* (1959, with Ralph Harris), *Everyman's Dictionary of Economics* (1964, 2nd edition 1975, with F.G. Pennance), *Charge* (1977), *Corrigible Capitalism, Incorrigible Socialism* (1980), *Wither the Welfare State* (1981), *Capitalism* (1990), and *The State is Rolling Back* (1994).

Hans F. Sennholz*, former Professor of Economics at Grove City College in Pennsylvania, is Director of *The Foundation for Economic Education* (F.F.E.) in Irvington, New York since 1992. He received several honorary doctorates and published more than 600 essays and articles on American economic and social policy. Among his books are: *Divided Europe* (1955), *Gold is money* (1975), *Death and Taxes* (1976), *Age of Inflation* (1979, also in Spanish), *Money and Freedom* (1985, also in Spanish and Polish), *The Politics of Unemployment* (1987), and *Debts and Deficits* (1987).

Manfred E. Streit*, Founder and Director of the Max-Planck-Institute for Research into Economic Systems in Jena, held chairs and appointments at European universities. He is a member of the scientific council to the German economics ministry and other advisory boards and institutes. He published some 120 articles and a number of books. Among these are *Theorie der Wirtschaftspolitik* (4th rev. and enl. ed. 1991), *Freiburger Beiträge zur Ordnungsökonomik* (with G. Wegner et al. 1995). Moreover, he is also editor of *Futures Markets: Managing and Monitoring Futures Trading* (1983) and *Wirtschaftspolitik zwischen ökonomischer und politischer Rationalität* (1988).

Gordon Tullock* has been the Karl Eller Professor of Economics and Political Science at the University of Arizona since 1987. He is the first recipient of the Leslie T. Wilkens Awards and a founder and past president of *The Public Choice Society* and of several other economic and scientific societies. His publications include *The Calculus of Consent* (first published 1962 with James Buchanan), *Economics of Income Redistribution* (1983, 2nd edition 1984), *Private Wants, Public Means* (reprint 1987), *Autocracy* (1987), *Economic Hierarchies, Organization and the Structure of Production* (1992), *The Economics of Non-Human Societies* (1994), *The New Federalist* (1994, also in Serbo-Croatian and Russian).

(*) Member of the Mont Pèlerin Society